THE WELFARE STATE
and Social Work

D0074473

Para o Peter

Aquele virar de costas ao irmão caído. Doentes dessa cegueira que é deixarmos sofrer pelos outros.

That sickness of turning our backs on our fallen brother. That blindness that ignores the suffering of others.

Mia Couto, *A River Called Time*

THE WELFARE STATE
and Social Work
PURSUING SOCIAL JUSTICE

Josefina Figueira-McDonough
Arizona State University

SAGE Publications
Thousand Oaks ▪ London ▪ New Delhi

For information:

Sage Publications, Inc.
2455 Teller Road
Thousand Oaks, California 91320
E-mail: order@sagepub.com

SAGE Publications Ltd.
1 Oliver's Yard
55 City Road
London EC1Y 1SP
United Kingdom

Sage Publications India Pvt. Ltd.
B-42, Panchsheel Enclave
Post Box 4109
New Delhi 110 017 India

Printed in the United States of America

Library of Congress Cataloging-in-Publication Data

Figueira-McDonough, Josefina.
The welfare state and social work : pursuing social justice / Josefina Figueira-McDonough.
    p. cm.
Includes bibliographical references and index.
ISBN 0-7619-3024-8 (pbk.)
    1. Social justice. 2. Social justice—United States. 3. Human services. 4. Human services—United States. 5. Welfare state. I. Title.
HM671.F54 2007
361.973—dc22

2006006358

This book is printed on acid-free paper.

06   07   08   09   10   10   9   8   7   6   5   4   3   2   1

Acquisitions Editor:	Kassie Graves
Editorial Assistant:	Veronica Novak
Production Editor:	Kristen Gibson
Copy Editor:	Teresa Herlinger
Typesetter:	C&M Digitals (P) Ltd.
Cover Designer:	Bryan Fishman

Contents

Introduction

There are plenty of good books on welfare policy, just as many on social work, and even a few on both. I have borrowed from many of these books with abandon. Why another one?

My purpose is not to provide exhaustive documentation but to take a critical look at welfare in the United States, its impact on people who are struggling for economic participation and political representation, and the roles of social workers in this contested terrain. The undertaking is ambitious, and the result may be more polemical than a mainstream academic take on welfare. Let me set out the reasons that led me to follow this road.

I recently attended several conferences bringing together politicians, human service leaders, social workers, student representatives, and grassroots activists concerned with growing social injustice. All of the participants were committed to halting and reversing this trend. My career has followed both social work and social science trajectories, and my strongest bond to social work is a belief in its social justice mission. The energy revealed in the gatherings rekindled my hope that progress toward social justice might be achieved even within a climate shaped by highly skilled and well-financed opponents.

As gratified as I was with the tone, objectives, and synergy of the meetings, however, some crucial elements stood out by their absence.

The presentations and discussions listed numerous instances of injustice, and they laid out inventive, piecemeal recommendations for dealing with them. But there was no map to interrelate these injustices, no guidelines about how they were reinforced by common institutional practices.

"Social justice" was a mantra used throughout the panels. Yet it was never defined, much less operationalized. A multitude of social wrongs was listed without spelling out what would constitute achieving social justice. Sometimes this led to wishful discussions about a thorough overhaul of government, capped by blue-sky visions of an ideal, egalitarian society. Strategies of intervention ran the gamut from organizing the deprived, coordinating volunteer organizations, and shifting administrative procedures, to lobbying local, state, and national government. But there was not much concern about the effectiveness of any one of these strategies for specific aspects of concrete problems. Nor was much attention paid to putting the pieces together to maximize change. Strategizing about the orchestrated deployment of interventions was never on the table.

None of this is meant to downplay the importance of these encounters. On the contrary, the ideas coming out of the discussions inspired this book. One of my objectives is to situate concepts of social justice not in universalistic terms but within the distinctive context of the United States. As appealing as grand principles may be, they easily degenerate into abstractions with little use for concerted action. The often-criticized dissociation between the notional commitment of social work to social justice and its implementation in practice stands as the prime example of this split-level mentality.

Principles of social justice come to life when they are understood against the historical antecedents of welfare policies and the institutional evolution of social work as a profession. Workable strategies need to be based on three questions:

1. How far have the actual achievements of welfare policies fallen behind the specific goals of social justice?

2. What characteristics of the welfare state have prevented us from moving closer to these goals?

3. What can we learn from other, more successful experiments in implementing welfare policy?

Questions like these help us locate the origins of social injustice, and they open horizons for improvement. Change agents have to be able to deal with the social and political forces that have created and perpetuate unjust conditions. This requires an understanding of power relationships and of how ideological presuppositions—the conventional wisdom about poverty and its remedies—are transmitted. It also requires a grasp of the effectiveness of different intervention strategies.

The themes of this book are social justice; the hesitant course of welfare policy and the social work profession in the United States; the meandering, partial inclusion of certain groups in social citizenship; the dangerous retrogression of recent policies; an evaluation of the impact of the liberal-democratic welfare state; and finally, an overview of policy practice.

My analysis of policies is hardly neutral. While I do not consider myself a disciple of Richard Cloward and Frances Piven, I admire their contributions to the field. Their contention that, in an asymmetric confrontation, neutrality equals support for the stronger party is particularly telling. Little David needed divine help against Goliath.

So my commentary is colored by how policies impact on the have-nots. A couple of reasons make this stance less biased than it may appear. First, a social justice perspective provides the overarching frame of the book. Second, the current dominance of ideologies that seek to rationalize and legitimize injustice calls for an antidote.

Part I is composed of three chapters that set the multiple themes of the book in a coherent framework. Chapter 1 reviews different outlooks on the justice mission of social work. These perspectives range from a call to active participation in destroying an unjust system to giving priority to the justice goal in social work interventions. Chapter 2 discusses selected theories of social justice consistent with the tenets of liberal-democratic regimes. Two commitments—liberty and equality—define market economies, and the theories come in two corresponding groups: one giving priority to freedom and the other privileging equality. Chapter 3 uses empirical indicators of distributive justice to assess the present situation in the United States against the conceptual backdrop put in place in the first pair of chapters.

The second part of the book reviews the history of welfare in the United States, from colonial times through the creation of the welfare state in the 1930s, to the demise of public assistance entitlements in the late 1990s. This part also traces the evolution of the social work profession from the second half of the nineteenth century onward.

Chapter 4 introduces an analytical framework for the historical review. The idea is to call attention to the institutional and cultural forces operating in each period. The framework is not only explanatory, but should also help alert activists to what they are up against at the present time. We examine how ideology, institutional path dependence, barriers to national policies, and the role of labor have all conditioned social citizenship.

A parallel approach is applied to stages in the transformation of social work. The push for professional status comes in for special attention, as does the impact of the welfare state in shaping career opportunities for social workers. This section also highlights the role of activists in upholding the justice goal of the profession and the political currents within which they function.

This historical review takes up five chapters. In addition to briefly laying out a framework for the historical presentation, Chapter 4 covers the period from colonial times to the Gilded Era and the heyday of the robber barons at the end of the nineteenth century. Chapter 5 looks at the first half of the twentieth century and the birth of the American welfare state in the mid-thirties. Chapter 6 examines the aftermath of World War II up to the Great Society programs of the 1960s. The surprisingly benevolent first term of Richard Nixon and the decline of the welfare state thereafter are the topics of Chapter 7. The focus of Chapter 8 is the welfare reform of 1996 and the loss of entitlements in public assistance.

Parts III, IV, and V concentrate on specific features of welfare policy and its impact on both clients and social workers themselves. They emphasize the consequences suffered by women and minorities of color over time, the limitations of recent social policies, and the comparative outcomes across different types of welfare regimes, seen from a cross-national perspective. It is against the environment shaped by the fluctuating fortunes in welfare policies that the tasks performed by social workers and the options open to the profession can be understood.

Part III is devoted to groups that the welfare system has discriminated against and at times simply excluded from benefits. Chapter 9 relates the tortuous story of the marginalization of women. Chapter 10 is devoted to African Americans, Mexican Americans, and Native Americans.

Part IV concentrates on the analysis of present-day policies and proposed reforms. Chapters 11 and 12 cover TANF—in effect, the replacement for AFDC in the Welfare Reform Act of 1996. Outcome evaluations and recommendations for adjusting the system are at the center of these chapters. The spotlight falls on the political unresponsiveness—the studied ignorance—of proposed reauthorization legislation regarding the body of knowledge accumulated in these evaluations. Chapter 13 covers Medicare reforms and President Bush's plan for privatizing Social Security.

Part V takes up a comparative evaluation of the American welfare state. Chapter 14 compares the American welfare regime with other types of welfare states within the Organization for Economic Coordination and Development (OECD) along several indicators of well-being. Chapter 15 spells out welfare issues emerging in postindustrial societies, including the United States.

The potential of social work as a force for a more equitable society is the core theme of Part VI. Chapter 16 lays out suggestions based on Chapters 1, 2, and 3, together with recommendations from various social work authors, regarding the profession's role in the twenty-first century. Obstacles to progressive change are also discussed. Chapter 17 centers on policy practice as a crucial intervention for the promotion of social justice. The chapter is not and does not aspire to be a manual of interventions. Many competent handbooks do just that. The goal is to identify the variety of policy practices, the strengths and linkages among these practices, and the optimal roles of social workers in selecting and implementing them.

As I've mentioned, the book is opinionated. Students should be encouraged to debate the positions it takes for and against policies and recommendations for reform. Dialogue of this sort should enhance the comprehension of what policies aim to do and what their consequences are. Conversation in this vein should also promote the civic engagement of social workers and the prospects for progressive change.

Acknowledgments _____

T he first impulse for this book came a couple of years ago from my colleagues on the committee on doctoral education at Arizona State University. Elizabeth Segal, Robert Moroney, Flávio Marsiglia, José Ashford, Nora Gustavson, Nancy Larson, and Ann MacEachorn approved a proposal for a new graduate course on welfare and social justice and asked me to develop the course. The course plan became the rough draft of a book proposal.

Several colleagues and friends helped me along the way. Ann Casebolt's suggestions on the book's first draft improved the original structure, Marie Provine enlightened me about public interest law, while Julia Figueira-McDonough's work in that field offered me some experiential glimpses. Armand Laufer reminded me of the new international directions of welfare in a global age. Other anonymous reviewers went with extreme detail through the book and offered criticism, praise, and suggestions that helped shape the final manuscript.

In the spring of 2005, Professor Fernanda Rodrigues invited me to lead a seminar on issues of social justice at the Catholic University of Lisbon. The participants' lively discussions brought to the fore new insights about the connection between ideology and social policy, as well as the distance between social work jobs and social activism. I am grateful to Fernanda Rodrigues, who organized the seminar, to Margarida Abreu, who supervised it, and to all the participants for the experience.

The editorial staff at Sage, Kassie Graves, Kristen Gibson, Teresa Herlinger, and Veronica Novak, were patient, supportive, and efficient. Grace F. McDonough helped me, with care and good humor, to straighten the figures in the book.

My greatest debt is to Peter McDonough. He stood firm through all my despairs and, more importantly, edited the whole book, transforming my rather dreary deductive style into a more gracious, Irish-inspired cadence. Furthermore, he typed tables, references, and inserts, and graciously allowed me to use photos from his period collection. In truth, this book might never have been completed but for him.

In addition, Sage gratefully acknowledges the contributions of the following reviewers:

Pranab Chatterjee, Case Western Reserve University

David G. Gil, Brandeis University

Ann Nichols-Casebolt, Virginia Commonwealth University

Mary Ohmer, Georgia State University

PART I

Making Sense of Social Justice

This section covers ideas about social justice in the context of a liberal democracy, exemplified by the United States. Founded on values of freedom and a government "of the people, by the people, for the people," these ideas are at the bedrock of the American way of life.

The first chapter considers goals of social justice as they are understood by social work professionals. The second chapter examines a representative selection of theories that focus on these core values. The third chapter uses empirical indicators of social outcomes to evaluate distributive justice in the United States. The evaluative perspective behind this exercise draws on a modern version of liberal democratic theory as portrayed by the philosopher John Rawls.

1

Justice as a Value in Social Work

Social workers once aided striking workers and helped bring about social change. What are we doing now? We are often caught up in political campaigning for a bill, proposition, candidates, etc. rather than focusing on the macro change.

—Natalia Ventura, Southern Chair of
the Social Action Council of California, 2005

Since the 1960s and 1970s, justice issues have received considerable attention in writings on social work. The spotlight has intensified even though radical critics consider the shift more rhetorical window-dressing than a program implemented in practice or supported through professional training (Reisch & Andrews, 2001; Wagner, 2000). Social justice and related themes stand out in the documents of major organizations—the National Association of Social Workers (NASW) and the Council on Social Work Education (CSWE)—that represent the profession and that shape the training of social workers.

The codes and standards of the NASW (2003) address professional ethics. Professional commitment centers on issues that stress human rights and interpersonal resources. The core values guiding the enterprise are service, social justice, personal dignity and worth, the importance of human relationships, and integrity.

The guiding notion is that "social workers challenge social injustice." Professionals are supposed to "pursue social change, particularly with and on behalf of vulnerable and oppressed individuals and groups." Social workers' reform efforts are to concentrate on issues of "poverty, unemployment, discrimination and other forms of social injustice." These activities seek to promote sensitivity to and knowledge about oppression. "Social workers strive to ensure access to needed services and resources, equality of opportunity, and meaningful participation for all people" (NASW, 2003, pp. 381–395).

Under the heading of "Social Workers' Ethical Responsibilities to the Broader Society," justice comes in for further operationalization. "Social workers should," the codes and standards document (NASW, 2003) states,

- promote the general welfare of society, from local to global levels, and the development of people, their communities, and environments. Social workers should advocate for living conditions conducive to the fulfillment of basic human needs and should promote social, economic, political and cultural values and institutions that are compatible with the realization of social justice.
- facilitate informed participation by the public in shaping social policies and institutions.
- engage in social and political action that seeks to ensure that all people have equal access to resources, employment, services and opportunities they require to meet their basic human needs and to develop fully. Social workers should be aware of the impact of the political arena on practice and should advocate for changes in policy and legislation to improve social conditions in order to meet basic human needs and promote social justice. (pp. 394–395)

A similar insistence on justice crops up repeatedly in other NASW declarations about economic programs, electoral politics, environmental policy, health care, housing, immigrants and refugees, international relations, and human rights.

The first formal statement of the Council on Social Work Education (CSWE) about curricula dates from 1962. In this, and in a number of subsequent documents, attention is given to social policy. However, it was not until 1992 that economic justice and populations at risk received explicit notice. By 1994, the need to promote social and economic justice in professional curricula was pressed still more clearly:

Programs of social work education must provide an understanding of the dynamics and consequences of social economic injustice, including all forms of human oppression and discrimination. They must provide students with the skills to promote social change and to implement a wide range of interventions that further the achievement of individual and collective social and economic justice. Theoretical and practice content must be provided about strategies of intervention for achieving social and economic justice and for combating the causes and effects of institutionalized forms of oppression. (CSWE, 1994)

Since then, curricular statements stressing issues of multiculturalism have become more common. Some commentators (e.g., Gilbert, 1995; Piven & Cloward, 1997) view the rise of identity politics as a distraction that undermines the struggle for human rights.

In sum, both the professional association and the accrediting body of the professional schools exhort social workers, in their role as change agents, to correct and undo injustice. The NASW uses the tentative "should." The CSWE prefers the imperative "must." The difference probably reflects the different scope of the organizations more than any practical variance in their commitment to justice. The NASW is much larger but more heterogeneous. The CSWE has a narrower, somewhat more focused mission, with sharper teeth through its powers of accreditation.

These documents leave no doubt about the overarching importance of social justice for the profession. But "overarching" can easily be translated into "generic bromides" and posturing. The task is to see how social work authors have emphasized one or another specific facet of these guidelines.

The approaches we will look at are representative of a range of formulations rather than exhaustive. I have selected a variety of works that stand along a continuum. Some positions claim that only certain interventions are consistent with the justice mandate. Alternative views adopt radical, reformist, and distributive ideas about justice in social work.

A Schizophrenic Profession?

The statements about justice issued by the NASW and the CSWE came late to a profession whose core method has been casework and, more recently, clinical practice. There seems to be a discrepancy between officially sanctioned principles and the courses offered in most schools. A similar gap appears between the justice ethic as a principle on the one hand and, on the other, values in tune with the jobs that social workers actually perform.

In a typical introductory class, students learn about the history of the profession. Mary Richmond and Jane Addams are identified as the founding mothers. While Richmond was the decisive figure in professionalizing social work, Addams and the settlement movement associated with her have remained at the roots of the justice thrust in the profession (Franklin, 1986).

Mary Richmond played a crucial role in bringing social work to professional standing. Together with the backing of the Russell Sage Foundation, her influence on the fledgling profession was decisive. Richmond's views took shape during her years of work with the Charity Organizations and at the John Hopkins Hospital in Baltimore. This experience helps explain her liking for both the practice of casework and the medical model of intervention. Her book on social diagnosis (Richmond, 1917) merged these two preferences and was instrumental in giving professional status and scientific credibility to the activities of social workers (Lubove, 1965; Reamer, 1994; Specht & Courtney, 1994; Wenocur & Reisch, 1983). This was the ground in which the therapeutic direction, with a few collectively oriented excursions, germinated, grew, and came to dominate the field (Wenocur & Reisch, 1983).

Jane Addams had more formal schooling than Mary Richmond, and she had close ties with the Department of Sociology at the University of Chicago. But she was suspicious of the move to professionalize social work. An activist reformer, Addams saw it as a threat to the progressive mission of the field. She feared that the search for professional respectability made social work vulnerable to cooptation (Franklin, 1986). Addams preferred community practice. Her vision of social problems was sociological rather than psychological. She aimed at changing policies on women's work, child care, health, housing, immigrant education, and integration. She pushed for the creation of juvenile courts.

Addams became involved in the politics of the Progressive movement. This was a commitment that "pro-profession" social workers made no secret of disliking. In addition, most social workers saw her tireless opposition to the entrance of the United States in World War I as unpatriotic. Addams eventually became a Nobel Peace Prize laureate, but her direct influence on social work's rise to professionalism was marginal (Franklin, 1986). Nevertheless, her ideas were absorbed into and have remained part of the identity of social work, even if they have taken the rather disembodied form of "values" that are rarely integrated in practice (Reisch & Andrews, 2001; Specht & Courtney, 1994; Wagner, 2000). Hers was a moral victory, not one that set an institutional course. So, a split developed between the individual-therapeutic slant of the profession and the justice and social change goals expressed in NASW and CSWE policy statements. The history of the profession shows a relentless, if not entirely linear, ascent of the therapeutic approach in training as well as practice.

How did the individual perspective gain so much ground? It is not as if, during the early days, there was a lack of practitioners to push a vision of clients within a larger community—the person-in-environment perspective. The preeminence of Mary Richmond notwithstanding, there were a number of reformers among pioneering professionals (e.g., Follett, 1909; Lindeman, 1921), and the staying power of the justice norm as a minority current is evident. Still, the puzzle remains. Why has the impulse toward justice lost out, in relative terms, compared to the therapeutic turn?

Although they differ in details, accounts of the origins and development of the profession are fairly consistent. Several factors combined to support "the triumph of the therapeutic." Besides the search for professional credibility, these include social demands for specific services, the priorities of funding sources, political pressure, and the dominance of a distinctive social ideology.

In a market economy like that of the United States, professional status matters. It is essential for gaining political, legal, and economic control of an occupation. Certification requires evidence of delivering a unique service, demonstration of its utility, and a rationale that justifies the necessity of that service. Furthermore, professional recognition has to be based on a body of knowledge. This entails elaborating a set of codified interventions that can be imparted to future professionals. Accreditation and licensing regulate the process. In short, in order to legitimize its claim of exclusivity in an occupational sphere, a new profession has to justify a unique approach and impart skills that address social needs.

The medical profession provided the outstanding template for social work in its embryonic days. Social work's typical method of intervention was casework with psychiatric overtones. In its desire to stand on its own—to distance itself from volunteer charitable work and from an auxiliary role within the medical orbit—social work was drawn to Freudian theories and, somewhat later, to what Specht (1990) terms popular therapies. The profession drifted toward clinical social work. This attraction did not take hold in a historical vacuum. These trends gained momentum in response to a real demand for such services—notably, the need to treat the traumas of wartime combatants.

But this is not the whole story. In the 1930s, during the New Deal, the demand for social workers grew with the expansion of public programs. Schools of social work responded by training students in the administration of services. In the 1960s, the War on Poverty provided an enormous stimulus to community organizers, and enrollments in community organization courses reached a peak (Reisch & Wenocur, 1986). Later, with the fading of the conditions that gave them birth, both types of incentives for the development of macro-practice fizzled. The slide continued even as advocates kept promoting macro-strategies of intervention (Dunham, 1940; Gurin, 1971; Lane, 1939; 1930; Ross, 1955; Rothman, 1968; Steiner, 1925; Woods & Kennedy, 1922).

Changes in the political climate, fashions in funding for different programs, bureaucratic hierarchies within service agencies, and the persistence of an ethos of individualism all converged to favor the therapeutic style. The 1950s, and particularly the McCarthyism that reigned at the time, had a chilling effect on reform movements and demands for fairness. Dissidents were viewed with suspicion and labeled as anti-American.

The 1960s represented a sharp break with the repression of the 1950s. But that notorious decade also generated a backlash. The cultural revolution amplified and united a conservative constituency. The counter-mobilization of the right could measure its success by how terms like "liberal," "civil liberties," and "left" became codes for symptoms of decadent, pathological, and self-indulgent inclinations and behavior (Schram, 1995).

In addition, programs of service delivery became more dispersed with the growth of private and for-profit agencies working under hard-to-supervise government contracts. The sponsorship of social programs through private foundations and the United Fund cemented a business/corporate alliance that limited the options of social workers and fragmented the claims of clients.

Finally, the therapeutic style jibes with the national culture of individualism (Ellwood, 1988). Americans are not inclined to search for social remedies in collective, communal approaches. Even when systemic failures such as economic recessions occur, the tendency is to neglect structural causes and to concentrate on promoting individual responses, "pluck" and personal initiative, against all odds.

The individualist norm evokes two long-standing beliefs that mesh with and encourage a therapeutic approach. People have the capacity to shape their lives under a variety of circumstances. Since people have this capacity, they are responsible for what happens to them. The role of therapy is to help individuals discover and strengthen their capacities, and to motivate them to use these endowments to solve their problems.

Given this force field of cultural prescriptions and organizational conditions, it is easy to see why the appeal of the justice ethic paled in social work practice. But we still have to answer the question as to why the casework/clinical practice perspective is considered to be *antithetical* to the justice principle. It is one thing to account for the popularity of one approach over the other. It is another to understand the invidious nature of the comparison and the enmity between the approaches.

The professional consensus is that the goal of social work is to better the life of the oppressed and the exploited, those facing barriers to self-fulfillment. The mission of social work is to turn the skills of the disadvantaged to their own advantage and, in so doing, to solve or ameliorate social problems.

Justice practitioners criticize social workers who approach such problems as clinicians, and they castigate them for assuming that clients themselves are the cause of the problems they experience. Clinicians, they argue, choose interventions to improve behavior by correcting individual shortcomings. A selective repertoire of interventions is designed to foster functional, healthy adaptation. The description is simplified, of course. Experienced caseworkers are aware of barriers over which clients have little control, and they try to lower them, even if on a case-by-case basis.

Yet even the characteristic social work approach of dealing with the "person in the situation" centers rather myopically on the individual, and his or her immediate environment—the family, the work setting, and so on. Another example illustrates the same point. "Human Behavior and Social Environment (HBSE)," a course required in all accredited schools of social work, emphasizes the first part of the title, with a subordinate role for the second (Carter et al., 1994; Figueira-McDonough, 1998b). Along similar lines, a recent book proposal on mental health, prepared by a number of distinguished social work scholars, was touted as the ideal text for HBSE.

The fundamental argument of justice practitioners is that systemic forces drive social problems. The justice mission of social work requires nothing less than that an unjust system be the target of change. The individual approach boils down to a version of blaming the victim that reinforces the status quo. It is as if, through a kind of collective hallucination, social workers have dismissed the "social" from their professional nomenclature. For justice practitioners, the honest and sensible methods of intervention, consistent with the principle of justice, include community organization, and policy practice and skills such as advocacy, grassroots organization, collective protests, and the like.

_____ Rescuing a Profession That Betrayed Its Mission

How valid is the idea that social work has fallen short of its mission? Specht and Courtney mount what is probably the most dramatic attack on the therapeutic strategy. Along with their criticism, they develop an ambitious program for implementing social justice that hinges on community organization (Specht, 1990; Specht & Courtney, 1994).

Specht and Courtney on the Shortcomings _____ of Therapy as a Social Work Method

Specht and Courtney acknowledge that the therapeutic turn in education and practice goes back a long way, having evolved over the course of the last century. Their principal concern is the ongoing love affair of social work with popular therapies, together with the growth of clinical work and its transfer to private practice. The gist of their criticism is that these techniques fail to address the structural context within which social problems emerge. The massive investment of human resources in individual treatment is misplaced and ineffective.

A corollary distortion stems from the population that therapeutic social work is likely to reach. The types of therapy that are deployed fit the anxieties of the urban middle class rather than the stresses of the poor. The standard menu of concerns includes identity crisis, the pursuit of self-advancement, and the like. Therapeutic services are often delivered privately, in a closed-door setting, where interaction depends on the skill of the therapist. Evidence for the effectiveness of these interventions has proven to be pretty thin (Saxton, 1991; Stiles, Shapiro, & Elliott, 1986).

Specht and Courtney direct their bitterest attacks at what they call "popular therapies" adopted by practitioners and taught in many schools of social work. Most of these are psychodynamic approaches associated with figures like Rogers, Maslow, Perls, and Pollack. Specht and Courtney deny that these treatments have theoretical coherence or research validity. The therapies, such as they are, grew out of utopian religious movements in vogue during the nineteenth century, and they came back in fashion under the guise of motivational/self-realization techniques during the pop culture years of the 1960s and 1970s.

As Specht and Courtney see it, the trend in favor of therapeutic intervention and clinical practice goes squarely in the wrong direction, turning social workers away from the poor, whom they were originally supposed to serve. By the 1990s, about one-third of the students entering schools of social work said they planned to go into private practice. The flight from welfare and public services continued unabated (Abel & McDonnell, 1990).

Redeeming Social Work

Critics like Specht and Courtney are aware that social workers distinguish between casework and psychotherapy. For caseworkers, personality change is not the goal, nor is the middle class their target clientele. The priority is to understand the client's problems from a social interaction perspective, to match needs with resources. Still, even if the approach worked for those in poverty, it would require an unrealistically optimal—that is, low—ratio of therapists to clients to deal with the problems of the poor on a one-to-one basis. Logistically and financially, the strategy would be infeasible. In short, it looks like a prescription for burnout.

The bottom line for Specht and Courtney is that traditional case-work scores low on efficiency and social utility. Social problems have social causes; hence, a collective response seems intuitively to be the way to go. At the end of the day, the focus should not be on the individual but rather on the process by which individuals participate in and utilize collective life.

Child abuse and neglect are cases in point. The availability of child care services in poor neighborhoods, accessible to all residents and with extensive and flexible schedules, together with self-help clusters of parents, would reduce the incidence of abuse and neglect. Parents would be able to put children in a safe place during periods of stress. At the same time, the self-help group would help them tune in to signs that lead to a loss of self-control. During periods of tension or depression, access to services would protect children and allow parents to recover. While admitting that certain cases might require individually targeted interventions, Specht and Courtney expect that their collective approach would drive down abuse and neglect in poor neighborhoods.

Loosely inspired by the settlement house movement, the community proposal differs from it in two ways. The community center would deliver locally coordinated *public* services, and the purpose would be to foster the active *participation* of residents. Social workers would be central to this project in delivering and coordinating services. Even more importantly, they would be crucial in facilitating the organization of grassroots groups and enabling their participation in the planning and policies of the community center. All this would bring social work back to its true mission of addressing social problems and empowering clients.

Critical Commentary

It is easy to see that the spirit of the Specht and Courtney proposal goes well with notions of social capital, grounded civic society, participatory democracy, inter-organizational synchronization, and collective effectiveness (Figueira-McDonough, 2001; Halpern, 1995; Putnam, 1993a, 1993b). But it has operational problems. As is often the case with such proposals, details about the structure of the community center, inter-service coordination, assumptions about community solidarity, and evidence of effectiveness of collective intervention are sketchy. On all these fronts, a variety of concrete precedents could be explored to move Specht and Courtney's ideal model closer to one that is open to experimentation.

Gil on Social Determinism and Constructing a Just Society

In the eyes of many, David Gil is the father of radical social work theory. In *Confronting Injustice and Oppression: Concepts and Strategies for Social Workers* (1998), Gil brings together his ideas and proposals for practice.

His point of departure is the observation that social workers have always been involved with victims of injustice and oppression, and they seem to grasp intuitively and emotionally the meaning of dehumanizing conditions. Yet there is also evidence of a lack of theoretical insight into the causes of suffering and into the strategies necessary to transform oppressive socioeconomic and political institutions. It is Gil's ambition to construct a theory of injustice, lay out strategies of social change for overcoming oppression, and highlight the implications of both for social work practice.

Assumptions and Evidence

Gil starts with a pair of assumptions. First, relations of dominance are not inevitable expressions of the nature of groups but the result of choices and actions. Because they are constructed, hierarchies can be changed through movements for justice. Second, relations of dominance permeate all spheres of life—the social, economic, political, and cultural. These hierarchies condition, as well, the consciousness and behavior of winners and losers. The net result favors the maintenance of the status quo. In sum, unjust societies can be changed. It is acceptance of the unjust system that is the major obstacle to change.

Gil puts together a historical analysis to support his first point, that relations of dominance reflect choice rather than the weight of inevitability. He contrasts societies, and periods of history, that rank high in egalitarianism, solidarity, and a fair distribution of resources with others that have been wracked by the opposite. While some of Gil's grand comparisons are oversimplified, a few corroborate the first assumption. Societies with excessive demographic growth, for example, may encourage emigration, or develop new public enterprises, or shorten the workweek in order to encourage a more equitable distribution of income. In short, what is built into history is not determinism but the lesson that social challenges can be handled in a variety of ways, some more conducive than others to social justice.

Gil adopts an organic view of society to buttress his second assumption about the pervasiveness of dominance. Not unlike that of Talcott Parsons's (1951) vision of systemic functions, Gil's perspective stresses the functional complementarity and interdependence of institutions.

Table 1.1   Key Institutions of Social Life

Stewardship (development, management, control, use, and ownership) of natural and human-created resources

Organization of work and production

Exchange of products of human work

Distribution of concrete and symbolic goods and services, and of social, civil, and political rights and responsibilities

Governance and legitimation

Reproduction, biological and social

Take as an example the restrictions imposed by patriarchal traditions on property ownership by women. This particular injustice spills over into limited access to employment, education and divorce, controlled authority over offspring, and barriers against the right to vote. Exploitation is typically not confined to a single area; it crosses over into multiple institutions and domains.

Types of Change

Long-range change consists of undoing instances of systemic injustice and putting just structures in their place. Since key institutions reinforce one another across the board, only a complete overhaul can reverse this vicious circle. The goal seems extravagant, but Gil musters historical evidence for such seismic change through collective resistance to the established order.

Controlled by elites, agencies of educational and media socialization give rise to and reinforce a phenomenon variously described as hegemony (by Gramsci) or false consciousness (by Marx). The process means acceptance by the oppressed of the ideology that advances their oppression. This belief is accompanied by the fear that any systemic change would make matters worse. In Gil's view, a good deal of missionary work is required to counteract ideological submission of this magnitude. Conversion necessitates a lengthy mobilization of critical consciousness, initiated and maintained by social movements in search of just alternatives.

However it comes about, the success of total system change would be measured by the elimination of multiple inequalities. So, for example,

- Natural and manufactured products are treated as a public trust available on equal terms to everyone
- Work and social protection are organized to meet individual and social needs
- Products are to be exchanged and distributed fairly according to needs
- Truly participatory democracy exists
- Socialization is shaped by egalitarian values

Short of systemwide reconstruction, certain transition policies may be viable. As intervening steps, their aim is to alleviate as much suffering as possible. The basic rule is to fight social oppression within prevailing cultural and legal conditions. Supposedly, this will allow for curbing deprivation, while the struggle for fundamental transformation proceeds. Gil treats bringing down unemployment as a prime example of transitional policy.

At the heart of structural inequalities is exploitation that occurs through the division of labor. There are huge inequalities in the prestige and rewards attributed to different types of work. For those at the bottom, doing the most undesirable work, "incentives" range from wages that keep them in poverty to threats of starvation from unemployment.

The appropriate transitional policy is the elimination of unemployment, together with fair compensation for work. This entails participation in the production of needed goods and services by all members of society, depending on their abilities. The legislature would periodically adjust the length of work depending on the ratio of workers to what has to be done. Productive workfare, when necessary, would be an option. The most undesirable work would be rotated among all.

Employment is a badge of social membership. Its role in determining self-identity, shaping the creation of social wealth, and influencing compensation is undeniable. In recognition of their contribution to production and reproduction, workers should receive adequate wages, health protection, and child care. Progressive taxation would be a key mechanism moving toward such reforms.

The Role of Social Workers

Gil insists that the mandate of social workers is to promote welfare—that is, conditions under which people fare well. So, social workers must understand and strive to overcome the sociostructural causes of "ill-fare" by examining the institutions that uphold them.

Gil knows full well that there are contradictory tendencies in social work. On the one hand, there are the tenets of human solidarity and mutual help, empathy for suffering, and the ethical values of justice. On the other, there is the need to ensure the strength of the profession and its organizational viability, even when this means concessions to an unjust status quo. Navigating these currents impels social workers toward dissonant roles:

Control—that is, enforcing dominant norms on the "undeserving poor"

Adaptation—treating the poor so that they adjust to their conditions

Reform—carrying out incremental policies from the top down in the name of reducing oppression and injustice

Structural transformation—spreading critical consciousness by forming collective movements to root out injustice

A justice perspective, according to Gil, would be consistent with the two latter imperatives. *Reform* coincides with Gil's notion of transitional, short-term policies, while *structural transformation* is indispensable for long-term change.

Critical Commentary

Injustice is socially determined. There is little room, in Gil's world, for individual causes. Yet systemwide change depends on individual conversion, and this conversion in turn depends on the dedication and zeal of those who possess critical conscience. Therein lies the catch. Gil's vision of an enlightened few implies a cadre-led hierarchy otherwise rejected by his theory.

Paulo Freire's (1990) method of encouraging oppressed people to reflect on their experience, exchange insights and feelings with one another, and imagine their way toward fresh perspectives on social claims is more consistent with a horizontal democracy than the "enlightened know best" command structure that Gil flirts with. In fairness, when he discusses the choice of means for change, Gil (1998) sounds a return to a relatively egalitarian standard of leadership:

> If this change of consciousness will lead to a non-violent or violent system change, only people affected by the particular unjust and oppressive realities, rather than distant supporters and observers, have a moral right to decide, for they alone may live or die with the consequences of their strategic choice. (p. 62)

The call for systemwide overhaul and long-range change is grandiose and sketchily operationalized. Weighed down by its own ambition and complexity, the scheme collapses in abstraction. Nevertheless, despite these shortcomings, Gil's presentation of transitional, short-term tactics remains an important contribution to policy practice.

Piven and Cloward on Welfare, Control, and Disruption

A political scientist, Frances Piven, and Richard Cloward, a professor of social work, are widely known in radical social work circles both as activists and authors. Mobilization for Youth, a landmark program of the War on Poverty, was their brainchild. Together with several Columbia University colleagues, Piven and Cloward spearheaded the program's implementation in New York City. In the 1980s, they initiated a movement that promoted voting in poor communities. The history of organized labor in the United States, the functions of welfare, the unfolding of poor people's movements, and critiques of welfare reforms are recurrent themes in their work.

The Failure of the Labor Movement

For Piven and Cloward, the route toward a fair and more equal society goes through the power of a labor party, supported by an active labor movement. They link persistently high and growing inequality in the United States to the absence of the first and the weakness of the second.

Early efforts to unionize were squashed by powerful industrialists during the second half of the nineteenth century. Under Franklin Roosevelt, the union movement gained some legitimacy, but the strategies promoted by government and adopted by labor leaders to win health and related benefits through contracts with employers weakened the movement and set workers against the expansion of benefits outside the unions. This accommodation defused the development of a militant labor movement in the European sense.

The political wheeling and dealing of conservative administrations—in particular, the Reagan administration—further sapped the unions, and globalization quickened the downward course. Public opinion turned against unions for putting American businesses at a disadvantage in the world market. Production costs inflated by union demands were blamed for the migration of industries abroad. Over the past decades, union membership has fallen from its high point in the 1950s to below 20 percent of the workforce. Against this trajectory, the dream of a working class democracy in the United States, Piven and Cloward (1997) conclude, was unachievable.

Welfare as a Control Mechanism

Among social workers, *Regulating the Poor* (1971) is probably the best known of Piven and Cloward's books. The focus is on welfare in general and public assistance in particular. The thesis is that the purpose of welfare is to control the working poor, not necessarily to help them or improve their social position. Piven and Cloward marshal historical evidence ranging from the Elizabethan poor laws to the development of comparable legislation in the United States. Welfare policy does not follow a progressive path, responding in linear fashion to the needs of the poor. On the contrary, it expands and shrinks depending on perceived threats to the status quo. Figure 1.1 gives a schematic depiction of their model.

The cycle starts with an unequal society, typical of capitalist systems in which competition is never fair. Early victories create differences in resources between winners and losers. The winners enter subsequent competitions with accumulated resources that guarantee future victories or at least bias outcomes in their favor. With economic power comes political power, and so we have a society bifurcated between the powerful and the powerless.

There is a catch, however. Those in power need the poor to do the work that creates wealth. They need docile workers to maximize production and decrease the costs of coercion. How can systemic problems be transformed

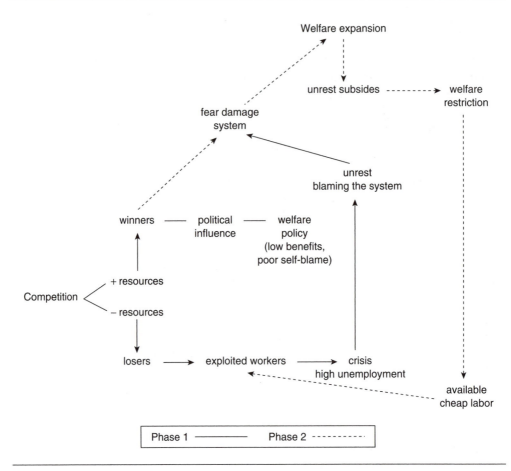

Figure 1.1   Welfare Cycle

into (the illusion of) self-generated pathologies? The answer is public assistance. These are programs designed to alleviate the misery and despair of the marginalized, by giving them a measure of insufficient help. Treatment concentrates on individual dysfunctions that reflect essentially self-inflicted problems. Tacitly, blame is shifted from the system to the person.

Sometimes, when economic crisis occurs and the number of the marginalized grows, as does their despair, this comfortable arrangement breaks down. The self-blame ploy loses plausibility. Outsiders start to attribute their predicament to the system's shortcomings. Protests, civil disruptions, and even mass violence follow. To protect their advantages and the system that provides them, elites are quick to make concessions to appease widening discontent.

As the situation returns to what passes for normal, and the need for cheap labor continues, rules specifying requirements for applications for social assistance are subtly and not so subtly adjusted upwards, and many who were receiving assistance find themselves expelled from the welfare rolls. Left without protection, the impoverished cannot bargain for better wages, and they accept the pittance offered them. This equilibrium settles in until the next crisis.

The Depression era in the United States is a showcase, Piven and Cloward argue, that confirms their hypothesis. Social assistance provided by the states before the 1930s was meager, a fact that became painfully obvious as soon as the Depression hit. By the beginning of the 1930s, the Hoover administration and Congress were well aware of the misery spreading across indusstrial centers like Detroit and agricultural states like Arkansas. But neither branch of government moved to respond to the emergency. It was the aggressive demands of various groups, disorders in a few cities, increased agitation by communist sympathizers, and a march on Washington by disgruntled World War II veterans that raised the awareness of the nation and led to the landslide electoral victory of Franklin Roosevelt. Fearing mounting disorder, some farsighted businessmen backed Roosevelt's election and his early social reforms (Gates, 1983).

As the economy slowly recovered, however, this support withered. Some workfare programs—the Works Progress Administration (WPA) was perhaps the most conspicuous—came in for attack on the grounds that they constituted government competition with private business. So, though high unemployment persisted for another year, the program was dismantled.

Social Workers and Strategies of Disruption

From the perspective of Piven and Cloward, social workers, as deliverers of remedial services, are handmaidens of the status quo. The professional neutrality professed by social workers is a fake. As an attempt to reconcile differences between parties with huge power discrepancies, neutrality becomes in effect a political act that favors the mighty. Social workers should be unequivocally on the side of the powerless—that is, the poor.

Their research on *Poor People's Movements* (1974) led Piven and Cloward to conclude that, within the political system of the United States, disruptive collective action—riots, protests, civil disobedience, and the like—constituted the only chance for the poor to turn social policy in their favor. These strategies have a chance when social dislocations make political realignments likely.

Since the poor are powerless, the only change strategies available to them are those of conflict. Powerlessness does not simply result from a lack of economic resources. It is also transmitted through the treatment the poor receive from various institutions, including those that are supposed to help them. Long delays in receiving service, continuous checks, and vigilance and suspicion are the norm. These experiences convey to recipients that they are worthless, and the feeling often gets internalized. The extremely low electoral participation of the poor reflects an awareness of their lack of power. Seeing themselves as outsiders, without access to formal channels, the marginalized are left only with "deviant" forms of asserting their claims.

So, according to Piven and Cloward, only spontaneous acts of collective protest that grab the attention of political parties when they are going through constituency realignments can be successful. The 1960s provide an exemplary, best-case illustration of this scenario. Southern whites began to abandon the Democratic Party, and blacks were courted to join up.

Critical Commentary

Piven and Cloward's stand on welfare has come in for numerous criticisms. The core of the programs instituted by Roosevelt has survived and grown over time. While ours remains a very unequal society, the United States is not simply a land of the very rich and the very poor. Piven and Cloward dismiss the role of the middle class and the power of the unions. Criticisms such as these are reasonable correctives to a simplistic model. This said, the theory still alerts us to certain dynamics and biases that have driven recent changes in welfare policy in the United States (Figueira-McDonough & Sarri, 2002).

The disruption thesis has been the target of particularly stringent criticism. Many observers of social movements reject exclusive reliance on disruption as a strategy for success. One representative of this position, the sociologist William Gamson (Gamson & Schmeidler, 1984) cites evidence from histories of the labor and the civil rights movements that contradicts Piven and Cloward's ideas. These movements cannot be reduced to spontaneous, violent expressions of despair. They gained real benefits for the poor through a repertoire of tactics. They managed to mobilize resources, develop effective long-term inter-organizational alliances, and introduce important changes in social policy.

David Wagner (2000), a radical social worker, acknowledges some of the dangers of cooptation that representatives of welfare clients face. But his research has also demonstrated that consumers of assistance have been effective if they belong to social movements that give them clout.

In *The Other America: Poverty in the United States*, Michael Harrington (1962) stripped Americans of the fiction of shared national affluence. His vivid depiction of poverty, in some places paralleling Third World conditions, fed into a strategy of reform that did not rely on disruption. Harrington, a democratic socialist, saw the poor he had encountered face-to-face as society's outsiders. Serious redistribution was needed to bring them into the American way of life. He did not believe that conventional, mostly voluntary channels of redistribution would work. In a society prizing individual competition, insiders would not willingly back redistribution on such a scale. Harrington held to the view that only the federal government had the power to promote the inclusion of the marginalized. His strategy was translated into the War on Poverty, launched during the Kennedy years. Bypassing state, county, and municipal authorities, federal grants were channeled directly to poor communities.

_____ Gilbert on Balanced Reform From Within

The reformism of Neil Gilbert (1995) contrasts dramatically with the radicalism of Gil, and Cloward and Piven. The inexorable expansion of welfare alarms him. The solution, he thinks, lies in transforming the welfare state into an "enabling" state. In view of an exponential growth in entitlements, the aging of the population, and resulting fiscal pressure, Gilbert looks on some such "Third Way" reform as unavoidable.

Structuralists like Gil define problems as socially determined, whereas Gilbert is inclined to attribute them to individual causes and only tangentially to the vagaries of the market. By and large, the thesis developed by Gilbert could stand as a blueprint for Clinton's 1996 welfare reform.

Excesses of Welfare Expansion

Three factors are behind the growth in welfare: the aging of the population, the breakdown of the family, and the sheer increase in claims on the state. The first cause is a demographic fact, widely discussed whenever Social Security reform is considered. Gilbert's recommendations are akin to some of the solutions common in these debates. Raising the retirement age is one; reducing tax deductions for retirees whose assets reach a comfortable level is another.

Gilbert's views on the second factor—family collapse—overlap with a proposition advanced by Charles Murray (1984). Single motherhood is an indicator of family breakdown, and welfare encourages this breakdown. The rapid growth of AFDC (Aid to Families with Dependent Children) caseloads in the 1960s, Gilbert admits, resulted in part from policies that set fairer admissions criteria. His critique focuses on how the originally temporary features of the program took on the characteristics of a permanent entitlement. Social Security Survivor's Insurance was supposed, in time, to protect widows with children. In Gilbert's view, had the government kept on that road, the outcomes for families and society would have been much better.

Gilbert gives extensive coverage to his third factor—the increase in claims on the government. He decries the proliferation of social rights as a contagion promoted by activists enamored of identity politics. Trendy zealots fabricate novel categories of social victims to whom protection is due. The call for policies to protect the homeless is one such fashion. Others include demands to protect abused children and women who are sexually assaulted. Gilbert claims that evidence of these problems is vastly, and deliberately, inflated to boost the emotional appeal of calls for reform.

Inefficiencies of Welfare

The decentralization of services, delivered in a maze of agencies through which benefits, in cash and in kind, wend their way, has a negative impact on the uniformity of criteria and evaluation of outcomes. Contracting out might lead to cuts in costs, but the lack of adequate supervision jeopardizes evaluation, especially with for-profit organization dealing in human services.

Gilbert cites benefits given to teenage single mothers as a typical inefficiency. Teenage girls are in a troubled period of their lives, and he sees becoming pregnant as one more sign of immaturity. "Kids with kids" have deficient parenting skills. Child abuse and crib deaths are the predictable results (Kleinman, 1993). Since teenage mothers are unusually inept caretakers of their children, they need to be under the watch of competent guardians. Teen mothers should be required to take parenting classes. Furthermore, they should go to school or they should work. If their performance does not improve, sending incompetent teen mothers to a halfway house should be considered.

The Costs and Unfairness of Wealthfare

Indirect and often invisible transfers along the lines of tax deductions and credit subsidies—such as tax credits, tax deductions on retirement, deductions and exclusions for housing, credit subsidies and tax expenditures for education, training, and employment and social services—disproportionately benefit the middle and upper-middle classes. These benefits cost a lot to the Treasury and mount up to a serious fiscal burden. Such expenses—*wealthfare*—are equivalent to welfare. They are social goods, not earned in market exchange, distributed by the government.

Mortgage interest deductions and rental exclusions cost more than twice as much as direct federal grants for housing and community development. The value of child care tax credits is twice as high for upper than for lower income brackets. The same happens with job benefits. High-paying jobs are more likely to include pension benefits than low-paying jobs. Taxpayers from the first group gain more than they should from pension-related tax deductions. Most transfer payments to the poor go to immediate consumption, while benefits for the better off tend to contribute to the accumulation of assets (Sherraden, 1991). In short, indirect and invisible gifts to the non-poor exacerbate inequalities created by the market.

The Enabling State and the Role of Social Workers

As far as Gilbert is concerned, the welfare state has no choice but to move away from entitlements toward the promotion of private responsibility, in the direction of what he calls the enabling state. Citizens are to be treated not as passive recipients of public benefits but as individuals capable of looking after themselves, with occasional assistance from the government.

Citizens who embrace American values, including stable and responsible family life and hard work, will eventually succeed. They will manage to become productive and independent. Some, because of personal incapacity as well as (ill-defined) social forces, may be temporarily or permanently unable to fulfill the ordinary responsibilities of citizenship. Training and temporary support, with incentives and punishments, will push the more capable toward independence. Longer periods of service provision, under strict controls, will achieve the same result for the less capable.

The objective of welfare is not redistributive. It is not a means to reduce social inequalities. Rather, the goal is to integrate everyone into the market. The distinctive function of the market is to foment economic development and social integration. This is the true road to social equity.

The importance of programs like WIN and other workfare programs for clients on assistance is that they link recipients' rights and social responsibility in order to achieve self-sufficiency. The assumption of civic responsibilities has to accompany any expansion of claims to benefits. These duties include taking available jobs, contributing to the support of one's family, learning enough in school to be employable, and respecting the law.

Behavioral Strategies

How do you get collaboration from people who, for a variety of reasons, cannot make ends meet and who see no opportunities to better their lives? The answer is carrot-and-stick behavior modification through incentives and punishment.

Take as a success story of work incentives the experience of some AFDC mothers. They left the program by getting a job, while retaining their access to Medicaid, food stamps, and child care benefits for one year, even if their job income would have disqualified them from those programs. By the same token, punishment, either by withdrawing benefits or increasing controls, would be meted out for nonconformity at any level—in family, in work effort, in training, or in moral behavior.

On the issue of unemployment, Gilbert's position is very close to Mead's (1986). Simply put, the unemployed must accept any job available. The ideal is to integrate people into the market economy and to ensure that the unemployed assume their responsibility as productive citizens.

Table 1.2 lays out the contrast between the traditional welfare state and the enabling state. Gilbert (1995) adds an important qualifier to the imperative of self-sufficiency:

> The new policies aim for a fairer balance between the right to welfare and the responsibility for self-sufficiency. The danger is that they will rely too heavily on the presumption of competence. Owing to personal incompetence, as well as to social forces beyond personal control, some people are temporarily or permanently unable to support themselves and meet the responsibilities of citizenship. (p. 83)

Table 1.2   Comparing the Welfare and the Enabling State

Welfare State	Enabling State
Expanding social rights	Linking rights to obligations
Relying on direct expenditures	Increasing indirect expenditures
Transfers in the form of service	Transfers in cash and vouchers
Delivery by public agencies	Delivery by private agencies
Policy focused on individuals	Policy focused on the family
Welfare benefits for consumption	Welfare benefits for investment
Reducing economic inequality	Restoring social equality

Gilbert separates welfare recipients into two groups. There are those who come to welfare due to some crisis in their lives, stay for a short time, have reasonable skills, and enjoy a certain family stability. For this sector, standard incentives and punishments will work in a relatively short time. However, the other group might have a more disorganized past because of drug addiction, brushes with the law, unstable or nonexistent family life, or spotty employment. For these individuals, strategies need to be tailored to their specific problems, over longer periods. Rehabilitation will depend on greater control, supervision, and intensive special services.

The enabling state would leave social workers with two roles. Some—case managers delivering routine behavior controls—would be suited to work with the first category of clients. A significantly greater variety of interventions, some demanding therapeutic expertise, would be needed for the second group. The mix of control and therapeutic interventions has proven to be hard to reconcile, as demonstrated by social work interventions in the criminal justice system. The scarcity of trained direct-service social workers in welfare agencies would make assigning different workers to different roles a nightmare.

Critical Commentary

Gilbert's concerns about the expansion of welfare are well taken, and his observations about the inefficiencies of welfare are justifiable. But his arguments against new claims are flimsy, and his views regarding cures for poverty seem forced into a preconceived framework.

Recall that, in his remarks on the expansion of claims, Gilbert charges activists with massaging data in order to elicit support for programs that they have already decided are desirable. He is very hard on reported evidence about the sexual abuse of children and rape. But the counter-evidence he introduces is just as weak.

This same problem of facile generalization taints his report on the dangers that teen mothers pose to the welfare of their children. Gilbert cites just one study to validate his conclusions. He suggests a further link between assumed abuse by mothers and the incidence of crib death. Several national and regional studies have found that children born to teenage mothers, in part because of their lack of access to prenatal care, are often underweight and frail (Ketterlinus, Henderson, & Lamb, 1990; Ventura & Martin, 1998). Besides this, we know that child abuse statistics are regularly biased, reflecting cultural construction and class vulnerability. The personal volatility imputed to teen mothers has not been found to be widespread (Horowitz, 1995; Walruff, 2002). The expectation that young mothers on their own will have a hard time handling the responsibilities of motherhood is plausible. But tarring these girls with unsubstantiated failings leads to punitive recommendations rather than the support they may need.

Gilbert sings the praises of self-responsibility and economic integration through work, but he neglects to mention how the market itself and the skewed distribution of economic rewards contribute to forms of institutionalized inequity that cause poverty. Individual causation—ineptitude, the wrong values, and the like—take the front seat. Strategies of intervention are cast around an image of the poor as people who do not quite abide by American standards of sturdy independence, work ethic, and family ethos. Behavior modification is needed to straighten them out. Once rehabilitated, the poor will be integrated into the market and become true—that is, productive—citizens. Some proposals along these lines, such as employment without choice, are hard to distinguish from those adopted by authoritarian governments.

Jordan on Struggling for Justice

The title of Bill Jordan's (1990) book—*Social Work in an Unjust Society*—captures the tension between the roles ascribed to social workers and their ethical commitment to justice. Jordan's approach differs from that of radicals like Piven and Cloward who stress the necessity of working outside and against the system. But neither does he subscribe to a belief that the profession's role is to prop up the status quo.

The Ethic of Social Justice and the Roles Assigned to Social Workers

Implicitly or otherwise, most jobs in social work come with a mission of control. Social workers are usually given coercive leverage over their clients. They can decide that certain requirements for a benefit have not been met. They can decide to remove children from their families. They can decide if a juvenile who has broken his or her parole should be sent to an institution. They can send a runaway child back to the family. In short, the positions held by social workers carry the authority to evaluate the behavior of clients and to enforce rules.

Rules supposedly represent a public morality; they are in place to enforce and maintain norms. A corollary assumption is that these goals or values represent the preferences of a majority. Social workers, then, find themselves in the position of enforcers. They can curtail the autonomy of clients.

The ethical dilemma disappears once clients are viewed as deviants, unable to fend for themselves in a rule-bound manner. But three considerations quickly make this solution much too simplistic. First, not all rules have moral content. Second, rules are standardized and abstract, while the situations that social workers confront are complex and idiosyncratic. Last, those involved in formulating rules are generally not representatives of a majority.

Moral reasoning is no substitute for knowledge of the law and social policy. Yet social workers handle tasks, day to day, in the field, precisely in situations where applying laws and policies is often ambiguous. Specific cases are open to a number of interpretations. Improvisation goes on all the time. The judgment, discretion, and skill of professionals all come into play to protect the public interest.

The interests of clients are at stake as well. Clients may be victims of injustices perpetrated by powerful groups who dominate decision making and influence the life chances and opportunities of clients. These "players" also condition the power and resources of social workers. Social worker–client transactions have to be understood within the ampler context in which policies originate. Only the guileless and utterly naïve would suppose that there is no real clash of interests between dominant groups, on the one hand, and the excluded on the other. A realistic expectation is that social workers are to act in conformity with rules formulated by those in charge, and only secondarily on behalf of the downtrodden.

Contradictions of the Liberal-Democratic System

The freedom and participation of individuals are ingredients essential to liberal democracies. This is the norm of high school civics textbooks. Be this as it may, Jordan concurs with the argument of some social justice theorists that there is a contradiction between property and personal rights (Bowles & Gintis, 1986). The accumulation of assets leads to the control of resources that others might need. The process gathers momentum. It allows the few to impose conditions for access to resources on the many.

Wealthy people, Jordan observes, are able to shape rules of distribution in their favor. They have a powerful say in setting wage and welfare benefit levels. As employers and landlords of the poor, they have enormous influence on remuneration and rents. They can become architects of economic marginality.

Some variations on the liberal theme (Bowring, 1843; Mill, 1912) express this link more clearly. Utilitarians, for example, assign to government the responsibility for structuring society so as to maximize production and optimize the distribution of welfare. The free market remains the best way to generate the largest possible income—with the added prescription that the resulting wealth be channeled to the whole population in fair proportions.

According to Jordan, the democratic side of liberal polities has serious fissures, too. Economic disparities impede access to political power. In reality, the majority principle excludes sizeable portions of the population. Political decision making may gain in efficiency, but at the cost of reducing outcomes to sheer competition, rather than consultation, cooperation, and compromise that are more in tune with genuine participatory democracy. These problems are endemic not only in the selection of representatives and decision making ostensibly by majority vote. They also characterize "expert" policies formulated without the participation of those affected by them. When applied to the poor, these arrangements tend to be paternalistic, shaped "for their own good."

Challenging the System From Within

Social workers face the dual challenge of responding to the here-and-now issues of clients and of evaluating options and strategies for dealing with the structural origins of those problems. Rules are not particularly case-sensitive. Besides, the connection between professional rules and social goals is often murky and even contradictory. Given these parameters, thought experiments require a good deal of ingenuity and imagination.

Compelled to apply the rules, social workers nevertheless have some freedom to interpret them. They can challenge their suitability for achieving one goal or another. They don't have to go by the book. They offer immediate counsel for the urgent needs of clients, and they open up access to resources designed to help them out. At the same time, their professional code specifies that social workers discern and respect the goals of clients themselves. They must also attend to the variable meanings of the problem, and their possible solution, that may arise out of the concrete social network in which clients find themselves.

Building mutual trust and identifying structural causes that may contribute to the client's problem are also part of the social worker's mission. Consciousness-raising of the latter sort resembles the strategy recommended by radical social workers. These efforts cannot be reduced to after-hours activism. They are to be carried on within the service agencies where most social workers do their work.

The justice-oriented social worker has two other commitments: to challenge the rules that hinder his or her clients' welfare, and to enhance the active participation of clients in decisions that affect them. This entails confronting the rules that infringe on or otherwise undermine publicly stated moral goals, such as those guaranteeing civil and human rights.

Similarly, social workers should build on the solidarity generated by common experiences and residential sharing in order to establish community centers where locals can gain an active voice in decisions affecting them (Figueira-McDonough, 2001). Reclaiming a degree of civic engagement that is a core expression of democratic values legitimizes such activities.

Critical Commentary

Jordan's proposals are more modest than those of radical theorists. The objective is not to dismantle the system but to draw on taken-for-granted principles—democracy, equal opportunity, civil rights and human rights—to correct the way the poor have been exploited, dominated, and rendered powerless. The approach sympathizes with the constraints imposed by social work practice in the trenches, and it sets forth strategies coherent with professional ethics. But detailed suggestions about how to implement such strategies remain to be specified. Jordan's preliminary map, enticing as it is, would benefit from the incorporation of experiential results.

Wakefield on Justice as the Organizing Principle of Social Work

In an important series of articles, Jerome Wakefield (1988a, 1988b) makes a useful distinction between disciplines and professions. Disciplines develop knowledge through theory and research; professions are supposed to change situations through interventions. The goal is to solve or prevent problematic situations. Disciplines are concerned with intellectual puzzles, professions with problems and solutions.

Plainly, professions base their intervention on knowledge derived from the theories and research of relevant disciplines. This borrowing forms a large part of their intake. But their practical activities follow from the values and goals that define their commitment to change. These are the norms, the desired outcomes, around which professions are organized.

Methods Versus Goals

Amid the reams of pages written about the organizing values of social work, the most direct statement comes from the professional codes of the National Association of Social Workers, cited at the beginning of this chapter. Two of these principles are central: (a) respect for the autonomy of the clients, and (b) contribution to social justice. Wakefield reiterates that these values are crucial to the professional identity of social workers.

Methods of intervention, he argues, have less importance. To prove the point, he assembles examples of methods that cut across human service professions. A typical arsenal of techniques includes those deployed in family therapy by social workers, counselors, family therapists, and clinical psychologists. The same "portability" holds at the macro level. Methods of community organization used by social workers and community developers are pretty much the same. All these professionals base their interventions on research conducted by social scientists. This is the provenance of constructs like psychological maturation, system and network linkages, inter-organizational connections, social capital, power structure, and so on. As knowledge expands and social contexts change, so will skills and methods of intervention. Dynamic adaptation of all human service professions is the only way to go. Fixing a profession around a supposed monopoly of intervention techniques is impossible and undesirable.

What distinguishes professions from one another, what gives them a unique identity, are their values or codes. Adherence to and promotion of these values are part and parcel of professional life. Success has to be judged in light of the commitment to the goals that the methods, whatever they may be, must advance. The rule applies to all professions. The goal of mental health professionals is to promote adjustment between the internal and external realities of clients. The methods and skills thought to be appropriate and productive have changed greatly—from scalding baths, to talk therapy, to behavior modification, to drug therapy. What is considered canonical one day may be quackery the next. Through all this, the remedial goal has not changed.

The Utility of the Concept of Distributive Justice

How do we put flesh on the abstract bones of self-determination and justice? Wakefield builds on Rawls's theory of distributive justice. True to its Kantian roots, the theory presupposes that we are all rational, and that we should be able to make decisions toward our own goals. Rousseau's notion of groups grounded on a social contract is also germane. This compact embodies an elemental trade-off. Individuals join social units and go along with their regulations in the belief that the group will be more efficient than scattered individuals in providing for their needs. This voluntary submission has a specific counterpart. It is the expectation that, downstream, social goods produced by the group will be distributed among all members.

Three principles determine distributive justice: (a) freedom—in other words, the right of all to the most extensive freedom compatible with comparable freedom for others; (b) equal opportunity, since economic and social inequalities can only be tolerated if positions that create them are open to all on equal terms; and (c) the difference principle—that is, social and economic inequalities are justified if and only if they function to benefit the least privileged. The principle of freedom accords well with the social work value of self-determination. The other two principles lie directly in the ambit of social work's justice ethic.

Legitimizing Psychotherapy as a Contribution to Justice

Principles of social justice are conventionally framed in terms of the distribution of economic goods. At first glance, the principles of equal opportunity and difference just mentioned appear to give credence to observers who assign priority to community organization and policy practice, stressing that these are the strategies that deal with access to rights and goods. Wakefield takes issue with this exclusivity of means. He reasserts the value of psychotherapy as a method at the service of justice.

Wakefield develops this idea from Rawls's insight that the psychological property of self-respect may be the most primary social good with which justice is concerned, independent of its economic implications. We gain self-respect by seeing ourselves as valued members of society and by being seen by our peers as such. Individuals with low economic and political status are likely to place themselves and to be positioned by others at the bottom of the pecking order. Low self-respect is thus a social construction. Lack of self-respect constitutes a barrier to freedom and equal opportunity insofar as it discourages individuals from pursuing these goals. Passivity can set in, letting others override legitimate desires and goals, and distancing those who are discouraged from the collectivity.

Wakefield extends this understanding of self-respect as a basic good to other psychological deficiencies that, he argues, are also socially created. His long list takes in a series of negative traits that result from bad experiences: low self-esteem, low self-confidence, low self-awareness, low problem-solving skills, low assertiveness, low self-organization, low social skills, and low emotional intelligence.

If social workers help individuals overcome problems in these areas and enable clients to pursue their goals by directing them toward opportunities, they are contributing to distributive justice. This is because justice so defined is nothing more than the distribution of socially created goods. Injustice, then, consists of social impediments in the way of reaching these goods. Justice-oriented therapists, in striving to remove or circumvent socially created psychological impediments, make a valuable contribution. By way of example, consider restrictions on the developmental needs of children. These may be biological, nutritional, or psychological, and they may be traced to the family situation, the surrounding environment, or some combination of both. Handicaps like these are attributable to failures of the social structure. The role of the psychotherapist is to foster viable personal development.

Obviously, policy advocacy and community practice are needed to redress some environmental and systemic conditions. Equal access to quality education is one such structural issue. If we are to live up to the equal opportunity principle, it is the institutional distortions of the education system that need fixing.

Critical Commentary

Wakefield's distinction between goals and methods is a helpful insight for social workers. So is his treatment of self-respect as a socially created phenomenon. The same goes for his depiction of psychotherapy as a justice-enhancing intervention.

Although Rawls's theory sets aside defects of nature because they do not meet his criteria of being socially created, we are becoming increasingly aware that many health problems are not matters of fate or bad luck. They are socially constructed. Polluted environments foster diseases. Insufficient food stunts growth and learning. Differential access to health services shortens the life of the least privileged. Lack of prenatal care affects what might otherwise be thought of as natural differences—for example, in intelligence. The market structure of health services in the United States leaves about 40 to 70 million citizens without health insurance. This constitutes a glaring failure of distributive justice, but it is one that Wakefield's model fails to address.

As a kind of afterthought, Wakefield makes allowances for clinical social workers who use their skills for other than justice objectives. The popularity of such specializations and the appeal of private practice are such that their place in the profession becomes justified. It is a mystery how this conclusion can be squared with the argument that values and goals, rather than methods and skills, organize and define a profession.

_____ Comparing Concepts of Justice in Social Work

The approaches we have examined treat social justice in markedly different ways, ranging from an ideal of equalization, to a social democratic order dominated by labor, to a liberal economic integration of responsible citizens under a free market. We have also looked at a couple of models that are less concerned with visionary goals, focusing instead on how to improve existing systems by challenging unfair policies or ensuring access to basic goods.

The more ambitious the justice model, the more sweeping the change goals and the more demanding the strategies recommended. The roles laid out for social workers in the creation of an egalitarian society are very far-reaching indeed. In contrast, by the standards of the labor socialism advocated by Cloward and Piven, social workers are dismissed as pernicious agents of the powerful.

Jordan's proposals require a complex response from practitioners. Social workers must assess the legitimacy of policies they implement, and they must empower their clients and protect their rights. Wakefield takes still another tack. By promoting goals over methods, he unifies the roles of social workers around the promotion of any activities that reduce injustice in the distribution of socially created resources.

Table 1.3 summarizes these diverse perspectives. It sorts out the authors' conceptualizations of what makes for a just and unjust society, outlines the changes and strategies proposed, and highlights the tasks assigned to social workers.

Table 1.3   Conceptualizations of Justice in Social Work

	Features of a just society	Features of an unjust society	Objectives for change	Strategies	Roles of social workers
Gil	Production of public goods for distribution based on needs Participatory democracy	Systemwide inequality Status quo ideology	*Long-range:* elimination of inequality *Short-term:* universal access to employment	Fight mass "false consciousness" Build just society through consensus or revolution	*Positive:* responsive to victims of injustice *Negative:* lack analytical and strategic knowledge of roots of social problems
Piven & Cloward	Labor socialism: a society shaped by labor to represent interests of labor	Any capitalist system serving interests of capital and exploiting workers	Promote democracy with labor participation Abolish welfare system that controls poor	*Desirable:* sustain the labor movement *Realistic:* use disruption during political realignment	Handmaidens of the status quo Controllers of the poor
Gilbert	Integrates citizens in the economy, requires social participation	Weakens citizens' responsibility by unfair, inefficient handouts	Move toward enabling state that promotes individual economic development and responsibility	Short-term help Accountability of outcomes through positive and negative reinforcement	Manage behavior conditioning Tailor interventions in cases of social handicaps
Jordan	Social policies reflect interests of the powerless	Policies made by and favoring the powerful	Participation of the powerless in decisions that affect them	Reform from within: challenge morality of rules and policies Uphold civil and human rights	Interpret adjustment of rules to cases Challenge rules that harm clients Organize clients for civic action
Wakefield	Based on distributive justice All have access to socially produced basic goods	Fails to provide access to basic goods consistent with level of development	Promote access to basic goods (e.g., food, shelter, education, health)	Professional methods that use any effective technique to promote justice	Increase distributive justice through interventions Promote self-respect as socially constructed basic good

2 Understanding Social Justice in Liberal Democracies

There is nothing so practical as good theory.

—Kurt Lewin

What is at stake in social policies that impact the lives of citizens? What assumptions, silent as well as spoken, underlie debates about issues of social policy?

Here we will explore some of the presuppositions and competing priorities that condition decision making on these controversies. In particular, we will examine the contradictions built into liberal democracies such as ours. We will see how a distinctive historical background has shaped the evolution of American political thought and its characteristic preference for freedom over equality. In addition, we will examine a variety of philosophical perspectives that reinforce or challenge this hierarchy.

_____ Liberal-Democratic Society and Its Contradictions

The search for social justice presupposes a functioning government. Except during times of drastic upheaval, social justice has characteristic links with the form of government in power. Different forms of government reflect and promote distinctive philosophies of social justice.

One school of theorists argues that any morally acceptable theory of social justice must begin with the notion of shared rights or common interests. There is something so fundamentally the same in all human beings that a theory of justice must, inevitably, be universal. Another perspective downplays universals. It argues that a social order is just if a country's policies and institutional arrangements are based on first principles.

Universality and first principles do not necessarily overlap. Although Immanuel Kant (1734–1804) claimed to support universal—that is, globally applicable—norms of justice, his principles were strictly individualistic, rational, and quite abstract. To say that the universal law of social justice requires you to act in such a way that your free will is compatible with the freedom of everyone else fails to spell out the concrete procedures and institutions that uphold those principles. It sounds like the biblical admonition to "do unto others as you would have them do unto you." The Kantian position is embedded in a Western, Enlightenment understanding of the supremacy of individual freedom. However this might be, it can be argued that the eminence given to human rights, the approval that the United Nations has accorded these rules, and the efforts on the part of international agencies to advance them around the world represent the full-scale emergence of universal social justice on the world stage.

Without doubt, cultures define rights differently. Some focus on individuals; some privilege communities. Whatever the underlying philosophy, specific institutional mechanisms vary across countries and affect the practice of social justice in their own ways. Rights emerge under discrepant historical circumstances, and they take shape with reference to disparate cultural beliefs. They are not born universal or stable (MacIntyre, 1981, p. 107).

The discussion that follows is geared to the liberal-democratic context. The idea is not to defend injustices perpetuated in this setting. The purpose is to lay out one model of social justice against which alternative ways of implementing freedom and equality can be compared.

The Roots and the Meaning of Liberal Democracy

If we grant that social organization requires some form of government, and that forms of government are linked with and reinforce philosophies of social justice, it makes sense to explore social justice as promoted in the United States by digging into its founding political values.

The United States exemplifies the prototype of a liberal democracy (Goodin, Heady, Muffels, & Dirven, 1999). What does "liberal democracy" mean in the United States? The quick response comes through in the declarations of political leaders to the effect that our country stands for freedom and democracy. The commitment of the American people to these values— our belief in their correctness—is so unshaken, the argument goes, that the country has a mission to spread them to other societies.

These principles are embedded in the Constitution. To a collection of colonies fighting against an imperial monarchy, populated by immigrants of whom many had fled persecution for their beliefs, the appeal of liberty and democracy was extraordinarily powerful. "Tyranny" was the archenemy.

But building "the first new nation" required more than allegiance to pleasant ideals and uplifting rhetoric. Good intentions did not guarantee implementation. The task involved devising rules to bring legitimate aspirations to fruition. In facing this practical challenge, the Founding Fathers were influenced by continental European philosophers as well as by Scottish and English thinkers—by Immanuel Kant, Jeremy Bentham (1748–1832), Adam Smith (1723–1790), and David Hume (1711–1776).

Celebrated as the philosopher of individualism and rationalism, Kant positioned himself at the same time as a great equalizer by attributing the capacity of choice to all of us. According to Kant, we all have the capacity to define our own goals and we should be able to choose the means to reach them. His influence was enormous on American ideology and, more specifically, on the formulation of this ideology in the Bill of Rights.

The ideas of Adam Smith proved comparably powerful during the formative years of the American system. It was Smith who conceptualized the architecture of an alternative economic order—namely, the competitive market. Open competition would not only create wealth but also lower prices and lead to a just distribution of assets. "The invisible hand," a self-correcting mechanism inherent in the competitive market, would guarantee harmonious outcomes, at least in the long run.

Others built on the theories of Kant and Smith to posit ways of ensuring that the well-being of the majority became a realistic measure of a government's success. The insights of these men coincide strikingly in promoting individualism and rationality. They share the expectation that these principles will advance the welfare of all citizens.

More of a political theorist than a metaphysician or economist, John Locke (1632–1704) reacted against capricious hierarchies—monarchies and aristocracies—that controlled and exploited their subjects. His proposal for a new start—a society of free citizens—meant keeping government small, limiting its role to maintaining order. Tyrannical rule was indeed the enemy. Locke's vision matched the thinking of fellow liberals perfectly, and it spoke to the fears of former colonists about powerful and presumably arbitrary government. The Protestant Reformation, more than 200 years old at the time of the American Revolution, also reverberated strongly across the Atlantic. Its rejection of the papacy and a strictly hierarchical church reinforced a widespread distaste for political as well as religious centralization.

Complementing what now would be called Locke's libertarian views were the populist ideals advocated by Jean-Jacques Rousseau (1712–1778). Influential in France and the United States, Rousseau's "social contract" became a cornerstone for both young democracies. Rousseau provided yet another philosophical basis for the growing belief that governments, far from being divinely ordained, as monarchies claimed to be, were instead human constructs—that is, compacts between rulers and ruled for the benefit of "the general will." The new perspective would find resounding expression later, in the words of Abraham Lincoln: a government "of the people, by the people, for the people."

The American Ideology

It was within this historical and cultural setting, shaped by innovative European thinkers, that a distinctively American ideology evolved. Successive waves of newcomers, arriving in the United States mostly from

Europe, were exposed to an amalgam of nontraditional ideas about politics and economics.

Several social scientists have explored the similarities of values and beliefs across different groups in the United States. Studies that focus on public opinion tend to uncover close to a consensus on general principles, with a much greater diversity of opinion regarding concrete cases. Our focus here will be on the common values. These norms fuel the political rhetoric that, in turn, defines the language in which social policies are discussed.

Ellwood (1988) and Edward Greenberg (1985) identify five values as vital to "the American mindset:"

- Individual autonomy
- Work ethic
- Family ethic
- Community autonomy
- Limited government

Individual autonomy refers to the belief that individuals have a significant degree of control over their destinies and that, at a minimum, they can provide for themselves. Since we live in a free society, the argument goes, you make your own choices, so you are responsible for the consequences. "Success" is evidence that you made the right choices, that you deserve the rewards and admiration that come with success. Conversely, failure is of your own making, and it is, therefore, "your own fault."

Work ethic is a virtue at the heart of both our conceptions about ourselves and our expectations about others. Laziness and idleness are signs of weak character. Diligence and "applying yourself"—in short, hard work—not only demonstrate character, but they also pay off. The more you work, the greater the material rewards. Wealth comes from disciplined effort, and poverty indicates laziness.

Family ethic is a group version of individual autonomy. Its standard is the nuclear family. This functional unit is sacred. The privacy of the family should not be invaded. By the same token, the expectation is that the nuclear family should take care of itself. The preference for a two-parent family stems in part from the belief that this form of organization offers optimal financial security for its members and can provide competent socialization for children—that is, bring them up properly.

Community autonomy reflects a sense of resistance against interference from outsiders. The belief—a mix of privacy and independence—is that community members should be the ones to take care of their own problems. Efforts to maintain schools under local control exemplify the urge for community autonomy.

The preference for *limited government* echoes the maxim that "the government that governs best is the one that governs least." The tradition goes back to the early days of the republic, even if this particular way of putting it first appeared in the nineteenth century. (Henry David Thoreau, the nonconformist author of *Walden Pond* whose theories of nonviolent resistance inspired Gandhi and Martin Luther King, coined the expression.) It is typically bundled with the economic ideal of "laissez-faire."

The popularity of minimal government—the long-standing idealization of a "night watchman state"—is remarkable in light of the growth in demands put on government. One of the most telling indicators of the appeal of this principle is how routinely presidents invoke it when promising to take government off the backs of citizens. The ongoing attraction of the "minimalist ideal" also comes across in the belief that private organizations are likely to be more efficient, better at getting things done, than their public counterparts.

Tensions of Liberal Democracies

For many of us, the content of liberal democracy is taken for granted. It is self-explanatory. It is part of our national identity. The American dream is, somewhat paradoxically, "just plain common sense."

A closer look at the principles of freedom and equality, the core ingredients of liberal democracy, reveals a dilemma. The two values cannot be maximized jointly. Privileging liberty tends to constrain equality. Conversely, giving priority to equality can restrict freedom. Laissez-faire societies often produce great social inequality, as happened toward the end of the nineteenth century. And democratic societies committed to equality are prone to develop an unwieldy, "all thumbs" apparatus of central control.

Numerous observers have taken note of the trade-off between the ideals of freedom and the demands for equality. Hayek (1976) declares outright that no plan for the distribution of benefits could be devised in a society where individuals are free, because individual responsibility for one's actions is incompatible with an overall pattern of egalitarian distribution. A. Pampapathy Rao (1998) claims that it is futile to speculate about freedom and equality without assigning priority to one over the other. He concludes that a society based on private property—a key dimension of freedom—gives an advantage to the wealthy, at the expense of achieving equality of opportunity.

Liberal democracies project a mixed message about a desirable society. The image is of a team in the same boat pulling together to brave the sea, at the same time that individuals compete for advantage. The implication is that goals of distribution should reflect both communal imperatives and individual aspirations.

The political scientist Hugh Heclo (1986) has argued that the American political tradition has embraced both readings of this goal. The historical record indicates, Heclo contends, that the welfare of citizens gets defined in two different ways.

The first understanding is *welfare as self-sufficiency*. Priority goes to individual freedom, property rights, and the protection of the individual against arbitrary government power. A self-interested pursuit of happiness is the standard for all. This reading of welfare puts great faith in the ability of ordinary people to know their own mind, to act independently, and to shape their own destiny. It is a conviction that is protected by civil liberties and by guarantees of a free market.

The second interpretation is *welfare as mutual dependence*. This applies rational criteria to the "self-in-group" rather than the "self-in-isolation." Under the first, *self-sufficiency* definition, the assumption is that if everyone pursues his or her interests and engages in exchange, the process will inadvertently (like Adam Smith's invisible hand) meet the needs of other people. Under the second, *mutual dependence* scenario, exclusive reliance on self-interest will eventually tear the social system apart. It is in the long-term interest of individuals to foster group solidarity. This perspective views government as a positive mechanism that provides public goods (e.g., schools, roads, defense) and promotes transfers (e.g., welfare payments) beneficial to the viability and prosperity of the community as a whole.

When Heclo estimates the balance between these working definitions of welfare, the success stories about self-in-group, *mutual dependence* that he musters turn out to come mostly from an agrarian America of early industrial times. He cites the common use of private property for pasture, hunting, and wood gathering. He also lists instances in which private property was transferred and even seized in the interest of communal needs, and he takes note of cases of limiting interest rates and setting prices for essential goods and services (milling, inn-keeping, and ferrying).

But these collectively oriented triumphs are in the minority. Heclo concedes that policies supporting *welfare as self-sufficiency* are winning out, though he questions the wisdom of this course in times of growing global interdependence. Under these circumstances, it is hard to link individual effort to outcomes. People feel they have less and less control over far-flung market forces, that events occurring beyond the boundaries of the nation-state can drastically impinge on their lives. The oil crisis of the 1970s was perhaps the most traumatic but hardly the only such wakeup call. Even so, the ideal of self-sufficiency is remarkably resilient.

The tension between the core principles of liberal democracy is reinforced by compartmentalizing freedom in the economic sphere from equality in the political sphere. Trying to resolve the dilemma in practical terms, commentators have been quick to point out the dubious assumption that the two spheres of the system can in fact be kept separate, insulated from one another.

Robert Dahl (1985) insists that economic inequality generates political inequality. Substantial differences in income and wealth correlate with differences in status, skills, control over information and propaganda, and access to political leaders. On the average, these capacities and opportunities, or the lack of them, build up from one generation to the next. The distribution of political assets becomes increasingly skewed. Procedural democracy alone—universal franchise, for example—cannot level the political field under these circumstances. It is slanted in favor of the economically powerful.

Rao (1998) extends Dahl's diagnosis. Capitalist states depend on business elites who use their freedom for their own benefit. Key issues in the political economy are worked out in the boardrooms and executive offices of state-size corporations. Talk about freedom is strategically aimed at diverting attention from this offstage style of shaping policy.

Claus Offe (1984) offers a more nuanced account of political inequality. Liberal democracy is, in effect, a capitalist government put in place to smooth the function of markets. Its ability to govern depends on revenues derived from capital investment and productivity. Government decisions, then, should favor industrial and financial interests. But in a democracy, political legitimacy comes from the people. To some extent, political decisions have to respond to popular demands. Yet middle class groups are better organized and more politically active than their lower class peers. The government tries to respond to and reconcile some middle class aspirations, while it can more easily put off radical demands from the worse off.

Both Rao and Offe highlight the limitations of the apparently pragmatic, divide-and-conquer resolution of the strains within liberal democracy. Giving priority to the principle of freedom in the economic sphere while relegating the equality principle to political procedures may seem like a tidy solution, but it is not automatically feasible. The challenge of defining social justice in liberal democracies cannot be dealt with by segregating the commitment to each principle into functional areas. The real question for most theorists of social justice revolves around justifications for, and criticisms of, the precedence of one principle over the other.

_____ Theories of Social Justice for Liberal Democracies

All these theories look at social justice in specific cultural, ideological, and historical settings. This approach encourages change agents and activists committed to social reform to analyze the culture and ideology within which they work. Attempts to nationalize health services, for example, have been notoriously unsuccessful in the United States because American voters often identify such programs with socialism (Schram, 1995). Evidently, such efforts cut against the American grain.

Questions about morality, of which social justice is a part, have traditionally belonged in the realm of philosophy. The theorists we are about to examine, regardless of whether they lean toward teleological or deontological approaches, try to break down this isolation of normative ethics from social philosophy. A common aim of the authors reviewed here is to provide a vision of a better society, a society that is more just, more legitimate, and more authentic (Phillips, D., 1986).

In varying degrees, the models of justice we are going to consider resemble ideal types. They are thought experiments that start by imagining a society with certain characteristics—e.g., liberal-democratic—and proceed to consider justifications as well as options for improving social justice, given that environment.

The theories reviewed here all struggle with issues of liberty and equality. Some give priority to liberty, others to equality. We will start with those that place individual freedom at the top of the agenda, then work our way, in rough order, toward those that privilege equality.

Giving Priority to Freedom

Robert Nozick on the Natural Right to Property and the Utopian Market

Laid out in his book *Anarchy, State and Utopia*, Nozick's (1974) entitlement theory belongs in the libertarian tradition. It is an offshoot of John Locke's proposition that freedom and property are natural rights that need to be protected from government interference.

Nozick (1974) argues that claims to property are not only legitimate— that is, good and proper—but also reflect natural rights. Transactions in free markets are fair because they are voluntary. In this respect, Nozick is concerned with procedural justice. His perspective is captured in this set of propositions: "If the world were wholly just, the following inductive definition would exhaustively cover the subject of justice in holdings [property]:

1. A person who acquires a holding in accordance with the principle of justice in acquisition,

2. A person who acquires a holding with the principle of justice in transfer from someone entitled to the holding, is entitled to the holding,

3. No one is entitled to the holding except by 1 and 2. (p. 151)

What matters is how market exchanges are carried out—that is, by free and fair procedures—not the pattern of distribution or the results of exchanges. In other words, process counts for more than outcomes.

According to Nozick, property obtained by violating either of the first two stipulations, and property held unjustly in light of his third principle, would have to be taken away and reparations made. He also concedes, as a postscript, that in rare emergencies the full right to property cannot be exercised. If, for example, a community is suffering extreme drought and the only source of water is on private land, then any absolute right to private property has to give way to the imperative of collective survival. On balance, however, Nozick opposes the intervention of the state in any form of redistribution, since this would violate individual rights. The supremacy of property rights advanced by Nozick finds a close real-world reflection in policies upholding "an ownership society" promoted by George W. Bush in his 2005 State of the Union speech.

Nozick's perspective rests on two presuppositions: (1) that property is a natural right based on an original claim, such as the claims of settlers in the Oklahoma Land Rush; and (2) the power of the market to distribute justly through the mechanism of the invisible hand. Critics have challenged both assumptions. Dahl (1985) argues against the presumption of property rights as natural. The right may be legally defensible but it is not constitutionally guaranteed. Dahl quotes Jefferson's view that the right to property is more social than natural—constructed rather than God-given. It is not so much prior to society as dependent on social convention. (Peterson, 1966, p. 338).

Other procedural questions can be raised: Who determines the legitimacy of the original claim? Entitlement to property requires that an ancestral point be fixed. Furthermore, how would issues of rectification and compensation be sorted out? The complexity of the problem should be evident in a relatively new country like the United States, where immigrants laid claim to territory that had been occupied much earlier by indigenous populations. The notion of "ancestral" property rights also ignores the fact that for a long time some groups have been prohibited from owning property.

The second foundational proposition of Nozick's theory is a belief in the social harmony and justice fostered by the market. The freedom of the individual is key and, following the vision of Adam Smith, equitable distribution is left to the workings of the market. It is this presumed outcome that deserves scrutiny.

Whatever the benefits of laissez-faire economics, it has not fostered the well-being of all citizens. Dahl (1985) acknowledges that the distributive results of the market were fairly beneficial, though narrowly defined, under certain conditions—during the mainly agrarian era in the United States, when citizenship was restricted, with women and minorities effectively excluded. However, from the mid-1870s on, as industrial capitalism became consolidated, the Supreme Court amplified the scope of the constitutional doctrine of "due process." The effect of these rulings was to insulate business from regulation (Brest, 1975). Over time, these changes created not an economically just society, but rather one of the most unequal of the twenty-first century.

John Rawls on Distribution, Freedom, and Basic Goods

John Rawls's *A Theory of Justice* (1971) has enjoyed great popularity in market democracies because it has provided a plausible rationale for the welfare state, within a capitalist framework. Individualism and rationality remain at the heart of Rawls's case. But, while giving priority to the principle of freedom, Rawls stipulates that all citizens are entitled to basic goods.

Rawls's theory descends from utilitarianism but goes beyond that lineage. Strict utilitarians consider a society just if its policies benefit the greatest number of its members. As a practical matter, if the GNP of India increased over the past decade, and the majority of the population benefited somewhat from it, the society would be considered just, even if huge economic differences persisted and a sizable portion of people went hungry. Rawls modified this "strict constructionist" version of utilitarianism by introducing the notion of basic goods—resources (food, shelter, clothing) indispensable for survival. An organized society is responsible for seeing that those who lack such goods get them, consistent with community standards.

Three procedural rules guide a just society in Rawls's view. First, each person is to have the right to the most extensive freedom compatible with a similar degree of liberty for all. This is the *freedom principle*. Second, social and economic inequalities are tolerated to the degree that they work to the greatest benefit of the least advantaged. This is the *difference principle*. Third, these differences are matched to—in effect, compensated by—offices and positions open to all under conditions of equal opportunity. This is the *equal opportunity principle*.

The first principle has absolute priority over the remaining pair, and on this point Nozick and Rawls agree. The second principle elaborates on the utilitarian theme by specifying that the advantages of those toward the top of the hierarchy of social positions—that is, the perks associated with leadership—can only be justified by the benefits that hierarchy brings to the least advantaged. The third principle comes closest to the ideal of equality by requiring equal access for everyone to advantageous positions.

One novelty of Rawls's theory is that it delineates government "branches" or functions for upholding a just social compact. The function of the *allocation* branch is to keep capitalism efficient. The competitive economy is fine-tuned through tax policies and subsidies. The idea is to fill in where pure efficiency criteria do not compensate for social costs. Government management along these lines would be unacceptable to Nozick, whose libertarian standards would consider taxes as theft.

The function of the *stabilizing* branch is to maintain sufficient effective demand. The goal is to ensure reasonably full employment—a desideratum inspired by Keynesian economics. The *transfer* branch secures a minimum of basic goods for each member of the community. In short, there is entitlement to assistance.

The role of the *distribution* branch is to ensure an approximately just distribution of income and wealth over time, by adjusting the dynamics of the market. The principal goal is gradually and continuously to correct the distribution of wealth and to prevent the concentration of power. Progressive taxes, inheritance taxes for the very wealthy, and tax credits for those with low income are all policy measures representative of this approach.

How would this type of community come about? How might the goals of the transfer and the distribution branches be reached? How would members of a society agree to the difference and equal opportunity principles? Rawls devises a procedure whereby supporters of a competitive, free, and open society would agree to a "mini-max" consensus that guarantees basic rights. A rational consensus could be achieved under conditions of a "veil of ignorance." Individuals, without knowing or being able to predict the position they will hold in a group, are asked to determine the minimum resources to which any member is entitled.

The following example, generated from the notion of a social contract, clarifies the strategy. Social groups grow out of a recognition that it is in the best interests of individuals to band together. Through a division of labor, groups can often produce more resources than individuals in isolation. Although becoming part of a group has advantages, it also puts demands on individuals.

Now let us assume that there is a major cataclysm and that a number of people find themselves in an environment similar to that in the film *Jurassic Park*. None of these people know each other. It quickly becomes apparent to these strangers that if they are going to survive, they will have to stick together. Their most immediate needs are for food and protection from dangerous animals.

To organize into a group, these individuals have to decide what would be the group's responsibilities toward the members and, conversely, what would be the members' obligations to the group. Remember, they are strangers. They know nothing about each other's skills and capacities. There are so many unknowns and the situation is so unpredictable that they have no idea about the eventual utility of their own skills and capacities for the group. They cannot anticipate what positions they might attain in the group, because the value of their potential contribution, relative to that of others, has yet to be determined. Under these conditions—that is, under a veil of ignorance—persons would act rationally by voting that every member, regardless of what his or her contribution turns out to be, would be assured a share of daily food and subsistence. In other words, they would be assured basic goods.

More complex and influential than Nozick's, Rawls's theory is just as individualistic and rational. In both cases, the state is not a party to the social contract, and society boils down to mutual agreement among individuals. Regardless of the difference principle, Rawls accepts differential compensation, so that his theory does not address economic inequality, at least not as an outcome. Furthermore, responding to basic needs in the Rawlsean sense comes closer to conceding humanitarian entitlements than redistribution (Phillips, D., 1986). The theory attempts to strike a balance between private wealth and public welfare. Accommodating equality while assigning greater weight to liberty forces a compromise that does not favor equality (Piven & Cloward, 1997).

Rao (1998) is especially virulent in his critique of Rawls. He comes up with a sardonic two-part example to bring home his criticism: First, you should be free to eat what you want to eat; this is the freedom principle. Second, you should eat in such a way that your crumbs should reach those without food; this is the difference principle.

Over a long career, Rawls clarified the rationale behind his principles and definitions. One of the objectives of the difference principle, he explains, was to offset advantages based on the lottery of natural gifts. Even then, however, inequalities generated by the need to compensate for more or less valuable benefits to the community cannot be reversed. From this perspective, the principle of democratic equality stands in some conflict with the accidents of natural endowment. Moreover, to prevent inequality in access to opportunities, Rawls recommends that states expand resources on education and training. Though not quite so explicitly, other basic needs such as health care provision and job entitlements, in consonance with the principle of equal opportunity and consistent with the standard of living of developed nations, are added as well.

Gewirth on Deriving Norms About Justice From the Web of Social Relationships

Reason and Morality (Gewirth, 1978) attempts to provide a rational justification for moral principles but, contrary to Nozick and Rawls, Alan Gewirth does not resort to hypothetical situations or mental experiments along the lines of the "state of nature," "original claims," or "the veil of ignorance." Instead, he logically derives his principles from the nature of social action.

Gewirth argues that moral principles can be found in the web of social relations, and that these rules can be extracted from social relations through reason, deductive as well as inductive. The essential ingredients of morality, of which justice is part, are common to all social ethics, founded in human interaction. Yet Gewirth shares with Nozick and Rawls an individualist, rationalist frame of reference. Like theirs, his perspective is Western.

Morally consequential action takes place whenever people shape their behavior for ends they regard as worth pursuing. The two distinctive features of human actions are that they are *voluntary*—you act out of free choice—and *purposeful*—you act intentionally. The decision to act purposefully in pursuit of a goal constitutes human action.

With this notion of human behavior in place, a normative structure for action can be derived. For starters, every agent implicitly makes a judgment about the goodness of his or her purpose and about the freedom and well-being associated with this goal. Next, in view of the goodness of a chosen goal, every agent implicitly claims the right to freedom and well-being. Finally, since the individual is a prospective agent who has purposes to fulfill, the chosen goal provides sufficient reason to claim the rights of freedom and well-being. Logically, such rights must be applicable to all prospective agents.

The purposefulness that interests Gewirth encompasses three types of goods. *Basic goods* are preconditions, physical and psychological, to an agent's performance. *Non-substantive goods* include whatever goods the agent has and regards as worthwhile. *Additive goods* are conditions that enable any person to increase his or her capacity for purposeful action and therefore his or her ability to reach more goals.

The only condition that Gewirth attaches to purposive action for it to have "value" is that it cannot impinge on the freedom of others. Particular goals differ, but the capabilities of action must precede any purpose. Otherwise, action is simply not possible.

So freedom and well-being are indispensable to achieving any purpose. These are rights to which people can make claims. If this right holds for the agent, it has to be true for all persons. By the same token, all citizens have duties related to the rights of freedom and well-being of others; these are fundamental—in effect, universal—human rights. You cannot assert a right for yourself without accepting the obligations that go with it. Rights are reciprocal.

By virtue of having purposes and pursuing goals, the rights to freedom and well-being are universal and egalitarian. The crucial precept for any agent "is to act according to the generic rights of your recipient as well as yourself" (Gewirth, 1978, p. 64). This constitutes the *principle of generic consistency* in human relationships. It is a revival of the "do unto others" rule.

However, the *principle of generic consistency* goes beyond requiring noninterference in the initiatives of others. It entails a duty to contribute positively to the well-being of others, considered as recipients of one's actions or possible actions. The desirable state is that "each person have rational autonomy in the sense of being a self-controlling, self-developing agent [who] relates with others with respect and cooperation, in contrast to being a dependent, passive recipient of agency of others" (Gewirth, 1978, p. 135). Positive duties place more demands on individuals than do negative obligations. Often they require institutional mechanisms for providing assistance to people who lack basic goods—that is, those who lack the psychological or physical preconditions for free and purposive action.

In sum, the *principle of generic consistency* has both direct and indirect consequences. The first application requires the individual agent to act in accord with the rights of freedom and well-being of all other persons. The latter involves rights and obligations developed through social rules and prescriptions.

Critics of Gewirth question the universality of the two principles and, hence, his assumption that consensus can be achieved around them. They point out that configurations of social rules emerge in different contexts at different times, and that the rights based on individualism and rationality, far from being universal features of the human condition, are culture-bound. The creation and consolidation of social norms and rules require attachment to a specific community, to a shared way of life and civic culture. The process cannot rely on a supposedly universal sentiment or logic (MacIntyre, 1981; Sullivan, 1982). (See Table 2.1.)

Nozick, Rawls, and Gewirth on Social Justice: Competing Views

While they vary in their treatment of equality, the primary principle for all these authors is freedom. A staunch libertarian, Nozick stands against all

Table 2.1   Selected Philosophies of Justice Within the Context of Liberal
                     Democracies

PART ONE: PRIORITY GIVEN TO FREEDOM

Nozick

Premises:

Basic Premise—
    Natural right of property based on legal transmission of original claims.

Derivative Premises—
    Distribution: Invisible hand of the market.
    Taxes and redistribution infringe on this natural right (Libertarian).
    Voluntary charity acceptable for those without property and unable to
participate in the market.

Outcomes:

    Progressively unequal and unregulated society. Charity the only response for
those without property or losing it in the market.

Welfare Type:
    Voluntary charities.

Critique:

How to determine the original claim?
    Legal transmission is socially defined, does not occur as a dictate of nature.
    Distribution does not occur naturally. People are often legally barred from
obtaining property.
    Laws can favor those with property.
    Those with property are in a better position to acquire more property.

Rawls

Premises:

    First principle: Freedom only restricted by equal exercise of freedom of others.
    Second principle:

    (a) Benefits of those who are advantaged are only permissible if they help the
         disadvantaged (*difference* principle)

    (b) All positions are open to everyone (*equal opportunity* principle)

    Distribution: Decisions about the distribution of basic goods would be made
under the metaphoric "veil of ignorance."
    Access to all basic goods (shelter, food, health) through a transfer institution.
Other institutions would deal with the efficiency and stability of the market and
avoid dysfunctional inequalities through taxes, incentives, and regulations.

Outcomes:

    An unequal society is acceptable, tied to proportional benefits contributed by
individuals.
    Benefits to disadvantaged individuals would count in justifying the rewards for
those in privileged positions.

Table 2.1 (Continued)

Access to education supplements related to the equal opportunity principle. This, and the institutionalization of basic goods, opens the opportunity for entitlements for the disadvantaged

Welfare Type:
  Entitlement to basic goods.

Critique:

The most important goal is freedom, and the weaker distribution goals remain subject to it.

Although the "veil of ignorance" is ingenious, it is unworkable. There are no standards about levels of inequality and levels of disadvantage. The level of entitlement to basic goods remains undefined. It will permit survival but not necessarily mobility or the reduction of inequality.

Gewirth

Premises:

Justice principles are generated by social relationships.

Purposive action to achieve goals is a just goal across all human communities. The prerequisites for purposive action—freedom and well-being—are also just.

The principle of generic consistency in human relations will safeguard both freedom and well-being:

  (a) freedom from non-interference obliges to contribute to the welfare of others as recipients of good, purposive actions, and

  (b) institutional assistance would be extended to those without conditions, material or psychological, for purposive action.

Outcomes:

Equality is not part of this equation, and any purposive action toward goals that do not limit the freedom of others in their purposive actions is just. So, any type of outcome within this framework is just. Nothing hampers the generation of great inequality.

Institutional assistance to those materially or psychologically hampered in the quest of their goals may or may not enable them to pursue their goals, depending on the type of assistance received.

Welfare Type:
  residual and rehabilitative.

Critique:

The assumption that the norm of purposeful action is universal seems problematic. It may simply represent Westernized values of individual freedom and rationality. The question is whether the theory is specific to a culture that values freedom and rationality rather than to cultures generally. It is not the common link of goal-directed behaviors to social interaction that makes them just. Rather, it is solidarity with a culture in a community that upholds the values of individual self-directed activity. The assistance provided for those who cannot contribute appears to be remedial, not compensatory.

compulsory transfers, such as taxes. He considers these transfers an infringement of rights, pure and simple. According to Nozick, entitlement is the
ultimate grounds for economic reward. Measures to rectify unjust property
holdings call for corrective action in favor of those who are rightly entitled.
There is no obligation to help citizens who are worse off than others. The
only acceptable means of help is voluntary. Charity is permitted, but the
poor have no legal or moral entitlement to help.

Differences in wealth do not enter into this calculus. People considered
entitled to great riches or poor people with meager entitlements are treated
equally. Since corrective measures based on original claims to property are
hard to specify and adjudicate (imagine the paper trail!), getting the legitimacy of original property ownership straight is just about impossible. All
this encourages a pattern of growing intergenerational inequality, with negative consequences for the principle of equal opportunity.

Consider the following example. In 1973, Nelson comes into the world
with a substantial trust fund. He grows up with his necessities and whims
abundantly satisfied. He attends the best schools. Eventually, he takes over
his parents' highly valued property. In the same year that Nelson is born, on
the other side of the tracks, Jim is born into poverty. During his formative
years, he goes without the barest necessities. He lives in a slum and attends
a local school, where teachers spend most of the time trying to impose discipline. There are not enough books for all the students, and often the school
year is cut short because of budget problems. In Nozick's view, this state of
affairs—the blatant contrast between Nelson and Jim—may be regrettable
but it cannot be considered unjust.

Rawls's difference principle addresses the issue of distribution. Some
people will, inevitably, accrue greater economic compensation because of
their contribution to the community. Such privileged positions are justified,
however, only if those who are worse off benefit from the activity of those
who get more. In addition, economically rewarding positions should be open
to all. Equality of opportunity is supremely important.

The "worse off" label conveys an exclusively economic meaning. How it
is to be measured is uncertain, in any event. It appears that the transfer
branch of government would be in charge of helping the worse off with general revenues obtained through taxes. Rawls clearly establishes a duty to
transfer funds to this group, but the objective of such help is not equalization. The rationale appears to be more modest—to meet basic needs.
Nevertheless, Rawls is relatively open in his handling of equal opportunity.
He exhorts governments to improve education and training for all. There is
a strong indication, as we have seen, that rights are tied to equal opportunity in the world according to Rawls.

For Gewirth, just as for Nozick and Rawls, the basic value is freedom. In
Gewirth's account, freedom takes two forms—choice and pursuing your
own goals—which he equates with the right to well-being. Since both freedom and pursuing one's goals are intertwined, the right to well-being would

seem to imply support for equality. This is not so, however, since well-being is individually defined.

Gewirth steps back a bit to resolve this problem. He proposes that basic goods are prerequisites to freedom of choice and to pursuing one's own goals. It follows, then, that all persons have the right to adequate food, shelter, health care, and so on. This right takes precedence over all other entitlements, because it underlies the possibility of action and its success. Social rules to supply basic goods to those persons who cannot obtain them by their own effort or who are psychologically or otherwise disadvantaged are a must.

It is clear enough that the institutional responsibility for leveling the playing field lies with the state and that funding is to come from general revenues. The problem is that Gewirth never specifies how basic goods should be distributed or how this entitlement should be honored in practice. His concern is not with inequality per se but with the prerequisites for exercising freedom in action.

In the end, none of these theories is much concerned with economic equality. They all assume that economic efficiency is the paramount value for society as a whole.

Bringing Democracy to the Forefront

Recently, several movements have grown up in reaction to the sway of individualism in American philosophical and social thought (Winfrey, 1998). Probably the most articulate is the communitarian movement (Bellah, Madsen, Sullivan, Swidler, & Tipton, 1985; Etzioni, 1995, 1996a, 1996b; Figueira-McDonough, 2001; Putnam, 1993a, 1993b, 2001). Following in the steps of Heclo, who argued that the United States has a communitarian as well as an individualistic tradition, communitarians point out that the emphasis of Western, or Anglo-American, culture on individualism must be balanced with a sense of collective responsibility, so that the social fabric can be protected. They contend that self-centeredness and adversarial relationships are weakening institutions such as families, volunteer associations, neighborhoods, schools, and indeed the nation itself.

Social justice theories based on the individual in isolation, the communitarian critique contends, are mythical fabrications. Moral principles are unavoidably interactive, not atomized, and individuality can only be expressed in how we relate to one another. We are born and grow into social relationships, and we assume certain responsibilities within this matrix of connections. These obligations go beyond the personal level. Doctors, social workers, and teachers, for example, accept responsibility for their clients in the exercise of their profession. They do not see themselves primarily as profit maximizers. Issues such as education, health care, social security, welfare reform, and environmental protection cannot be approached solely within the contractual framework of the market. How they affect families, neighborhoods, schools, and other institutions must also be taken into account.

Communitarians view group identity as a cornerstone for the development and implementation of collective goals and as a corrective to the ethos of self-interest. The need for solidarity reflects not only the fact that people are embedded in social networks, and therefore interdependent, but also that civilized society hangs on such bonds. What's more, communities not only constitute an all-purpose social cement. According to the communitarians, they also have the potential to act as repositories of democracy (Etzioni, 1995, 1996a, 1996b). It is this capacity for acquainting ordinary people with hands-on involvement in public issues that makes it possible to move from procedural democracy to participant and presumably more communal democracy.

All of the authors we are about to consider take this idea a step further. Their central contention is that democracy, in an interdependent society, cannot be limited to politics as conventionally defined; it has to include the economic sphere as well.

Clark and Higgins, and Winfrey on Correcting Markets and Expanding Public Goods

Regulations are corrections to the market that are designed to counter the laissez-faire tendency favoring cumulative inequality. Strong defenders of economic competition, Clark and Higgins (1973) also recommend certain compensatory measures for "raw" capitalism. The following story, adapted from their book, illustrates their starting position clearly:

> John and Jim are two men who fish from the same shore. John builds a canoe and his catch is now twice as large. Jim asks John to use the boat and agrees to give 1/4 of his catch to cover John's cost of building the boat. Since Jim will get twice as many fish, it is worthwhile paying for the use of the boat. Other fishermen see the benefit the boat renders, so they also build boats for hire. They will keep this up to the point when each gets a modest gain. John, the ideal entrepreneur, also hires other fishermen to use his boat to fish for him. To motivate them, he has to promise to increase the share of the catch that they can keep. The more boats, the greater the share John has to give to the hired fishermen, and the smaller he can keep to himself. Finally, there is a greater abundance of fish so that it can be sold more cheaply to a greater number of people. (p. 27)

This fable crystallizes the virtues of the ideal market. Innovation increases production and benefits the innovator. Imitation increases competition and spreads the benefits to others, so that all benefits level out more or less equally. Finally, the product becomes cheaper because of competition, and more consumers can afford it. It is a win–win situation all around.

Clark and Higgins are quite aware that the idealized market has been distorted in practice. The tendency is to produce large inequalities, thus defeating the original distributive functions of the model. While acknowledging the faults of the market system, Clark and Higgins admire its productive efficiency. Rather than opting for dismantling it, they engage in a corrective effort with the intent of strengthening democratic goals. Their chief concern is to establish fair competition and simultaneously increase the well-being of workers. They see market regulations as a set of policies to be devised by the state. Here is a sample of the measures they propose:

- Effective trust legislation, to prevent the growth of corporate monopolies or oligopolies
- Tariff legislation opening markets to cheaper goods
- Corrective taxes and subsidies
- Conservation of natural resources
- Shortening the workday and providing better pay (as improvements occur in methods of production, the worker should benefit from the results)
- Compensatory and preventive protection for dangerous and injurious occupations
- Emergency employment during periods of recessions and depression
- The principle of "eminent domain," used to shift polluting businesses out of residential areas
- Weakening of the divide separating capital from labor by facilitating access of workers to stock ownership

Such corrective measures, Clark and Higgins believe, are feasible in view of mechanisms (the referendum, the recall, the short ballot, direct primaries, and so forth) associated with a democracy-by-the-people. They view their agenda, lengthy as it may be, as a doable as well as necessary set of corrective measures.

Winfrey's contribution (1998) stresses the growth of public goods in a mixed economy. Public goods—the classic examples are defense and roads—are consumed jointly; they are accessible to all citizens. If the goods are considered entitlements, the tax bill can be adjusted, so that marginal benefits equal marginal costs.

Winfrey realizes that in a democratic society, agreement about entitlements, such as welfare, and assessments of their benefits relative to costs, run up against predictable problems. The norm of allocative efficiency applies. The gist of allocative efficiency is not generosity. It is to provide the most welfare at the smallest cost. Issues dealing with social problems are typically translated into policies that calculate quick solutions and employ stringent outcomes—in other words, that minimize waste. A common result is rejection of programs that do not satisfy a cost/benefit calculus.

The constraints on decisions regarding public goods are political and governmental. The first challenge is to devise a set of political institutions that allow citizens to voice their preferences regarding public goods. The second problem reflects the risks and difficulties associated with government implementation, such as these:

- Insufficient information for officials to make sensible estimates of the marginal costs and benefits of public goods (e.g., cutbacks in rehabilitation services in prisons)
- Imperfections in the administrative process that encourage short-run incentives for bureaucrats to be efficient rather than effective (e.g., removal of clients from welfare rolls to achieve a favorable quota)
- Flaws in the legislative process that allow special-interest groups to have undue influence (e.g., health insurance organizations versus national health plans)

Many policy practitioners have welcomed this diagnosis (e.g., Jansson, 1999; Piven & Cloward, 1997). But there is considerable disagreement about how to deal with questions of political feasibility. Ideological misperception and feelings of powerlessness are serious obstacles to increasing public goods that will benefit the most vulnerable. Some critics note that proposals of the type advocated by Winfrey give insufficient attention to the weakness of procedural democracy in achieving reforms committed to egalitarian values. Since citizens who benefit materially from the market tend to translate their economic advantage into political power, they are likely to oppose reforms that run against their interests, and to do so strongly and effectively. In short, Winfrey suffers from political naiveté. Less pessimistic observers argue that the way to counter the uneven balance of power would have to involve "a long march through the institutions"—coalitions of organizations with common interests.

Phillips on the Social-Democratic Option

In the last chapter of *Toward a Just Social Order*, Derek Phillips (1986) embarks on an empirical search for a just economy. The blatant inequality produced by corporate capitalism as practiced in the United States is a far cry from the fair market envisioned by Adam Smith. Although remarkably efficient in generating wealth, the market's glaring disparities in distribution jeopardize the well-being of large sectors of the population, who often lack access to health care, adequate nutrition, housing, and education.

Derek Phillips believes that a focus on distribution is a dead-end pursuit. It ignores the hidden forces that create and govern the pattern of distribution. He agrees with Marx that a just social order depends ultimately on the structure of production in an economy.

When the socialist movement emerged in the nineteenth century, its rallying cry was to carry democracy forward into the economic sphere, in order to improve the condition of the poorer classes (Clark & Higgins, 1973). The original idea was to implement democracy in business and industry. A primary option was to use the state to control the economy. Even if such a model achieved a fairer distribution of income, goods, and services, however, Phillips states that it is economically inefficient. Then, too, civil and political liberties tend to shrink with centralization in decision making. Phillips also points out that an entrenched elite of fat-cat bureaucrats emerges, perpetuating inequality in both income and services.

In search of an alternative system that respects individual rights of choice and equality, Phillips follows a teleological approach. That is, he engages in a kind of reverse engineering. He starts by looking at the consequences of adopting a given economic order, then works his way back to the institutional arrangements that, he infers, best produce the observed results. The political model that meets his criteria (choice and equality) has the following characteristics:

- Natural resources (coal, oil, iron, forest, electricity, transportation, etc.) are nationally owned. This entails either substantial planning on the part of the state or large-scale, state-owned enterprises.
- The remainder of the economy is in the hands of private, medium-size enterprises.
- Citizens have freedom of choice in work, in associations, and as consumers.
- The selection of representatives is a prerogative of voters, not of the apparatus of political parties.
- All persons have generic rights (entitlements) to adequate food, shelter, and health care. The distribution of economic goods and services involves a two-tier scheme. The first tier can be fulfilled in either one of two ways:
  (i)   Guaranteed welfare rights (state provision of medical care, education, housing, employment), or
  (ii) The state redistributes wealth and income to assure that everyone is able to obtain an adequate level of goods and services.

The second tier refers to residual rights, that is, salaries and wages. Regarding these areas, Derek Phillips (1986) reformulates and extends Rawls's difference principle. "An unequal distribution of economic rewards is morally permissible," he reasons, "if it does not lead to concentrations of wealth that are demonstrably detrimental to the exercise of other people's rights (e.g., political participation)" (p. 403). What Phillips implies here goes beyond Rawls's difference principle. Equal distribution cannot really occur until generic rights have been assured.

This mixed system of distribution, usually labeled as social democratic, stands apart from others by trying to reduce social inequalities without curtailing basic freedoms. To maintain such a system of universal access to generic goods requires a program of redistribution through steeply progressive taxes. Those with higher incomes and wealth pay proportionately more in taxes. Denmark, Sweden, Norway, and Finland are examples of nations following this model.

Common criticisms of the model are that it stifles markets, that progressive taxes discourage investment, and that protective legislation makes labor prohibitively expensive. The unavoidable result, this line of criticism contends, is a growing number of inactive workers. Unemployment insurance creates an ever-expanding, untenable burden on the state. The imbalance between inputs and outputs makes for a dysfunctional system. The entire operation appears to be headed in a downward spiral. The only way out is movement toward a more liberal, market-driven economic order.

Supporters make the point that there is no evidence that such downturns occur in social democracies at times of international depressions or during the expansion of world economy. In other words, the social-democratic system remains competitive under a variety of conditions (Esping-Andersen, 1996; Goodin et al., 1999). It does not have any inherently self-destructive dynamic.

Zucker on Democratic Distributive Justice

Ross Zucker calls into question what he considers to be the false dichotomy between a liberal economy and political democracy. In *Democratic Distributive Justice* (2001), Zucker narrows in on the difference between true and nominal democracy.

A substantive democracy, according to Dworkin (1981), is obliged to enforce equal treatment and, even more, to promote equality of resources. A political system cannot qualify as substantively democratic unless it fosters a just economic order. This standard goes back to the definition of democracy as rule of, by, and for the people. Democracy cannot be "for the people"— it cannot be a democracy—if it maintains conditions of social injustice.

There are two ways to achieve substantive democracy. One is to formulate a decision rule through which individuals decide their own rights. Another is to deduce a right through a course of reasoning about how citizens can claim a right. Zucker follows the second path.

Economic output is the result of a complex interdependence between capital, work, and consumption. These components cannot be atomized, because it is their systemic interdependence that maintains and generates growth. Reliance on the notion of markets purely as composites of individuals is a misleading fiction. Actions that sustain the economic circuit are generated by socially connected forces. Capitalist systems, Zucker argues, exhibit not only an overt dimension of individualism. They also have a less obvious, communal dimension that requires us to rethink how an alternative distribution of rewards and benefits might work.

Self-seeking individuals in an exchange system have to "grow into" the requirements of mutual dependence, which supports the system. The reconciliation of social determination and self-determination is necessary for a realistic theory of rights. Material rewards should not rest only on individual economic contributions but also on entitlements tied to membership in the community that upholds the system. The economic ensemble is made up of diverse contributions that form and cohere into an interdependent network. In Zucker's world, these contributions come from three main sources: capitalists, workers, and consumers.

The argument is based on the primacy of social groups and, in particular, their superiority over isolated individuals in producing resources. While Rawls uses a similar logic to justify the group's responsibility for ensuring the provision of basic needs, Zucker goes further. He calls for an equal distribution of socially generated resources. His argument is that credits and recognition should be given to all economic agents who contribute to the creation of value—to consumers as well as producers—as a matter of entitlement. In recognition of the communal nature of the contributions that go into exchanges, Zucker calls for the right to a proportional share of part of the national income.

Zucker's rationale is buttressed by economic demand theory, which attributes an essential role in development to consumption. It counters the supply-side position, which sees capital as the crucial factor. John Maynard Keynes (1935) is the classic proponent of the demand school of economic thought. It was Keynes who blamed the failures of the capitalist economy on its inability to provide full employment and on its arbitrary and inequitable distribution of wealth and income.

Keynes's vision of the structural nature of unemployment, of the need for full employment as a means to reduce inequality, promote consumption, and strengthen the economy, can be read as a recognition of the collective properties of the market. If communal rather than individual contributions are responsible for much of the growth in wealth, reducing inequalities becomes a matter of matching rewards to contributions. The macroeconomic perspective that sees the collective ingredients of market operations provides justification for redistribution, while a microeconomic perspective does not.

In contrast to other theorists, Zucker bases his position on rights to shares of resources to economic contributors rather than on transfers to meet basic needs. Welfare, for example, consists of income transfers to the poor that may marginally make up for a deficiency of resources. But it has no systemic effect on diminishing inequality. Zucker considers welfare of this type to be more humanitarian than egalitarian.

The right to a fair portion of national income may mean one of two things: a right to well-being or to the equal pursuit of a common goal. Some people, one might argue, do not seek to maximize wealth. They are happy enough with a decent living. The problem with this hypothesis, Zucker responds, is that it misconstrues the nature of wealth, and it leads to false inferences about the pursuit of wealth as a common end. While some members of a capitalist society may be uninterested in wealth, they cannot be expected to be content with just getting by. Seemingly modest requirements—an automobile, refrigerator, toaster, oven, television, stereo, microwave, a variety of clothes and furniture, vacations, restaurants, recreation, entertainment, college education, computer and Internet connections, advanced medical treatment, and so on—presuppose a prodigious system of wealth generation. We are no longer talking about bare-bones subsistence. The bar defining a comfortable standard of living has been raised. Since practically everyone in a capitalist system seeks wealth in the sense just described, a community of economic ends—a modern-day "pursuit of happiness"—is a fact of life.

Zucker (2001) argues that a communal basis for a right to part of national income exists beyond doubt, even if an ingrained culture of individualism blinds us to this right. Distributive justice is based on a right derived from communal contributions to a share of part of the national income. Granted the interdependence of capital, labor, and consumption in building the economy, these follow from the community propensity to consume as an aggregate. The multiplication of wants through advertising, diffusion, and a keeping-up-with-the-Joneses effect increases the quantity of goods that consumers buy. Goods derive much of their value, indexed by prices, from the willingness of consumers to pay for them. So consumer decisions reflect and contribute to the same ends as those of producers. Consumption is not just consumption; it is an economic contribution. Customers are active partners in the creation of wealth. They account for a significant part of total wealth that is produced. This wealth should be divided among all citizens. Distribution as a right reflects contributions to the production of wealth, and it serves in fact as an impetus to further growth in the contribution of consumers: the more consumption, the more investment; the more investment, the more production.

Zucker's formulation is fairly recent, and it has yet to receive much critical review. The schematic fashion in which it has been presented here necessitates a simplification of the original version. Zucker does not serve up a blueprint. This said, on balance, the theory lacks concrete suggestions as to how the value of community consumption, compared to the contributions of other economic actors and functions, would be calculated—nor, for that matter, is it clear how individual contributions are to be estimated.

On the other hand, no one has criticized Zucker for failing to think outside the box. His theory has the makings of a fresh perspective on what goes into economic equilibrium. Supporters welcome an approach that links diverse components of an interdependent economy directly to benefits. This represents an innovative break from the standard market calculus. Zucker makes a logical case for the right to benefits based on contributions to the economy. By highlighting the communal nature of consumption, he attempts to establish a new generic right that promises to reduce inequality and increase substantive democracy.

Dahl on the Priority of Participatory Democracy

Robert Dahl's (1985) *A Preface to Economic Democracy* argues that the right to self-government trumps the right of property. Calling into question the self-definition of the American republic as a beacon of democracy, Dahl observes dryly that "to say that democratic institutions and political rights have shown a certain capacity of survival is not to argue, however, that political equality is alive and well in the United States" (p. 52).

Dahl is aware of the possibility that massive departures from political equality may be the price we pay for the achievements of corporate capitalism—for greater efficiency in economic affairs and greater liberty in political life, relative to the inadequacies of other "isms." But vigorous defense of this line of thought requires assent to a couple of doubtful propositions. One is that property rights have an inalienable status. The other is the reduction of the right of self-government to procedural democracy.

Some relatively tame criticisms of the presumptive natural right to property came up in our discussion of Nozick's libertarian theory. Dahl's critique is pointed. He underlines the difference between instrumental and inalienable rights. These often get confused in arguments over rights, even though they have radically different implications for the democratic process. Consider the following:

- If property is an instrumental—that is, contingent—right and self-government a fundamental and inalienable right, then the former is subordinate to the latter.
- If private ownership is a natural and inalienable right, it could be that property rights are superior to the right of self-government. If this were so, the democratic process could not infringe on property rights.

Democracy can be seen as a danger to property, or property as a threat to democracy. In the first instance, the concern is that those without property, being more numerous, might join together to form a majority that bans or severely restricts property rights. The flip side of this is that economic resources can be converted into political resources, destroying or vastly diminishing the prospects for political equality.

The solution to the dilemma turns on whether the ownership of property is or is not a natural right. Although liberty—the principle from which property rights flow—is founded on a right to do as one chooses, it is not an absolute, since the exercise of freedom cannot infringe on the freedom of others. To the extent that economic inequalities impede the access of others to needed resources, as defined by the standards of the society, property rights have to be regulated. Furthermore, to the extent that the concentration of property spills over into unequal political rights, a skewed distribution of this sort would work against equal participation in self-governance.

The instrumental right to property as a component of economic freedom underwent a historical transformation, as did the idea of fair competition. "By 1900," Blum (1963) explains, "man became economic man; democracy was identified with capitalism; liberty with property and the use of it; and equality with opportunity for gain, and progress with economic change and accumulation" (p. 39). Hardball conservatism successfully transformed the Jeffersonian ideal of agrarian republicans, one that privileged small to medium-size farms and enterprises, into corporate ownership. Enshrining the corporate economy in the ideology of the early republic made it look acceptable. An economic order that fostered inequality in the social and political spheres gained legitimacy by an ideological sleight-of-hand.

For Dahl, the inconsistency between corporate capitalism and the commitment to democracy persists. His position is that the democratic process—the right to self-government—is among the most sacred of moral rights. It outranks property rights, not to mention the unlimited acquisition of private property. The *demos* (the common people) and their representatives are entitled to decide, by means of democratic procedures, how economic enterprises should be owned and controlled.

A democratic government might need to regulate economic freedom in order to protect fairness in competition and to guarantee equal political rights. Equal political rights, in turn, depend on the distribution of material resources and the extent to which economic order itself favors equality of wealth and income.

At the core of a democracy is a belief in the right—inalienable for citizens—to govern themselves. The practical validity of the claim rests on certain assumptions about the nature of decision making "of the people, by the people, for the people." Dahl spells out these principles in the following terms:

- Society needs to reach some decisions binding on all
- This involves setting the agenda and making final decisions that become binding
- The process should include only persons who are subject to those decisions, since laws cannot rightfully be imposed on others by persons who are not themselves obliged to obey those laws
- The good of each person is entitled to equal consideration (this is the weak principle of equality)
- The burden of proof must always lie with anyone who wishes to establish exceptions to the principle (this is the principle of liberty)
- All adult citizens are equally qualified to decide which matters do or do not require binding collective decisions (this is the strong principle of equality)
- In general, scarce and valued resources should be fairly allocated. Fairness sometimes requires that each person's need or desserts be taken into account. At other times, it requires that each person receive an equal share or equal chance. When the claims of different persons to a scarce resource are equally valid, the resource should be divided equally, if it is divisible. If not, then each claimant should be entitled to an equal chance of getting it (this is the elementary principle of fairness).

Using these principles, Dahl (1998) draws up criteria for participant democracy. He fleshes out political equality in terms of equally weighted votes, effective participation, enlightened understanding—enough time for the discovery and evaluation of your own preferences—control of the agenda, and inclusiveness.

Dahl also insists on a distinction between fundamental and inalienable rights. Inalienable rights are essential to democracy, fundamental rights to liberty. In this way, he sets up a moral hierarchy with democracy at its peak. The system is open to regulating economic freedom through the democratic process.

Dahl puts considerable effort into developing the principles behind the democratic process. On the downside, however, he says little about concrete strategies for redressing the current system of inequitable property accumulation, and his treatment of how to insulate the democratic process from unfair economic influence is sketchy.

Table 2.2   Selected Philosophies of Justice Within the Context of Liberal Democracies

PART TWO: PRIORITY GIVEN TO DEMOCRACY

Clark, Higgins, Winfrey

Premises:

Basic Premise—

Market regulation and the expansion of public goods are the conditions for a just society.

Derivative Premises—

Anti-trust legislation, taxes, subsidies, conservation of resources, pollution control. Protection of workers' well-being and partial ownership of companies (e.g., stock funds), emergency employment in times of economic crisis.

Expansion of public goods, i.e., goods that are of common interest and used by all the community, including welfare. Such goods should not be subject to market-like assessments of costs/benefits.

Reforms can be brought about through democratic mechanisms such as referenda, recalls, direct primaries, and short ballots.

Outcomes:

A more regulated market to avoid excessive inequality, protection from environmental hazards, and assurance of workers' rights. The expansion of entitlements to cover common needs of all citizens.

Welfare Type:

Universal programs in such areas as health, education, child care, and social security.

Critique:

The mechanisms of reform assume a much more participant and egalitarian democracy than the one likely to exist in a liberal market economy. Given the inequality of resources, powerful opposition against regulation would filter into the

(Continued)

Table 2.2 (Continued)

political arena. Expansion of public goods would require a strong consensus among citizens and the re-education of policy makers about social issues.

Phillips

Premises:

Basic Premise—
    The goal is to carry democracy to the economic sphere.

Derivative Premises—
    Natural resources and public goods are nationally owned and managed by state agencies.
    Direct voting, entitlement to general goods for basic needs, and moderate to low inequality are standard.

Outcome:

    These specifications describe the social-democratic systems of Northern Europe. Often characterized in the United States as socialist, they have a free market with democratic procedures.

Welfare Type:

    Universalistic, i.e., all citizens have access not only to social security but also to a variety of services based on common needs (health, education, child care, and the like). These universal programs are funded by progressive taxation.

Critique:

    The model may limit freedom of the market, making it less efficient, and limiting growth. Furthermore, it is expensive, and heavy taxes may stifle entrepreneurship.

Zucker

Premises:

Basic Premise—
    Substantive democracy requires a just distribution of economic resources.

Derivative Premises—
    Economic output and growth result from a complex interdependence of capital, labor, and consumption. Without consumption, there is no demand, and without demand, there are no jobs or profits. While capital is needed for investment and workers are needed for production, all citizens are consumers.
    So part of the benefits from production should be distributed equally among all citizens who consume and pay for the products and services.
    Individual benefits would go to workers and the owners of capital, and consumer benefits would flow to the community of consumers.
    The right to an equal share of the national income will augment consumption and give a further impetus to the economy.

Outcomes:

The general entitlement would increase the resources of all citizens, benefiting the disadvantaged and, to a certain extent, decreasing inequality, since what is available for private benefits is curtailed.

Welfare Type:

In principle, given general equal entitlement, none would be necessary.

Critique:

How would the division between communal and individual benefits be calculated? How would it work during times of economic crisis not caused simply by underconsumption? How would you deal with sizeable individual needs such as catastrophic illnesses?

Dahl

Premises:

Basic Premise—
The right to self-government is superior to the right to property.

Derivative Premises—
Liberty is a fundamental but not an absolute right; it cannot infringe on the fundamental rights of others.

To the extent that large inequities infringe on the rights of others to obtain resources deemed socially necessary, economic inequality leads to unequal political participation.

This runs counter to equal participation in self-government, which is an absolute right. It also limits capacity of people to serve their self-interest.

Citizens and their representatives should decide how the economic enterprise should be owned and controlled, according to democratic principles of fairness.

Outcome:

Dahl envisions a society that rejects the separation between a free economy and procedural democracy. The absolute value of democracy requires a substantive democracy that shapes the economy, as part of the inalienable right of people to govern themselves. Structural decisions about the economy would be made through political participation, adjusted in terms of fair distribution of resources. Inequality would be low.

Welfare Type:

Entitlements automatic to people falling below a level necessary for political participation and economic well-being.

Critique:

How democratic procedures might infiltrate the economic sphere is not clear. Nor is it clear how some complex economic decisions could be decided by popular vote. On the other hand, desired outcomes might be decided by all citizens, with the government accountable for bringing these goals about.

Regulating Markets, Increasing Public Goods, Equalizing
Benefits for Community Consumer Activity, and Promoting
the Ascendancy of Democratic Over Freedom Rights

Clark and Higgins, Winfrey, and Phillips see regulation of the market—
in particular, protecting the distribution of certain essential goods from pure
market transactions—as a way of enhancing equality and preventing further
social disparities. They also share the belief that such reforms can be brought
about through democratic processes.

Phillips's empirical approach provides a real-world anchor in a turbulent
sea of theorists. His research on market democracies enables him to identify those variants—namely, social-democratic systems—with an egalitarian
profile. He then links the policies and institutional mechanisms—treating
natural resources as public goods, for example, guaranteeing across-the-
board entitlement to basic goods—favored by social-democratic countries
for moving toward equality and substantive democracy. While Phillips's
conclusions are not radically different from those of the other analysts, his
recommendations are comparatively operational.

Dahl follows a more deductive route. He sets out to demonstrate that
democracy is a higher good than freedom. The precedence imputed to
democracy over liberty has an important consequence. It means that the
design of economic structures should be worked out democratically. Dahl
has a harder time than Phillips with the operational task of "getting from
here to there."

Zucker goes down still another road. For the most part, he is uncon-
cerned with the debate over liberty and democracy. His central focus is on
rights to economic benefits. Consumers are a vital factor in economic development. It follows, so he argues, that in the aggregate, consumers deserve a
corresponding share of benefits. Such benefits, if given equally, would boost
the well-being of the entire community and decrease the maldistribution of
individual rewards.

Freedom Versus Democracy:
Priorities in the United States _____

American political culture assigns priority to liberty. The coming chapters
(3 through 9) will present a historical review of welfare in the United States that
gives abundant evidence for power of this core tenet of the American creed.

The main contours of a distinctively American perspective on social
equity should be plain enough already. Recall the charity model that Nozick
proposes as a remedy to poverty. With a few variations (e.g., at the state
level and in piecemeal economic regulations), this was in fact the dominant
approach to "the social question" in the United States for generations,
through the early decades of the twentieth century. It was only in the 1930s,

with the deepening of the Depression and the rise of the New Deal, that ideas similar to those given theoretical shape by Clark and Higgins, and Winfrey took hold.

Later, in the 1960s, the Great Society promoted under Lyndon Johnson came up with a weak imitation of the social-democratic model. By the beginning of the 1980s, and accelerating through the opening of the present century, there has been a powerful return to the "freedom first" presumption. The effects of this turnaround—in particular, worsening inequality—have been alarming. Proposals for substantive democracy of the sort advocated by Robert Dahl, and ideas like those set forth by Ross Zucker, favoring an equitable distribution of benefits for all contributors to economic development, have yet to be seriously considered, much less given trial runs.

3

Evaluating Distributive Justice in the United States

Ill fares the land, to hast'ning ills a prey
Where wealth accumulates and men decay.

—Oliver Goldsmith, *The Deserted Village* (1770)

Expanding the Welfare State Concept

The English policy analyst Richard Titmuss (1958) looked at welfare from a fresh perspective. In everyday American parlance, "welfare" means public assistance. The definition is narrow and its connotation pejorative. The negative ring is associated mostly with the dependence of welfare on general revenues—on taxes paid by hardworking citizens who themselves are not welfare cases, or do not see themselves as such. In most other advanced industrial societies, however, universal programs erase the invidious split between contributors and recipients.

Titmuss defines social security as occupational welfare. The contributions of workers sustain the system, and for this reason benefits are generally considered to be a right. But in fact, the contributions of younger generations supplement retiree benefits, and Medicare—a program attached to Social Security—is partially funded out of general revenues. In any event, it is the principle of participation, however partial, that exempts Social Security from the lowly status of public "assistance" and that legitimizes it as an entitlement.

By international standards, occupational welfare—particularly the regressive reforms associated with it—and the absence of a national health policy look weak and patchy in the United States. Backers of the American system contend that the negative grade is misleading. The United States looks like an outlier because of its unique form of public/private collaboration. Once contributions from private as well as public sources are factored in, the sum total of services and cash benefits delivered to Americans matches and sometimes actually surpasses the sustenance and help provided by other welfare states.

Gottschalk (2000) gives a vigorous defense of the hybrid arrangement. In this system, benefits are tied to jobs, not citizenship. Employers administer the private side, with the support of government. The government sets rules and guidelines, and provides incentives and tax breaks to private employers, who in turn offer pensions, health insurance, and disability benefits. These payouts and services are negotiated through labor contracts for about two-thirds of the workforce. The officially public pieces of the welfare state—Social Security, Medicare, and Temporary Assistance for Needy Families (TANF)—fill the gaps that the private sector leaves unattended.

The partnership has always been voluntary for employers, who receive tax breaks for running their programs. The system has never covered all workers, and it is falling apart. Its foundations rest on a stable industrial workplace that is crumbling in postindustrial societies. The partnership was not designed for an economy whose hallmarks are employment mobility and rapid turnover in technology.

A significantly more ample notion of welfare traces its lineage to Titmuss. Welfare consists of any benefits that are not earned through market trans-actions but instead are given free by the government in the form of incen-tives, tax cuts, or grants-in-aid. The switch in viewpoints is simple but it has seismic implications for how welfare and its costs are understood. The "pas-sive" loss of established sources of revenue—through tax breaks, for example—affects the account balance of the public treasury just as "active" expenditures on public programs do. Both costs constitute welfare. The drawdowns attributable to incentives and the like, however, are usually hid-den from public view. Spending on welfare programs, narrowly construed, is much more visible. Public spending in either form has its defenders. Supply-side theorists favor tax cuts; demand theorists prefer welfare grants.

State-supported higher education is a public benefit given to the middle class. Tuition payments cover only part of the costs of land grant universi-ties, for example. Taxes paid by everyone—even by those who cannot afford tuition payments as well as by those, at the opposite end, who send their children to private universities—go to pay the remainder. Another hidden welfare benefit is the tax deduction for interest paid on mortgages. The larger the mortgage and, as is likely, the more expensive the property, the more substantial the tax break.

In 2000, special tax rebates cost the government over $55 billion. Corporate welfare—"wealthfare"—encompasses preferential benefits for giant corpora-tions. Twelve corporations with earnings of more than $12 billion between 1996 and 1998—Texaco, Goodyear, Colgate-Palmolive, and MIC WorldCom, for example—received $535 million in tax credits or refunds. The oil and gas industries get similar write-offs for depletion of reserves. Mining and timber industries use public lands at nominal fees. Airlines, defense contractors, and commercial agriculture have received, and continue to receive, federal subsidies. Some—the sugar and pharmaceutical industries are prime examples—keep

Table 3.1   The Upside-Down Home Owner Subsidy

People who make the most get the biggest subsidy because they borrow more and are in higher tax brackets.

Income Categories	Percentage Who Claim Deduction	Average Deduction	Average Tax Savings at Marginal Tax Rate
$10,000–$25,000	11%	$432	$65
$25,000–$50,000	33	1,704	256
$50,000–$75,000	63	4,028	1,128
$75,000–$100,000	81	5,991	1,677
$100,000–$200,000	90	8,430	2,163
$200,000–$500,000	93	12,845	4,624
$500,000–$1 million	91	16,863	6,678
$1 million to $5 million	68	21,928	8,684
$5 million & above	62	25,528	10,109
Average Deduction	27%	$2,319	N/A

Source: IRS, Statistics of Income for Year 2000.

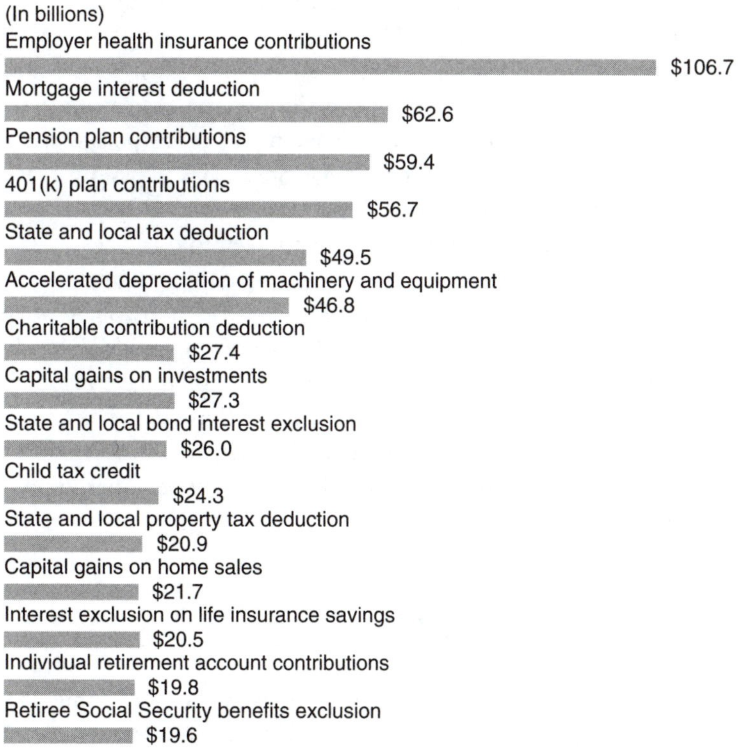

(In billions)
Employer health insurance contributions $106.7
Mortgage interest deduction $62.6
Pension plan contributions $59.4
401(k) plan contributions $56.7
State and local tax deduction $49.5
Accelerated depreciation of machinery and equipment $46.8
Charitable contribution deduction $27.4
Capital gains on investments $27.3
State and local bond interest exclusion $26.0
Child tax credit $24.3
State and local property tax deduction $20.9
Capital gains on home sales $21.7
Interest exclusion on life insurance savings $20.5
Individual retirement account contributions $19.8
Retiree Social Security benefits exclusion $19.6

Figure 3.1   Federal Government Major Tax Breaks

Source: U.S. budget for fiscal 2005.

Table 3.2   Middle Class Pays So the Rich Can Pay Less

Income Category (in thousands)	Share of Alternative Minimum Tax	
	2003	*2010*
$30–$50	0.2%	1.1%
$50–$75	1.2	7.2
$75–$100	2.1	14.0
$100–$200	15.9	36.3
$200–$500	43.0	30.7
$500–$1,000	13.8	4.2
$1,000 or more	22.5	6.0

Source: Tax Policy Center.

prices high with the help of tariffs that reduce competition (Barlett & Steele, 2002; "Corporate Welfare Runs Amok," 2005; Johnston, 2003).

In short, the ampler definition of welfare includes the targeted distribution of unearned income from public funds. The process takes two basic forms: One involves directly distributing governmental payments and services. The other exempts citizens from contributing to the treasury in several specific ways—mortgage deductions, for example, or corporate write-offs and the like. By this definition, the United States has a plainly regressive system of redistribution. The country has a welfare state that reserves many of its benefits for the comfortable and the very well to do.

The alternative minimum tax (AMT) was originally designed in 1969 as a way to prevent wealthy Americans from using deductions, shelters, depreciation allowances, and a variety of other loopholes to pay ridiculously low taxes or, in some cases, no taxes whatsoever. This should have made the tax code more progressive. Since then, however, inflation creep has caused the AMT to fall most heavily on the middle and upper-middle tax brackets, as shown in Table 3.2, with proportionately less stringent penalties imposed on the true upper crust.

Dimensions of Distributive Justice

The second chapter gave an overview of a variety of philosophical approaches to social justice within the context of liberal democracies. How can these theories be used as standards of evaluation? A fair approach is to select the theories that are in accord with "the American way"—in other words, that give priority to freedom—as the criteria by which to assess the operations of welfare in the United States. The theories of Novick, Gewirth, and Rawls generally fill this bill. But Novick does not consider welfare to be a legitimate function of government at all, and Gewirth's principle of "generic consistency in human relations" has yet to be cast in operational terms. This leaves us with Rawls's theory as a standard for evaluating the American welfare state.

Rawls defines basic goods as those that all members of society should have access to. They are "basic" because they are essential to survival—*food, shelter, and health*—as defined by the standards of a particular society.

Remember that while freedom is Rawls's primary principle, the difference and the equal opportunity principles set some conditions or boundaries on it. The *difference principle* requires that *the rewards of citizens in higher positions be reflected in benefits for the less advantaged*. The equal opportunity principle requires *open access to available positions* on the part of all. In postindustrial societies, this corresponds very closely to access to educational opportunities.

Rawls does not call for equality in the sense of equality of results. But he does propose that economic and social institutions guarantee access to basic goods and education as preconditions of equal opportunity. He attributes to government a role in avoiding dysfunctional inequalities, through *taxes, incentives, and regulations*.

It is from this perspective that we will examine the extent to which the United States has used welfare policies to curb or undo inequality. Rawls's ideas about distributive justice shape our assessment of the operations of the American welfare state.

How Does the United States Rate on Distributive Justice?

Basic Rights: Food, Shelter, and Health

Hunger

In the early 1960s, Michael Harrington's documentation of widespread hunger in the United States shocked the nation. Hunger was so extensive in certain areas that it reached levels comparable to conditions in the most destitute parts of the Third World. Great improvements have been made since then. The Food Stamps program became one of the most successful of federal initiatives. Can it be said that hunger has now been eliminated in the United States? Apparently not.

According to a 2004 report from the U.S. Department of Agriculture, more than 12 million American families (11.2 percent of all households) struggle, not always successfully, to feed themselves. At some time during the year, these households do not have enough money or other resources to get enough food for all their members. The estimate is that some 3.9 million Americans go hungry at some point in the year. Others get emergency relief from food programs, community food pantries, and emergency kitchens. The Center for an Urban Future found that, in New York, 550,000 families—fully a quarter of all working families in the state (more than half of them formed by married couples)—had incomes too low to cover basic needs (Fisher, Colton, Kleiman, & Schimble, 2004; Herbert, 2003).

Homelessness

Persistent homelessness is the most direct indicator of the failure to provide shelter to all. Conceivably, given the existence of public and private shelters, the threat to survival might be minimal. But the inference would be quite out of line with Rawls's theory, which defines "survival" in terms of the concrete requirements for integration in a particular society. Homelessness is a condition—a status—that spills over into other areas: getting a job, attending school, avoiding undue risks to health and security, and maintaining a minimum level of privacy and stability.

The McKinney Act of 1987 is the only piece of legislation addressing this social problem. None of the multiple revisions of the act—in 1988, 1990, 1992, and 1998—have generated enough resources for emergency allocations for shelters and transitional housing. Furthermore, the different versions all turn a blind eye to underlying causes.

Since the end of the 1980s, debate has raged over how to count the homeless. Estimates range from over 3 million to a low of 125,000. Several definitional problems enter into these huge discrepancies: Who exactly is to be considered homeless? What are the statistics to be used for? How is homelessness measured, once it is defined? And how exactly is the information to be collected? How do you enumerate a population whose "places of residence" are nebulous at best (Corday & Piton, 1991)?

The National Law Center on Homelessness and Poverty (2004) released a count in 2004. The Center's report indicated that at any given time, there were about 840,000 homeless. Over a year, there are between 2.5 and 3.5 million, of whom 1.35 million are children. A survey of 605 cities conducted by the U.S. Conference of Mayors (2002) shows that the time people remain homeless has lengthened. Requests for shelter went up by an average of 13 percent in 2003, with the result that more homeless were turned away for lack of space.

A representative national sample of homeless people using services provides more background information on the homeless. Table 3.3 gives some of the findings from a study fielded in the late 1990s (Burt, 2002).

Table 3.3 Basic Demographic Characteristics of Current Homeless Clients (in Percentages)

	Age		
	All	Men/children	Women/children
Race	25–40	35–44	25–34
W	41	58	34
B	40	32	45
Prior Residence			
Central cities	71	64	70
Marital Status			
Married	9	63	15
Single	48	15	46
Education			
Less than high school	38	54	53
High school	34	25	20
Present Spell			
Homeless for more than 6 months	30	37	22
Prior spells homeless	49	56	49
Partner/spouse	10	74	18
House emergency	63	83	81
Causes of Homelessness			
No rent money	15	33	20
Job loss	14	6	—
House violence	4	—	18
Work past month	44	39	27
Food stamps	37	59	74
Hunger*	40	37	40
No medical insurance or Medicaid	55	61	27

*Some days in past month without food

Source: Reprinted from Martha R. Burt. Homeless Families, Singles, and Others: Findings from the 1996 National Survey of the Homeless Assistance Providers and Clients, in *Housing Policy Debate,* 12(4), pp. 737–780. © 2001 Fannie Mae Foundation, Washington DC. Used with permission.

Data on place of origin and racial breakdown—the proportion of African Americans and those originating from the inner cities—are clear tip-offs to how homelessness afflicts the most destitute. Even so, a third of the homeless have completed high school, and 44 percent have worked during the previous month. These characteristics suggest a modicum of stability among at least some of the homeless population.

Still, in another one-third of the cases, homelessness was attributable to the loss of work or the failure to pay rent. Access to health and food was very poor, the frequency of spells of homelessness was high, and their duration was protracted. Education among the homeless with children was lower than for the whole sample, and so was their labor force participation while homeless.

There are clear differences between homeless men and women with children. Men are four times more likely than women to be accompanied by their spouses or partners, and they are over three times *less* likely to have access to health care.

The homeless with children have greater access to emergency housing and Food Stamps than others. Yet they report levels of hunger similar to those experienced by those without children. Finally, the causes of homelessness are different for males and females with children. Failure to meet rent payments drove over one-third of the men into homelessness, while domestic abuse was a major cause for 18 percent of the women.

Access to Housing

The demand for housing on the part of low-income families greatly exceeds the supply. Spatial mismatching between affordable housing and the location of job opportunities compounds the crisis for working families. Seventy percent of poor employed adults and children who live in rentals face high costs and location problems (Sard & Waller, 2002). Rents correspond to about half of their income, and these families typically live in substandard apartments in rundown buildings, in unsafe neighborhoods. Only one-quarter of these families are eligible for direct assistance (Swartz & Miller, 2002).

There are 4.2 million low-income renters receiving assistance through public housing and Section 8. Roughly 1.3 million are tenants in public housing, 1.6 million use Section 8 vouchers to find housing in the private market, and 1.3 million live in privately owned but subsidized properties (project-based Section 8). TANF emergency housing assistance is limited to 5 years over a lifetime (O'Dell, 2004). According to the National Low Income Housing Coalition (2002), the minimum national median salary needed to afford a two-bedroom housing unit in 2002 was $15.21 per hour; this is the "housing wage." Table 3.4 shows the discrepancy between rental costs and the incomes of many working families in California.

Table 3.4   The Housing Wage

Hourly Wages (40-hour week) Needed to Afford a Dwelling

| | *Number of bedrooms* | | | |
	zero	*one*	*two*	*three*
California	$13.35	$15.69	$19.69*	$27.00

*fair market rent: $1,024

| | *Wages in California* | | |
	Hourly	*Annual income*	*Percent of income for 2 bedrooms*
Minimum Wage	$6.75	$14,040	87.5%
Poverty Wage (federal)	$8.85	$18,408	66.8
Median Wage	$14.72	$30,619	40.1
Family Wage	$18.64	$38,771	31.7

- A single earner at minimum or poverty level (e.g., a single mother or couple with two to three very young children) cannot afford the rent.
- A single median wage earner with two children can afford the apartment by sacrificing other necessities.
- Two earners with at least one having a median wage can afford the apartment.

Source: National Low Income Housing Coalition (2004, press release). Based on an unpublished paper for community scholars by Limor Bar-Cohen (2002). http://www/NILHC.org.

In 2005, according to a study conducted by the National Low Income Housing Coalition, a full-time worker at minimum wage could not afford a one-room apartment *anywhere in the United States* (Pelletiere, Wardrip, & Crowley, 2005).

Health Care

Previous chapters laid out the private/public system of health care in the United States. Public programs such as Medicare, Medicaid, and the State Child Health Insurance Program (SCHIP) cover the elderly and disabled, the medically indigent, and children, respectively. For the working population, voluntary, publicly subsidized programs run by employers may offer health benefits.

Recent statistics showing a growing percentage of families without health insurance testify to the weakness of the system. Forty-five million Americans—15.6 percent of the population—lack health insurance. This number is nearly twice the population of Canada. Sixty percent of the uninsured are full-time workers, and 16 percent are part-time (DeNavas-Walt, Proctor, & Mills, 2004; Jost, 2003). (See Figure 3.2.)

The health care deficit persists because individuals do not meet the criteria for public health programs, or because they cannot pay the growing cost of premiums and co-payments of work-related health programs, or because they do not have on-the-job health benefits and are unable to pay the typical annual premium for family coverage—about $9,068. Health insurance premiums have grown faster than wages, as Figure 3.2 shows.

The United States spends a higher fraction—15 percent—of its gross domestic product on health than other OECD (Organization for Economic Co-operation and Development) countries—$5,440 on a per capita basis. The jump in health costs between 1997 and 2002 affected all OECD countries, but it was accentuated in the United States, at about 2.3 percent, as compared to other nations offering universal coverage, where it was about 1.7 percent. A comparison between the United States, the United Kingdom, and Canada, shown in Table 3.5, highlights the close association between access to care and income in the United States (Jost, 2003, p. 215).

Lawrence Jacobs and James Morone edited a volume entitled *Healthy, Wealthy, and Fair* (2005), in which they launch a forceful criticism of

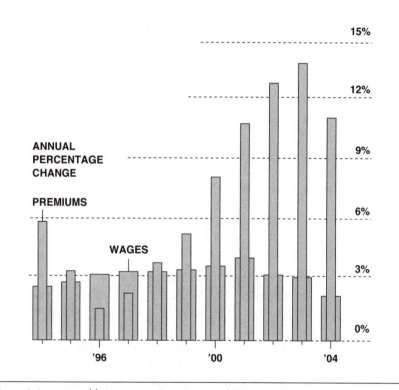

Figure 3.2   Health Insurance Premiums and Wages: 1995–2004

Source: Findings from the Kaiser/Hewitt 2004 Survey on Retiree Health Benefits #7194. This information was reprinted with permission of the Henry J. Kaiser Family Foundation, a nonprofit, independent national health care philanthropy and is not associated with Kaiser Permanente or Kaiser Industries.

Table 3.5   Responses Regarding Negative Health Decisions Due to Cost (%)

	Canada	UK	USA
Did not fill prescriptions	13%	7%	26%
Did not get medical care	5	3	26
Did not get tests/follow-up	6	2	22
Did not get dental care	26	19	35
Had problems paying medical bills	7	3	21

Source: Adapted from Jost (2003, p. 215). Based on the 2001 international policy survey by the Commonwealth Fund/Harvard Harris.

American policy regarding the right of access to health. They compare outcomes across nations as well as within the United States.

The life expectancy of American females at birth ranks 17th, and males rank 20th, among the industrialized OECD countries; the country ranks last among the 13 wealthiest nations on overall infant mortality, low birth weight, and life expectancy for babies and infants. People die younger in Harlem than in Bangladesh. The leading causes are unrelenting stress, cardiovascular disease, cancer, and untreated medical conditions among the poor—not murder and drug overdoses, often played up by the media. Jacobs and Morone (2005) quote a recent report by the Institute of Medicine that blames gaps in insurance coverage for 17,000 preventable deaths a year. Health bills, they point out, are the major cause of personal bankruptcy filings.

Jacobs and Morone credit SCHIP for permitting Medicaid to reach 20 million children and the Robert Wood Johnson Foundation for being instrumental in inducing state governments to place health clinics directly in schools. The Earned Income Tax Credit (EITC) is responsible for lifting millions of low-income workers and their children out of poverty. In doing so, the tax credit has improved their chances of access to health care. In spite of these steps forward, however, Jacobs and Morone conclude that a universal program, as provided by other postindustrial societies, is needed to grant all Americans the right to health care.

Educational Opportunities

Economic participation is tightly linked to education in postindustrial societies where technological development proceeds at a breakneck pace. According to Rawls's equal opportunity principle, the level and distribution of education are critical.

The United States has been an educational pioneer. It became the first country to require 12 years of formal schooling—the K–12 formula. The GI

Bill that came in the wake of World War II made the United States the first nation to provide widespread college education. School integration during the 1950s was a crucial step toward equal opportunity. The Great Society reforms of 1965 extended federal mandates regarding education in order to help poor performers and the children of deprived families. Twenty years later, evaluations showed progress in high school graduation rates—from 56 to 74 percent of all 17-year-olds; a reduction was also apparent in the white–black gap in dropout rates among 16- to 25-year-olds—from 13.2/27.9 to 12.2/14.9 percent, respectively (Jencks, 1991).

Equal access to education is still unfinished business. While rapid progress in forging a large middle class by upgrading education is a source of pride, the overall statistics conceal the fact that a significant portion of the population, especially in the inner cities, is losing ground (Wilson, 1991). OECD data (2003) on public education helps to delineate the strengths and weaknesses of the educational system in the United States at the beginning of the twenty-first century. (See Table 3.6.)

Among OECD countries, the United States—in absolute numbers, not as a proportion of the GNP—spends the most for public higher education and is nearly at the top in expenditures on primary and secondary education. In addition, teacher contact hours at every level are higher than in other countries.

However, the teacher–student ratio is below the median, and so are the mean scores on science tests taken at age 15, even if students in the United States test considerably better in reading proficiency. In most OECD countries, the inverse relationship between long-term unemployment and education is evident: the lower the education, the higher the probability of joblessness. However, the rate of unemployment at each education level is lower in most of the developed countries than in the United States.

The data from the 2003 OECD survey suggests that a greater investment in public education, as a proportion of the GNP, might drive down the student–teacher ratio, especially in the area of science. Scores on science testing have a higher standard of deviation in the United States than elsewhere, indicating a very wide spread in attainment. In other words, the problem in American education is one of distribution. The United States has outstanding public schools that are centers of excellence. It also has dilapidated schools, strapped for money, packed with students without hope for a better future. Large numbers of students from poor families are not getting the resources they need to do well in school. Poverty is becoming more concentrated, and school districts in poor areas do not have the revenues to counterbalance the downward spiral (Reich, 2003).

Is No Child Left Behind, the program passed in 2001, an adequate response to this crisis? The stated purpose—to raise the proficiency of students who fall behind—seems to make sense. But implementation has fallen short of the goals. Funds have not come through on the scale that was promised. The standards used for evaluation are confusing and limited. The "improve or else" approach to evaluation encourages schools to manipulate

Table 3.6   Public Education in the United States and OECD Placement

	USA	OECD ranking
Expenditures		
primary/secondary (per student)	$8,144	3rd
tertiary (per student)	22,234	1st
% GNP primary/secondary	3.5	12th
% GNP tertiary	0.9	18th
% money going to public schools	89	12th
Staff		
ratio teaching staff/1,000 students	64.4	18th
contact hours (primary)	1,139	1st
contact hours (middle school)	1,127	1st
contact hours (high school)	1,167	2nd
Students		
science test means, 15-year-olds	499*	13th
reading proficiency, 15-year-olds	12.2**	7th
Unemployment, ages 25–64*		
less than high school	36%	13th
high school	22%	15th
college	14%	20th

* Mean value. Standard deviation = 7.03. Standard deviations for countries with higher means varied from 1.5 to 5.5.

** Percentage at the 95th percentile

*** Rankings refer to countries with less unemployment than the United States at each educational level.

Source: OECD *Education Survey* (2002, Tables B1.6, B2.1b, D3.3, D4.1, A6.1, A7.1, A7.2, A10.2c, A10.26).

test results rather than innovate. In addition, many of the studies that inspired the simplistic thrust of the policy have turned out to be inaccurate (Schrag et al., 2004).

Appropriations are almost a third less than what was authorized by Congress—about $6 billion under the mark. By default, the costs of No Child Left Behind fall on the states and the cities that cannot afford them. Unaccompanied by more contextual and formative vehicles of assessment, evaluation standards are rigid. A compromise with the states produced a hodgepodge of tests that were not comparable. Classes have become laboratories for testing. On the ground, the goal is to avoid penalizing teachers and schools with low test results.

Finally, the experiments that were used as pilot projects to shape the program were found to be less than scientific. The "Houston miracle," attributed to then superintendent Rod Paige, who became George W. Bush's first-term Secretary of Education, looked like a success. But it was built on a stratospheric dropout rate of 60 percent. Class sessions were reduced to test drills. Cheating was rampant in the reporting of results, and the students did poorly in tests other than those mandated by the district. On the internal tests, more than 80 percent of Houston students were proficient in reading, but only 25 percent passed the National Assessment of Educational Tests (Special Report on Educating America, 2004).

The goal of No Child Left Behind—improving the nation's schools and its human capital—is consensual. What is needed is a thoughtful reform that rectifies the concrete disparity between goals and the methods of reaching them. Just as important is an understanding of who the children at risk of school failure are. Indicators of the well-being of children, shown in Table 3.7, provide a useful starting point (Mather & Rivers, 2003).

Abundant research confirms that the seeds of academic failure are sewn long before high-risk students enter the schools. The demand for quality child care is growing, both for infants and preschoolers (see Chapter 10). Yet, in 2001, only half of the preschool children living below the poverty line actually attended preschool centers. To be sure, older children should also be helped. But the sorry state of child care indicates the need for progress based on more than just honing testing skills.

Table 3.7   Key Indicators of Child Well-Being, 2000

	United States	
Indicator	Number	Percent
Children in poverty	11,746,858	16.6
Children in extreme poverty (below 50% poverty level)	5,274,343	7.4
Children in low-income families (below 20% poverty level)	26,806,452	37.8
Children* in single-parent households	16,812,254	23.3
Population ages 16–19 who are high school dropouts	1,566,039	9.8
Population ages 16–19 who are not in school and not working	1,423,283	8.9
Children ages 5–17 who have difficulty speaking English	3,493,118	6.6
Children ages 5–15 with one or more disabilities	2,614,919	5.8
Children living in high-poverty neighborhoods	14,746,918	20.4

Source: Ann E. Casey Foundation, A Kids Count/PRB Report on Census 2000.

Table 3.8   Relationship Between Parents' Education and Children's Cognitive Abilities

Standardized OLS (Ordinary Least Squares) Regression Coefficients

	Coefficient for 16- to 25-year-olds	*Coefficient for 25- to 65-year-olds*
Denmark	0.29	0.31
Norway	0.24	0.34
Sweden	0.23	0.39
Belgium (Flanders)	0.39	0.33
Germany	0.27	0.17
Netherlands	0.32	0.48
Portugal	0.34	0.47
Canada	0.34	0.47
USA	0.48	0.48

Source: International literacy survey data reported in Esping-Andersen (2002a, p. 28).

Overcoming the impediments that poor children face in schooling is an urgent issue. International research on the correlation between the education of parents and achievement of children, as teens and young adults (summarized in Table 3.8), documents the problem. While the challenge confronts all postindustrial countries that depend increasingly on an educated workforce, the data show that the problem is particularly grave in the United States. Here, parent–child correlations are very high. As a consequence, the future success of children is very directly contingent on parental education. The offspring of better-educated parents have a head start, and the converse holds true for children of parents with lower educational achievement. The success of No Child Left Behind, and with it the attainment of equal opportunity education, hinges on the ability to improve the prospects of students whose parents have inadequate schooling, and who grow up in settings where aspirations are stifled by dead-end experiences.

The Income Gap and the Difference Principle

Nowhere in his writings does Rawls call for economic equality. However, his difference principle states that the rewards that accrue to individuals in advantaged positions have to be counterbalanced by benefits for the most destitute members of society. This is close to John F. Kennedy's idea that "a rising tide floats all boats." The expectation is that growth in well-being among the higher-ups should also entail improvement in the situation of those toward the lower echelons, even if inequality between the two groups remains.

According to the difference principle, the emergence and growth of the welfare state should have been accompanied by a relative increase in the economic well-being of the poor. But comparative data contradict this expectation. Over the last two decades in the United States, the income gap has steadily increased. The richest have done exceptionally well relative to those at the middle as well as the bottom of the pay scale. Contrary to what has happened in other periods of prosperity, the disparity in income did not abate during the boom times of the late 1990s (Danziger & Gottschalk, 1993). The trickle-down effect was reversed.

Figure 3.3 highlights income growth among income groups between the late seventies and 2000. According to 2003 data from the U.S. Census Bureau, 20 percent of the wealthiest Americans control 50 percent of all income, while the amount of income controlled by the bottom 20 percent has dropped to 3.5 percent.

The contrast between the remuneration of CEOs and that of employees reflects still more dramatically the exponential distancing between classes. Within a 10-year span, the economic rewards of CEOs went from being 42 times the average factory worker's pay to 419 times. The ratio in the United States is 475:1. In Germany, it is 21:1; in the British Isles, 24:1; in France, 15:1; and in Sweden, 13:1 (Blackburn, 2002, p. 201).

The concentration of wealth was also accompanied, in 2003, by an uptick in the poverty rates. Since poverty in the United States is calculated in

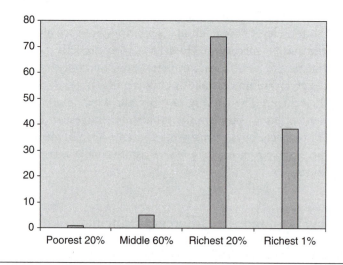

Figure 3.3   Distribution of Income Growth Among Income Groups, 1979–2000

Growth rates (%): Poorest 0.8; Middle 5.1; Richest 74.0; Top rich 38.4

Source: US Census Bureau, *Income Inequality,* Tables 1 & 2 (revised May, 2004). *Income Earnings and Poverty,* American Community Survey, 2004.

absolute terms, this means that a greater proportion of the population falls below survival standards (DeNavas-Walt et al., 2004).

Another anomaly is that, as of this writing, the federal minimum wage has not been changed since 1998 in a society that embraces the work ethic—this in spite of inflation in the cost of basic goods. It is legal in the United States to pay full-time workers poverty wages. In 1968, the minimum wage was 86 percent of the living wage, and in 1970, it was 80 percent. In 1998, it had come down to 68 percent. These calculations were done more carefully in 2001, to take into account place of residence and state-approved minimum wages (Pearce, 2002). In Los Angeles County, for example, the minimum wage corresponds to 14 percent of what a family with two children needs to get by (see Table 3.4).

The evidence is overwhelming that in the United States, the difference principle of distributive justice has been disregarded. If wealth, including a variety of assets, had been used for these determinations, rather than income, the conclusion would have been still more devastating.

Institutional Strategies to Prevent Dysfunctional Inequalities

In Rawls's view, taxation might be a means to reduce inequality. How does the tax code work in the United States, for or against this end?

Corporate as compared to personal taxes have declined over the past six decades. Supply-side economists see nothing wrong with this trend as long as it encourages investment, creating in turn more jobs, and hence a more equitable distribution of rewards. Damning as they are, these figures do not take into account the perfectly legal tax-dodge called "corporation inversion": Corporations set up a company in a tax-free zone, such as the Bahamas, calling it a subsidiary of a foreign corporation (Lowenberg, 2004).

Its name notwithstanding, the 1997 Taxpayer Relief Act made the personal tax code more complicated and less fair at the same time. The Act envisioned $95 billion in cuts over 5 years and $275 billion over 10 years. Almost half of these tax savings went to the wealthiest 5 percent—to those households with incomes over $135,000 at the time and assets in excess of $650,000. The reforms reduced capital gains taxes as well as levies on estates. The top 5 percent got 62.4 percent of the savings with the capital gains cut, and 25.6 percent went to the other 15 percent of the upper quintile. The remaining 80 percent of the population received 5.9 percent of the total cuts. Estate taxes now are levied on only 2 percent of the largest holdings. This has reduced the tax bill on the richest estates by $10 billion (Citizens for Tax Justice, 1999).

It is estimated that the tax cuts of 2001 and 2002 will cost the U.S. Treasury $3.6 trillion between 2001 and 2014. The tax code continues to be decidedly regressive. In spite of a modest boost in the EITC for poor working families, and small breaks for the middle class, it works disproportionately to the advantage of those in the top 1-percent bracket (Gale & Orszag,

2004; Johnston, 2003). The tax cuts not only aggravate inequality, but also cut into public spending on education, health, housing, job training, and the like. The government provides tax breaks totaling $741 billion a year. While some of these are designed to ease the lives of children and the elderly, most are not (see Figure 3.1).

In sum, with Rawls's theory of distributive justice in view, the bottom line is this: The United States has failed to distribute access to basic goods—especially health care—at a level consistent with the abundant resources of the country. There are still striking shortfalls in the achievement in educational opportunity, and there is no evidence of adhering to the difference principle. Instead of using taxes as a tool to curb dysfunctional inequality, from the 1980s on, the government seems to have been bent on widening the income gap.

Part I: Suggestions for Exercises _____

Students should read the following dialogue adapted from Bill Jordan's foreword to his book on social work in an unjust society (1990).

Clients were holding a demonstration against a major social service department in a major city, in the aftermath of the victory of the opposition movement. A social worker, working as a community organizer in a nearby community, was chosen to be their spokesperson to the director. Below is the record of their conversation.

Spokesperson: Now that the opposition movement is entering upon the negotiation stage, we are opening dialogue with all social services agencies. We want to discuss your department's position in a number of issues.

Director: How can I be of help?

S: The opposition movement is calling for democracy, freedom, and social justice. But a good deal of hostility has been expressed toward agencies delivering social services. The people are highly critical of the part your agency has played in the last 15 years. Not so much the social workers, you understand—the hostility is toward its policies and practices. Some people blame the leadership. . . .

D: We use the higher possible standards of professional integrity . . . value each client . . . do our best to promote human potential . . . through rigorous assessment of need. . . . support of all times for the family. . . . of course, terrible constraints on resources. . . . no longer the provider, just the enabling authority . . . difficult to monitor all the services we contract out through competitive tendering . . .

S: Yes, quite. None of us has been free to do what is right in these past years. But what concerns us is the future, and the part that social services can play in building a better society. Do you, I wonder, share our values and aspirations?

D: Our professional ethics are quite clear. Every human being is of equal value, regardless of creed, age, or abilities, and each has the right to self-fulfillment. Society should provide the greatest possible benefit for all individuals. The professional social worker should develop knowledge and skills to bring systematic and disciplined practice to his or her clients' needs, and each has the obligation to provide the best possible service. That is the basis of the international code of ethics and our own national code.

S: This sounds good. Perhaps we should discuss a bit more what it means in practice. From the point of view of the users, it has often felt like being under a watchful eye of authority, being carefully watched and controlled, and being jumped on as soon as they step out of line. This is what the parents and young people in poor areas say. As for the women, they feel like they are reminded of their responsibilities to care for the children and the elders and with little help or support. And as far as resources are concerned, for all of them it has felt like being strictly rationed. First there are all those questions about how much money they have, and what relatives are available to help. Then there is the long wait—waiting for something to get worse, or to break down altogether, before they get the service. This is what the people with handicaps and their carers say.

D: You must understand that detailed assessment of each individual and family is the cornerstone of our professional skill, whether it is an assessment for a statutory intervention or to provide a service. How can we tailor our intervention or our resources to the individual needs, or give the right package of care if we have not the proper assessment? And of course there is the budget. Central government is very strict on budgetary control, as you know, and its guidelines are firm on how we should spend in relation to various priority groups and needs.

S: Do you think that this is just?

D: I'm not sure that it's my part to say. Whatever I think, in the last resort, it's the government—the elected government—that says what justice is about. It's a question for politicians, not officials. This government says, and lots of people agree with them, that people should be responsible for themselves, financially and morally, if they can. It says that an agency which undermines that kind of individual responsibility, for one's self or one's family, is doing harm. We can't simply ignore or overrule the government's view on social justice.

So we have to try to target help to those in greatest need, the ones who are least successful, least able . . .

S: Yet the effect, you see, is that people feel they are being regulated and controlled. They do not have any say or any choice. They are not in prison and they are allowed to speak but they are not free. Like those people that have to wear electronic devices on their ankles, and report to the police every day.

D: Oh well, you will have to speak to the Chief Probation Officer about them.

S: Yes, we a meeting him today. We see his service very much like yours. They say that they are for offenders' rights and freedoms, but the people see it differently. The whole machinery of the state, what we used to call the welfare state, seems to be treating people as demanding and disruptive, trying to keep them down. You both seem to be looking for the specially dependent and dangerous ones to isolate or punish them as an example to the rest, to make them work harder for less. That's the way it seems.

D: Let me get this straight. You are saying that we don't respect people's freedom, or help them to get a decent life. But they are coming to us, more and more of them, for help. We are overwhelmed by people's needs, every day, in all our services, and I guess it is the same in probation— people begging for a hostel place, or a letter to help them get money from Social Security or whatever. From our point of view, we're doing the best we can, under new very tight restrictions, and with legal duties to protect certain vulnerable people—the victims, if you like, of crime and abuse. What are we supposed to do?

S: Yes, we have all struggled with these problems. It is not a question of blame—our society has been going along a wrong road, and we have all been going down that wrong road together, getting lost and getting hurt. Now we are looking for another road. We want you to help in the process, and we want to find what our services have to offer in a new way.

D: Haven't I said enough about values and objectives? Haven't we tried to do our best for those in need?

S: Let me tell you what we don't seem to see from your service. First, we don't see clear statements or actions on injustice. I know you have taken positions on specific issues—racism in the criminal justice system, child sexual abuse, the rights of the carers, and so on—but there isn't an overall position on injustice. We don't hear you say, quite clearly and unequivocally, that there should be no economic exploitation and no political domination in society. We don't hear you say that wealthy and powerful people, individuals and groups, should not be able to exclude or subordinate the poor and powerless, or coerce them against their will. And as our movement has suddenly gathered strength and found a voice, we do not see you at our demonstrations in the streets. We see more people from the churches than people from the social services, which is a shame. Are you afraid to speak out, or don't you recognize the injustice that I am speaking about?

D: Not afraid exactly. More muddled really, and a bit compromised. But perhaps especially, not seeing an alternative. We were all radicals in our way, back in the sixties and seventies, but all that got sat on, and even the politicians on the left distanced themselves from it, and from us. We had to buckle down and accept change, things like privatization and contracting services. And some of it has been very good, you know. Some very good quality care and very satisfied customers, better than we could do when we run the whole show. I guess we look back to the time when we had our chance, when public services were growing, resources were expanding, and we thought . . . well we blew it. So now we have to admit it, we haven't got all the answers, we didn't do it so well, a lot of people run a mile from state services, they had do anything rather than come to us, and I can't blame them. So, who are we to shout the odds? Something like that, maybe.

S: We've all had these doubts at times. It's part of the government success—to make us believe that everything else has been tried and failed, to make us feel guilty, and to cut us from everyone else who feels the same. To tell us that we can only be responsible for ourselves, to look after ourselves, and that doing right just means keeping the rules that it makes for us. Making us forget that we are all in the same boat, that we can support each other, can share and act together, can gain strength by depending on each other, rather than trying to stand alone. I always thought that those were the fundamental values of social work—to give support, to share, to listen to others' points of view, to get a fair deal for all, as members of the same community, because we all belong together.

D: Well yes, but we don't belong together, do we? There are many things that divide us. Our roles, our legal responsibilities, our interests—as home owners, taxpayers, citizens, and whatever. And in some ways, I have to say anti-racism and anti-sexism and all the other isms seem to divide us even more, or make us more aware of the divisions. So we just fall back on ourselves, and on keeping the rules, because that is safer that way.

S: It's true that for many of us the main block is a sense of isolation and helplessness. But if it's like that for you and your workers, what's it like for the service users? Okay, you had defeats for your unions, attacks on your resources, restructuring changes in the law, privatization and all the rest. But poor people, black people, single parents, people with handicaps, they have been treated like the enemy. It has been like a war on them—a battle to keep their self-respect, their identity, and some organizations to support each other, to stay in some control of their lives. And in the end, it's by seeing that we belong together, that there is strength through cooperation and sharing, that we have come through, and the movement has grown.

D: I still don't understand.

S: There is something else missing from your list of values, and from the way your department works. You don't say, or you have stopped saying, that it is all about individuals and their needs. All that stuff about individual assessments—what about people needing each other, not just in families, but in groups, associations, clubs, churches, and communities? What about people having an equal voice in running their own society as a kind of a club, because they are members? What about democracy? What do you mean by democracy in your department? Sometimes it seems to us that you mean the same as the guy who says the local counties should meet once a year to hand out contracts for all their services. We mean that people should rule themselves, have a real say in those things they share as citizens, or as service users. You can't privatize everything, you know; you can't give each person their own bit of ozone layer or the ocean; and why should you want to? Sharing things with other people is good—it is a benefit, not a cost, of being a member. Everybody for themselves is no way of running things. We all end up valuing nothing unless we own it, unless we can buy it and sell it, unless we can keep others off it. So we end up putting no value on other people, as well as no value on the things we have to share with them. So we end up seeing nothing, with us having everything and them having nothing.

D: That's not quite fair, because we have been trying all these years to see that people, the outsiders, the neglected and rejected ones, got something. It may not be much, but it's something.

S: That's true, but it is something they get at a terrible price. Not in money. To get it, they have to prove that they've failed. That they are desperate, that they are broke, that they have done something wrong, or they are deranged, or just that they can't cope. And then what they get isn't what other people want. It's something for the other failures, or the other deviants, or deranged people. It isn't a way back into society, it's often a way out, and when they get it it's still harder to get back.

D: But wait a minute. You know that we have deliberately been kept short of resources by this government. We've been put in a terrible position. Either we give adequate amounts to a few and none to many or we give everyone in need short rations. It's simply a question of arithmetic. When our resources are at a desperately low level, our clients have to prove that they are desperate to get anything. We don't want it to be like that—it's a straightforward consequence of the shortage of funding.

S: And this is helping them?

D: You sound as if you want to blame social work and social services. It makes me feel that everything we've been trying to do all these years has been a waste of time, all wrong, more harm than good. Is that what you're saying?

S: There have been hard years and some wasted years for all of us, and we've all done things we regret, and that we wouldn't choose to do again. That's not the point. The only question is this: have we got something to offer to a better society, and to search for justice for all?

D: What is justice?

S: Our movement doesn't pretend to have a ready-made answer to that question. The important issue for us is whether you are willing to ask it, and to listen to those people out there when they try to answer.

1. Ask for volunteers among your students to enact the dialogue in the insert. You might want to split the director's lines among three managers, and the spokesperson's lines among three social workers. This would allow for the participation of six students and a more dramatic presentation.

2. Ask students to select a different part of the insert and comment on it. This could be done orally or in a short paper.

3. Students could prepare a major paper showing the links between the dialogue and the following:
   a. Different philosophies of justice
   b. Different social work theories of justice

Source: From Jordan, B., *Social Work in an Unjust Society,* reprinted with permission from Pearson Education.

PART II

Interpreting Welfare in the United States: Beyond Exceptionalism

The late onset and slow development of public welfare in the United States, compared to the earlier start and extensive coverage of such programs in other market economies, make for an intriguing historical puzzle. A common explanation goes under the name of "exceptionalism." The history of the American welfare state is supposedly unique, for a variety of reasons.

The absence of a feudal past meant that Americans faced fewer of the status rigidities typical of "Old Europe." In addition, political democracy, limited though it was to white males, took hold before industrialization got underway. This opening took some of the sting out of the class resentments characteristic of systems—again, like those of Old Europe—in which workers were barred from the franchise until they forced their way in under the aegis of militant socialist and communist parties. For a long time, too, through the eighteenth and most of the nineteenth centuries, the continent-size country offered cheap land that promised immigrants a stake in a better life. Territorial immensity, and federalism, also gave leeway to regional interests. If all this wasn't enough, the mélange of religious and ethnic identities that immigrants brought with them also diluted class consciousness (e.g., Klass, 1985).

The late start of the welfare state in the United States, compared to Western Europe, is shared by other new market democracies. Yet welfare in nations with historical characteristics similar to the United States—Canada, for example, or Australia—developed much faster and reached levels of inclusiveness similar to those in older countries.

So we need analytical tools that explain not only the underdevelopment of the American system but also its uncertain path. We need to specify the intricate connections between welfare and social work. Then we can establish the back-and-forth—the changing direction of influence—between them at different periods. Identifying cycles of activism, withdrawal, and resistance is important for tracing the development of the profession, and for coming to grips with the elements of continuity and conflict in the professional identity of social workers.

The purpose of Chapters 4 through 8 is to consider rival explanations for the vacillating welfare state. We will pay special attention to the reciprocal and contrasting forces that have shaped the development of the profession of social work across different historical periods.

Building an Analytic Framework

In an important article that appeared during the Reagan administration, Catherine Jones (1985) pointed out that, while welfare states coexisted with market economies, their links with these economies varied regardless of their spending levels. In short, there are different kinds of "welfare states." Jones distinguishes between *welfare* capitalism and welfare *capitalism*. In the first case, welfare is the important outcome, and capitalism is the means chosen to achieve it. In the second instance, keeping capitalism afloat is the main goal, and welfare is contingent on or adapted to that goal. The first system, with the accent on welfare, is geared toward redistribution. The second strives to maximize productivity and minimize the impact of welfare on it.

The dichotomy places Reagan's social policies unambiguously in the second category. But the categorization itself tells us little about the social forces that made for that result. Further analysis ties the emergence and evolution of welfare to two contrasting political ideologies: progressive and social control.

The Progressive Perspective

The way of looking at the growth of public welfare that has come to be called "progressive" draws heavily on a handful of developmental ideas, in particular, the expansion of democratic rights and the logic of industrialism (Quadagno, 1987). The implicit assumption is that the development of welfare goes hand in hand with economic growth. Several suppositions about social change underlie this perspective:

- Historical evidence shows that the instinct of mutual help is inscribed in human nature.

- Mutual assistance, and the interdependence of social systems, press toward the integration of groups.
- The acquisition of knowledge leads to an understanding of the social origins of many problems and increases our ability to resolve them (Rochefort, 1981).
- Industrialization and urbanization concentrate social problems but also provide the organizational and financial resources for responding to them (Wilensky & Lebeaux, 1958).
- Political maturation is plain to see in the expansion of rights in liberal democracies. Witness the evolution from civil rights to political rights and subsequently the emergence of social rights. Social citizenship takes in economic welfare and security (Marshall, 1950).
- Lastly, because industrial productivity depends on large and stable flows of human capital, it is in the interest of business leaders to support educational and health programs proposed by the welfare state (Rimlinger, 1971).

The core contention is that there is an intrinsic harmony between economic development and progress in welfare. The research of Kirsten Gronbjerg (1977) lends some credibility to the convergence thesis. When she compared states in the United States during the late 1960s, Gronbjerg found that those ranking higher in urbanization, industrialization, and education had a more developed sense of common identity and mutual responsibility, and that they supported relatively generous welfare outlays.

The demand-centered theories that dominated the postwar years reinforced the belief that welfare benefited the economy. Consumption could even out business cycle fluctuations—notably, unemployment—that depressed demand if left alone. Economic equilibrium was predicated on sustained growth, which in turn promoted and depended on the expansion of welfare (Quadagno, 1987).

Social workers were to implement the welfare provisions of this organic, optimistic model. Their role was to assist individuals to fit in a system where balanced growth depended on adjusted, productive workers. Their functions were to be administrative and rehabilitative: the professional delivery of public welfare services and the recovery of individuals who could not, or would not, fit.

The Social Control Perspective

While classical Marxism has always expressed a dislike for welfare, more precise criticisms come from modern socialists (Rochefort, 1981). Social control theorists criticize several major assumptions of their progressive counterparts as a preface to offering alternative interpretations of their own:

- The state is not autonomous. Under capitalism, it operates in a context of conflict between capital and labor. The twofold role of the state is to promote capitalist interests while preserving social harmony.

- Institutions such as welfare agencies grow not from humanitarian commitments but from material conditions.
- Society is a round-the-clock theater of conflict between various interests, and capital has the upper hand.
- The latent functions of welfare are not to help needy citizens but to dull their class consciousness and blunt their capacity for demanding their rights. Simultaneously keeping the lower classes dependent on handouts and defining them as deviant are strategies that favor these goals.

Claus Offe (1984) has carefully developed the first and last of these propositions. The state in a market situation exists to promote and protect capitalism, on which it depends for revenues. However, in democratic countries, the state also depends on the support of citizens, and it needs to take their interests into account. The upshot is welfare that provides some security to the middle class, while offering marginal assistance to the lower classes, provided they behave. According to Piven and Cloward (1971), these carrots are more cost-effective than exclusive reliance on the stick of outright coercion.

Seen in this light, social workers are handmaidens of the control system: They obediently administer welfare programs. They are instrumental in correcting the supposed deviance of their clients. They help clients adjust to their social condition and so deflect potential conflict. In short, they smooth things over. Political and economic power relationships remain unchanged. Welfare programs work to ensure profitability and stability in the private sector. The state does not strenuously promote welfare. At most, it compensates for selected "negative externalities" of industrial growth.

A More Complex Explanation

The symbiosis—the intimate connection—between the economic and the welfare systems is a theme common to progressive and social control outlooks. The theses and their variants have been criticized for overgeneralization, simplification, attachment to unverifiable theories, and disregard of historical evidence.

Evidence for a happy mutuality between welfare and industrialism in the United States is hard to come by. Only one national welfare program—old-age insurance—has emerged in the United States. This hardly constitutes proof of a grand, strategically cunning alliance. Less industrialized countries have achieved universal programs of health care, old-age pensions, family allowances, and more comprehensive public assistance.

The energy crisis of the 1970s that produced "stagflation"—high unemployment and inflation at the same time—shattered the growth-dependent optimism of Progressives. This trauma redirected economic policy away from high-rolling Keynesianism toward a stricter monetarism. Cuts in welfare and tax reductions for businesses were designed to alleviate the crisis by promoting investment. The link between capital and welfare began to look very tenuous. Conversely, other market democracies have constructed vast protective umbrellas for their citizens. This strategy raises doubts about reducing welfare to a mechanism of social control. Both theories fall short of explaining the actual behavior of welfare states.

Historical sociologists (Quadagno, 1987; Skocpol, 1980) have looked at the facts closely. They insist that a variety of intervening variables affect the behavior of states. Whether, as the Progressives claim, governments harmonize the demands of multiple groups or do the bidding of an economic ruling class, as the social control theorists believe, depends on complex conditions that neither of these schools bothers seriously to consider. A glance at the following variables clarifies how welfare policies actually take shape:

- *Bureaucracy.* Public sector bureaucratization, centralization, and dependence on direct taxation are the best predictors of growth in welfare programs (Gates, 1983; Heclo, 1974). For example, in the 1930s and 1940s, a relatively weak central government in the United States depended on deals with private business to pull off parts of its welfare agenda (Gottschalk, 2000; Hacker, 2002; Howard, C., 1993).
- *Ideological foundations.* The beliefs, religious as well as secular, that underpin a national political culture are crucial in framing new experiences and setting the country on a consistent course (Goodin, 1980).
- *Political learning.* Previous decisions constrain the institutional options considered to be practical at subsequent times. Policy making is therefore "path-dependent" (Pierson, 2004). Traditional charities and the legacy of the English Poor Laws have had a lasting effect on public assistance in the United States (Luna & Figueira-McDonough, 2002; Wagner, 2000). The influence of antecedent state and local welfare programs is likewise evident in national policies promulgated during the 1930s.
- *Political parties.* The presence of a mass-based Socialist Party supported by a powerful labor movement is a strong predictor of growth in welfare. During the Depression in the United States, the Democratic Party stood for northern labor, but it also represented landed whites in the South. These divergent interests weakened the party's effectiveness in promoting the welfare agenda of the New Deal (Piven & Cloward, 1982).

Taking into account conditions like these can help us understand the restricted and uneven evolution of welfare in the most affluent country in the world. Whether social policy outcomes at different periods turn out to be closer to the progressive or social control predictions depends on specific interactions among the degree of state centralization, inherited ideological fashion, rigidities carried over from past legislation, and the strength of labor.

Analytic frameworks that try to make sense of the origins and development of social work are less sophisticated than historical approaches. From the outset, two lines of thought and action have been discernible. One corresponds with the progressive view of welfare just outlined. It stresses individual change and adjustment. The other sees social problems like poverty, inequality, and injustice as systemic. The first, comparatively psychological approach tends to be described as conservative despite the "progressive" label. "Radical" is more often attached to the second, relatively sociological interpretation.

Labels can only take us so far. For different historical periods, we need to examine the following:

- The influence of social workers of both persuasions on welfare policy, whether through contestation or collaboration
- The bases of the power of social workers (or their lack of it) in the profession
- How social policy conditions types of intervention
- The impact of political contexts and social forces in promoting or restricting the direction of professional activity

4

The Fragile Roots of Welfare in the United States

From Colony to the Gilded Era

No man in this land suffers from poverty unless it be more than his fault—his sin . . . If men have not enough it is from want of provident care and foresight, and industry and frugality.

—Henry Ward Beecher, nineteenth-century
preacher (cited in Morone, 2003b)

The Legacy of the English Poor Laws and the Shaping of a National Ideology in the Eighteenth Century

Poverty in North America grew in part because England used the colonies as a dumping ground, lowering the numbers of the incarcerated and other undesirables in the mother country by shipping criminals, vagrants, orphans, and the unemployed overseas. Many such immigrants found life harsh in America; many were unable to escape poverty.

As the colonies searched for remedies, they drew on the poor laws familiar from Elizabethan times. In the name of local responsibility, towns operated as key units of government, and local taxation was a principal source of revenue. Small towns doled out charitable handouts to the needy. As in England, a system of foster care was instituted for those without families. Foster families received cash incentives or tax credits. Strangers, by contrast, were treated punitively. Communities excluded blacks and Native Americans altogether.

As mobility increased, the colonial treasury began to reimburse localities for expenses in managing the poor. At the same time, with the spread of Calvinist precepts, a sharp distinction between the worthy and unworthy poor evolved. The contrast was based on the work ethic. The able-bodied poor were deemed unworthy. They had the obligation to work or starve. Indentured servitude was one way to satisfy this obligation. Another way, for younger cohorts, was apprenticeship. The fear was that even charity extended to the worthy poor would undermine the work ethic. It had to amount to less than compensation for work. This became known as "the least eligibility principle" (Wisner, 1945).

So, the elements of English charitable customs were resettled in the North American colonies. The process of importation is a clear example of path dependence. Prior institutional solutions became habits that shaped subsequent options. But America was not England. Other influences conditioned the ideology of the emerging republic as well, and these in turn were to condition the future of welfare in the United States.

Poverty grew exponentially in the second half of the eighteenth century due to seasonal work, the return of settlers from inhospitable areas, economic depression, and a steady rise in the number of illegitimate offspring. (Children so classified made up about one-third of births per year [Jernegan, 1931a].) Colonial life grew in complexity. It became more difficult to find jobs, and the prosecution of criminals expanded. Workhouses, many of them built by an expanding class of developers, become a welcome solution.

Religious groups, prosperous citizens, and fraternal associations based on occupational and ethnic ties took to the spirit of humanitarian reform spurred by the War of Independence. Private organizations were created to supplement the meager public system. However, neither public nor private assistance was extended to Native Americans or African Americans (Trattner, 1999).

Such innovations reflected the ideas of the time. National leaders absorbed these beliefs and integrated them into the constitution of the new republic. The citizenry quickly made them their own. The features of this creed that were to become important over time for welfare policy include

- Kant's philosophy of individual worth, choice, and responsibility
- French ideals of democratic government
- Locke's defense of limited government and local autonomy
- Adam Smith's gospel of economic competition and the sacredness of the free market
- The separation of state and religion

The separation of church and state fostered religious toleration, as Thomas Jefferson and like-minded leaders hoped it would. It also encouraged—based on shared Christian values—ideals such as the centrality of the family and the secularization of virtue, at the core of which was the work ethic. The implementation of democratic ideals was circumscribed at the time. Only those of the right race and gender who were literate and had a modicum of property enjoyed suffrage.

The Nineteenth Century: Seismic Changes and Moral Certainties

The 1800s took in bewilderingly rapid geographic expansion and industrial growth. Practically from the outset, a new doctrine—*manifest destiny*—marked the nineteenth century. One way to bring order to this enormous outburst of energy is to examine the historical profile of the country before and after the Civil War.

Antebellum Society

The Louisiana Purchase (1803) extended the borders of the United States from the Mississippi River to the Pacific, leaving aside the Southwest and Western regions of the continent. Four decades later, the Southwest became part of the United States. Provoked by the invasion of Mexican land by American ranchers and the massacre by Mexicans of white settlers at the Alamo, the Mexican War of 1846 ended in a resounding victory for the United States. The defeated government ceded territory that included what is now California, Nevada, New Mexico, Colorado, Wyoming, and Arizona.

Expansionism gained ideological cover through racist nationalism, propounded in the new doctrine of manifest destiny. God had assigned Anglo-Saxons the task of developing the North American continent. The promised land became a laboratory for building a utopian society fusing capitalism, Protestantism, and democracy. Native Americans were killed or removed to territories west of the Mississippi. Despite guarantees written into the Treaty of Guadalupe Hidalgo, the forced or illegal removal of Mexican peasants and landowners proceeded apace. White settlers and public officials welcomed the policy. State and federal governments tacitly accepted and permitted aggressive strategies of occupation (Heidler & Heidler, 2003; Horseman, 1981; Weinberg, 1935).

The federal government did not have the bureaucratic capacity to manage this sprawling territory. It adopted the expedient of auctioning off large tracts of land. Though bidding was open to all, the immense size of the properties meant that only the wealthy could acquire them. Then, with the idea of speeding up a coast-to-coast infrastructure of communications, more land was granted to railroad developers, who later sold the properties at a high profit.

Frontier expansion did not contribute much to the redistribution of land. Many poor settlers had grubstakes; they occupied land without title. Preemption laws allowed squatters to buy smaller properties at low prices with easy payments. Still, most of the frontier stayed in the hands of the wealthy. As early as 1820, one percent of the population controlled one-quarter of the wealth. By 1850, the wealthiest one percent controlled half (Jansson, 2001).

Meanwhile, the land rush attracted more and more immigrants from Europe. They were needed to settle the new territories, and they worked as well in the burgeoning manufacturing industries.

Until 1830, about 9 Americans out of 10 lived in towns of no more than 2,500 inhabitants. After that time, urban growth began to take off as new industries—textiles, shoes, and food processing—emerged. These operations were relatively low-tech and very labor-intensive. Within just two decades after 1830, four million immigrants, pushed out of their homelands by poverty and pulled in by the economic boom, came to the United States (Specht & Courtney, 1994). Almost all of them stayed.

Penniless immigrants, especially those with families in tow, could not readily pack up and move westward. If males did go off on their own, they left their families behind with no income. For those who stayed around the East Coast, factory work meant a 12-hour day, chronic risk of accidents, and low wages. Strikes were frequent but rarely successful. Unions were weak, prosecuted by the courts and vulnerable to the violence of goons and strike-busters in the pay of bosses. The fledgling market ran into serious recessions in 1819, 1837, and 1857. Misery spread through the cities: crowded housing, wretched hygiene, an array of infectious diseases, high mortality, cast-off street children, and crime (Griffin, 1965).

Continuities in Response to Need

The United States underwent rapid demographic expansion throughout the nineteenth century. So did its underprivileged population. Remarkably, the pattern of response, initiated in colonial times, remained consistent with the values that had crystallized years before during the preindustrial period, around the birth of the republic. The states and townships placed restrictions on outdoor relief—essentially, at-home assistance—and increased indoor assistance, which required the placement of the needy in institutions. Private welfare services favored character-building methods (Friedman, 1982).

Private and public measures like these for remedying pauperism cannot be understood without appreciating the unbounded opportunities offered by the country as well as the virtuous discipline that presumably led to success. In 1821, in the midst of the country's worst depression to date, the New York Society for Prevention of Pauperism earnestly declared that "no man who is temperate, frugal and willing to work need suffer for lack of employment" (cited in Trattner, 1999, p. 54).

The mindset that encouraged such views on misery and success hardened when faced by the fact that the poor, especially in New York City, came from a hodgepodge of strange cultures. They looked different and they had different habits. The Irish, who arrived from rural backgrounds, were fond of alcohol and raucous singing. Most were Catholics, and they had lots of children. The caricatures of shanty Irish and bibulous, brawling Paddies that appeared in metropolitan newspapers made the immigrants look as if they were at a lower stage on the evolutionary ladder. The image did not go down well with Protestant, Anglo-Saxon settlers and their descendents.

Destitution, then, was a kind of character flaw. It reflected slovenly morals. The public welfare authorities leaned toward deterrence. Issued in 1824 by the secretary of state of New York, the Yates report recommended that poorhouses be constructed in every county. Resettlement statutes were also strengthened to reinforce residence requirements for welfare. New York City, which had to deal with the most serious problems of pauperism, obtained state money to enlarge its poorhouse and its house of correction.

Treatment of the destitute in these poorhouses—also called alms- or workhouses—was inhumane. Rigid schedules were imposed for all activities, which consisted mostly of long hours of uninterrupted work. Character-building lectures were added from time to time. The diet was kept at starvation levels. By 1850, the houses were popularly known as living tombs or social cemeteries (Cray, 1988).

Policies of this severity surpassed the strictures of the deterrence methods traditionally used to force the unworthy poor to work. The policy built directly on the dour views of the Rev. Thomas Malthus, the first professor of political economy at Oxford University in England and the model for Mr. Scrooge in Charles Dickens's *A Christmas Carol*.

The approach tallies with a belief in class superiority and with a determination to roll over any obstacles toward a model society, as set forth in the doctrine of manifest destiny. For Malthus, social hierarchy mirrored differing evolutionary capabilities. Positions at the top of the pyramid reflected the superior talents of those reaching such positions. These competitive qualities would be transmitted to their descendants. Society as a whole benefited by yielding authority to those equipped to make the best decisions. Naturally, those who wound up at the bottom of the social pyramid were the weakest, who contributed least. They were a drag on the system. Helping them only created a greater, and unnecessary, burden on society. Allowing the impoverished to breed augmented the least desirable elements, and this "population bomb" (as it came to be called in the twentieth century) threatened to bring the entire system crashing down. The rational alternative was equivalent to a triage decision made in a foundering lifeboat: let them die (Glass, 1953). The ultimate purpose of poorhouses, it has been argued, was to get rid of the poor by keeping them invisible and letting them starve (Wagner, 2000).

However, even if private organizations embraced or went along with the notion that loose morals were at the root of poverty, most of them did not throw the poor overboard. They persisted in trying to salvage the poor by converting them to virtue, that is, to middle class norms. Many of these institutions worked under the auspices of prosperous citizens and local notables. Good deeds earned them respect and status. Others were run by religious groups vying for local ascendancy (Wagner, 2000).

Private assistance, then, aimed for rehabilitation. Total institutions, many of them targeting children, suited this goal. Isolation from the baneful influence of the streets was the first step in acculturating orphans and strays. Children were generally more docile and instructable than adults. Houses of refuge and homes for wayward children received delinquent and neglected youths. Orphanages took in orphans or poor children whose parents could not maintain them. Institutions for the feebleminded and the blind also grew up at this time. All of them provided moral education and, to varying degrees, educational and vocational training (Downs & Sherraden, 1983; Hawes, 1971).

The temperance movement was the most dramatic moral crusade. It saw alcohol as the chief cause of poverty and a host of attendant ills such as violence, unemployment, and family disintegration. The movement would settle for nothing less than ridding society of "the demon drink." By 1833, it had 6,000 chapters. Between 1840 and 1850, fifteen states enacted prohibitions against the sale of alcoholic spirits. Twenty years later, these "blue laws" were rescinded, but the movement underwent a powerful revival early in the twentieth century, culminating in a constitutional amendment that enforced prohibition until finally it was overturned with the onset of the Great Depression (Tyrrell, 1979).

Innovative Directions

Three programs born during the antebellum years deviate from the pattern of minimal relief. They fostered types of assistance that surpassed the strictures set by the poor laws. These innovative movements can be considered antecedents of later social work orientations.

The purpose of the Sunday school movement was to bring religious/ethical instruction to poor children. By 1835, the American Sunday School Union had its own, nondenominational administrative staff and it could boast of having recruits in the tens of thousands. Thousands of middle class teachers were brought in for the effort, trained, and supervised.

Like many institutions of the time, the Sunday schools strove to help children and adolescents internalize principles, such as honesty and industry, through regular moral instruction. But their methods were less Draconian. They did not beat or starve children into obedience. The schools avoided physical punishment, and they adopted a system of rewards, punishments, and peer pressure very similar to present-day behavioral conditioning. In addition, instead of isolating the children, the Sunday school movement searched out community support (Boyer, 1978).

In the 1850s, Charles Loring Brace launched the Children's Aid Society of New York. Although his initiative has received considerable criticism in recent years, Brace's forthright stance against institutionalizing children merits praise. His idea was to enlist country families willing to adopt New York street children. His vision reveals an understanding of developmental and emotional needs, as well as of the stability that adoption could bring to the children (Brace, 1872).

The plan was not carefully implemented and it fell short of its goals. But none of this diminishes the breakthrough accomplishment that Brace

Photo 4.1 Midwest Railroad Station Point of Arrival for Some of Charles Brace's Children

Source: From the private collection of Peter McDonough.

engineered. Historians who have documented the exploitation that such children suffered have failed to compare these troubling outcomes with the fate of children who left institutions at that time or with those who stayed on the streets of New York. In short, they considered no control groups. Some of Brace's vision remains in programs that send deprived street kids to rural areas or to camps in the summer. His legacy can also be seen in the easing of adoption by foster parents, a reform that takes into account the advantages of stability for the children.

In the mental health field, Dorothea Lynde Dix stands as a role model for social workers interested in policy practice. Her campaign on behalf of the indigent mentally ill was triggered by two episodes: a visit to an asylum for the mentally ill in England and her experience at the East Cambridge women's jail in Massachusetts, where she taught Sunday school.

The first experience showed Dix how humanely mentally ill people could be treated and how enlightened the English caretakers were about mental illness. The second experience drove home to her how cruelly the mentally sick were treated in American prisons. Starting in Massachusetts, she traveled from state to state documenting the treatment of the indigent mentally ill in prison, and she produced numerous case studies. Helped by a physician with great foresight, Dix requested that the legislature provide for the treatment of the indigent mentally ill. Her request was approved on the second submission.

Dix was a whirlwind of reform. She interviewed thousands of mentally ill persons and visited 300 county jails and 500 poorhouses. More than 33 other mental health facilities were established in the following decades. Her success came not only from sheer persistence but also from the undeniable quality of her surveys. All this earned Dix many allies. She took her crusade to Washington, where several congressmen signed on to help her produce a bill that would have provided federal land grants to states for the purpose of building mental health facilities. Though it won congressional approval, the bill succumbed to an 1854 veto by President Franklin Pierce, who deemed its provisions unconstitutional (Gollander, 1993).

Another outstanding achievement of the antebellum period was public education. At the start of the century, education for the well to do was conducted primarily through private tutoring. Middle class students went to boarding schools or religious day schools. A few charity schools reached the urban poor.

By 1860, a national network of public primary and secondary schools was in place (Katz, M., 1968). Also, just before he was assassinated, Abraham Lincoln signed into law the Land Grant Act, which opened up inexpensive higher education dedicated to "the practical arts." This was the origin of many of the state colleges and universities that helped power economic development and social mobility.

Critical Commentary

With the exception of the nationwide spread of public education, a profile of the antebellum period does not substantiate the Progressive model of a benevolent, incremental alliance between industrial growth and the expansion of welfare. On the contrary, social control strategies prevailed. In his valuable work *The Reluctant Welfare State*, Bruce Jansson (2001) depicts the industrial development and the rapid expansion of the frontier of this period as lost opportunities. One might ask, were there viable alternatives?

To answer this question, it is important to note that responses to dire need were clearly path-dependent. Already limited public programs became increasingly punitive. Private assistance took off, shaped by an ideology drenched in upper and middle class values. Moral conversion was the answer to pauperism. A fledgling union movement could not bring together a disorganized, barely surviving, and ethnically diverse workforce. Nor could it stand up to the courts or the armed reaction of factory owners.

The weakness of the federal government also militated against any harmoniously combined evolution of economic growth and welfare. By 1829, the number of federal government employees came to a grand total of 352 (Jansson, 2001). Given the obsession with preserving state and local autonomy, the federal initiatives that did emerge ran into economic and organizational resistance. The policy of selling large tracts of land in the new territories reflected, at least in part, these constraints. The government sold off properties it could not administer on its own. The veto that squashed Dorothea Dix's bill was also symptomatic of the limits on the national government's role in welfare. According to the constitutional interpretations then in vogue in the Supreme Court, such programs were unacceptable exercises in political overreaching. The bureaucratic and political-cultural preconditions for the development of welfare were missing (Quadagno, 1987).

Finally, although political suffrage was extended to most white males, the representation of all citizens was inadequate. Land speculators and agricultural interests wielded decisive influence. Whatever its relevance to other societies, the expectations of Marshall (1950) regarding a stately evolution from civil to political rights and on to social entitlements look far-fetched for the nineteenth-century United States.

Puritanical values and the inheritance of the English Poor Laws explain the cult of character-building strategies during this time. The extremes of inhumane treatment meted out to minorities and the poor also grew out of the doctrines of Manifest Destiny and Malthusianism (Hofstadter, 1992). Certain tenets of American political culture—notably, the conviction of racial superiority—encouraged acceptance of these two harsh doctrines.

The few innovative strategies, though hardly radical, stand as examples of how American ideology can evolve in a progressive direction. The Sunday school movement clearly abided by the character-building precepts of the time. Yet it succeeded in promoting more advanced, humane, and professional methods that look, in retrospect, not unlike empowerment strategies.

The ideas put into practice by Charles Brace pinpointed the importance of family setting and stability for child development. Dorothea Dix's legacy for policy practice highlights the significance of disseminating hard data in a pragmatic culture for the sake of reform. Finally, public education gave tangible impetus to the strongly held value of equal opportunity.

Arguably, both progressive and control interpretations fit the case of public education. Better-educated workers are productive workers, indicating the coincidence of interests between the economy in the aggregate and the welfare of individuals. On the other hand, the disciplinary style of schools may contribute to the inculcation of docility (Katz, M., 1968). Even then, however, unforeseen side effects of literacy, such as critical thinking, are difficult to contain.

The Civil War and Its Aftermath

On the eve of the Civil War, regional interests pulled the national government in different directions. Industrialists in New England wanted high tariffs to protect their products from foreign competition. Southern plantation owners wanted low tariffs to reduce the costs of importing industrial products (few of which they manufactured) from abroad and to make the distribution of cotton and tobacco, which they exported, cheaper. The Midwest wanted subsidies for transportation networks to move their agricultural goods. The Southwest competed for railroad and turnpike construction funds.

The North and South also competed over the frontier territories. The South wanted to extend slavery, and its way of life, to these lands. For their part, the Northern states were interested in supporting the movement of their inhabitants, with a quite different tradition of small family farms and free labor. Efforts on the part of the federal government to resolve this simmering conflict by designating some states-to-be as "free" and others as "slave" did not work. As new arrivals poured in from the North and the South, armed conflict exploded (Jansson, 2001).

At stake was not only the slavery issue. The political strength of the parties supporting the North and those flirting with secession of the South also came into play. The traditionally democratic South interpreted the 1860 electoral victory of Abraham Lincoln, standard-bearer of the newly founded Republican Party, as a body blow to its national influence. Secession followed, and that triggered civil war.

Abolitionists had grown in number and importance prior to the outbreak of hostilities. Yet the Civil War was not fought primarily over the freedom of slaves. The appeal of abolitionism was part of a larger, dispersed movement of social liberation. The role that women played in the ranks of the abolitionists evolved from the 1848 convention on women's rights. This first feminist movement centered on universal suffrage. Women, free African Americans, and radical leaders fought for a racially equal society.

All the same, many northerners considered slaves as representatives of an inferior race. They were to be treated humanely, but they were not up to full citizenship. African Americans residing in the North suffered educational, residential, and on-the-job discrimination. Many of the philanthropic organizations that worked in the South after the war treated freed slaves with the same biases as those directed at the supposed character deficiencies of poor whites (Franklin, 1970).

The Limits of African American Freedom

The Emancipation Proclamation, issued in 1863 as the Civil War raged on, officially abolished slavery in the rebellious states. Still, even after the war, support for granting full citizenship to African Americans was sparse. In 1865, the War Department established the Bureau of Refugees, Freedmen, and Abandoned Lands, popularly known as the Freedmen's Bureau. Since welfare activities were assigned to local governments, funding was limited. The expectation was that private agencies would attend to new initiatives. The work of the Bureau boiled down to confiscating and distributing abandoned land, and to supervising labor contracts with former slaves. The officers in charge lacked legal training, so that even these tasks were poorly carried out. Of the 3 million African Americans who were promised 40 acres of land apiece, 2.5 million received nothing. They were forced to work as tenant farmers or sharecroppers.

The agenda that Lincoln had in mind for after the war gave priority to national healing. The devastated South was to be treated with great tolerance and few demands. After his assassination, however, his vice president, Andrew Johnson, a Southern sympathizer, took over. The rights conceded to African Americans were not enforced. Southern legislatures adopted "black codes" that limited mobility, rights of assembly, and free speech of freed slaves. They legalized whipping for disrespect or insurgency, and passed Jim Crow legislation (McPherson, 1982).

Civil rights legislation and a series of constitutional amendments were enacted after the victory of the North: ratification of the Thirteenth Amendment abolishing slavery, the Fourteenth Amendment giving full personhood and equal protection to African Americans, the Fifteenth Amendment establishing universal suffrage for all adult males, the Civil Rights Acts of 1870 and 1875 providing for enforcement of anti-discrimination in public facilities and schools, and the Ku Klux Klan Act making the infringement of civil rights a federal offense. But when the Freedmen's Bureau and Union troops left the South, the southern democrats found ways to circumvent the legislation or used the Ku Klux Klan to disregard its provisions. The Supreme Court reacted mildly to such infractions, handing down opinions in line with a restrictive interpretation of civil rights. Economic worries provoked by the recession of 1873 absorbed northerners much more than concern over the troubles of the backward South (Trattner, 1999).

The Making of the Gilded Era

Despite frequent recessions, American industry expanded in a rush during the postwar years. Getting underway some decades after the first industrializers in Europe, the burst of manufacturing in the United States drew on up-to-date technology. This was "the advantage of backwardness." Access to cheap labor was virtually endless. Ten million immigrants arrived between 1860 and 1890. High tariffs, minimal safety regulation, and low taxes accelerated the leap forward. The United States became a leading power among industrialized nations.

Supreme Court decisions of 1885 and 1900 curbed the right of the federal government to regulate, and to collect income taxes from, corporations. The Sherman Antitrust Legislation of 1890, originally designed to tame corporate monopolies, was interpreted by the courts in such a way as to permit control of union federations (Cochran, 1961).

Protection of corporate behemoths exacerbated the concentration of wealth. The great fortunes of the century were amassed by families like the Rockefellers, the Vanderbilts, the Carnegies, the Morgans, and the Astors. Their holdings and grandiose lifestyles rivaled, and indeed surpassed, the possessions and comforts of European monarchs. On the other hand, a huge underclass continued in deplorable conditions, working 10- to 12-hour days, subject to very high accident rates, and exposed to unemployment in times of recession. By one account, as many as 1 out of 4 urban workers found themselves unemployed during this period. Between these two extremes, a modest middle class, calculated to be 16 percent of the population, who owned and managed small enterprises, was threatened by the competition of the giant conglomerates (Boyer, 1978; Katz, Ducet, & Stern, 1982).

On the political side, large economic interests lobbied and made generous contributions to both parties. They obtained the passage of anti-union, anti-regulatory, and anti-tax legislation, and government contracts flowed in their direction.

Unions and Welfare

Workers' organizations were a lame counterpoint to the corporations. Having started by organizing craftsmen and other skilled workers tied to a local base, unions were tardy in reaching the crowds of unskilled laborers. After 1880, strikes became more frequent, even though they continued to be beaten back by the bosses and their private troops, and by the police. In 1893, Eugene Debs, a socialist, was able to organize the American Railroad Union (ARU) under centralized leadership. The ARU included about 150,000 members, both skilled and unskilled.

In 1894, workers at the Chicago-based Pullman Sleeping Car Company went on strike, protesting pay cuts. ARU members boycotted trains to which Pullman carriages were attached, halting rail traffic from Chicago to the West Coast. Though no violence had occurred, the newspapers labeled the strike a rebellion. When President Grover Cleveland ordered troops to the area, a confrontation ensued that lasted over the next few months. The strike went on despite a federal court injunction. A grand jury indicted Debs for conspiracy to interfere with interstate commerce, and he was locked up for 6 months (Brommel, 1978; Radosh, 1971).

In short, government harassment, the difficulty of organizing oncoming waves of immigrants, and a series of recessions that left many unemployed all worked against the unions.

Three developments characterized welfare after the Civil War: the first federal program, the growth of character-building programs, and the slow emergence of a new understanding of the socioeconomic causes of poverty.

The federal government authorized social spending on pensions for veterans of the Civil War and their widows. The pension program continued to make substantial outlays well into the twentieth century, covering just under 30 percent of the elderly population (Skocpol, 1995).

There is some debate about the generosity of the veterans and widows pension program and whether it can be considered a precursor to national welfare. Jansson (2001) notes that the federal budget at the time was paltry. Even in 1920, only 5.5 percent of the GNP was allocated for all public spending at all levels of government. In the end, regardless of how many veterans were covered, this was a wartime program, as was the Freedmen's Bureau, not a welfare program. This was how it had to be understood in light of the Supreme Court's dislike of federal involvement in welfare. The War Department was undeniably under federal authority.

The Charity Organization Societies appeared in the second half of the nineteenth century. Recessions, especially in 1870, left the cities in disarray, with as many as 3 million people unemployed, homeless, and hungry. Philanthropic organizations responded by setting up soup kitchens and emergency shelters. The openhandedness of these groups grated against the character-building creed, and by 1874, nine states had boards of charities in place in order to monitor and rationalize voluntary giving. The boards, in turn, organized the National Conference on Charities and Corrections (Warner, 1894).

In 1877, the first Charity Organization Society (COS) was established in upstate New York, in Buffalo. Others came into being in cities across the nation. The emergence of the COS impacted the movement for the institution of scientific charity. Their purpose was to supervise, coordinate, and investigate the poor who applied for help. Efficiency and self-help were watchwords. The COS got busy with the prevention of cheating and receiving assistance from multiple organizations. Most cities soon created a COS to bring order to charitable activities, not to give relief grants outright. They employed many volunteers—"friendly visitors," they were called—to evaluate the worthiness of the poor and keep registers of applicants for relief and the help they received.

The COS added systematic surveillance to a generalized mistrust of the lower classes and their morals. The institution was looked upon as an efficient way of converting the shiftless to middle class virtues by emphasizing self-help. The poor needed "not alms but a friend" (Brenner, J., 1956; Trattner, 1999; Wagner, 2000).

The new settlement movement, led by social-minded intellectuals and others who had the chance to visit Europe (Great Britain, Germany, and France, where national welfare programs were being developed), began to challenge the view that character flaws were the cause of poverty. Influenced by the "social gospel" movement, educated young women and men questioned the moral deficiency account. Many of them shared a commitment to aspects of socialist utopianism.

Amos G. Warner and the Chicago Federation of Settlements were both instrumental in reversing the traditional view. In 1884, Warner, later a Stanford University professor, published *American Charities*. This important book drew attention to the social and economic causes of poverty. In the same year, Graham Taylor, a minister's son, started the settlement movement. For the time, his was a radical take on cooperation across the barriers of class and race, and he argued forcefully for the integration of research into community practice.

If the cases are those who have merely applied for relief, the first thing to be ascertained is how many of these applicants ought to have relief of any sort. A table of nearly 28,000 cases investigated by the Charity Organization Societies in 1887 gave these returns:

Worthy of continuous relief	10.3%
Worthy of temporary relief	26.6%
Need work rather than relief	40.4%
Unworthy of relief	22.7%

A more exact view of the same thing may be obtained from 8,294 cases in three large cities—Baltimore, Boston, and New York—in 1892:

Need of work rather than relief	35%
Not in need of relief	9.1%
Should be disciplined	5.8%
Should have visitation and advice	7.4%
Need direct relief	42.7%

Source: Adapted from Warner (1919/1989).

Critical Commentary

Why, in the midst of the upheavals of the second half of the nineteenth century, was no major advance made in welfare? This is Jansson's (2001) main question. Answering it returns us to those intervening, contextual factors that conditioned resistance to social change.

The failure to give African Americans full citizenship may have been related to the huge loss of life suffered in the Civil War and to military costs that drained the national treasury. The trouble with this explanation is that in other times and other places (France after World War I, England after World War II), great *improvements* in social programs grew out of similar circumstances. The ineffectiveness of the Freedmen's Bureau and the thwarting of legislation favoring the rights of African Americans cannot be imputed solely to a desire on the part of political leaders to placate southerners in defeat and maintain peace in the Union.

The weakness of the federal government and its flimsy management capacity were heavy impediments. Because the Supreme Court had ruled that national social policies were unconstitutional, the federal government had to implement the programs of the Freedmen's Bureau through a poorly equipped War Department. In the absence of a strong central bureaucracy, local governments were left to implement constitutional amendments. The limited benefits distributed to veterans and war widows were politically feasible. The

Subjective and objective analysis of causes of poverty:

Subjective

Characteristics

- Indolence
- Lubricity
- Specific disease
- Lack of judgment
- Unhealthy appetite

Habits

- Shiftlessness
- Self-abuse and sexual excess
- Abuse of stimulants and narcotics
- Unhealthy diet
- Disregard of family ties

Objective

- Inadequate natural resources
- Bad climatic conditions
- Defective sanitation
- Evil associations and surroundings
- Defective legislation, defective judicial and punitive machinery
- Misdirected or inadequate education
- Bad industrial conditions: changes of trade, unfair taxation
- Lack of protections for emergencies
- Class exploitation
- Immobility of labor
- Inadequate wages and irregular employment

Source: Adapted from Warner (1894).

expenditures were connected to war. There, the federal government had undisputed authority.

The further constraints that the Supreme Court imposed on the federal executive had to do with an extremely narrow interpretation of the purview of government. Tying the hands of the executive branch benefited wealthy corporations. This was the effect of decisions that cut their taxes, blocked their regulation, and protected businesses from the Sherman Antitrust laws. Here we see not only the fear of a powerful federal government but also a firm belief that competition in industry should run free. The likelihood that some Supreme Court justices were true believers in the free market fails to explain why they believed less zealously in the right of free association for unions.

Economic wealth that favored both parties was converted into political might. This transfer goes a long way toward explaining the adoption of policies that benefited the well off and hurt the interests of workers. President Cleveland did not hesitate to send military force to confront the Pullman strikers in Chicago. Police interference in other strikes was considered routine and appropriate at the time.

The Charity Organization Societies (COS) lent some efficiency and greater control to the dispensation of largesse to the poor during the economic twists and turns of the century's later years. Not coincidentally, the COS enjoyed the support of grand entrepreneurs. The patrons of the COS in New York City were William Astor, Andrew Carnegie, J. Piedmont Morgan, and Mrs. Cornelius Vanderbilt (Trattner, 1999).

Two variations on the long-standing belief in character-based poverty were added. One, already evident in the punitive treatment of the poor in workhouses, became more widespread through the theories of Herbert Spencer (Beer, 1969). Spencer's views did not differ much from those of Thomas Malthus, a fellow Englishman. They acquired an aura of scientific validity by extrapolating from the research of Charles Darwin on natural selection in evolution. Those who are successful, Spencer observed, are "the fittest." It is to society's advantage that the fittest hold more resources and greater power, since they are the ones who contribute most. The unsuccessful, evidently, have lower capacities. They should, therefore, hold lower positions or perhaps even be marginalized. More resources in their hands would be wasteful, and more power would be dangerous.

Social Darwinism converged with Calvinism to glorify the rich, whose success spoke of their virtues as well as their capabilities. The well to do were to be admired, not envied. They were role models, and many people fantasized after their good fortune. Since the attainment of great success was a matter of individual effort rather than differential opportunities, everyone could legitimately aspire to it. The myth proved powerfully attractive. It ranged from the message given every elementary school student—that anyone can become president—to the mythical example of Horatio Alger, who worked his way up, overcoming humble origins. The myth helped melt class resentment in the United States (Hofstadter, 1992).

The germs of a counter-ideology sprouted at the end of the century. Grating economic disparities, radical ideas brought by some immigrants, the writings of major socialist thinkers, a social gospel propagated by some Protestant churches, and news about how other nations were addressing "the social question" all contributed to this development.

At the end of the nineteenth century, Jane Addams and Mary Richmond—the founders of social work—stood in opposite corners. Mary Richmond took a job in 1888 with the Maryland COS. Apparently, she agreed with the philosophy of the friendly visitors: "If you are going to be a friend, fertile in helpful suggestions, sympathetic and kind, you cannot be an almoner too." By 1889, Jane Addams had opened Hull House, a Chicago settlement center. Addams felt that a negative, pseudoscientific spirit pervaded the COS agents: "Don't give, don't act, don't do this, don't do that; all they give the poor is advice—and for that they probably send the Almighty a bill" (Trattner, 1999, p. 97).

These outlooks forecast the therapeutic and the social change directions for social workers in the next century. By the end of the nineteenth century, path dependence exerted a powerful influence on ideas and institutions in welfare. Turning points going far back in American history could not be easily undone, even after huge changes in the size and makeup of the population, in national borders, and in economic growth appeared to make these customs obsolete.

The weak central government inherited from colonial and postcolonial times continued to be strapped financially and administratively. Private organizations still handled most services to the poor. The belief that poverty was self-made and that it reflected deviance from righteousness not only persisted as a religious conviction but was also reinforced by social Darwinism. Functional incapacity was added, like injury to insult, to the moral inferiority ascribed to the poor.

While many workers' movements were strangled, a few strikes were successful. The American Federation of Labor (AFL) was formed in 1886. Without support from either of the major parties, various socialist groups advocated views about the rights of workers and the causes of poverty that ran counter to the dominant ideology.

5

The Ambiguous Ancestry of Welfare and Social Work, 1900–1950

As immigration and industrialization accelerated through the early years of the twentieth century, the devastating toll exacted by the depression of 1893 to 1896 awakened Americans to the sufferings of millions of unemployed. The destitute jobless depended on soup kitchens for sustenance. Misery on this scale rattled the belief that poverty originated in the character deficiencies of the poor or their sheer lack of ability. Attention turned to the incapacity of the economic system to provide a minimally adequate distribution of material benefits. Out of such traumas, a reformist movement grew. Almost immediately, a counter-reaction set in, mobilized by those who benefited from or who remained convinced of the legitimacy of the system.

The Progressive Era

The Multiple Goals and Constituencies of the Progressive Movement

Disparate goals went under "the big tent" of the Progressive movement. At best, the medley of reforms looked like a loosely woven quilt.

Spread by urban pastors, the "social gospel" inspired the moral branch of the movement. Their notion of charity broke away from puritanical, otherworldly ideals. They took to heart the need to alleviate the pain and suffering of the poor through concrete measures in the here and now. Social gospelers also decried the impact of poverty on family stability and the social development of children.

Other Progressives were dismayed with corruption in public administration. They railed against the prevalence of bribes, political cronyism, and the inefficiency that accompanied these vices.

Charles Booth began his pioneering research on poverty in 1886, in East London and then, over the next 17 years, extended it to all districts of the city. Carefully identifying different levels of poverty, Booth's work stood in contrast with other studies based on subjective and moralistic standards. His approach was painstakingly empirical. He measured age, access to employment, family size and composition, resources needed for maintenance, community opportunities or lack thereof, and birth and mortality rates (Booth, 1902–1904/1970).

Booth's studies were conducted block by block throughout London. This coverage enabled him to derive an estimate of the types and distribution of classes for the whole city that was a gift to policy makers. Contrary to the conventional wisdom of the time, Booth found the following classes:

- The lowest class—occasional laborers, loafers, and semi-criminals
- The very poor—casual laborers, characterized by hand-to-mouth existence and chronic want
- The poor—irregular employment or regular, ill-paid employment
- The comfortable working class, with regular and fairly paid employment
- The middle class and above, well paid and regularly employed, with assets

Booth's example had a major impact on social welfare research in the United States in the late nineteenth and early twentieth centuries. The heyday of this type of study in American social work was between the turn of the century and World War I. Louise Moore's (1907/1970) early study of household budgets made use of a longitudinal method of supervised account keeping on the part of selected families. In *Standards of Living Among Workingmen's Families*, Robert Chapin (1909/1970) adopted the retrospective approach of relying largely on the families' memory of expenditures. Chapin introduced the systematic formulation of minimum estimates for each category of expenditure and the use of a dietician's judgment to analyze the adequacy of food expenditures. From such data, Moore and Chapin calculated the minimum standard for a living wage for a normal family in the early 1900s (Zimbalist, 1977). The U.S. Department of Agriculture used this procedure, with minor improvements, in the sixties to define and measure rates of poverty in the United States.

Some social service workers joined the Progressive movement in seeking more public funds for their agencies and backing legislation to improve housing and health. For still other groups, the central goal was to improve the security of workers. This meant pushing for a minimum wage and health benefits, and cutting the length of the workday. Politically minded reformers wanted to cleanse the system of patronage and give more say to voters. The top priority of some radical and socialist-leaning leaders was the rights of unions and the use of militant labor to dismantle an unjust capitalist order. In addition, many small commercial and industrial outfits clamored for the regulation of large corporations who were driving them out of business through unfair competition.

Some but not all of these interests overlapped. Even those with broadly similar goals were liable to go off on their own in pursuit of their favorite cause. Small factions attracted followers with fairly narrow goals, without much interest in supporting wider reforms. Those in the moral camp, for example, typically nurtured objectives in line with the social service group, but fighting for broader legislation did not excite them. Within the social service coalition itself, one faction pressed for more funds for its programs, while another backed the expansion of private programs. Still others were inclined to view assistance as a social right (Hofstadter, 1963).

Strategies and Outcomes

Because the Supreme Court had barred federal intervention in welfare policy, the Progressive movement targeted state and local governments. The strategy required a huge effort and produced scattered outcomes—a flaw that several critics pointed out. Victories gained in one state might or might not spill over into others. The problem did not necessarily reflect any political ineptitude on the part of the Progressives; it was built into the institutional constraints of the time. Some Progressives realized that success depended on implementation at the national level. The Constitution, they noted, had been drafted when the nation was overwhelmingly agricultural. The document did not reflect the conditions and needs of an industrial society (Beard, 1965).

The movement's hope of gaining the attention of national-level decision makers fixed on Theodore Roosevelt, a Republican who in 1901 succeeded the assassinated William McKinley in the presidency and was reelected in 1904. "Teddy" sympathized with the reform agenda. In 1908, when his term was up, he mounted an unsuccessful bid for his party's nomination against his conservative successor, William Howard Taft. In 1912, Roosevelt's supporters, with Jane Addams prominent among them, convinced him to become the candidate of the recently formed Progressive Party. Roosevelt's campaign split the Republican vote and handed the victory to the Democrats. Woodrow Wilson was elected president.

To the consternation of conservatives who had supported his candidacy, Wilson turned out to be receptive to parts of the Progressive agenda—to child labor laws, for example, banking regulation, and women's suffrage. Many Progressives and labor unions supported his reelection in 1916. However, the political forces aligned against the Progressives remained strong. They kept up a barrage of attacks, accusing Progressives of disseminating pro-socialist, anti-constitutional, anti-free market—in sum, anti-American—tendencies. These attacks, abetted by the courts, blunted or reversed the few successes that the Progressives achieved (Hofstadter, 1992).

Maternal Welfare

A number of concerned ministers, service reformers, and women activists pushed through legislative initiatives—mothers' pensions, local juvenile courts, and a national-level Children's Bureau—that some historians have called "maternal welfare." These groups mobilized against the disruptive effects of poverty on families and its consequences for younger generations (Leff, 1973).

Mothers' pensions were mandated in almost all the states. The program represented a breakthrough in government assistance directed to outdoor relief. But it covered only widows, who were considered morally deserving. Thus, the number of mothers covered was quite restricted, and the benefits provided were so skimpy that they undercut child care functions, since most widows had to work to survive.

If children deprived of maternal care were the concern of legislators, why were other single mothers not covered, and why were minorities excluded? Two explanations come to mind. By the moral standards of the time, widows were considered far more worthy than women abandoned by the fathers of their children. Besides, since most non-protected women in poverty were either immigrants or minorities, their offspring did not count as much as "real Americans." Another possibility is that this program was allowed as a token exception. It served as a symbolic, materially minimal nod to the moral high ground.

Many states established juvenile courts. Their rationale was to segregate children who had committed crimes from their adult counterparts. Progress in the study of human development buttressed this separation. Children and young adolescents had yet to attain the cognitive level to assume full responsibility for their acts. A related theory was that, precisely because they were at a lower stage of moral development, young people were relatively malleable and could be rehabilitated through well-designed programs. The juvenile judge would act as a surrogate parent, exercising the power of *parens patriae*. The judge was to evaluate the background and the behavior of the juvenile and decide on the program he or she needed for rehabilitation.

The "child-saving movement" had enormous influence on the creation of juvenile courts. Some historians consider it a strategy designed to assimilate hordes of immigrant children. Parents from different cultures whose customs did not accord with those of nineteenth-century America were raising poor immigrant children. Since the courts had authority over cases of parental neglect and abuse, it was easy to remove children from their parents and resocialize them. In fact, during periods of economic distress, many parents did nothing to resist this strategy. The procedure was also in line with the demand for an ever-increasing, disciplined labor force (Bellingham, 1986; Platt, 1969).

The Children's Bureau, a national program, was established in 1912. It had a meager budget, and its functions were limited to data-gathering and dispensing advice. Lacking the mandate or the resources to implement policy, the Bureau avoided political controversy. Nevertheless, for all its prudence, the major initiatives of the Children's Bureau—legislation to curb child labor and the Sheppard Turner Bill, which provided federal funds for states to run women's and young children's clinics—were passed but eventually defeated. The first was done in by the standard argument about the unconstitutionality of federal intervention in welfare. The second went down to defeat under charges of socialized medicine from the American Medical Association (Hacker, 2002).

Workmen's Compensation

In one form or another, all states passed workmen's compensation laws. The level of accidents in factories that had introduced mechanization without providing safety measures was staggering. The estimate is that at the time, about 35,000 workers were killed and many thousands more injured each year (Hacker, 2002). To obtain redress, workers had to sue companies. Although workers lost the vast majority (85 percent) of cases, it was a costly process for industry as well. The laws established state funds that received revenues from a payroll tax levied on employers. More workers were covered than previously, but the level of compensation was very low. Furthermore, the immunity that employers enjoyed from being sued reduced incentives for improving workplace safety (Castrovinci, 1976).

Other Achievements

One of the lasting reforms of the Progressive Era was the meritocratization of civil service careers, promoting professionalism in public administration. Various states also instituted aftercare services for mental patients released from hospitals.

Critical Commentary

The significance of the Progressive movement is not confined to its rather modest legislative achievements. It represented the first important impulse for social reform in the United States with lasting repercussions.

Why was policy reform so subdued? Part of the reason must be the ramshackle integration of the groups allied to the movement, and their neglect of a concerted political strategy. The Progressives were not strong enough to pose a revolutionary threat. Nor did they have well-organized supporters or powerful political allies. In large part, their momentum appeared to come from their moral positions, based on the appeal to right wrongs. Can reliance on calls to "do the right thing" be attributed to the naïveté of the Progressives, as many historians claim, or were there specific conditions that impeded their efforts?

With regard to the decentralization and administrative underdevelopment of the national government, nothing much had changed since the nineteenth century. The federal government's ability to draw on direct taxation was practically nonexistent. The Supreme Court reversed and eliminated certain projects advanced by the Progressives on these issues. Reform programs were forced to follow a piecemeal, state-level approach.

A major exception to the power of conservative intransigence on this score was the passage, in 1913, of the Sixteenth Amendment, which created the personal income tax in modern form. Though such taxes had been collected as an emergency measure during the Civil War, they had been phased out in 1872. Now, after the election of Woodrow Wilson in 1912, and with the support of Progressives alarmed by the concentration of wealth and conservatives anxious to stabilize the sources of government revenues, the required three-fourths of the states ratified the amendment (Chace, 2004). The tax rate began at 1 percent of income, minus deductions and exemptions, and rose gently to 7 percent of incomes above $500,000.

Unions, which might have provided a strong impetus for reform, were not serious players for two reasons. To begin with, the number of unionized workers grew. But these organizations were hardly representative of the huge urban proletariat. The masses of immigrants who arrived in the United States toward the end of the nineteenth century and during the first decades of the twentieth were extremely difficult to organize. While Anglo culture fretted that the "teeming multitudes" would damage the moral fiber of Americans, industrialists depended on cheap labor. For their part, eager for any employment and tied to their ethnic groups and to habits of patronage and clientelism, most newcomers could not be counted on to push for social reforms.

Secondly, the leaders of the strongest union—the American Federation of Labor (AFL), whose founder, Samuel Gompers, famously replied "More!" when asked "What is it you people want?"—stayed away from political causes and plugged away at negotiating wage and benefits contracts. Woodrow Wilson won the allegiance of Gompers by promising to improve the legal status of organized labor (Hofstadter, 1963).

The Progressive movement developed a significant critique of both unbridled capitalism and corrupt democracy. Progressives submitted the presuppositions favoring the superiority of the well to do—an ideology that had hardened over the decades—to scathing attack. Paradoxically, however, reforms influenced by the movement, especially maternal welfare, were implicated in that ideology. They bore signs of the negative stereotyping of the poor that were common to nineteenth-century thinking. Intoxicated by economic success, which evidently confirmed the supremacy of the market and the truths of the Constitution, resistance to reform waxed triumphant through the 1920s. Participation in World War I heightened a patriotism that contributed to righteous complacency (Chace, 2004).

Social Work, 1900–1920

By the end of the nineteenth century, the Charity Organization Society (COS) and the settlement house movement had already drawn up two directions for social work: individual help and social action. Both sets of activities were designated "social works." At times, the expression was synonymous with "good works."

By the early twentieth century, due in part to a change in the ideology of COS, the settlement houses and charity organizations had reached a rapprochement. A survey of working conditions in Pittsburgh, directed by Paul Kellogg, followed by others by the Russell Sage Foundation, controverted the Victorian views of poverty identified with COS.

Two examples marked this newfound collaboration. In 1909, Jane Addams was chosen as the first woman president of the National Conference of Charities and Corrections (NCCC). Secondly, in 1912, the two publications that once represented each movement, *Charities* and *Commons*, merged into *Survey*, under the editorship of Paul Kellogg, a resident of the Henry Street Settlement in New York. Nevertheless, the two movements also kept up their rivalry. Reflecting this dissension, Mary Richmond continued to argue that settlement work suffered from a lack of clarity, while Jane Addams questioned the efficacy of the COS (Drew, 1983).

The COS may have moved away from Puritanism and social Darwinism, but the embrace of scientific charity ratified efficiency as a fundamental objective. Upgrading the processing and classification of cases suited the standards of industrial bureaucracy. Mary Richmond, who had been an assistant treasurer of the Baltimore COS and then Director of Social Work at the Russell Sage Foundation, became the acknowledged leader in organizational processing techniques. Richmond established casework as *the* intervention method for social work, and she specified the guidelines for conceptualizing social diagnosis (Franklin, D., 1986).

The overall effect of these developments was to reorder the priorities of the COS and to encourage the shift from friendly visitors to professional social workers. In a speech given at the Conference on Charities and Corrections in 1901, Richmond clarified the process of helping a person in the "situation." She defined "situation" to include aspects of the person's environment, and the speech had a great impact on the curricula of the emerging programs. By 1904, the COS set up a one-year graduate program at the New York School of Philanthropy. In 1917, Richmond's book on social diagnosis drew out parallels between social work and medical intervention, and it contributed decisively to acceptance of the professional status of social work. Only two years earlier, Abraham Flexner, an expert in medical evaluation, had denied that social work was or could be a profession. Events surrounding World War I also shaped the future of the profession.

The Red Cross asked Mary Richmond to establish the Home Service to respond to the traumas of servicemen and the family disruptions caused by the war. By 1918, a total of 40,000 social workers were employed in home services all over the country (Black, 1991). Two years later, the war over, the Home Service program was dismantled. But the approaches the program used—casework and psychiatric social work—flourished. The Public Health

Service and the Veterans Bureau adopted psychiatric social work as their major practice.

Clifford Beers, a previous mental patient, authored *A Mind That Found Itself* (1909), a book that triggered interest in mental health. This was followed by a study, conducted by the NCCC and the New York School of Philanthropy, assessing the situation of mental patients released from mental hospitals. The results demonstrated an acute need for aftercare services. The survey findings were instrumental in promoting the aftercare legislation adopted by various states. By 1911, social work services were integrated into New York mental health hospitals (Trattner, 1999). Mary Richmond, at the helm of the COS, continued to press for private welfare and individual intervention. She emulated the medical model of careful documentation, diagnosis, and rehabilitative intervention.

The settlement house movement represented the other structural facet of social work. A wide range of intellectual and political currents, from the social gospel to socialism, fed into the settlement house movement in the early years of the century. Many of the women residing in these settlements were active in other social movements of the Progressive Era. Their work represented quite a departure from the traditional COS style. They were part of a group of well-educated women—including Jane Addams—from affluent backgrounds, brought up in families with political connections.

The attraction of the settlement houses stemmed from an awareness of the inequities that produced and reproduced poverty. The settlement houses stood for a desire to make a difference in the communities where poor people lived. Marriage and family life did not attract many of the settlement house residents, nor were they enthusiastic about the charity work assigned to "respectable" married women. They also felt limited by traditional female professions, such as nursing and teaching. In short, they rebelled against the stereotypes imposed on their gender, and they empathized with others oppressed by inequality. A grasp of the sources of economic and social inequality informed their commitment (Hofstadter, 1956).

Different kinds of settlement houses sprung up. Not all of them, some critics have observed, were staffed by idealistic, educated women, and some opted to use control strategies on their clients (Karger, 1987). Still, many settlement houses pursued innovative participatory approaches that were dedicated, at the same time, to social reform. Hull House, organized and managed by Jane Addams and her coresidents and friends, is the best-known prototype of the movement (Hofstadter, 1956).

In 1889, Jane Addams and Ellen Gates Starr founded Hull House in the blighted neighborhood around Chicago's South Halstead Street. Immigrants swarmed into the area. The programs that Addams and Starr developed in concert with the community made education an essential tool for achieving reform. Their goals and strategies contrasted sharply with the approach of the COS. Local participation in planning and implementing activities, leadership formation, and respect for cultural diversity were the means toward a varied agenda through which settlement house residents expressed their commitment to democratic principles in the delivery of services. Another departure from conventional social work was the alliance of Addams and her colleagues with other movements (labor, feminists, pacifists, socialists) to achieve reforms across the board for workers, for women, and for children (Addams, 1910).

Addams supported Teddy Roosevelt as a candidate for the Progressive Party and campaigned on behalf of his candidacy for president. This was viewed by many social workers as a breach of professionalism, even among supporters of the Progressive agenda. Addams had already come in for criticism because of her resistance to social work professionalism; she feared that this development would rein in activism and make social workers vulnerable to cooptation by the status quo (Franklin, 1986).

Addams and her colleagues searched out the systemic causes of poverty and injustice and vigorously advocated for social reform. If industrial conditions were putting workers at risk or were driving them below the level of material decency, it became obvious to them that state regulation was needed to correct such situations. They allied themselves openly with various groups—some of them radical—to achieve change, and they were not shy about using political clout in the service of their objectives. Activism in this mold played an important role in some of the social policies of the Progressive Era. However, the impact of Addams and her allies on the evolution toward social work professionalism was at most indirect (Elshtain, 2002; Trattner, 1999).

By the end of the 1920s, both Mary Richmond and Jane Addams had lost their sway over the profession. The effort that Richmond put into gaining professional status for social work proved insufficient, and her influence waned. Jane Addams's agitation against the war had made her unpopular. When Addams and Richmond ran for the presidency of the National Conference of Charities and Corrections, both lost (Specht & Courtney, 1994).

Social Regression, Disaster, and the Birth of the Welfare State During the Interwar Years

The Roaring Twenties

American participation in "The Great War" stifled the reformist impulses of the Progressive Era. After the war, resurgent industrial growth, now directed toward a market avid for consumer goods, not only confirmed a long-standing faith in the economic system but also amplified belief in the trickle-down effect. Capital investment created jobs, facilitating further investment that would benefit the workers. This virtuous circle gave renewed impetus to policies favoring laissez-faire.

Photo 5.1   Patriotism, World War I

Source: From the private collection of Peter McDonough.

Photo 5.2   Mass Production in the Prosperous Twenties

Source: From the private collection of Peter McDonough.

A string of Republican presidents during the 1920s—Warren Harding, Calvin Coolidge, and Herbert Hoover—believed devoutly in this formula. At the same time that they backed a free market and nonintervention by the state in areas of welfare, they approved of wealthfare as a matter of national economic interest. As had happened during the previous century, the police and National Guard troops were deployed to harass union militants. Court injunctions and firings were regularly used against union activists and leaders. Companies manipulated their workforce by creating make-believe unions, submissive to their authority, and negotiating wages and benefits through them.

In the midst of their love affair with new technologies, Americans held fast to features of the old morality. In 1919, the Eighteenth Amendment was passed, nationalizing the prohibition of alcoholic spirits. The Immigration Act of 1924 not only limited the number of immigrants but also set quotas to favor inflows from Northern Europe over those from Southern and Eastern Europe. The preference accorded to Anglo-Nordic immigrants echoed the racial and ethnic arrogance that had appeared a century before in the doctrine of Manifest Destiny. Immigration from putatively inferior cultures would bring disorder and moral contagion. Immigration from Asia was halted, first by the Chinese Act in the late nineteenth century and, early in the twentieth century, by a complete prohibition of immigration from Japan.

The Great Depression

The prosperity of the 1920s hid a continuously high rate of unemployment (reaching 13 percent) and a decade-long depression in agriculture. At least one-third of the population actually lived in poverty. The trickle-down theory that justified the primacy of capital for the sake of investment fostered instead accumulation in a few hands. Assets were often used for speculation rather than investment. Low wages, high unemployment, and agricultural depression drove down purchasing power. In practice, the trickle-down effect was not working. This short circuit became a major cause of the Great Depression that hit the nation with the crash of the stock market in October of 1929 (Edsforth, 2000).

Fifteen million people lost their jobs, and hundreds of thousands of farmers lost their land. Public response to the immensity of the disaster was slow and ineffective. Local officials had no institutionalized means of relief at their disposal. Still devoted to the rehabilitation of the poor, private agencies were not equipped to deliver appropriate services (Paradis, 1967).

Victims and non-victims alike, as well as social workers, volunteers, and local public officials, all knew that a coordinated response was urgently needed. However, President Hoover clung to his belief that the market would bounce back. In his judgment, government help to corporations would bring the downward spiral to a halt, and volunteer organizations like

Photo 5.3   Okies on The Way to California

Source: From the private collection of Peter McDonough.

Photo 5.4   Casual Workers on a Break

Source: From the private collection of Peter McDonough.

the Red Cross could best handle the clamor for social assistance. Unwavering in his convictions, Hoover dismissed the grim statistics and the demands for help pouring in from the states. Nonintervention by the federal government in social assistance remained the bedrock of his creed. In the face of inaction, disorder spread. Prodded along by radicals and communists, so did disillusionment with the economic system (Sobel, 1975).

The Birth of the Welfare State

Meanwhile, unable to get help from the federal government, the Democratic governor of New York, Franklin Roosevelt, asked state lawmakers to help local authorities meet the needs of the unemployed. The Temporary Emergency Relief Administration, an independent agency, was quickly set up with Harry Hopkins, a social worker, as executive director. Fearful of greater instability and aware of his record in New York, some powerful businessmen backed Roosevelt's presidential candidacy in 1931. FDR's promise to act quickly against economic deterioration also gained broad popular support. He won by a landslide.

The new president did in fact move rapidly to help out the victims of the Depression and strengthen the economy. By creating "temporary programs to deal with the crisis," Roosevelt circumvented the Supreme Court's resistance to a federal role in welfare. In fact, when Social Security legislation passed in 1935, FERA (the Federal Emergency Relief Administration) and CWA (the Civil Works Administration) were discontinued. Other agencies like the Civilian Conservative Corps (CCC) and the Public Works Administration (PWA) stayed alive as, respectively, the National Youth Administration and the Works Progress Administration.

The Roosevelt administration launched more such "alphabet soup" programs. The Federal Deposit Insurance Corporation (FDIC), the Securities and Exchange Commission (SEC), the Federal Home Administration (FHA), and the Regional Development Planning (RDP) all remain in existence. Their aim was to prevent the panic and losses dramatized by runs on the banks, to avoid stock market crashes, to avert evictions by facilitating home ownership, and to develop selected agricultural regions. Two other programs, the National Industrial Recovery Act and the Agricultural Adjustment Agency, gave the government enhanced regulatory powers over price setting and labor contracts. The Supreme Court declared them unconstitutional before the decade was over (Edsforth, 2000; Jansson, 2001).

The passage of all these programs in so short a time reflected the nation's sense of emergency. But the temporary assistance measures were not revolutionary, in spite of their number and the significant role of the federal involvement. Under Harry Hopkins, FERA gave grants-in-aid to states and localities, specifying that every 20 employees be supervised by a social worker. Means tests were required. Rules for eligibility and benefits were established locally or by the states. The various workfare programs covered about one-third of the unemployed, and wages were set below those in the private sector.

Because these temporary programs did not live up to the ambitious promises made by Roosevelt to reverse economic decline, the administration set up a Committee on Economic Security, headed by Hopkins and Frances

Perkins, Secretary of Labor who, like Hopkins, was a social worker. Their mandate was to develop a social security proposal. Many economists, including Wilbur Cohen, the future Secretary of the Department of Health, Education and Welfare, were members of the committee.

Initially, the plan was to build a structure of social insurance similar to the systems put in place in industrialized Europe during the late nineteenth and early twentieth centuries. But internal disagreements, political maneuvering, and professional priorities resulted in a much more limited two-tier proposal, passed in 1935 (Cates, 1983). Southern legislators wanted farm laborers excluded. Pressure from the American Medical Association took health insurance off the agenda. The fact that early threats of popular uprising had subsided gave these interests leverage (Piven & Cloward, 1971).

The design embedded in the 1935 Social Security Act showed the influence of two systems of protection: one modeled on private insurance and the other rooted in the poor laws. The social insurance law—the part of the Social Security Act dealing exclusively with insurance—reflected the private model, and it created two programs. Old-age insurance (OAI) was federally regulated and administered; unemployment insurance (UI) was federally regulated but run by the states (Gates, 1983, pp. 13–16).

The OAI called for worker contributions through a special tax. Funding for the UI came from employer contributions to the federal treasury, set as a percentage of the payroll. Ninety percent of that contribution was returned to the states to administer. Farm laborers, seasonal workers, immigrant workers, and domestic servants were excluded from these protections (Cates, 1983; Douglas, 1939).

The formula for OAI self-funding was not redistributive. It was, in fact, regressive, placing proportionally stiffer taxes on low-wage workers. As for the UI, employer costs could be passed on to consumers. Nonetheless, though coverage was not universal, enactment of these programs showed a commitment on the part of the government to face the socioeconomic sources of poverty driven by old age and structural unemployment. They were popular because they covered working people, and so paid homage to the work ethic. Since the program was self-funded by the participants, OAI benefits came to be seen as rights.

Public assistance reflected the second model, going back to the poor laws. It was geared to the deserving poor—those who were blind, or too young, or too old to be employed. So the government crafted such programs as Aid to Dependent Children, Old-Age Assistance, and Assistance to the Blind. Federal matching grants went to the states, and the programs were to be managed locally. The states set criteria for entitlement and the level of benefits. Since the funds came from federal and state general revenues, the program was viewed as charity. Means tests and proof of "good behavior" were the norm. Recipients were, in effect, dependents.

In 1936, the Wagner Act guaranteed unions the right to organize. It provided for a National Labor Relations Board (NLRB), an independent agency charged with mediating conflicts between employers and employees. The Wagner Act generated an upsurge in union membership, but the NLRB's mediation efforts had only a modest impact. Strikes proved to be more effective than mediation in getting a hearing for workers.

In 1937, the Wagner-Steagall Act established the Housing Authority to provide low-interest loans to local authorities for public housing.

Critical Commentary

The economic boom of the 1920s gave a boost to conservative ideologies and policies, just as happened during the final decade of the nineteenth century. The Progressive movement could not provide an equivalent counterweight. The 1920s, like the 1890s, ended in a depression.

Economic collapse eroded faith in capitalism, and the Hoover administration's failures threatened to deplete the political system's reservoir of legitimacy. Demonstrations of unemployed workers, veterans, and farmers multiplied. Socialists and communist sympathizers contributed to organizing this swelling of discontent. Their numbers were not large but their leadership in organizing protests was visible.

Some industrial and financial leaders saw all this as a precursor to revolutionary upheaval. Hoover's policy of appealing to private charities and offering subsidies to stimulate business was clearly not working. Nervous businessmen supported Roosevelt and many of his proposals as a way out of the rush toward cataclysm. This is the setting in which the New Deal's early legislative proposals were accepted (Piven & Cloward, 1971). By 1935, business panic had receded. The willingness to entertain seriously redistributive social security policies waned. This set the stage for the two-tier legislation that treated workers as first-class citizens but relegated non-workers, even if worthy, to the lower ranks. The path dependence built into institutional history and the "stickiness" of values was preserved.

Powerful interests, economic as well as political, had to be catered to in order to reach legislative outcomes. Despite this, the intellectual landscape of the early years of the New Deal covered a range of approaches to reform. Some were rooted in the Progressive movement, others in the management experiences of mobilizing for World War I. For a time, diverse ideas managed to coexist—a mélange encouraged by Roosevelt who, with a studied casualness, often asked his battling advisors to "meld it all together." While many shared an assumption that the big problems were bound up with the very structure of modern capitalism and that it was the government's mission to control the flaws of that structure, such as monopolies, few New Dealers were genuinely hostile to capitalism. Some called for policies that would redistribute wealth and income. Others favored centralized planning as a way to counter the power of corporations. Still others envisioned business consortia and associations as mechanisms to curb the destabilizing impact of competition. Only a tiny group of radicals saw the Depression as the death knell of capitalism and called for a total overhaul of the economic system.

Pragmatism reigned, pushing towards the most viable and quickest solutions to the woes of the Depression. The government took on regulatory responsibilities and the task of stimulating weak spots in the economy. With the New Deal, an American welfare state was born, and protective legislation for labor was enacted (Brinkley, 1995).

Without a doubt, the government at last reached a modicum of centralization, and the unions finally could operate without fear of repression. However, in contrast to other Western countries, these two developments were limited and late. Welfare was more restrictive than in other industrial nations. Some of the programs—notably, public assistance—were run by the states and they adhered to traditional principles, inherited from the poor laws, regarding deservedness, investigation, eligibility, and control. Means testing and normative checking of behavior were standard features.

In the end, the Social Security Act established a mixed public/private arrangement rather than a public welfare state. Social insurance benefits are not tied to citizenship, nor are they fully administered by the central government. They are tied to jobs, administered by employers, and supported by public policies. The unions function as active participants in an intricate web of private and public benefits. Unions negotiate contracts with employers that cover not only wages but also pensions and other benefits. This arrangement accounts for roughly a third of social benefits in the United States. The state actively promulgates rules, writes regulations, and offers incentives to organize the private sector safety net. The public pieces of the welfare settlement fill the gaps that private partners cannot or do not fill (Gottschalk, 2000).

As it happened, it was corporate pension plans that flourished in the immediate aftermath of Social Security legislation. Employers lobbied to expand tax breaks for private pensions, and they recast their plans as supplementary benefits for higher-income workers (Hacker, 2002).

Behind the scenes, business groups, insurers, pension consultants, and conservatives in Congress worked to codify laws that allowed publicly subsidized private plans to be generously integrated with Social Security. In practice, such plans provided little or no benefit to the workers whom New Deal reformers had sought to help. After the passage of old-age insurance, private pension plans began to grow. Employers tailored these plans to white collar workers. A feature of the tax code that allowed corporate contributions to pensions and interest income on trusts to escape taxation encouraged the bias toward privatization (Hacker, 2002).

The dependence of the government on the private sector also reflected the chronically underdeveloped condition of public bureaucracy, and this legacy ultimately held back the reach of the New Deal. The Lockean defense of small government, part and parcel of American political culture, restricted the growth of "big government."

At the same time, organizational modernization led to greater efficiency in business. So, when President Wilson had to deal with the unprecedented administrative demands of World War I, he turned to private organizations to oversee contracting out. The War Industries Board was a brief experiment in quasi-centralized mobilization and national planning that was disbanded soon after the armistice was signed.

The Roosevelt administration followed a similar route to implement New Deal programs. The National Industrial Recovery Act essentially delegated public policy to industry. One of the consequences of this public–private interdependence was to perpetuate the administrative weakness of the government and its dependence on business (Eisner, 2000).

To a large extent, social movements impelled successful policies. Powerful agrarian organizations had a strong voice in formulating agricultural policy. Labor's rank-and-file made itself heard in the Wagner Act. Social workers and women's organizations lobbied skillfully for welfare state policies (Brinkley, 1995). The policies of the New Deal strengthened the identification of the Democratic Party with labor, at the same time that this alliance narrowed any opening for the emergence of a militant labor party.

Social Work in the Twenties and Thirties

After World War I, most social workers opted for psychiatric social work, and courses in psychiatry dominated the curricula of the pioneer schools. Most of these schools were tied to private agencies. During the 1920s, three journals—*Social Work Casework*, *Child Welfare*, and *Social Services Review*—issued their first numbers. Several professional organizations, including the American Association of Social Workers and the American Association of Psychiatric Social Worker, were founded at the time. The National Conference of Charities and Corrections become the National Conference of Social Work (Trattner, 1999).

The creation of the School of Psychiatric Social Work at Smith College was part of this trend. As the school's cofounder Mary Jarrett (1919) stated in "The Psychiatric Thread Running Through All Social Case Work," the study of mental health is fundamental to casework, since the adaptation of the individual to his or her environment depends on the mental makeup of that person.

By 1925, psychotherapy had become the go-to method in social casework, and the social environment component of casework lost ground. The mental hygiene movement was influential in moving social workers in this direction, but other factors played a role as well. Since 1915, when Flexner, the expert on medical evaluation, had denied social work professional status and consigned social workers to the standing of an auxiliary occupation, on the margins of professionalism, social workers and their leaders searched eagerly for a theory and method of intervention that would make them undeniably professional and autonomous.

Psychotherapy offered a conceptual and scientific-sounding method of intervention. It propagated a systematic view of the relation between conscious and unconscious processes that were supposed to affect human behavior, and it had developed a canonical list of procedures for diagnosis and intervention. It also allowed social workers—until then working under the supervision of psychiatrists—to operate independently, since the exercise of psychiatry did not require a medical degree. The turn to psychotherapy paid off. Social work appeared as a distinct occupation in the 1930 census.

Focused on rehabilitation of the personality, this type of social work was not far from the methods used by the "friendly visitors" of the nineteenth century. Like them, psychotherapists held the view that individual treatment was the key to curing poverty. The friendly visitors were on a mission to improve the character of the poor. Basing their interventions on a "technical assessment" of psychological problems, social workers in the twenties concentrated on the emotional deprivation and maladjustment of the poor.

The chicken-in-every-pot optimism of the 1920s did not encourage much attention to social reform. Private social agencies proliferated, specializing in health, child guidance, family services, and the like. But to say that the new profession was unenthusiastic about social reform, and leave it at that, overlooks signs of social work radicalism that, although weak, was not dead.

The anti-war stance of many Progressive activists was unpopular, and this blocked alliances that might have been used to promote reform. The military reacted directly. In 1922, a widely distributed pamphlet originating from the War Department's Chemical Warfare Service traced the interconnections among 15 pro-peace women's organizations. The presumed evildoers were part of a "Spider Web Conspiracy." The pamphlet not only questioned the women's patriotism but also accused them of being communists and dupes, out to destroy American institutions (Reisch & Andrews, 2001).

The climate of repression and reprisals discouraged a new generation of activists from pressing for Progressive-style reforms. Julia Lathrop, the director of the Child Bureau and once a resident at Hull House, wanted to implement legislation that created clinics for mothers and their children across the nation. The act was passed in 1921. However, in spite of reliable research demonstrating critical need, the legislation was subsequently withdrawn on the grounds that it was a socialist measure.

Though severely repressed, the radical spirit of social work activists was passed on through their associations and allied social movements, and it was ready to respond to the challenges of the 1930s. Contrary to their colleagues, who were increasingly devoted to psychotherapy, radical social workers were already alarmed by trends in unemployment during the second half of the 1920s. In 1931, Edith Abbott reminded educators that knowledge of the structure and functioning of society was as indispensable to social workers as physiology was for physicians. Anthropology, sociology, and economics, as well as administration, should be part of social work training. In her presidential address to the National Conference of Social Work, Grace Coyle spoke in the same spirit of the role of poverty in an array of problems: physical and mental illness, unemployment, inadequate shelter, family insecurity, and hunger. All of these were related and they undermined the development of children (Trattner, 1999).

Professional social work organizations rejected or remained indifferent to social activists. The most important factor superseding the commitment of the profession to personality adjustment seems to have been the demand for social workers in the implementation of New Deal programs.

The prominence of social workers at the policy level within the Roosevelt administration was remarkable. Harry Hopkins orchestrated all the early emergency programs, and he was in on the founding of Social Security. Frances Perkins was Roosevelt's labor secretary. "Molly" Dewson headed the Women's Division of the Democratic National Committee. Audrey Williams was the director of the National Youth Association. Katharina Lenroot and Martha Elliot were members of the Children's Bureau. Jane Hoey worked in the Social Security Administration, and Ellen Woodward worked in the FERA and WPA (Trattner, 1999). The profession had become part of the machinery of state.

For the most part, the American Association of Social Work and the National Conference of Social Work endorsed the goals and proposals of the New Deal. Some were critical of its programmatic timidity. Mary Van Kleeck, who had been director of the Department of Industrial Studies at the Russell Sage Foundation, was appointed to the Federal Advisory Council of the U.S. Employment Service within the National Recovery Administration. Van Kleeck left the position in 1933 when Roosevelt eliminated some of its provisions, and she became a critic of his policies (Brenden, 1993). In 1934, in a speech to the National Council of Social Work Education, she declared that without change in the political structure, poverty would not be prevented, nor would living standards improve. She argued in defense of a social-democratic solution.

Van Kleeck's speech resonated among the "Rank and File," a grassroots movement of social workers tied to labor. Its members met in discussion and consciousness-raising clubs, grappling with the distance between social workers and clients and the contradictions between capitalism and their daily experiences (Fisher, 1990). In 1935, the Rank and File had 15,000 members, two times more than the American Association of Social Workers (AASW) (Fisher, 1990). These social workers fought for a more generous, inclusive social insurance and a fully developed welfare state.

AASW followers believed that unionization violated their professional ethic. But the Rank and File movement supported and was active in the Association of Federation Workers (AFW), which in 1936 became affiliated with the CIO as the Social Service Employees Union (Reisch & Andrews, 2001). After 1936, with fascism looming in Europe, they joined mainstream social workers in supporting Roosevelt and his policies (Klehr, 1984).

While social workers with a socialist bent kept alive an awareness of the limitations of the welfare state as realized under the New Deal, their primary impact was to enlarge the focus of the profession, especially in training. Public welfare was included as an area of practice. The goals of clients, the renewal of group and community methods of intervention, and the integration of social environment in all practices came in for greater attention (Figueira-McDonough, 2001).

6

From the Aftermath of World War II to the Great Society

Holding Back the New Deal

Progress on the welfare front slowed considerably as the resources of the Roosevelt administration were funneled into the war effort against Germany and Japan. Rumblings about the socialist overtones of New Deal policies grew louder. After being elected three times, Roosevelt himself came under attack as a dictator indifferent to democratic traditions. In 1938, the House Committee on Un-American Activities was formed (known at that time as the Dies Committee), and Representative Martin Dies charged Frances Perkins and Harry Hopkins with fomenting class hatred (Caute, 1978).

During the war, radicalism was often taken as a sign of disloyalty. Suspicion of their patriotic credentials blocked pro-reform activists from office and many positions of authority. The jingoistic rhetoric and paranoid tactics used against socialists and radicals decades earlier, during the First World War, came back to haunt their successors during the Second.

Economic Success and Social Conservatism

The United States came out of the global conflict as a world power. Its own territory was unscathed. Its military superiority eased access to cheap raw materials, mostly from developing countries, and this helped boost American productivity, while the country's two potential competitors, Germany and Japan, lay in ruins.

Russia was the other new great power. The Yalta Conference, held toward the end of the war, had granted the Soviet Union a free hand in Eastern Europe. The USSR and the USA represented diametrically opposed material and ideological systems. The communist ethos of equality and economic planning was pitted against the market capitalism of liberal democracy. As Russia expanded and tightened its influence over Eastern Europe, the United States became alarmed at the prospects of a spillover into Western Europe. Launched in 1948, the Marshall Plan was its major strategic response. It provided economic assistance to Western European countries on the hunch that while poverty might cause communism, prosperity would strengthen adherence to liberal democratic ideals. The Marshall Plan was the lynchpin of the policy of containment.

So the Cold War began. Each country vied for allies while building up military establishments and nuclear arsenals that kept aggression in check through a system of "mutually assured destruction" (MAD). It was against this backdrop that the jingoism associated with war turned into anticommunist hysteria (Schrecker, 2002).

The economy of the United States entered boom times. Jobs were plentiful. Exports shot up, and domestic policies spurred growth in home construction and automobile manufacturing. Immediately after the war, the Truman administration signed legislation that provided easy home mortgages for family ownership. The *Autobahn* system he saw in Germany impressed General Dwight Eisenhower, and a coast-to-coast network of interstate highways, funded under federal auspices, became one of the legacies of his presidency.

These housing and transportation measures fueled suburbanization, and they were also a boon to the auto industry. The GI Bill underwrote higher education for returning veterans and helped upgrade the occupational structure. A large middle class, including more and more white collar employees, defined a new American lifestyle. Home and car ownership, job security, and consumerism were its hallmarks.

New Deal liberals and activists believed that the failures of laissez-faire capitalism indicated a need for ongoing reform. By 1940, most of them had made their peace with the economic system, clinging to state action as a way to compensate for the inevitable flaws of capitalism (Brinkley, 1995). The

Photo 6.1   Symbols of the New American Lifestyle

Source: From the private collection of Peter McDonough.

Photo 6.2   The Suburban Middle Class Dresses Up

Source: From the private collection of Peter McDonough.

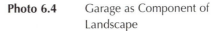

Photo 6.3   The New Affluence

Source: From the private collection of Peter McDonough.

Photo 6.4   Garage as Component of Landscape

Source: From the private collection of Peter McDonough.

government had a responsibility to protect the health, stability, and progress of industry. A favorable business climate would help the market sustain full employment. Wartime experience muted hostility to capitalism by dramatizing its productivity. Postwar consumerism legitimized Keynesian fiscal policies. The transition from a producer-oriented to a consumer economy looked remarkably smooth.

President Truman was concerned about deficits built up from expenditures for the war, and Congress was weary of added expenses tied to New Deal programs. Besides, with the economy generating plenty of jobs, welfare expansion lost one of its prime rationales. Unions worried that the inevitable drop in government spending after the war would lead to recession, as happened in 1919. At the prodding of the unions, a full-employment bill passed in 1946. However, apart from setting up a Council of Economic Advisors, the language of the legislation was vague and failed to specify action on the part of the government. The outbreak of the Korean War, a byproduct of the Cold War, also restricted reform (Bailey, 1950).

The Eisenhower presidency, from 1953 through 1960, witnessed some extension of social insurance and public assistance. Both became more family-friendly. Social insurance benefits were extended to the disabled, widows, dependent children, and survivors. The Aid to Dependent Children (ADC) program became Aid to Families with Dependent Children (AFDC), but a proposal for the establishment of a Department of Health, Education and Welfare was defeated.

The Dismissal of the Labor Movement

After the Wagner Act of 1936, union membership shot up from 3 to 10.5 million, and production was soon geared to military purposes. Labor leaders sought to devise more significant roles for the union movement.

An early proposal focused on creating industrial councils. Walter Reuther, the head of the United Auto Workers, formulated the most daring of these efforts at union democracy. His plan had three components. The first step was to convert comparatively idle automobile plants to airplane production. The second was to distribute different parts of the manufacturing and assembly process across various companies, a maneuver that would force them into a federated whole. Finally, with these steps in place, Reuther envisioned the creation of industrial councils composed of representatives of industry, labor, and government (Brinkley, 1995).

The attack on Pearl Harbor propelled the United States into war, and the imaginative promise of this novel proposal became a dead letter as the government assumed powers to direct both industries and unions. The administration and the unions came to a three-part accord, involving (1) a union promise to abstain from disruptive labor actions for the duration of the war, (2) a wage freeze for the duration of the war—with a one-time adjustment, called the "little steel" formula, to make up for the previous 16 months of inflation, and (3) a government guarantee of the institutional stability of the unions, stating that workers hired in the union plants would become union members. But as living costs increased, wildcat strikes and walkouts spread. In 1943 alone, such actions involved 3 million workers, and they turned public opinion against the unions (Brinkley, 1995).

While visionary leaders like Reuther and some union members tried, through the industrial council proposal and the promotion of interest in a labor party, to forge a more participatory mode of worker involvement in the economy, other leaders took a different tack. The perspective of Sidney Hillman, head of the Amalgamated Clothing Workers of America, was that labor had to present itself not as an adversary to capital and the middle class but as a partner sharing many interests with them (Brinkley, 1995). The Congress of Industrial Organizations (CIO) set up a political action committee so that labor could campaign effectively on behalf of Democrats sympathetic to workers. By cementing an alliance with the Democratic Party, and by abandoning the larger goals of industrial councils and the ideal of a labor party, Hillman crushed the chances of an independent workers movement.

The Birth of the Civil Rights Movement

The civil rights of African Americans in the South were a charade. Local and state governments had succeeded in silently overturning or abrogating post–Civil War legislation. Political equality was nonexistent. Most African Americans no longer lived in the countryside. They flocked to segregated neighborhoods in metropolitan areas, and their collective awareness of racial mistreatment rose exponentially. In the North, where millions of African Americans had migrated since 1950, discrimination was rampant in housing, work, and police control.

The humiliation of African American veterans made this divide all the more unbearable. Harry Truman had integrated the military, yet racial discrimination pervaded civilian life. Because of their race, men who had risked their lives for their country could not lodge where they chose, could not send their children to the schools they wanted; were barred from eating in "Whites only" restaurants; and had to sit in assigned places, toward "the back of the bus," in public transportation. In 1954, the Supreme Court's decision in *Brown v. Board of Education* declared segregated education unconstitutional, but its implementation required federal troops in parts of the South.

Many barriers stood in the way of schooling for African Americans, but there was a strong tradition of educated ministers within the black community. The ingredients of a movement were present: outrage, communication through television and word-of-mouth that spread news about injustice and its causes, and leadership positioned for change (Gamson, 1990). In 1955, in Montgomery, Alabama, civil rights associations inaugurated a bus boycott led by Martin Luther King, an African American minister. It was the first major step toward mobilizing a mass movement.

Critical Commentary

The New Deal gave the federal government a role, one that had long been missing, in welfare. Federal expenditures for public welfare reached 8 percent of national income. Before 1935, outlays for assistance were borne almost exclusively by localities and states. After 1935, the burden of local governments constituted only 20 percent of total disbursements. State-level social expenses were set at 39 percent, and the federal government's contribution at 41 percent.

Centralized agencies developed, especially to manage Social Security. In 1953, the Department of Health, Education and Welfare finally came into being. Even so, the percentage of national income spent on public welfare in the United States was still about two-thirds less than similar expenditures in European countries. Moreover, the birth of the welfare state in the United States lagged about 30 years behind Europe.

The New Deal was a breakthrough for a country that had resisted public welfare so tenaciously for so long. However, the conditions that overcame this resistance—the Great Depression, the protests of the 1930s, the fear of upheaval if government did nothing—failed to defeat an entrenched ideology. An ethos that protected the private sector strongly influenced the debate over social insurance in 1935. The two-tier result was social insurance for workers combined with public assistance for deserving non-workers. By 1937, opponents of the New Deal became more vocal, criticizing the socialistic bent of "brain trusters" and accusing Roosevelt of trying to pack the Supreme Court with his sympathizers.

To the deficits generated by World War II were added expenditures for the Korean War and the Cold War military buildup, and all this became red ink used to justify the near stagnation of welfare programs. The economic success of the postwar period took the edge away from unions and radical activists pushing for more extensive social rights. The national obsession with communism discouraged Progressives and put a damper on movements for change (Theoharis, 1971).

Union leadership at the highest levels was divided. The lack of a grand strategy diverted the movement from programs that would include the poor, not just union members. Visions of a European-style labor party evaporated. McCarthyite-like persecution stigmatized those who favored industrial councils and an independent workers' movement as unacceptably left wing. Mainstream Americans of the time were equivocal about unions. Legislation and numbers appeared to be on the side of workers, but support leaned toward the non-adversarial camp of labor. It was this camp that tilted the balance in favor of an alliance with the Democratic Party, thereby wiping out the possibility of a militant labor party. As a prudential style of bargaining over wages, benefits, and work rules won support, broader economic and political issues were dropped. With unemployment rates low, and with good chances of negotiating favorable contracts, the unions lost interest in fighting for universal welfare programs. In terms of both population coverage and benefit levels, welfare claims languished.

The fate of private welfare was much less dismal. As taxes rose, employers saw an opportunity to deflect increases through workers' retirement pensions and health benefits. Here, regulations and requirements were minimal, and tax deductions quite easy to obtain. The 1942 Revenue Integration Act allowed corporations to factor in Social Security benefits when setting up tax-favored pension plans, even when low-wage workers were excluded or received meager private benefits. Employers with private plans had a motivation to support Social Security, because increases in Social Security benefits correspondingly offset the costs of private welfare. Employers, pension sponsors, and life insurance interests worked strenuously if invisibly to influence congressional negotiations (Hacker, 2002). As a result, private welfare doubled by 1945. "Old-age insurance," one commentator observed, "represents acceptance of approaches to social welfare created by private businessmen" (Quadagno, 1987, p. 641).

The Clark Amendment of 1944, sponsored by Republicans and anti–New Deal Democrats, would have allowed employers who offered or intended to operate private plans to opt out of Social Security. Had it passed, the amendment would have killed Social Security.

The 1940s were a period of stagnation for Social Security and of expansion in private pensions. This stagnation pushed labor unions, and even political leaders, to press for private plans as temporary substitutes for public programs. By the end of the decade, coverage under private plans rose from 6 percent to 20 percent of the nonagricultural workforce (Hacker, 2002, p. 8).

The government's encouragement of collective bargaining gave organized labor a stake in seeking valuable social benefits from employers rather than from the government. Structured in this way, the game produced two outcomes: Labor was tied to a system of health and pension insurance, based on benefits linked to jobs, that eclipsed demands for public social insurance. Second, employers became more willing to push for public social insurance, with the intent of integrating it, to their advantage, in private pension plans.

In 1943, adherence to private welfare designs led to the defeat of a comprehensive program of social insurance—the Wagner-Murray-Dingell Bill—authored by the Social Security Board and promoted by Northern Democrats along with elements of organized labor. The net effect was to consolidate political support for a tax regime favorable to corporations. This turn of events put a stamp of approval on policies that legitimized private options at odds with publicly stated goals and that often marginally supported or altogether excluded the very workers for whom federal old-age insurance had been created.

Skepticism about private plans rose in the 1950s, however. Scandals brewing out of the misuse of pension funds by the Teamsters and some other unions brought on congressional investigations of labor officials and fund managers. The uproar alerted the public to the special tax treatment given to private pension schemes, and insistent calls for government regulation followed.

Social Work in the Postwar Period

Both world wars had broadly similar effects on the social work profession. Social workers were called on to meet the needs of servicemen and -women and their families. Psychological trauma and mental health problems generally became urgent priorities.

In the years following the Second World War, most social workers returned to psychotherapeutic interventions and away from public welfare. Later, with the apparently widespread affluence of the fifties and the breakup of immigrant ethnic communities, poor Americans became less visible. Social workers flocked to mental health hospitals and mental health agencies, targeting their services to the middle class, often for a fee. These institutions offered better pay than public welfare agencies (Cloward & Epstein, 1965).

Although psychotherapy was a major part of their training, humanistic psychology filtered steadily into schools of social work, and it eventually became a dominant force in casework. Carl Rodgers, Abraham Maslow, Fritz Perls, Otto Pollack, and others were the new gurus of clinical social work. Their recurrent theme was how to build and reconstruct the self through positive reinforcement (Specht & Courtney, 1994). Psychic well-being became the gold standard, replacing attention to the social environment in casework and reducing the focus of intervention to individual personality and practitioner–client relationships (Specht, 1991).

The demand for certain social work skills also expanded in public welfare. In most states, casework was needed for recipients receiving monetary benefits. This took in surveillance to ensure meritorious behavior. The prevalent idea was that clients had to be taught appropriate moral habits, and to cultivate psychological insight and self-reflection, in order to get off welfare.

Three factors—an ethos of individualism, the yearning of the profession for greater status, and the threat of McCarthyism—help explain the popularity of clinical social work.

From the earliest days of the republic, as we have seen, a deep commitment to individualism reinforced the conviction that free men and women bore responsibility for their problems. Remedial approaches stressing personal inadequacies fit this view perfectly. As a young profession reaching for status, social work welcomed an approach that targeted the middle class as well as the downtrodden. In the repressive fifties, this type of practice highlighted the technical proficiency rather than the political overtones of the profession.

*"Perhaps we should take a fresh look at the methods of
the much maligned Spanish Inquisition."*

Exhibit 6.1

Source: © 2005 Mick Stevens from cartoonbank.com. All rights reserved.

In pursuit of the grail of professional status, some social workers warmed up to the model of the liberal professions—notably, medicine—and sought to privatize the exercise of clinical practice. In 1951, Josephine Peek and Charlotte Plotkin, affiliated with Columbia University's School of Social Work, did a study of private social work in New York City. They found that most of the social workers in this field had a master's degree, frequently attended seminars and workshops on psychotherapy, and were members of the National Psychology Association for Psychoanalysis and the American Association of Psychiatric Social Work, but not of the National Association of Social Workers (NASW). Their clients came mostly from the middle class. Autonomy, together with pay and the rewards of status, were commonly cited as the prime motivations for working in private practice (Specht & Courtney, 1994).

Oddly, in spite of the low level of identification of private clinical social workers with the NASW, the organization established minimum standards for private practitioners. The national association thereby conferred legitimacy on this practice as social work.

Some social workers argued that a real difference existed between case-work and personality-focused practice. The goal of casework was tied to the agency's mission. This purpose covered the community of clients and took a social interactive perspective toward understanding the social relations in which clients were embedded (Dore, 1990). Social workers who had worked hard for the New Deal kept alive the view that the goal of the profession was to advocate for the poor and for a more equal society. Many of them suffered persecution for their activities.

The McCarthy era transformed the House Un-American Activities Committee into an inquisition. In the name of patriotism and anticommunism, McCarthyism adopted many of the same repressive tools used by the totalitarian system it professed to combat. Thousands lost their jobs. Millions curtailed their social activism, fearing to be dealt with as traitors. Calling attention to pressing needs in health, housing, and civil rights could be interpreted as a sign of disloyalty.

Social workers affiliated with the Rank and File movement were the first to be hit. About 150 college and university teachers appeared before the investigating committee, and more than half of them lost their jobs. A listing of social workers who were scrutinized and the reasons for their investigation indicates how severely the liberal and radical wings of social work were attacked (Reisch & Andrews, 2001):

In 1938, Bertha Reynolds was forced to resign from Smith College and was ostracized by the profession because of the socialist orientation of her lectures and writings.

In 1945, Charlotte Towel, author of *Common Human Needs,* in which she defended welfare services as citizens' rights and the obligation of a caring society, saw her book criticized and further publication forbidden.

In 1947, Jacob Fisher, editor of *Social Work Today,* fell under suspicion because of his links with the Social Service Employees Union.

In 1948, Jane Howey was fired from the Bureau of Public Assistance for protesting recent cuts.

In 1948, Inabel Lindsay, dean of the School of Social Work at Howard University, came under investigation because of his support of Henry Wallace, the presidential candidate of the Progressive Party.

In 1948, Marion Hathaway, professor of social work at the University of Pittsburgh, who had presented a paper entitled "Economic Bill of Rights," was accused by the media of socialist tendencies and threatened with dismissal.

In 1948, Eduard Lindeman, a member of the American Civil Liberties Union at Columbia University, and Benjamin Youngdahl, dean of Columbia's School of Social Work, were investigated. (pp. 87–134)

Social work retreated from its advocacy of social justice and focused most of its energies on building up the profession. Practitioners united under the National Association of Social Workers, striving to create a nonthreatening image of professionalism. The Association of Group Workers, which had encouraged compromise, self-government, democratic leadership, and resistance to illegitimate authority, became a victim of this move. It morphed into an organization for the advancement of group therapy.

Social action become apolitical, redefined in the late fifties as interagency coordination and the promotion of client–agency interaction. In short, "professionalism came to represent an intellectual status that denied the class division within society" and placed individualism at the center of its practice (Wenocur & Reisch, 1983, p. 692). The impact of McCarthyism on social work and on the development of social welfare was to be felt for years to come.

Lonely and courageous voices such as those of Whitney Young, then dean of the School of Social Work in Atlanta, tried to remind colleagues of their social justice mission. In a speech delivered at the National Conference of Social Work (NCSW), Young told his audience that social work had arisen out of an atmosphere of righteous indignation. Yet, he observed, some of those responding to the urge toward professionalism had forgotten their initial crusading impulse. He exhorted social workers to reclaim this lost heritage. At the commencement ceremonies of the Columbia University Graduate School of Social Work in 1956, Agnes Meyer encouraged the newly minted professionals to be the social conscience of society and take on the task of community reorganization (Trattner, 1999, p. 311).

The Promise of the Great Society

Most liberals remember the sixties as the golden age of American social history. But social radicals are more likely to view the decade as a missed opportunity for structural change.

Prelude to the Social Reforms of the Sixties

In 1960, by a very narrow margin, John Kennedy was elected president. Kennedy owed much of his victory to African American voters. He had not presented himself as a social reformer. Still, in his fight for the nomination in West Virginia, Kennedy showed concern for the conditions of miners, and for the poverty of the elderly and the unemployed, and he promised programs that would ease their problems. He also could not remain indifferent to the burgeoning civil rights movement in the South and to the voters who had elected him.

First publicized in a favorable review by Dwight McDonald in *The New Yorker*, the graphic and groundbreaking research of Michael Harrington about poverty in *The Other America* (1962) awakened the public to the magnitude and depth of a national problem. Harrington, an activist once attached to the Catholic Worker movement in New York, movingly described the forgotten places in America where families went to bed hungry and children lived in Third World conditions. Together with images showing African Americans besieged by attack dogs and cattle prods during civil rights confrontations, Harrington's exposé tarnished the reputation of the United States as the beacon of democracy and "justice for all." American credibility as leader of the free world was shaken.

It is hard to predict how Kennedy would have reacted to these long-term conditions had he lived and been elected to another term. His slowness in advancing civil rights legislation suggests caution about alienating Southern Democrats rather than concern with a flawed democracy.

Kennedy's most remarkable social legacy may be the Mental Retardation Facilities and Community Mental Health Centers Construction Act. While some of the motivation behind this legislation might have stemmed from Kennedy's experiences with his mentally ill older sister, research supporting deinstitutionalization of mental patients and the protection of their rights came from two different sources. World War II veterans who had been treated in mental hospitals testified to the inhuman conditions they suffered during hospitalization, and the discovery of effective drugs that could allow mental patients to return safely to their communities was also a decisive contributor. The Act was approved as an alternative that promised to lower the costs of treating the mentally ill. But budgetary cutbacks severely impeded its implementation (Goodwin, 1997).

Legislative Successes

Lyndon Johnson assumed the presidency after Kennedy's assassination in 1963. One year later, he was elected in a landslide, with a Democratic majority in Congress. Johnson's legislative successes on the social front matched Roosevelt's during the mid-thirties. Like Roosevelt, Johnson extended social programs into areas previously outside the purview of federal policy, such as schools and health. The 1964 Civil Rights Bill required desegregation of public facilities, and it prohibited discrimination in hiring practices of any organization receiving federal funds. The attorney general was empowered to file suit to desegregate schools. Federal authorities could directly administer elections when there was evidence of voting discrimination (Stern, 1992).

Johnson's most extraordinary successes were in the area of health care, where earlier legislation had been systematically defeated. Medicare and Medicaid were created as Titles XVIII and XIX of the Social Security Act. Medicare was to be administered under Social Insurance and was designed to serve retired workers. It had two components: Part A, mandatory and financed by payroll taxes on workers and employers, covered hospital services. Part B covered doctors' services. It was voluntary and financed by monthly premiums from elderly persons and general revenues. Medicaid was designed for welfare recipients and those near poverty—the medically indigent. It was funded by a federal grant and administered by the states.

In the past, the American Medical Association (AMA) had been the major opponent of public health insurance. The AMA's acceptance of Johnson's Great Society legislation was contingent on a provision that allowed doctors to charge rates under Medicare that were higher than the maximum fees authorities would reimburse. The elderly would have to make up the difference by drawing on their own funds for services in Part B of the program. The direct result of this agreement was a large increase in the clientele for physicians among seniors, without curtailment of medical fees.

The same compensatory rationale did not hold for Medicaid, and only a very low percentage of physicians chose to work with this program. The economics of the system required doctors to see many clients for short examinations, in what came to be known as "Medicaid mills."

The new health policy perpetuated the two-tier system present from the creation of public welfare in the United States. There was one system for insured workers (Medicare) and another for the poor (Medicaid). Nonetheless, access to health care by the elderly and the poor improved considerably (Davis & Shoen, 1978).

Having been majority leader in the Senate, President Johnson had extensive experience in dealing with Congress, and this served him well in winning approval for his health care measures and other social legislation. He was an able compromiser, seasoned in the ways of marshalling bipartisan support and accustomed to tweaking the legal language of bills. Johnson amplified his stock of goodwill by presenting many of his initiatives to Congress as if they were based on blueprints handed down by Kennedy. It also helped that the Supreme Court, headed by Chief Justice Earl Warren, had already demonstrated its commitment to civil rights and social fairness and was in tune with Johnson's social agenda.

The Older Americans Act (OAA) of 1965 had a positive impact on services for the elderly. The OAA authorized the development of a national network of Area Agencies on Aging (AAA) to coordinate such services as nutrition programs for the housebound. The Elementary and Secondary Education Act, establishing federal help to public schools with high numbers of low-income students, improved education among African American children. The Food Stamp Act allowing welfare recipients to purchase stamps at 40 percent of the full cost of food, was one of the most successful programs in combating hunger. Another important step was the increase in matching federal funds to states for the AFDC program. This raised benefits in the poorer states. Since the increase was tied to the level of state poverty, and the southern states had the lowest income level, conservative Southern Democrats supported the measure.

The War on Poverty

The illusion of an affluent society triumphant in the fifties was dethroned by research that documented great inequality. The richest 20 percent controlled 45 percent of the nation's wealth, while the poorest 20 percent had barely 5 percent. What's more, absolute levels of poverty rivaled those found in the poorer developing countries. The careful empirical work of economists like James Morgan at the University of Michigan in *Income and Welfare in the United States* (Morgan, David, Cohen, & Brazer, 1962) combined with the impact of Michael Harrington's powerful accounts of poverty to startle Americans out of their complacency.

Harrington presented his findings through a dramatic narrative. *The Other America* became a surprise best seller. In part this was due to Harrington's close-up depiction of families of all races, trapped in poverty by a cycle of neglect and injustice. Among the dispossessed were thousands of displaced farmers, unemployed miners and laborers, older citizens awaiting death in shabby institutions, and marginally employed service workers. Among children in the poorest families, malnutrition was rampant. Bringing these excluded sectors into American society, Harrington concluded, would require the effort of an extremely powerful ally—the federal government.

In 1963, before the War on Poverty got underway, Mollie Orshansky of the Department of Agriculture devised a standard for measuring absolute poverty. Orshansky based her study on previous research showing that low-income families spent one-third of their income on food and the remainder on all other basic needs—for example, housing. The cost of a survival diet multiplied by three constituted a survival income (Orshansky, 1965). From then on, statistics on poverty in the United States reflect the number of people whose income does not reach the standard of survival.

One way to understand the War on Poverty is as a national-level strategy to bypass the sectional divisions of the Democratic Party and to avoid the mistakes of past social policy experiments. A look at how the goals of urban renewal had traditionally been displaced is instructive. Urban renewal was supposed to improve poor neighborhoods and housing in inner cities filled with low-income residents. This goal got sidetracked at the hands of a coalition of businesses and city governments who promoted their own interests for profits and power (Halpern, R., 1995). Funds went into vast business centers and government buildings. The program veered away from its original goals because resources were funneled toward state and city officials. The War on Poverty responded to this diagnosis by allocating grants directly to poor communities (Piven, 1974).

By its very name, the War on Poverty reflected a nineteenth-century vision that poverty was an evil that could be eradicated. The War on Poverty included a variety of programs—the Job Corps for unemployed youth, Legal Aid, and Community Action Agencies (CAAs). The Office of Economic Opportunity (OEO) was created to coordinate the various programs, and Sargent Shriver, a brother-in-law of John Kennedy and first director of the Peace Corps, took on its leadership. From the onset, the OEO was a bureaucratic nightmare. Personnel had to be recruited quickly for an organization that still had to be put together. There were few resources for mandated functions such as training to process grants, the evaluation of proposals, grant selection, and financing.

The task of the CAAs was to plan and coordinate local programs for the poor, including such popular initiatives as Head Start. Under the principle of "maximum feasible participation," the CAA boards were required to be representative of the populations they served. In many cases, they were transformed into advocacy bodies. Before he became a senator from New York, Daniel Patrick Moynihan (1969) labeled the situation "maximum feasible misunderstanding." Others, however, have highlighted the merits of community grassroots involvement. The experience informed, empowered, and politicized residents of poor neighborhoods, and the fuller participation of African Americans in mainstream politics can be traced to the experiential learning that took place in the sixties (Fisher, R., 1984; Naples, 1991, 1996, 1998; Wellstone, 1978).

Constraints and Defeat

In earlier times, children and mothers in need had frequently been kept out of welfare programs because of race or marital status. Now, fairer criteria drove a huge increase in welfare rolls, especially for programs like the AFDC. The costs of these programs doubled from 3 to 6 billion dollars. For conservatives, this raised the specter of lazy mothers, unwilling to work, addicted to a life of dependence.

Partly in response to these alarms, Johnson proposed the Work Incentive Program. (The acronym was quickly changed from WIP to WIN—the Work Incentive Network). The program was supposed to train and encourage welfare recipients to search for work. Lawmakers gladly supported it. Exemptions were plentiful: age of the child, access to child care, family well-being, distance from training centers, and so on. Very few women actually went through the program. Later, an incentive program was adopted that proved more successful: it allowed working welfare mothers to keep their welfare checks up to a certain salary level.

During Johnson's presidency, the American intervention in Vietnam grew rapidly, without the explicit approval of Congress, and so did its costs, both human and financial. In 1964, Johnson had drastically cut taxes, and fiscal conservatives worried about possible budget deficits. Even though Congress had not officially sanctioned the war, and even though the military consumed about 70 percent of discretionary funds, while social programs took about 28 percent, it was social programs—especially the War on Poverty—that took the budgetary hit.

Anti-war demonstrations became more frequent and more rancorous. Riots across a string of cities put the effectiveness of Johnson's welfare programs in doubt. Once again, the War on Poverty came in for criticism, and the already underfunded program gave way to Model Cities. This effort, created by the Demonstration Cities and Metropolitan Development Act, was more rigorously structured, without the grassroots participation that characterized the War on Poverty (Jansson, 2001).

Critical Commentary

Federal policies expanded into new social areas, but only a few of them—Part A of Medicare, food stamps, and the War on Poverty—were centrally administered. All the other programs were implemented at the state level with matching federal funds. Part B of Medicare was a mixed bag, run in the private health market and supplemented by general revenues. The Department of Agriculture administered the Food Stamps program. The OEO, with insufficient funds, managed the War on Poverty. But for the creation of the Department of Health, Education and Welfare in the 1950s, growth in the centralization and bureaucratization of public welfare was modest.

Private welfare did not shrink as public programs grew. In part this was because some of their activities incorporated public insurance programs. Lyndon Johnson tried to revise the tax deductions and guidelines that integrated work-related benefits with Social Security. The idea—to reverse the upward distribution of private welfare—met with little success.

Medicare and Medicaid, the cornerstones of health policy, protected the poor and the elderly but left the adult population and their children at the mercy of the market. As private insurers spread into the workplace, health care became a private benefit. Employer contributions to health plans were treated as non-taxable (Hacker, 2002). Health benefits for workers were thus encouraged through blanket tax exemptions. Since these plans were voluntary on the part of employers, people employed in jobs without a health plan either went to public clinics or bought health insurance on their own.

Daniel Patrick Moynihan (1969) argued that the Johnson administration had squandered an immense opportunity offered by the civil rights movement—namely, the chance to pass a full-employment and income maintenance program that would permanently solve the problem of American poverty. A venture on this scale would have approached the social-democratic welfare states of Northern Europe and would have called for extensive government intervention in labor and income markets.

To what extent would American political culture have supported or rejected such ambitious structural reforms? In light of the weakness of the progressive wing of the Democratic Party and the cooptation of labor by private welfare, reaching that target would seem unlikely. In the years following World War II, the labor movement had been transformed from a social-democratic insurgency into a more narrowly focused interest group, and the Democratic Party was in transition, still burdened by a strongly reactionary southern wing.

A structural war on poverty had to target the systemic sources of poverty. It would have entailed extending state control over capitalist institutions and markets. There was not much political support for this, either from labor or from progressive Democratic constituencies. The War on Poverty was a misnomer. It did not tackle the root causes of poverty. It was underbudgeted, undermanaged, and did not support or channel the rising demands from community action activists (CAAs).

The War on Poverty came to be identified as a program for African Americans, since many living in the poorest urban communities were black. The anger that exploded in urban riots looked to conservatives like proof of the failure of all welfare programs, especially those benefiting African Americans. This judgment compounded prejudice directed against African Americans and the poor in general. Once again, blacks and the poor were "outsiders" and "others." They did not belong, and they were assumed to be deviant.

The War on Poverty followed a well-worn historical path. It offered cures for poverty disconnected from its structural and economic causes—from lack of work, decent pay, and opportunity. Many northerners supported the civil rights movement, reacting with revulsion to images of peaceful marchers under police attack, going over in dismay reports of the harassment and outright murder of young white supporters gone South to help in the struggle. But their sympathy weakened when Martin Luther King traveled to Chicago and denounced the treatment of African Americans in northern cities. With the riots of 1968, the situation deteriorated still further. Race became more divisive than class (McNight, 1998).

This dynamic generated a pair of consequences. First, the lack of material progress among African Americans and the unfulfilled promise of the War on Poverty gave rise to more militant groups such as Black Power, the Black Panthers, and the Black Muslims. They shared some characteristics: a mistrust of whites, cultural pride, engagement in negotiations from a position of power, and a view of the ghetto as a colony. Second, many lower–middle class and working class people, attached to Christian moral precepts, resented the youth movement and the women's movement, not to mention government programs helping African Americans. This resentment blossomed in anti-poverty and anti–affirmative action legislation that defined many of the goals of Johnson's Great Society as anti-American and reverse discrimination.

The radical youth movement harbored young people, mostly from middle class and upper–middle class backgrounds, who rejected materialism, consumerism, the nuclear family, and other shrines to the American Way. They claimed to be rejecting their parents' values—married life, the pursuit of economic security, monogamy, and patriarchy. They vowed to stand up against the demands of production, and against bureaucracy, rationality, and hierarchy as well. They rallied against hypocrisy, racism, poverty, technocracy, and imperialism. Their search for authenticity—the thirst to be true to oneself—was thought to be an important step along an evolutionary process (Isserman & Kazin, 1989). The counterculture prompted many young people to get involved in social causes, such as the civil rights movement, the Peace Corps, and the campaign against the war in Vietnam. But self-realization was the prime motivation, some analysts contend, rather than concern with social change (Swidler, 1986).

In an interesting analysis, Elaine Tyler May (1989) suggests that the new generation's aspirations were in fact a modified version of the aspirations of their suburban parents. Secure in their employment, either unionized or white collar, these parents had succumbed to the seductions of consumerism. They had submitted to bureaucratic hierarchies in the workplace. Their homes, housing nuclear families, became the core of their lives, their vehicles of self-realization. Shopping, recreation, and social activities centered on the family. It was in these activities that adults could escape the tedium and oppression of work.

According to May, young people raised in these settings were searching for individual freedom in their own way, with the same purpose of self-realization as their parents. Participants in the youth movement were trying out different expressions of individualism, not countering its centrality or seriously flirting with building up communal attachments or revamping social structures. They played with many alternatives, but anti-individualism was not one of them.

All sorts of movements flourished: the feminist movement, the gay rights movement, the Mexican agricultural laborer movement, the welfare movement. For these last two, the Legal Aid program sponsored by the War on Poverty was crucial. The program helped advocates to challenge denials of eligibility for or dismissals from the AFDC, and it boosted welfare rolls. By protecting the civil and the working rights of strikers, the program was also of great value in Cesar Chavez's farm workers movement. Legal Aid paved the way for extending the full protection of the law to the poor.

Social Work in the Sixties

While inequality was high at the onset of the sixties, the economic growth of the previous decade had enlarged a middle class intent on further mobility. Prosperity fostered a belief that those unable to improve their condition in the preceding decade were either functionally incapable or deviant. Revelations of the extent of poverty and the treatment of blacks in the South shook these certainties, however. Many otherwise complacent citizens acquiesced in the spate of welfare reforms.

The 1962 amendment to the Social Security Act gave federal funds to the states to provide intensive social casework services for AFDC recipients. This was envisioned as a way to reduce their dependence and to cut back on welfare rolls that had doubled during the fifties. The amendment drove up demand for social workers, and non–social workers were called in to fill positions for which social workers were not available.

Other programs were established by the Economic Opportunity Act in 1964 and by the WIN program in 1967. These measures enabled the states to provide a more comprehensive array of social services: casework, day care centers, job training, and community organization. The programs encouraged the use of grassroots personnel. In practice, they drove up the demand for social workers even further (Trattner, 1999).

The NASW represented only social workers with master's degrees. The association focused on how to fill gaps in the employment opportunities opened by these programs, without decreasing the professional status of its members. A resolution of the first challenge was the integration of the bachelor's degree in social work into the organization and the accreditation of social work bachelor programs by the CSWE.

However, the rehabilitation from dependence on welfare that casework intervention was supposed to achieve did not materialize. By the end of the decade, federal grants to the states grew from 19 million dollars to 740 million (Specht & Courtney, 1994). Although the welfare rolls grew mainly because of population movements, the increase in unemployment, and the displacement of agricultural labor, the ballooning of expenditures discredited belief in the efficacy of casework (Trattner, 1999). Nonetheless, the income maintenance programs of the welfare system were separated from personal social services, and the states were allowed to contract services out to private providers.

By the late sixties, the profile of social workers in the public agencies had altered dramatically. Social workers with bachelor's degrees took positions as case managers. Some with master's credentials took administrative positions, while others went back to private organizations as caseworkers or to private clinical practice serving the new middle class.

This was only part of the new professional landscape. In a time of turbulence, rights movements, and new programs, social work radicalism was bound to reemerge. Many social workers took to heart participatory democracy and the redistributive ideal of opportunities at the core of the War on Poverty. After the success of the civil rights movement and the ignition of the youth movement, opportunities for change seemed at hand. Young social workers and students embraced social justice movements and programs. The most attractive to social workers were the Community Action Programs and the National Welfare Rights movement. Both supported participation of the poor in planning and fighting for their goals.

An earlier program inspired and led by social workers prepared the way for these experiments. Mobilization for Youth, a program funded by the Ford Foundation, applied Cloward and Ohlin's theory (1960) that delinquency was not the result of individual or family dysfunction but rather of blocked opportunities. Cloward and other social workers from the School of Social Work at Columbia University were involved in implementing the program (Brager, 1999). Some members of the team followed the approach of Saul Alinsky (1946), a sociologist/community organizer. Alinsky argued that mass confrontation and disruption were the only tools available to the poor to assert their claims in an unequal society. Since poverty is a form of oppression, gaining access to legitimate goals justified the use of such means.

Social workers involved in Community Action Programs (CAPs) were committed to grassroots organization, sharing and enhancing the power of the community in planning for services, demanding rights, and advocating for themselves. Similarly, Legal Aid, another program under the umbrella of the War on Poverty, asserted the entitlement of poor mothers and their children to public assistance. It did so by challenging AFDC decisions in court cases regarding non-eligibility and withdrawal of benefits.

The positive results from such encounters gave welfare clients confidence to form the National Welfare Rights Organization (NWRO) in 1966. Three years later, the organization had 22,000 active members and 523 local groups. One of their purposes was to claim the "right to live" within the Equal Protection Clause of the Fourteenth Amendment. The argument challenged the difference between passive and active rights. The NWRO pressed to overcome the charity ideology that informed public assistance, and it backed moves for a guaranteed income (Goodin, 1985; Trattner, 1999).

Many social workers provided technical assistance to the movement—on bureaucratic rules, for example, advocacy, and political coalitions. They created a sister "Social Welfare Workers Movement" (SWWM). This movement focused on the decentralization and deprofessionalization of services, exposing social inequities and the dehumanizing procedures of the welfare system, the promotion of political participation of the poor, and coalition formation and grassroots organization. The relationship between the two organizations was tense, though SWWM tried to be supportive. The NWRO's battle with the welfare establishment targeted social workers, who were viewed as its enforcers (Reisch & Andrews, 2001).

The NWRO espoused confrontational and disruptive tactics, emulating the more aggressive black movements. Its membership became mostly black and unrepresentative of the welfare population as a whole. The experience was another example of the rising eminence of race over class. The NWRO's identification with African Americans, and its almost exclusive reliance on confrontation, made this pioneer organization the target of conservative wrath. By the end of the decade, its power had declined. The SWWM did not last any longer, but it revived leftist theories about social change, participatory democracy, grassroots control of community agencies, and redistributive economic policies. Young people who entered the profession during the sixties were comparatively open to these views and resisted the professional tryst with individual intervention (Wenocur, 1975).

In contrast to their ascendancy during the Progressive and New Deal eras, few social workers rose to positions of influence in the government or in the movements and programs of the sixties. But the spirit of the decade had some impact on the organized profession. For example, in 1961, the NASW endorsed universal disarmament, and "Social Workers for Peace and Social Justice" was created under its auspices. In 1968, the NASW sponsored a National Social Action Workshop, "The Urban Crisis: A Challenge to the Profession/Strategies for Action." In 1962, the CSWE recognized community organization as a legitimate specialization for social work, and adopted an accreditation standard banning discrimination for race, ethnicity, and religion.

Though radical strategies were still frowned on, an article by Jack Rothman, a professor of social work at the University of Michigan, on "Three Models of Community Organization" (1968), included social action as one of the models and listed mass organization, confrontation, and disruption as its strategies. Still, even some social workers who supported community approaches repudiated radical strategies. From their point of view, these methods were more like feel-good manifestations of temperament—in effect, acting out—than thoughtful, goal-oriented strategies. The supposition was that serious social change could only occur by way of a long march through existing institutions (Specht, 1968). Other social workers dismissed the attention paid to macro-systems, in contrast to the interpersonal problems that most of them dealt with on a day-to-day basis.

The timidity of the profession in facing the issues of the time and getting involved in advocacy for justice issues, such as guaranteed income, has been attributed to its investment in an over-professionalized career model and to fears of radicalism still alive from the McCarthy period. At first glance, with the Warren Court strongly defending civil rights—including radical beliefs— the explanation seems weak. Still, it is true that the FBI under J. Edgar Hoover kept files on thousands of activists, including Martin Luther King (McNight, 1998).

Courses on social change, community action, and advocacy were made available to social work students, and the number of students specializing in community organization reached its peak—around 10 percent of all students—at this time (Reisch & Wenocur, 1986). Doctoral education also grew in this and the following decade, along with a diversity of theoretical and research approaches, enriching the uniformity of curricula in the professional schools.

Many minority students entered the field. Social work authors repudiated the popular culture of poverty theory, which claimed that the poor were entrapped in poverty by their own culture (Banfield, 1970; Glazer, 1971; Moynihan, 1965). They stressed a "strengths" approach to poverty. The orientation goes back to Jane Addams's effort to validate and uphold the culture of immigrants, seeing hidden resources in their communities.

7 The Weakening of the Welfare State Gains Speed

Tax cuts loaded on the side of the rich ignore the evidence of history that such cuts do not provide the type of investment society needs most and do not trickle surely down to embrace the general welfare.

—Lane Kirkland, President of the AFL/CIO,
testifying before the House Budget Committee,
May 4, 1981 (Hearings on Taxation, 1981)

In 1968, as Lyndon Johnson was deciding not to seek a second term, three candidates were in the running for the Democratic nomination: Hubert Humphrey, Johnson's vice president; Robert Kennedy, who had been Attorney General during his brother's administration; and Eugene McCarthy, the Democratic senator from Wisconsin. After mounting a spectacular challenge in the early primaries that drove Johnson to call off his candidacy and that spurred Kennedy to enter the race, McCarthy saw his campaign dwindle to that of a gadfly, a critical keeper of the antiwar flame.

Both Humphrey and Kennedy had progressive agendas and credentials. But Humphrey could never disown the legacy of the war he inherited from Johnson. Discontent spilled over dramatically, covering television screens across the nation, in the clash of antiwar demonstrators with the Chicago police during the Democratic national convention. When Robert Kennedy was shot down in the Ambassador Hotel in Los Angeles just after winning the California Democratic primary, Humphrey's road to the Democratic nomination was clear.

The Republican nominee was Richard Nixon, who appealed to "the silent majority." This broad swath of the electorate was made up largely of middle and working class whites. Viewing many Great Society programs as coddling African Americans, they were irritated by big government, the erosion of American values, and the disorder they saw around them. Nixon's platform of conservative fiscal policies, small government, law and order, and morality spoke loudly and clearly to their concerns (Rieder, 1989).

The Seventies: Expansion and Stagnation

Nixon was elected in 1968 by a narrow margin. Though critical of the programs of the Great Society, he was keenly aware that his mandate was shaky and that he had to work with a Democratic majority in Congress. To consolidate his position and boost support for Republicans, Nixon refrained from moving against the social policies of the previous administration. He struck out on a different course, aiming to surpass the Democrats' domestic accomplishments with greater efficiency and less mess. Nixon recruited moderate Republicans along with one key Democrat, Daniel Patrick Moynihan, who had been a central player in the Great Society. Moynihan became director of Nixon's Urban Affairs Council.

The Failure of the Family Assistance Plan (FAP)

The President's Commission on Income and Maintenance, which included Moynihan, proposed a complex program to take the place of public assistance. The Family Assistance Plan (FAP) was probably the most daring reform in the history of American public assistance. For starters, it included a guaranteed income, and covered the working poor as well as welfare recipients. Contrary to many state regulations, complete families could apply for welfare to avoid the unintended breakdown of the domestic unit resulting from AFDC requirements. The proposal also included strong work incentives. Welfare benefits would not be withdrawn until wages reached a given level and even then, only partially, until a "decent income"—above poverty level—was reached (Trattner, 1999, pp. 339–340).

President Nixon endorsed the Family Assistance Plan and the House passed it, but both conservatives and progressives in the Senate blocked it. Conservatives balked at the huge costs that it entailed, and progressives disapproved of the work requirements and the low benefits. In a public hearing, the National Welfare Rights Association (NWRO) vociferously opposed the plan.

The greatest obstacle, in the view of organized groups representing the poor and for the Senate as well, was the very complexity of the Family Assistance Plan. It required calculations of appropriate incentives, and it sought to harmonize an array of programs such as Food Stamps and Medicaid administered by various departments—Agriculture; Labor; and Health, Education and Welfare (HEW)—with different criteria. The labyrinthine nature of the organizational mechanisms and the coordination problems they implied contributed to the failure of the proposal.

AFDC remained the traditional public assistance program, with all that entailed for differential access and benefits across the states. Faced with a double-digit increase in AFDC rolls, in 1971 Congress passed the Talmadge Amendment to the WIN program. Several components of the original program—training, job search counseling, and family support—disappeared. The sole intent of the amendment was to force the poor to work. Only single parents with preschool children were exempt from the work requirement. AFDC mothers now became firmly entrenched among the undeserving poor; they were to be made to work for their benefits.

SSI, Food Stamps, and COLA

The creation of the Supplemental Security Income (SSI) program signified a rapprochement between public assistance and Social Security. Previous public assistance programs that had been administered by the states—Assistance to the Blind (AB), Old-Age Assistance (OAA), and Assistance to the Totally Disabled (APTD)—were federalized under SSI and centrally managed by the Social Security Administration. Although funded by general revenues, payments went directly to beneficiaries through social insurance checks, without the stigma attached to public assistance handouts. The Food Stamps program was also federalized, reducing differential benefits across the states and strengthening federal control over the system.

In spite of periodic increases in Social Security, inflation had left retired workers with very scanty benefits. With the support of Congress, Nixon engineered a 20 percent upgrade in benefits and, most importantly, an automatic cost-of-living adjustment (COLA). These measures, taken together, made for the greatest increase and reform in Social Security since its inception. The reforms won the political support of a new and powerful interest group—the American Association of Retired Persons (AARP).

Work Protection

In 1973, the Comprehensive Employment and Training Act (CETA) subsidized hundreds of thousands of jobs, in both public and private nonprofit organizations, for the unemployed. Begun in the same year, the Earned Income Tax Credit (EITC) provided families with dependent children who earned $4,000 a year or less a refundable credit.

These policies represented a clear departure from previous programs. They were not concerned with psychological and community rehabilitation. They were patterned instead on an economic definition of poverty, and their remedial focus was on work effort. A similar rationale stood behind the 1970 Occupational Safety and Health Act (OSHA) that increased federal oversight over the work environment.

Special Populations

The 1973 Rehabilitation Act accorded protection against discrimination to physically disabled persons. In 1974, the first child abuse prevention measure was enacted, the Child Abuse Prevention and Treatment Act (CAPTA). In the same year, the Juvenile Justice and Delinquency Prevention Act regulated differential treatment between status offenders (those whose behavior is considered deviant only because they are minors, e.g., running away, alcohol drinking, truancy) and delinquents (those who have broken the law), and set up legal procedures for both groups. Well received by women, the 1970 Planned Parenthood Services Act was criticized by some as a ploy designed to reduce the size of poor, single-parent families (Buchanan, 1973).

The Social Service Amendments (Title XX) to the Social Security Act allocated $2.5 billion annually to the states. The funds could be used with considerable latitude. They might be dispersed to public assistance beneficiaries or, on a fee-for-service basis, to anyone else. This was the first time that the federal government funded social services for the non-poor (Jansson, 2001).

The Local Fiscal Assistance Act

In an attempt to counter the trend toward the centralization of social policy, the Local Fiscal Assistance Act of 1972 instituted general revenue sharing. It was introduced as an effort to reverse the flow of power and resources from states and communities to Washington. The idea was to direct power and resources back to people across America. General revenue sharing returned moneys to the states without strings attached. The federal government used special revenue sharing to consolidate 130 conditional grants-in-aid to the states into six areas: urban community development, rural community development, education, law enforcement, transportation, and manpower training.

State and community officials reacted enthusiastically to the Act. It helped fill their coffers while at the same time cutting back on guidelines for programmatic implementation. It was a simple matter to divert funds to routine expenditures for road repair, fire protection, and parks and recreation. As little as 2.7 percent was devoted to social programs, including health care (Berkowitz, 1991).

Nixon's Successors: Ford and Carter

If these reforms were geared to gain popular support, Nixon's landslide victory in 1972 proved the strategy right. With his stock of political capital built up from the election and the end of the Vietnam War, Nixon seemed poised to return to his conservative roots. His veto of child development legislation was a precursor to this switch. Even though the number of working mothers compensating for male wage stagnation was on the rise, Nixon opposed the legislation on the grounds that it was anti-family. Nothing, he argued, could substitute for a mother's care. Public child care in the United States would be tantamount to the socialized child care offered in China. It was wildly un-American.

The Watergate scandal, breaking in 1973, eventually forced Nixon's resignation and put off further moves toward conservative social policy. An overall assessment of Nixon's domestic achievements shows how remarkable this period was.

Social spending was twice as high as it was during the Kennedy-Johnson years. In 1986 dollars, the comparison is between $27 billion under the Democrats and $54 billion under Nixon (Stockman, 1986, p. 140). The most striking accomplishment was the reduction of poverty among the elderly, a drop directly attributable to Nixon's reform of social insurance. By the end of the seventies, poverty among Americans 65 and older declined from around 30 to 15 percent. If in-kind benefits such as Food Stamps and Medicaid are added, the poverty level goes down to 5 percent. In 1975, the percentage of the general population living below the official poverty line was at its lowest level ever: 11.7 percent (Plotnick & Skidmore, 1975).

Social policy came to a standstill in Nixon's second term. Gerald Ford, who became president after Nixon's resignation in 1974, systematically vetoed all social legislation. But the string of vetoes cannot be attributed just to his social conservatism. Ford's priority was to overcome stagflation, a combination of high unemployment and inflation. During his term, unemployment was the highest—9 percent—it had been since 1941, and the GNP had fallen as sharply as it had in 1929 (Trattner, 1999, pp. 351–355).

Running for the presidency as an outsider, Jimmy Carter, the governor of Georgia, promised to meet the problem of stagflation head-on. Several circumstances contributed to the failure of his administration. The oil embargo of 1973, an Arab reprisal for American assistance to Israel, had already led to double-digit inflation. The ongoing loss of manufacturing jobs in the face of new technologies and industrial flight toward cheaper labor markets aggravated unemployment. Carter's lack of familiarity with the ways of Washington and his ineptitude in dealing with Congress outweighed any outsider edge. Many of his domestic initiatives went nowhere.

The predicament of the United States on the international scene impinged on Carter's domestic options. His administration's response was to cut money for social programs and increase the military budget. Welfare reform proposals regularly failed in Congress. Carter missed an opportunity to support the Humphrey-Hawkins Full Employment and Balanced Growth Act. After tortuous negotiations, the bill passed with its contents so deformed as to render it meaningless. Carter's presidency ended with the humiliating failure to rescue Americans who had been taken hostage in Iran (Rosenbaum & Ugrinsky, 1994).

Critical Commentary

Why did a conservative president like Richard Nixon promote so many innovative social policies? A common explanation is that the advances made during Nixon's first term were a political response to his narrow electoral margin. Not only had Nixon lost to John Kennedy by a hair's breadth in 1960, but he was later defeated in a run for the governorship of California. He was nothing if not sensitive to close calls and political upsets. This learning experience helps explain Nixon's desire to gain the hearts and minds of the working class and to demonstrate that he could outdo the Democrats at their own game of social improvement.

A second interpretation is that since he had to work with a Democratic Congress, Nixon's ambition was to show that Republicans could do as well as or better in social policy than their peers across the aisle. Still another perspective situates his policy decisions as a reflection of beliefs about federal control and managerial rationality. The ultimate goal behind the delivery of services was to enhance the economic capabilities of workers and the deserving poor (Buchanan, 1973).

The various diagnoses are not mutually exclusive. Centralization had a powerful logic behind it, given the dilapidated and uneven architecture of welfare across the American states. Standardization was especially pertinent to SSI and Food Stamps, programs toward the lower tier of Social Security— that is, public assistance.

On the other hand, AFDC programs remained untouched by administrative efforts to reconfigure access on more equal terms, and their curious insulation from reform raises questions about how the beneficiaries of AFDC program were viewed. The Talmadge amendment to the WIN program reinforced the impression that impoverished, single caretakers of children were profligate and irresponsible, not among the deserving poor. The image of dependence/addiction attached to these recipients in the fifties had taken hold. They were welfare junkies who needed to be compelled to earn their benefits. The historical link going back to workhouse times was embedded in the presidential veto of child care, and it remained a powerful force.

Programs inherited from the sixties that challenged the barriers faced by the poor in a highly competitive and unequal society were returned to the states, with little or no federal oversight. This might have been politically astute, but the move also reflected the low value attributed to the programs. The provisions of the Social Services Amendment of the Social Security Act were similarly ambiguous. They could be taken as an attempt to eradicate the stigma of these services or as a sign of the government's willingness to increase welfare to the middle class, or both.

A common thread running through the social legislation of this period was that it did not concern itself with psychological or community rehabilitation. Rather, poverty was defined in economic terms. The poverty rate reached its lowest level in the United States in the mid-seventies, even if the quickest decrease had taken place in the sixties. The COLA and the rise in retirement benefits that went with it had a dramatically beneficial effect in this regard, and the success of such policies refuted the myth that "throwing money at the poor does not solve the problem."

Up to the early 1970s, the dependence of the Social Security system on private welfare stayed as strong as ever, especially in the area of health. By the mid-seventies, however, the growth of private pension plans had slowed significantly. The rise of public benefits, the stagnation of real wages, the decline of organized labor, and the shift from manufacturing to service jobs all contributed to the change. In the 1980s, the proportion of Americans covered by "defined contributive plans" went from 11.5 percent to 36.5 percent while the number of traditional-benefit pensions grew slowly from 33 to 40 million (Poterba, 1997, p. 186). With defined contributive plans, benefits simply reflect accumulated contributions plus interest. These financial mechanisms grew more rapidly than traditional benefit pensions, under which workers received fixed retirement allowances based on past earnings and Social Security benefits.

Health care costs began skyrocketing in the 1970s, and the government had to swallow a large part of medical inflation. As the economy deteriorated, employers and insurers tried to control costs on their own. The National Planning and Resources Development Act of 1974 instituted a new regulatory program designed to encourage more efficient use of health resources. These moves brought about a rift with the medical profession's interest in maintaining income and autonomy.

Nixon had been pushing the idea of health maintenance organizations (HMOs). The HMOs were supported by corporations and insurers but resisted by physicians. A bill to aid their development passed Congress in 1973. The HMOs were prepaid group plans that integrated financing and medical care. They employed panels of doctors, either on salary or on a fixed, per-patient fee basis.

The Employee Retirement Income Security Act of 1974 (ERISA) included a clause specifying that all employers providing health plans would be exempt from state laws related to employee benefits. Self-insured health plans operated by employers and union management trusts were not subject to state laws. This meant that the legal remedies that state courts normally provide for aggrieved or insured parties were rendered inoperable. Despite minimal requirements for tax-favored private plans, federal tax subsidies had increased to $100 billion, half of the Medicare outlays, by the mid-seventies.

At the end of the 1970s, a decisive increase in Social Security benefits and the centralization of welfare programs helped drive down poverty in the United States. These developments strengthened public insurance at the cost of private pensions. At the same time, public health policy faltered. Health care stayed bundled with private employer and union plans. Indeed, as health costs shot up, the states footed the bill through tax subsidies to businesses, without increasing regulation. As health insurance became more expensive, many working Americans were forced to let theirs lapse. Thus began the increase in the number of citizens without access to medical care (Hacker, 2002).

The COLA reflected the "gray power" of the newly organized elderly constituency. Conversely, the erosion of public insurance for workers and the growth of private welfare reflected the downward slide of the unions. Through much of the postwar period, collaboration between organized labor and large employers had been based on economic expansion that satisfied the interdependent interests of both parties. With the recession of the seventies, this marriage of convenience fell apart.

Supply-side economists from Princeton University, the National Bureau of Economic Research, and the University of Birmingham in England offered a way out of the recession. They proposed rolling back corporate taxes to promote investment and in turn create jobs. Jimmy Carter presided over the first regressive tax reform since the Roosevelt era, when taxes, especially during World War II, had become steeply progressive.

The supply-siders urged businesspeople to take the lead in economic recovery and allowed them ample leeway in dealing with labor. Publicity campaigns depicted unions as fostering policies—e.g., increasing tariffs on imported goods—that were contrary to consumer interests. A prevalent news flash of the time showed irate automobile workers taking sledgehammers to cheap Toyotas. Scandals and criminal prosecution of union leaders for corruption also hurt the unions. The commitment of Democratic legislators to labor became less than whole-hearted (Schwartz, 1983; Tolchin & Tolchin, 1983).

Social Work in the Seventies

Commentators like Specht and Courtney (1994) have interpreted the distancing of social workers from public welfare programs as a sign of selling out to misguided professional aspirations—in effect, social climbing—wedded to individual therapy. But other forces were at work as well. Critical postmortems on the failures of 1960s-style interventions to drive down, much less eradicate, poverty resonated in mainstream social work. Casework was abolished as a requirement for welfare recipients, and that had the effect of discrediting the profession's claim to solve social problems (Trattner, 1999). Likewise, the involvement of social workers in the community action programs identified with the War on Poverty was written off, at least to some extent, as ineffective. These activities looked like symptoms of the excesses of the late sixties.

Retrospective evaluations in this vein may be unfair. The profession never claimed to be able to "cure" poverty through casework, and it is unrealistic to suppose that social workers could have forestalled the outbursts of rage welling up from centuries of discrimination. Against this background, uncertainty pervaded the profession, and this may well have sent social workers on a search for alternative interventions that permitted more circumscribed evaluations.

Reactions to the performance of radical social workers during the sixties took three directions. Some professionals simply disowned radical activism. Others criticized radical activists as ineffective professionals. A third option involved integrating a modified radical activism into the profession.

Several liberal leaders took issue with the in-your-face tactics of the radicals. They deplored the street theater and the odd alliances. Such actions were unprofessional and counterproductive (Specht, 1968). Some blamed the demise of the Family Assistance Plan, the first policy establishing a guaranteed income and protecting the working poor, on the strident protests of the NWRO and their allies. The diagnosis was that radicals were as much at fault as conservatives in blocking reform. Pursuit of the perfect wrecked any chances of attaining the good. Proposals like the FAP, though not flawless, might have opened a new direction for the development of welfare over subsequent decades.

Conversely, radicals defined professionalism itself as antithetical to the principles of activism for the sake of justice. Social workers themselves were a big part of the problem. Institutional welfare was a form of social control. Service agencies did not have the true interests of clients at heart. They overlooked the structural origins of problems in the socioeconomic system. The oppression of clients in the name of professionalism was routine. In sum, the organizational bias, theoretical framework, and careerism of professional social workers impeded equal, cooperative practice across individual, family, community, and political systems (Brake & Bailey, 1980; Cloward & Piven, 1975).

The integrationists believed in transformative practice. They argued that social workers could empower clients individually and interactively. The cultivation of skills in critical thinking would help clients build alternative, self-controlled services. Heightened critical awareness would foster both individual and structural responses to oppression (Freire, 1973; Knickmeyer, 1972; Leonard, 1975; Needleman & Needleman, 1974).

Many social workers continued on or returned to the psychiatric path of the 1950s. Mental health services grew, and so did the percentage of social workers in this field, which was twice as large as in any other specialization. The Title XX amendment opened opportunities for counseling to the middle class as well as the poor. Furthermore, job openings in private agencies shot up as services for delinquency rehabilitation, disability, and family support were contracted out. Private practice became more and more popular during the seventies. A survey of Master's in Social Work (MSW) students found that between 20 and 30 percent of them were interested in pursuing private practice and considered psychotherapeutic techniques the most important of the practice methods (Abel & McDonnell, 1990).

In the wake of comparatively radical departures in the thirties and the sixties, the profession drifted back, as if by default, to individualistic approaches that had a long, path-dependent lineage. In 1971, the NASW's Academy of Certified Social Workers put in place a national examination that was required for the certification of its members. A survey of NASW chapters confirmed that fully two-thirds of their legislative priorities during the late seventies were dedicated to licensing and third-party payments. Only one-third had to do directly with social problems and services (Lause, 1979). The National Federation of Societies for Clinical Social Work (NFSCSW) was established and, in 1979, the

American Association of State Social Work Boards (AASSWB) came into being to coordinate state-level licensing procedures (Barker, 2003).

Did commitment to the active promotion of social justice end with the sixties? Without doubt, the activist thrust was blunted in the seventies, but it did not reach a dead end. Radical ideas and issues that gained attention during the previous decade left some imprint on the profession.

The Catalyst Collective, made up of young white social workers, propagated a new form of radicalism. The journal *Catalyst: A Socialist Journal of the Social Services* kept up criticism of the profession and kept alive the goal of restructuring the socioeconomic system. For 2 years, the Radical Alliance of Social Service Workers of New York attempted to coordinate like-minded groups to achieve change within the social service field. Intended to promote unity, the group broke up into factions. The National Federation of Student Social Workers (NFSSW) organized a conference in 1976 in Philadelphia, to coincide with the bicentennial, on "Revolutionary Tactics for Human Services." They showed much enthusiasm but had little impact (Reisch & Andrews, 2001; Wagner, 1989).

These groups strove to maintain a socialist commitment among their adherents but their influence on mainstream social work was minimal at most. Still, the experience of the sixties had some discernible effect on the profession. The 1976 NASW code of ethics included "an ethical imperative for social workers to engage in political action on behalf of vulnerable populations." In 1971, the Educational Legislative Action Network (ELAN) was formed in the NASW. Five years later, the Political Action for Candidate Election was established within the NASW (Barker, 2003).

The most significant impact of the sixties on the profession came from movements of minorities of color and women. In the NASW, minority caucuses of African Americans, Puerto Ricans, Asian Americans, and Native Americans emerged. Within the CSWE, the creation of commissions on the status of women, on race and ethnicity, and later on gay men and lesbians testifies to the carryover of the sixties.

As early as the middle and late sixties, the African American influence was evident in the profession and its schools. The feminist movement flourished and made itself felt somewhat later, in the seventies. Women in agencies and schools brought to the fore the inequalities in gender positions and compensation. Feminist theories modified methods of practice and teaching. The search for interventions dealing with women's problems focused on gender inequality, and the effort tended to favor structural remedies over psychological rehabilitation. Reacting to male hierarchy and domination, feminists pushed for egalitarian dialogue with clients and students. Favoring phenomenological research, they stressed the importance of experience in the construction of knowledge (Figueira-McDonough, 1998b).

Identity politics moved social work into new and important areas of debate. Some radical social workers (e.g., Reisch & Andrews, 2001) express concern about the fragmenting potential of identity issues on change within the profession and the political environment. Their case has some validity. To what extent a layered radicalism might converge around oppression and reinforce class identity remains a significant question.

The growth of doctoral programs also changed the profession. Research became increasingly salient as a guide to intervention, and a broader range of theories were brought to bear in social work curricula. The Group for the Advancement of Doctoral Education (GADE) was created in 1977. In the same year, the NASW started publishing the *Journal of Social Work Research and Abstracts*. The effect of this trend on the trajectory of the profession remains to be determined (Barker, 2003).

Reagan and the Precipitous Undoing of Public Assistance

An Inspirational Pro-Business and Anti-Welfare Leader

At the beginning of the eighties, the United States was still battling stagflation. Its economic dominance had begun to slip with the oil embargo. The country had been humbled by the hostage crisis in Iran, and it had not forgotten the historical defeat in Vietnam. The Carter administration's failure to cope with these problems fueled distrust in government.

Promoted by staunch Republicans and propelled by his record as the anti-tax, anti-welfare governor of California, Ronald Reagan became a formidable candidate. His message of reconstructing the country through a downsized government, delivered amiably and with conviction, evoked solid American beliefs. His recitation of these values and images—patriotism; the nuclear family; self-help; cohesive neighborhoods; local autonomy; a laissez-faire market; and a small, nonintrusive government—resonated with the traditional national ethos and reassured the struggling middle class.

Countering Jimmy Carter's call for Americans to adjust to and accept limits on the country's power, resources, and potential for growth, Reagan promised a revival of the "city on the hill." This was the Pilgrims' vision of the land as a beacon to the rest of the world. Reagan's model implied a return to the end of the nineteenth century or to a mythical version of it that never was. It was an appealing fantasy of restored moral and economic grandeur (Reagan, 1983).

Ratification of the policies pursued in the first term of Reagan's presidency came from the academy. Milton Friedman, a Nobel laureate from the University of Chicago, endorsed supply-side economics and deregulation. These ideas were enthusiastically publicized by George Gilder (1981), a conservative commentator. Supply-side economics opened the way to tax cuts for corporations and wealthy individuals, and to deregulation.

As for social policy, a string of cuts in welfare programs was justified by Martin Anderson (1978), a senior fellow working at Stanford's Hoover Institution. Poverty in the United States, Anderson contended, had disappeared. Later, Charles Murray (1984) claimed that welfare actually hurt the poor, creating a cycle of dependence and stifling their innate entrepreneurial spirit. Reagan's vice president, George Bush, drew selectively on cases of self-help during times of natural calamities to proclaim the superiority of volunteer organizations over public assistance. He maintained this position through his own term as president (Phillips, K., 1990), refining it with the phrase "a thousand points of light."

Gifts to Business, the Expansion of Defense, and Cuts in Public Assistance

The 1980 elections gave Republicans control of the Senate, and President Reagan's cabinet was dominated by businesspeople who shared his conservative philosophy. The war on the welfare state began in earnest.

The 1981 Omnibus Budget Reconciliation Act (OBRA) made deep cuts in social programs while offering tax breaks to corporations and wealthy entrepreneurs. It also provided lavish funding for the president's Star Wars initiative to build a missile defense system. Deregulation encouraged speculation and business and bank mergers, at the same time that it weakened environmental and workers' safety protections.

The rationale behind deregulation and tax cuts for business looked simple: to increase investment and create jobs. But the trickle-down prediction did not pan out. As unemployment grew and public assistance programs were pared, the absolute number and the percentage of Americans living in poverty increased from 24.4 million (11.5 percent) in 1978 to 35.6 million (15.3 percent) in 1984 (Phillips, K., 1990, Appendix C).

The New Federalism, a reform modeled on Nixon's revenue-sharing policies, eliminated 57 federal programs. Seven block grants were instituted to take their place. This reform followed one facet of the revenue-sharing model by granting the states further autonomy. The new twist was that it provided less federal money.

In tandem with this pruning, benefits were cut and eligibility was tightened in means-tested programs—in Food Stamps, AFDC, and disability—and the duration of unemployment insurance coverage was shortened. The Comprehensive Employment Training Act (CETA), the public service program for unemployed workers, was abolished. These decisions eliminated 400,000 families—a drop of 17.4 percent—from the rolls. About 1 million lost their eligibility for Food Stamps, a drop of 14.3 percent (Piven & Cloward, 1982).

At this point, unemployment, economic restructuring, and entrapment in poverty had crystallized into a new phenomenon—the underclass. The term pointed to urban areas, densely populated by minorities, with extremely high rates of unemployment, dilapidated schools with stratospherically high dropout rates, substandard housing, and family incomes below the poverty line. These people were not just poor; they were chronically poor. Clearly outsiders, they were trapped in poverty (Auletta, 1982; Devine & Wright, 1993; Figueira-McDonough, 1993, 1995, 2001; Katz, 1989).

Federal spending on AFDC in 1980 amounted to less than 1 percent of the national budget while military expenditures took up 25 percent. The severity of cutbacks in public assistance, alongside the generosity shown toward defense, had more to do with ideology than economic necessity. Reagan's view of poverty, based on stereotypes of laziness and bad character, went back to the nineteenth century. He customarily portrayed AFDC recipients as cheaters, and he was fond of telling anecdotes about the welfare queen, a black woman who collected benefits under different names. Through all this, the president's Star Wars program with its benefits for the defense industry at once boosted the military budget and increased the deficit, even as the leadership of the Soviet Union was signaling a rapprochement with the West.

Besides the policy decisions affecting AFDC and Food Stamps, a series of other programs fell under the knife. The litany of reductions is chilling: child nutrition, 28 percent; social services, 22 percent; compensatory education, 17 percent; public service jobs, 99 percent; training programs, 35 percent; rent subsidies, 5 percent (Piven & Cloward, 1982). Housing and Urban Development (HUD) funding for construction of public and controlled-rent housing was nearly eliminated. It is no mystery why, starting in the eighties, homelessness ballooned to crisis proportions (Halpern, 1995; Jansson, 2001; Rossi, 1989).

Tax cuts and deregulation failed to show dividends for unemployment or inflation. The anti-inflationary policies of the Federal Reserve Bank tightened the supply of money, and hence the availability of loans, by raising interest rates. Productivity went down, wages and salaries shrunk, exports decreased, and the deficit expanded. The country was crossing the worst recession since the Great Depression.

Meanwhile, under pressure from religious and humanitarian organizations like the United States Conference of Catholic Bishops, Congress restored some of what had been cut from public assistance. Legislation was enacted to increase SSI benefits and readmit many disabled people who had been removed from the program. The government funded an extension of the period of unemployment insurance and sent a $97 billion relief package to the states, with $4.6 billion earmarked for the creation of 300,000 to 600,000 public service jobs and $5 billion being sent to 27 acutely distressed states (Trattner, 1999, pp. 369–370).

Social Security Reforms

Early on, the Reagan administration had tried to impose cuts on Social Security, but policy makers quickly withdrew in the face of gray power counter-mobilization, most effectively organized through the American Association of Retired Persons. Whatever the politics of the situation, the realities presented by the growth in costs and the demographic imbalance between fewer contributors and more beneficiaries prompted the setting up of a study commission. A number of the commission's recommendations—taxing some benefits received by well-off retirees and phasing the retirement age upward to 67 by 2027—garnered bipartisan support and were enacted in 1983 (President's Commission on Pension Policy, 1981).

Medicare expenditures had more than doubled between 1970 and 1980, from $15.2 to $38.3 billion. In order to control part A of Medicare, which covered hospital care expenses, the program adopted a policy known as "diagnosis-related groups" (DRGs). The objective was to decrease hospital stays. Each diagnosis prescribed a specific number of days of hospital time. If a patient were discharged from the hospital ahead of time, the hospital would receive the extra amount linked to the diagnosis. If the patient stayed longer, the hospital had to cover the costs associated with the "overstay." The incentives pushing for early releases were plain, and some of the human costs—for frail elderly or those without supportive families—could be high (Demkovitch, 1984).

Federal state medical expenditures more than doubled between 1970 and 1980, from $10.9 billion to $25 billion. Washington's response to the inexorable upward shift in costs was to issue directives that created incentives for the states to sign contracts with clinics and hospitals offering the lowest bids. Medicaid budgets were also driven skyward by a spillover effect from the restrictions of Medicare with respect to old-age health needs. Medicare did not provide coverage for convalescent, nursing, or home health care. When the elderly had depleted their assets on such care, they became the charges of Medicaid.

After the extinction of CETA, the Job Training Partnership Act (JTPA) was enacted in 1982. The states received funds with relatively few restrictions. Contracts were awarded to job-placement agencies and other local organizations. These agencies got a fee for each person placed with private business. The program did not provide training or day-care subsidies, and the reimbursement policy encouraged a revolving door pattern in placements (Corrigan, 1983).

Labor's Slippery Slope

At the outset of his first administration, Ronald Reagan struck a blow against the union movement by replacing striking air controllers with military personnel, destroying the Professional Air Traffic Controllers Organization (PATCO). At the time, the union had 14,500 members with an average income of $30,000.

Reagan's hard-line position set a precedent. Strikebreaking underwent a resurgence through the rest of his administration. Corporate executives adopted tougher negotiating positions and developed more aggressive strategies in riding out strikes. Various changes undermined labor. Sharp reductions in unemployment insurance, complete elimination of public service job programs, and the weakening of the Occupational Safety and Health Administration all worked against unions. The same anti-union bias went for appointments to the National Labor Relations Board and the Department of Labor. Donald R. Dobson, for example, was once the chief management lawyer for the Wheeling-Pittsburgh Steel Corporation. Hugh L. Reilly was a former attorney with the National Right to Work Legal Defense Foundation, an organization specializing in bringing suits against unions (Edsall, 1984, 1989).

Reagan's Second Term and Bush's Presidency

By 1984, the economy had improved, and Reagan easily defeated Walter Mondale, the Democratic candidate who had been Jimmy Carter's vice president after serving as senator from Minnesota. Reagan's personal charm contributed to his landslide victory, and Mondale's charisma deficit was such that talk show hosts took to referring to him as "Norwegian Wood." Reagan also enjoyed the support of the Christian right and its offshoot, the Moral Majority, with an extensive, smoothly managed grassroots network.

The top priority of Congress was to control the unprecedented deficit, the mounting national debt, and the Strategic Defense Initiative, popularly known as Star Wars. In 1985, Congress passed the Balanced Budget and Emergency Deficit Control Act.

Tax reform was another top priority during Reagan's second term. The tax code underwent simplification. The number of tax brackets was reduced, and the tax brackets themselves, which inflation had made extremely regressive, were brought up to date. These adjustments took some of the burden off the middle class. But at the same time, the progressive nature of the tax code was undercut. The effective rate at which the wealthiest Americans were taxed went down to 33 from 50 percent, a figure only slightly higher than that imposed on the middle class and working class brackets.

Finally, the Family Support Act of 1988 provided modest funds to the states for training programs and child care. These were supposed to help AFDC recipients to enter the labor force and to force estranged parents to pay child support. The money collected from absent parents did not in fact help families. It reverted to the state public assistance programs, to defray the cost of benefits awarded to recipients (Figueira-McDonough, 1994a).

Ronald Reagan has become known as "the Teflon president," not because he could do no wrong but because, even when he did, blame failed to stick to him. But a series of scandals toward the end of Reagan's second term sidetracked many of his domestic initiatives. In what became known as the Iran-Contra Affair, some key officials had tried secretly to sell weapons to Iran in exchange for releasing American hostages. In turn, they funneled the profits from these sales to the Contras, rebels who were battling to overthrow the Sandinista government in Nicaragua. All this behavior was illegal, since it contravened decisions explicitly made by Congress. The uproar at these revelations and the subsequent investigation led to the punishment of some of the culprits. But the president, already in the early stages of Alzheimer's disease, was spared.

In 1980, when he was competing against Ronald Reagan for his party's presidential nomination, George H. W. Bush had dubbed supply-side theorizing "voodoo economics." But the two were quickly reconciled, and Bush served as Reagan's vice president. In 1988, he handily defeated Michael Dukakis, the former governor of Massachusetts, winning the presidency after a campaign marked by attack advertising and low voter turnout.

Bush's administration paid scarce attention to domestic economic problems. Deficits, unemployment, and social programs were not high on the agenda. As welfare rolls expanded and the states, under the new federalism, found it harder to cope, social programs were frozen or benefits reduced. The states were unable or unwilling to expand the training programs and child care services of the 1988 Family Support Act. As Herbert Hoover had done 50 years before, Bush kept his faith in the ability of private organizations to respond to social problems. These were his "thousand points of light." The United Way scandal that broke in 1992 severely tested this confidence. The top official of this major charitable operation was found to be receiving an exorbitant salary, to have engaged in illegal financial deals, and to have charged private expenses to United Way accounts.

Meanwhile, fresh indicators of extreme poverty—homelessness, unemployment, deterioration of underclass communities—registered the highest levels since the Great Depression. Enraged at the acquittal of police officers who had beaten Rodney King, an African American, residents of South Central Los Angeles took to the streets in a repetition of the 1965 Watts riots. Studies conducted after the riot revealed that little or no improvement had occurred in the community since the first riot 27 years before.

Few social policies took shape between 1988 and 1992. In 1990, Congress passed, and the president signed, the Americans with Disabilities Act (ADA). It was drawn up with the purpose of helping people with disabilities get into the labor market by guaranteeing them certain accommodations in the workplace. After some resistance from the administration, the minimum wage was raised from $3.35 to $4.25 an hour. This still left full-time minimum-wage earners with a family of four below the poverty line. Finally, in response to the inability of the states to cope with the growth in public assistance rolls, waivers were authorized allowing them to experiment with alternative forms of control.

President Bush, who had formerly directed the CIA, felt more at home dealing with defense issues. He invaded Panama to overthrow Manuel Noriega, the country's longtime dictator. To counter Saddam Hussein's invasion of Kuwait, he orchestrated and won the Gulf War against Iraq in a month's time. A large coalition of allies backed the invasion, which operated under the jurisdiction of the United Nations. These triumphs boosted presidential popularity. However, economic disarray on the home front drained the political capital of the president, who confessed to being baffled by a question—"Would you like paper or plastic?"—posed at the check-out counter during one of his very infrequent trips to a supermarket. The economy continued to sour. In 1992, Bush lost the presidency to Bill Clinton (Katz, 2001; Phillips, K., 1990).

Critical Commentary

The New Federalism enshrined block grants as the mechanism for national contributions to state-run social programs. These grants are annual allowances, fixed by federal authorities, that let states decide how they are spent. Wrapped in the rhetoric of local autonomy, the maneuver actually increases the financial responsibility of many of the states whose constitutions require balanced budgets. Although the states are free to set the levels of benefits and the requirements for access to services, defederalization was accompanied by huge cuts. All this has conspired to entrench an inequality of benefits rather than national standards across the states. AFDC and service programs designed to help those in poverty took the biggest hits under the New Federalism. Decentralization on this scale has had dramatic consequences during times of economic crisis when, for a growing number of adults and their children, means-tested programs have been the only form of relief.

Cutbacks in AFDC, together with similar reductions in Food Stamps and SSI, were carried out in the name of reducing a relentless increase in deficits. However, tax cuts awarded to corporations and individuals in high economic brackets and defense expenditures contributed to an extraordinary growth in the deficit. The math is straightforward. Tax write-offs for wealthy individuals and corporations, and subsidies for new business equipment, increased the deficit by $749 billion. Military expenditures contributed another $226 billion. Through all this, welfare cuts drove the deficit down by a comparatively paltry $50 billion. By the end of Reagan's presidency, the total increase in the deficit stood at $925 billion (Edsall, 1989; Phillips, K., 1990).

It is worth considering the different motivational assumptions behind the two types of cuts. Tax breaks for the wealthy made sense on the assumption that beneficiaries would do the right thing. They were expected to plough their extra savings back into productive investment. The belief behind the cuts in social programs was that the poor needed to respond to hardship by working rather than seeking handouts. It was a carrot-and-stick scenario, born again. Rewards are the proper incentive for the better off; only punishment is effective with the poor.

This split between the worthy and the undeserving accords with the path first tread by the Puritans. Poverty and wealth are self-made. Material failure reflects character flaws. Material success validates one's qualities and virtues. Individuals made it or failed to make it on their own, by their own boot-straps. Malthusianism and social Darwinism added apparently scientific confirmation to the religious conviction that, in the larger scheme of things, the poor get the fate, sad as it might be, that they deserve. The roots of poverty lay in a deviant, separate culture. It was through this miasma of stern morality and sentimentalized folklore that political emergencies were interpreted. Real or manufactured, crises like Reagan's Star Wars obsession or Bush's Panama invasion and month-long Gulf War deflected attention from efforts to promote social inclusion.

Policies sanctioned by supply-side economics also reflected the increasing political strength of the business class. New alliances were fashioned through Chambers of Commerce and the National Conservative Political Action Committees (Edsall, 1984). Think tanks like the National Bureau of Economic Research, the Hoover Institution, the Cato Institute, and the American Enterprise Institute attracted benefactors.

"Luck, son, is when preparation meets nepotism."

Exhibit 7.1

But a divided Democratic party eased the passage of supply-side–inspired policies as well. Sensing the decline of the unions and trying to skirt close identification with welfare, some New Democrats switched their attention to the suburbs and the middle class. Especially in the House, they often sided with Republicans and Southern Democrats. They finessed accusations of left-wing tendencies by styling themselves as centrists (Edsall, 1984).

The power of organized labor, essential to any progressive coalition, had been steadily declining. Union membership started heading downward after its peak in the 1950s and 1960s, from about 36 to 13 percent of the workforce in the 1980s. During their heyday after World War II, the unions forged a deceptively beneficial collaboration with big business through contracts for wages and benefits. But well before the first Gulf War, industries began moving to the South, where "right to work" legislation that encouraged a non-union workforce prevailed. Or they moved low-skilled production work abroad. Textiles and shoe manufacturing were prime examples. The "don't kill the goose that lays the golden egg" alliance frayed, and labor relations became more contentious. The commitment of the unions to a broad workers' movement, never very strong, weakened further. Labor leaders stuck with a defensive strategy. Rather than trying to extend benefits to the workforce as a whole, they focused on protecting their own members as much as possible (Cameron, 1982).

The Employment Retirement Income Security Act of 1974 (ERISA) was the last serious effort to regulate private welfare. In 1981, the Presidential Commission on Pension Policy had recommended requiring all employers to offer a minimum pension to all workers. President Reagan peremptorily dismissed this mandatory pension proposal (Hacker, 2002).

The benefits disbursed by employer-sponsored programs varied widely. Coverage was higher in unionized firms, in public employment, in larger companies, and in manufacturing. The likelihood of an employer offering a pension plan decreased sharply toward the lower rungs of corporate income, as did the probability that a worker would be covered at all.

Only 1 percent of total workplace retirement benefits go to older Americans in the lowest 20 percent of the income profile, while nearly 57.5 percent go to those in the top fifth (Hacker, 2002, pp. 157–160). It is clear that one purpose of ERISA, to shift benefits towards lower-paid employees, failed. At the same time, tax breaks and incentives were given to employers' plans, integrating Social Security into private pension plans. Not only did Social Security retain regressive features; the conditions of private old-age insurance became even more regressive.

According to provisions incorporated in ERISA in 1974, employers who offered self-insured health plans were exempt from state laws that governed the scope and character of benefits. This led to the growth of self-insured plans underwriting workers' risks and to the evasion of state regulations and taxes. Labor as well as business groups effectively countered attempts to redress this imbalance. All this indicates how entrenched employer-provided health insurance had become by the 1980s and how difficult it was to regulate the system. Meanwhile, the number of Americans without health insurance went up and up (Hacker, 2002).

Inequality grew. The Social Security tax (FICA) withheld from paychecks was plainly regressive. During the period of 1982 to 1985, the FICA went up but it did so in such a way that it cost lower-income wage earners more than those who were better off. Thus, the added cost for those with incomes of less than $10,000 was $1,340. For those earning over $80,000, the extra tax came to only $490. Between 1960 and 1984, social insurance taxes went up from 15.9 to 36.8 percent. At the same time, corporate taxes actually went down from 23.2 to 7.8 percent. Excise taxes dropped from 16.8 to 10.5 percent. In short, Social Security fell more heavily on those earning lower incomes. Income and capital gains taxes favored those with higher incomes (Edsall, 1989).

Together, these trends exacerbated the gulf between rich and poor. The lowest quintile (20 percent) of the population shared 4.7 percent of the national income. The highest quintile controlled 41.6 percent. The uneven distribution of wealth, covering a variety of assets such as property, bonds, stocks, savings, trusts, and life insurance, was still more dramatic. One quarter of national wealth—that is, of capital assets—was in the hands of 1 percent of the population (Edsall, 1984; Piven & Cloward, 1982).

Cuts in welfare, Social Security, and labor protection raised the poverty level from 11.5 percent in the mid-seventies to 15.5 percent in the mid-eighties. The solutions that states improvised to deal with their own budgetary shortfalls under the New Federalism compounded the problem. Between 1977 and 1988, the inequality in family income grew considerably. Table 7.1 shows the joint impact of wage stagnation among the working class and favorable tax concessions to the wealthy. It lays out the change, in percentages and dollar amounts, across income categories grouped by deciles, from the top 10 to the bottom 10 percent.

Table 7.1   Changes in Estimated Average After-Tax Family Income, 1977–1988

Income group	Average income		% of change	Income change ($)
	1977	1988		
1 (poorest)	3,528	3,175	−10.5	−371
2	7,084	6,990	−1.3	−94
3	10,740	10,614	−1.2	−126
4	14,423	14,266	−0.4	−57
5	18,043	18,086	+0.2	+33
6	22,009	22,259	+1.1	+250
7	26,240	27,038	+3.0	+798
8	32,568	33,282	+5.4	+1,718
9	39,286	42,323	+7.9	+3,087
10 (richest)	70,498	89,783	+27.4	+19,324
Of the richest 10%:				
Top 5%	90,756	124,651	+37.3	+33,895
Top 1%	174,498	303,900	+74.2	+129,402

Source: Congressional Budget Office, *The Changing Distribution of Federal Taxes: 1975–1990.* (October, 1987 [1987 dollars])

Social Work in a Regressive Era

As was the case in previous decades, the response of the profession to the slashing of social services and benefits and the relegation of the poor to the status of "others" was far from uniform, even within the representative organizations.

By the middle of the 1980s, membership in the National Association of Social Workers topped 100,000. Most were MSWs, with similar percentages working in private and public agencies. Nearly 15 percent were employed by for-profit organizations (Jansson, 2001, p. 344). Mental health, together with health and family and children services, were the favored sectors.

The labor market for social workers was moving in two different directions. Many public agencies had declassified their jobs in such a way that requirements for training in social work were dropped. On the other hand, many private organizations required not only a social work degree but often a professional license as well.

The NASW responded to the second trend by establishing the National Peer Review Committee in 1983. The association trained social workers to evaluate the work of other social workers, with an eye to promoting accountability and meeting the quality-control standards of government and third-party funding organizations. In 1984, the NASW Delegate Assembly focused on vendorship issues. The association sponsored a lobbying program between 1985 and 1986 directed at similar developments at the state and national levels (Sherraden, 1990).

However, professional organizations did not overlook the experience and influence of activists within its membership altogether. In 1987, the NASW established the Center for Social Policy and Practice to coordinate the exchange of information, education, and policy data regarding social work and social welfare. The conferences, policy statements, and newsletters of the Center frequently attacked the conservatism of the Reagan and Bush administrations. The Center backed a national health policy and allied itself with the Children's Defense Fund and other organizations in the family field. The position papers of the Delegate Assembly took progressive stands on AIDS, long-term care, and the rights of children (NASW, 1991).

NASW's support for Carter in 1980 was strongly opposed by the Radical Association of Social Service Workers (RASSW), who viewed both contenders, Carter and Reagan, as unacceptable. As the full impact of the Reagan revolution dawned on its members, the position taken by the association came to be seen as less controversial. The opposition of the NASW to OBRA, the Omnibus Budget Reconciliation Act, won the respect of activists. The RASSW attacked the 1981 OBRA, participated in the Solidarity Day, fought institutional racism in human services, and maintained its links with labor. Radical social workers also had to contend with fragmentation in their own organization. Through all this, the radicals kept up their cry for a socialist political solution and stood firm against reform within established institutions.

One successful strategy of neo-conservatives was to brand radicals, the left in general, and even the American Civil Liberties Union as un-American. As often happens when they are pigeonholed, people choose other labels for themselves and their ideas. "Radicals" became "progressives." Renaming the *Catalyst: A Socialist Journal of Social Services* as the *Journal of Progressive Social Services* exemplified just this reaction. The made-over progressives supported institutional reform, but class was no longer an exclusive part of their analytical repertoire. The arsenal was expanded to include race, ethnicity, gender, and sexual orientation (Reisch & Andrews, 2001; Schram, 1995).

At the Bertha Reynolds Centennial Conference in 1985, more than 150 social workers endorsed a call to establish the Bertha Capen Reynolds Society (BCRS), inspired by Marxist, feminist, and anti-racist ideas. Local chapters sprouted and members participated in demonstrations against cuts in services. Peace rallies were also popular, as were protests against government repression of public-assistance clients. By the 1990s, membership in the BCRS numbered 500. The society espoused mutuality in professional–client relationships; integration of the political into practice; alliances with clients in their confrontations with agencies; coalitions with other progressive movements; and an ongoing, independent critique of the welfare state (Withorn, 1986).

Since many social services had become decentralized, action at the local level became more viable and effective. Some social workers turned activist practice toward involvement in advocacy and the nurturing of broad-based political coalitions.

Two long-time activists embody this approach. Trained at the University of Michigan, Nancy Amidei (1982) was an energetic social worker and an exceptional speaker. Working both in Washington, D.C., and in Washington State, she pushed for welfare rights and programs to meet the needs of the homeless. In her view, it is the historical mission of social workers to give equal priority to helping individuals and to fighting for justice through the advocacy of structural change.

Maryann Mahaffey (1981), a professor at Wayne State University and ex-president of the Detroit City Council, became known for organizing mass opposition against militarism and the social policies of the Reagan administration. Important allies in this local activist practice were the National People's Action, Labor/Community Strategy Center, Acorn, Grassroots Leadership, the Center for Third World Organizing, and the Piedmont Peace Project (Figueira-McDonough, 2001).

On the whole, social work curricula did not absorb these models of integrated change (Falk, 1984). They were inclined to follow historically familiar prototypes. Ecological perspectives built on Mary Richmond's "person in situation" paradigm, including both environment and policy as setting the context for direct practice. Interest in diversity led to the development of culturally sensitive interventions. The adaptation of feminist theories to practice was extended across oppressed groups. Macro-practice courses were the main venues for promoting structural interventions. In spite of CSWE's requirement that all students take some macro-practice courses, most schools offer two separate micro and macro tracks. Typically, students majoring in individual or direct practice may be required to take just one course on social policy or macro-practice (Figueira-McDonough, 1994b).

The number of students opting for micro-practice is often three times larger than those in macro-practice. The result is some marginalization of macro faculty in curricular matters. This has predictable effects on the practice of future social workers. The Association for Community Organization and Social Administration (ACOSA), created in the early 1980s, became an important nucleus of development, exchange, and networking for macro faculty (Figueira-McDonough, 1995).

8 The End of the Millennium and the Demise of Entitlement to Public Assistance

A Centrist President in a Conservative Government

Bill Clinton presented himself as a "New" Democrat. He offered, so he contended, a third way between the radical flank of his own party and conservative Republicans.

Various ingredients went into shaping this position. In order to build a winning coalition, Clinton felt that he needed to appeal to relatively conservative southerners as well as comparatively liberal northerners. He also knew that during the past 12 years, when they held the presidency, Republicans had managed to link the Great Society legacy of the Democrats with a tax-and-spend brand of big government that benefited the poor and African Americans at the expense of the working and middle classes. Clinton saw an opportunity to win some of these Reagan Democrats back to the Democratic fold.

Implementing the third way required a balancing act. The trick was to reconcile giving priority to the economy—to job creation, infrastructure renewal, stimulus packages, and bringing down the deficits inherited from Reagan and Bush—while paying serious attention to social programs, including health and education, and the environment. The makeup of Clinton's cabinet reflected these rival pulls. He appointed conservative pragmatists like Senator Lloyd Bentsen and Robert Rubin to the Treasury and to head up his economic team. He put deficit hawks like Leon Panetta and, later, Alice Rivlin in charge of the Office of Management and Budget. In counterpoint, committed liberals—Robert Reich and Donna Shalala—took over at the Labor Department and the Department of Health and Human Services.

The Failure of Health Care Reform

During his campaign, Clinton had vowed to push for health care reform. By the end of the 1980s, the system had not only become very expensive, absorbing about 15 percent of the GNP, it also left about 40 million Americans without coverage. Ten million of these were children. The others were adults who could not afford insurance and were not eligible for Medicare or Medicaid.

Estimates were that reliance on private health insurance companies, with their administrative and marketing overhead, added 20 percent to total costs. To make matters worse, because they had no access to primary and preventive care, the uninsured did not seek medical services until their condition had already deteriorated. In terms of both cost and inclusiveness, the Canadian and European systems looked far superior (Katz, 2001).

In 1993, the president put Hillary Rodham Clinton in charge of a task force to develop a health reform proposal. The goal, stated up front, was universal health coverage for all Americans, including legal residents. People would be entitled to a comprehensive package of benefits, even if they were unemployed and regardless of whether they had preexisting illnesses. The plan was to be financed by employers, whose share of contribution would be 80 percent, and employees, who would pay for the rest. The federal government would provide subsidies to help the poor, the unemployed, and small businesses pay their share. There were also to be subsidies for prescription drugs and long-term care for the elderly not covered under Medicare (Trattner, 1999, p. 394).

Regional Health Alliances (RHAs), created in each state, would manage competition. As huge purchasing pools, the RHAs would have the economic clout to help consumers save money on their premiums. A National Health Board would oversee the quality of care, and would impose selective cost controls on physicians, hospitals, and insurance premiums.

A *New York Times*/CNN poll taken a few days after the proposal was made public indicated that 57 percent of the American people favored it. Before the details of implementation could be worked out, however, Republicans branded the plan as another big-spending, big-government scheme of the Democrats. But it was the health care industry, and especially health insurers, who supplied the truly formidable opposition. They weighed in with an intensive media campaign, using fear tactics to insinuate that the program would bring down the quality of medical care and that patients would be deprived of choices, especially in the selection of physicians. The scare tactics over the elimination of choice hit home, in spite of the fact that insured citizens already received most of their care from HMOs that imposed restrictions—some notoriously severe—on choice. Indeed, the percentage of those covered who were under HMOs would grow to 90 percent by the end of the decade.

The attacks worked. The proposal died even before reaching the stage of legislative debate (Hacker, 2002).

The Contract With America

In 1994, midway into Clinton's first term, the Republicans took control of both the House and the Senate. The most aggressive of the conservative leaders was Newt Gingrich, a professor of history and congressman from Georgia, who became Speaker of the House.

Gingrich chaired GOPAC, a private organization, favored by very wealthy donors, that funded Republican campaigns. Through GOPAC, he targeted 50 House districts and engineered the election of like-minded Republicans.

Gingrich's ultimate goal was to undo the New Deal and build a "conservative opportunity society." A network of think tanks, foundations, and talk shows promoted conservative ideas. The Heritage Foundation and the Cato Institute were prominent among these organizations. So were pro-family research shops like the Family Council, the Eagle Forum, Concerned Women of America, the Christian Coalition, and National Empowerment Television. The conservative resurgence attracted a number of high-profile personalities: televangelist Pat Robertson, radio talk show host Rush Limbaugh, and best-selling authors Charles Murray and William Bennett—the last of whom had been "drug czar" under George H. W. Bush (Jansson, 2001).

Gingrich brought many of these elements together in the "Contract with America." Standing side by side with dozens of conservative colleagues, he launched the program with great fanfare from the steps leading up to the House of Representatives. The manifesto covered nearly all of the causes dear to get-tough conservatives. The Contract with America called for tax cuts, a $500-per-child credit for families earning up to $200,000, repeal of the marriage tax penalty, a balanced budget, a constitutional amendment banning abortion, term limits on Congress, higher earning limits for seniors on Social Security, anti-litigation reform, reduced regulatory power, more punitive crime legislation, and the elimination of social services in prisons.

The lengthiest passages of the Contract with America dealt with measures for strengthening the family and weakening welfare. Drawing inspiration from the Christian Right, the family section came out for strict child support enforcement, higher tax incentives for adoption, greater parental control over education, stronger child pornography laws, and tax credits for family members who care for elderly parents or grandparents. The section on welfare encapsulated a litany of reforms close to conservative Republicans:

- Denial of welfare to teenage mothers
- Denial of higher payments to mothers who give birth to children while on welfare
- A strict 2-years-and-out provision for public assistance recipients
- More stringent work requirements as incentives to individual responsibility
- A cap on spending for AFDC, SSI, and public housing programs, and a consolidation of nutrition programs (Food Stamps; Women, Infants, and Children [WIC]; and school lunch programs) into block grants to the states

The Contract with America also recommended that states should be allowed to opt out of the current AFDC program by converting their share of AFDC into fixed annual block grants (Gillespie & Shellhas, 1994).

Budget Battles and the Passage of the Personal Responsibility and Work Opportunity Reconciliation Act (PRWORA)

Fierce battles over the budget raged between the White House and Congress during 1994. The conflict reached a peak with the Omnibus Budget Reconciliation Act, passed by Congress in 1995. The bill sought to eliminate the entitlement status of AFDC, Medicaid, and Food Stamps. Clinton vetoed the measure and the government, technically without authority to spend money, shut down for 43 days.

The prolonged impasse ended in compromise. Liberal Democrats criticized Clinton for conceding too much, especially after Treasury Secretary Rubin had eliminated the deficit and a budget surplus had been achieved. Even so, in a fiscally austere and socially conservative environment, Clinton was able to secure some initiatives consistent with progressive democracy.

For example, he used tax reimbursements to fund most of his education initiatives off-budget through the EITC (Earned Income Tax Credit). Project Hope gave families with incomes in the lowest quintiles up to $1,500 in tax breaks for their children's first 2 years in college. The Lifetime Learning program gave tax credits of $1,000 to the same group for the last 2 years of college. Education Savings Accounts allowed for a $500 yearly deposit and withdrawal of savings and interest for postgraduate education free of taxes.

Clinton won several other important victories (Jansson, 2001):

- The Family and Medical Leave Act (fixed at 6 months)
- The lifting of the ban that kept federally subsidized family planning clinics from discussing abortion with clients
- Guaranteed free and universal immunization for children
- Extension of unemployment compensation to the states most affected by the prolonged recession
- An increase in the number of those entitled to the EITC
- Allocation of $1 billion for medical care and housing assistance to street people
- The addition of $6.9 billion to the 1994 crime bill for social services
- The prohibition of discrimination in mental health coverage by private insurers
- Creation of the Children's Health Insurance Program, which gave grants amounting to $20 billion to the states to provide health coverage to uninsured children. (pp. 369, 338–393)

If the limitations of working with a socially conservative majority in Congress are taken into account, and if these constraints are thrown in with the subsequent threat of removal from office for lying about an affair with a White House intern, it would seem that Bill Clinton preserved the core of his commitment to social policy. But it is the passage of the Personal Responsibility Act of 1996 that will represent Clinton's legacy in this field. There is, as we will see, a wide gap between the Clinton who, as a presidential candidate, criticized the AFDC waivers given by the prior administration, and the restrictions on benefits that resulted from them, and President Clinton's 1996 legislation. It was this act that handed even greater freedom over to the states in the management of a program from which entitlements had been removed.

Temporary Assistance for Needy Families (TANF)

In one stroke, the Personal Responsibility and Work Opportunity Reconciliation Act (PRWORA) reversed six decades of federal social legislation. During this time, destitute and dependent citizens—especially mothers and their children—had a safety net, a minimal level of financial assistance. The PRWORA changed all this.

The Act consisted of nine titles covering public assistance, SSI, eligibility of immigrants for public benefits, child care, child nutrition, and Food Stamps. Temporary Assistance for Needy Families block grants (TANF) replaced AFDC. Federal grants to the new program were to decline by $55 billion over the next 6 years. After 2002, Congress could slash federal contributions and let the states have primary responsibility for the programs.

Eligibility limits were set at 2 consecutive years and a total of 5 years over a lifetime. Under TANF, the states had to ensure that adult recipients participated in work or work-related activities. By 1997, a total of 25 percent of the family caseload was expected to participate in the prescribed activities, and 50 percent by 2002. Federal funds for minor parents (younger than 18) were cut if they were not in school or living in an adult-supervised setting.

Otherwise, PRWORA gave the states ample latitude in setting the rules about levels and types of benefits (cash or in-kind). For example, time limits could be shortened; assistance to teen parents denied; provision of benefits to new residents could be kept, for up to 1 year, at the level of the states from which they had migrated; and persons with drug convictions could be barred from assistance. This flexibility in implementation produced wide differences in eligibility and benefits among TANF recipients across the states (Hansen & Morris, 1999).

Presidential advisors like Mary Jo Bane, Peter Edelman, and Wendell Primus resigned in protest. They had worked closely with Clinton to reform public assistance in such a way as to mainstream recipients toward decent-paying jobs. They wanted to attain this goal by developing strong training and education programs accompanied by accessible child care (Bane & Ellwood, 1994). They felt defeated when the president signed off on what they considered retrograde legislation.

Why did Clinton sign the Personal Responsibility and Work Opportunity Reconciliation Act into law? The simplest answer is that he felt compelled to bolster his centrist position to get reelected. Senate Majority Leader Bob Dole, who would become the Republican presidential candidate, was already fulminating against "welfarism," and Ross Perot, the maverick entrepreneur, was threatening to repeat the populist surge that won him about a fifth of the popular vote in the 1992 presidential election.

Dick Morris, a longtime political consultant of Clinton's whose clients included Republicans as well as Democrats, argued that "ending welfare as we know it" would distance the president from the Democratic dinosaurs associated with the New Deal. However, straightforward as it seems, this explanation is partially contradicted by the significant support that his presidency enjoyed at the time (Weaver, 2000). It is still unclear how much a sense of electoral expediency contributed to the fateful decision.

Critical Commentary

James Morone (2003a) and R. Kent Weaver (2000) have developed a different take on the welfare reform of 1996. Morone points out that the 1994 midterm elections put Republicans in a position of overwhelming dominance. They controlled both houses of Congress, captured the legislatures in 11 new states, and held the governorships of 32 states. This presented a golden opportunity to prove once and for all Charles Murray's thesis that welfare wrecked the lives of the poor, trapping them in endless generations of dependence. It was a tragic cycle, for both mother and child, that cried out for correction. Furthermore, the push for root-and-branch welfare reform responded to the traditional desire for autonomy on the part of the states, for decentralization, while slashing federal expenditures. The biggest targets of the reforms were AFDC and Medicaid.

Weaver (2000) emphasizes that Clinton had little political capital to offset Republican strength. The best he could hope for was a modest compromise. The expenditures for Medicaid were six times those for AFDC. Clinton decided to sacrifice AFDC, the much smaller program, and save Medicaid. About one-third of Medicaid funds go to subsidies for nursing homes and prescription drugs for middle class elderly on fixed retirement incomes. Clinton made the program look like a supplement to Medicare, calling it "our parents' program." The ploy gave him some wiggle room to protect Medicaid, even as he gave in on revamping AFDC. The Republicans, wanting a quick victory, accepted the deal.

The trade-off highlights the vulnerability of the decentralized AFDC. This was the only program that the Contract with America submitted to a complete overhaul. TANF focused on poor recipients outside the economic mainstream. The threats of punishment written into the measure clearly defined the poor as undeserving.

In the end, TANF did not go quite so far as mandating the removal of all children of assistance recipients and their confinement to asylums. This was one Gingrich proposal that was eventually dropped. Gingrich could not convince enough of his colleagues that single mothers were morally deficient and likely to bring their children up as useless, dangerous citizens who would threaten their peers and be a burden on the state. With few provisions for training, education, and child care, the work requirements of TANF would at best, in good economic times, move welfare recipients to join the working poor. The "work or starve" rule was a path followed from nineteenth-century times.

Restrictions on public assistance and the revival of the work-or-starve principle would have infringed on human rights. So Congress made a few adjustments. The Omnibus Consolidation Appropriations Act was passed in 1997, and in 1999 the Ticket to Work and Work Incentives Improvement Act became law. The measures clarified the ground rules for the access of legal immigrants to public assistance programs. They also codified rules for dispensing Food Stamps and Medicaid to families who had recently left the rolls, and they laid out guidelines on access to Medicaid or Medicare for citizens with disabilities who had joined the workforce.

The most credible 5-year evaluation (1996–2001) of TANF shows that while the rolls have decreased, most previous recipients who left welfare work at low-wage jobs with few benefits. Because they lost Food Stamps and Medicare, many are worse off than before. The situation is still more desperate among African Americans and immigrants. A telling indicator is the number of "children only" recipients, whose mothers were ruled ineligible due to sanctions or because they receive SSI benefits, or who have immigrant status, or the children live with non-parents. The number of these children has increased considerably.

What would happen when recession hits, when work is harder to come by, and the lack of benefits in many jobs leaves the poor without a safety net? This is the key question for many researchers. Under such a scenario, previous recipients might max out the time limits on their benefits, and more new poor people would turn to welfare. A policy that might avoid human disaster in good economic times, when low-paid jobs are at least available, could result in catastrophe when the economy stalls or turns downward (Weil & Finegold, 2002). This is a problem we will take up in Chapter 11.

The 1993 Health Security Plan attempted to provide affordable health security to all Americans. Its goal was to achieve the early aspirations of the Social Security Act of 1935. The plan was never approved.

This failure represented the fifth defeat of similar initiatives in the twentieth century. By the end of the 1990s, the number of medically uninsured had grown by another 5 million, to a total of 45 million. This corresponds to the combined populations of the country's five largest metropolitan areas—Los Angeles, New York, Chicago, Detroit, and Philadelphia. Private, work-related health insurance was entrenched from the 1970s on.

The doomed 1993 health bill did not reject private health insurance, but it specified that employers would pay a larger share, and it envisioned regulations that would assure a level of coverage and control insurance costs.

Three powerful interests—the health insurance business, accustomed to minimal regulation; the American Medical Association, whose members were traditionally free to set their own fees; and employers, who received incentives and tax breaks from the government without much oversight—united against the proposed regulations and controls to defeat health reform. Without a national health care system, the United States remained alone among postindustrial societies.

In the 1990s, private insurance shrank, and many Americans were inadequately protected or at risk of losing their coverage. Sixty-three percent of the workforce had some form of health protection connected to their jobs. The majority of the plans were run by HMOs, and they imposed annoying and sometimes severe restrictions on their clients (restricted choice of physicians, waiting periods, and so forth). A private, voluntary, decentralized, and limited health system was maintained.

The work-based retirement programs that took off in the mid-sixties continued their upward trend. In the late nineties, caps on income for tax-favored Individual Retirement Accounts and 401(k) accounts were liberalized. Roth IRAs, as they became known, required account holders to pay taxes up front, thus avoiding future taxes on their accounts, including estate taxes. At the time, 70 percent of Americans had incomes low enough to open traditional IRAs. The effect of the changes associated with Roth IRAs was to make tax-favored accounts more readily available to upper-income households. Between 1997 and 2002, Roth IRAs accounted for $1.8 billion in lost tax revenue.

In the nineties, 401(k) accounts became one of the most popular vehicles for private retirement savings. As they took off, and as the Roth IRAs skyrocketed with them, the stock market boomed. This astonishing prosperity inspired conservatives to talk seriously about the privatization of Social Security. Unlike traditional private pensions, which are voluntary for employers, but generally not for employees, the newer accounts, such as Roth IRAs, are voluntary for individual workers. Participants have real control over investment choices. The problem is that the fallout from bad financial luck hits participants directly, and there is no safety net (Hacker, 2002).

The trend toward private pensions favoring the top two quintiles accelerated. According to Congressional Budget Office estimates, about half of the extra income from the tax advantages of these plans ($100 billion or 70 percent in tax subsidies) will go to the top income quintile, with only 12 percent to the bottom three quintiles (Orszag, 2000, p. 3).

So, health reform with universal coverage was not achieved, and private protection—health benefits and pensions—became weaker and more unequal. The upshot was that the rights of the working class were more precarious, and the poor lost federal protection—that is, entitlements. The states instead offered them time-limited and highly discretionary assistance and workfare.

Since the mid-seventies, the war on welfare has intensified. A worldview that ignores inequality and sees the poor as the "other" accompanies this assault like a battle hymn.

The roots of this ideology run deep in American political culture. The paths implicit in past decisions have turned social policy toward a weak welfare state. Both legacies, together with the growth of a private system of unequal welfare, plus the decay of the labor movement, have facilitated a reversal of the New Deal. The uncertain identity of the Democratic Party has played an important role in this decline (Reich, 2004).

Conservative Republicans have shown remarkable unity. For the most part, they have been single-minded in their fight for certain moral principles—for personal independence, small government, and traditional family values—and in their promotion of a social Darwinism that ascribes virtue to economic success and moral laxness to poverty. They have demonstrated exceptional organizational skills, in addition to their customary flair for fund-raising. They have succeeded in recruiting and electing officials nationwide, uniting in the process evangelical Christians, southern and western blue collar whites, NASCAR dads (and moms), and big business. The grand coalition is held together more by what its members oppose than on the basis of shared experience. The ideological cement is one in which foreign enemies, domestic poverty, minority demands, crime, and homosexuality must be met with stern punishment and religious or quasi-religious orthodoxy. A defensive righteousness stands behind the conservative renaissance.

By the same token, the Democratic Party seems to have forgotten the 1930s. Democrats are inclined to embrace single issues rather than a consistent worldview. They spend more time responding piecemeal to accusations from the right than constructing a proactive path. Many Democrats have drifted toward the center, willingly criticizing liberal orthodoxies and apologizing for past Democratic programs such as the War on Poverty (Edsall, 1989; Reich, 2004; Rieder, 1989; Toner, 2004).

The fissures in the Democratic Party first appeared during the 1968 presidential campaign, when many working class whites in the North as well as the South supported the presidential bid of Alabama's conservative Governor George Wallace. The enthusiasm for Wallace reflected a political backlash against the rapid advance of social policies in the sixties.

A decade later, voters rejected the pessimism of the Carter administration and responded to the uplift orchestrated by Ronald Reagan. A selective repertoire of American values came into play to restore a damaged national pride and legitimize the economic policies of an inspirational leader. Unions were presented as culprits behind the daunting challenges of globalization. Less and less popular, the unions lost membership. Democrats fell almost completely silent in their traditional defense of labor. By the time of the presidential primaries in 2004, the only steadfast supporter of the unions, Senator Richard Gephardt, went down quickly to defeat.

Two other forces contributed to hard times for progressives. Democrats as well as Republicans became increasingly addicted to Political Action Committees and the money these organizations raised from wealthy donors. In addition, polishing the style and message scripted by Ronald Reagan, the Republican Party continued to wrap its policies in the banner of American ideals. Democrats and the left (e.g., Reich, 2004; Toner, 2004) lament that the party took these developments onboard uncritically and lost on both counts. Republican donors generally have deeper pockets, and the merchandizing of values perfected by the Republicans left the Democrats in a painfully defensive posture. On the whole, Democrats failed to connect their side of the policy debate—equal opportunity, workers' rights to decent earnings, rights to health care, fair taxation, and so on—to an equally convincing ideological story. Democratic proposals came out looking rather timid, as if inspired by public opinion polls rather than principle. The party lost contact with its base constituents (Lakoff, 2002).

Some Democrats appear to have accepted the notion that liberalism, social-democratic ideals, and concern for civil rights are un-American. The temptation has been to emulate the competition and to accept a Republican understanding of bedrock American values. Traditional principles of just reward for work, equal opportunity, and democratic participation have been practically erased from the party's memory banks. The weakness of the Democrats in the past decades reflects a failure of political memory and imagination. They have not shown Americans how to take back democracy from increasingly concentrated wealth and power.

Social Work at the End of the Millennium

What impact has the war against welfare and the poor had on social work?

Examining the initiatives of the major association representing the profession during this period suggests a stronger commitment to burnishing professional status and encouraging numerical growth than to resisting the assault on welfare. According to Abramovitz (1998), most social workers remained "strangely silent while the punitive welfare reform bill worked its way through Congress and the state legislatures" (p. 521). For all this, the record also shows a growing interest in social policy issues.

In 1990, the NASW created a classification called School Social Work Specialist, to be followed by other specializations through all state affiliates. This move was modeled on developments in other liberal professions. Along the same lines, the Academy of Certified Baccalaureate Social Workers (ACBSW) was instituted a year later. Another step toward solidifying the status of the profession was the 1996 Supreme Court decision, in *Jaffee v. Redmond*, declaring that social workers in federal courts have rights of privileged information with clients (Barker, 2003).

In a move promoting the old core of casework, the NASW published *The Person in Environment Setting* in 1994. The objective was to enable social workers to classify and code problems of psychosocial health and environmental functioning.

Two years later, the NASW revised its code of ethics to include two principles relevant to justice. The ethical principles stated that social workers challenge social injustice ("social workers pursue social change particularly with and on behalf of vulnerable and oppressed individuals and groups of people") and reaffirmed the social workers' ethical responsibility to the broader society ("social workers should act to prevent and eliminate domination of, and exploitation of, and discrimination against any person, group or class on the basis of race, ethnicity, national origin, color, sex, sexual orientation, age, marital status, political belief, religion or mental or physical disability") (NASW, 1996, pp. 394–396). Social Workers for Peace and Social Justice joined other organizations involved in human rights around the world.

At the outset of the nineties, the CSWE had established a Progressive Symposium. In 1994, the CSWE (1994) included "Promotion of Social and Economic Justice" in its curriculum guidelines:

> [P]rograms of social work must provide an understanding of the dynamics and consequences of social and economic injustice, including all forms of human oppression. They must provide students with skills to promote social change and implement a wide range of interventions that further the achievement of individual and collective and collective and economic justice. Theoretical and practice content must be provided about strategies of intervention for achieving social and economic justice and for combating the causes and effects of institutional forms of oppression.

The possibility that these resolutions regarding the justice roots of social work were more rhetorical and gestural than factual has not escaped several observers (Abramovitz, 1998; Reisch & Andrews, 2001; Wagner, 2000). To be sure, there are members of the profession who live by this ethic, but they continue to be a struggling minority. A review of *Social Work Abstracts* published by NASW Press in 1998 and 1999 reinforces this impression. An astonishingly small percentage—only 4 to 5 percent—of the abstracts address issues related to social change such as welfare or social reform, labor, movements, inequality, structural intervention, political economy, poverty, policy practice, social security, community intervention, organizational change, client–social worker mutuality, unemployment, welfare state, social action, activism, policy, social development, power, entitlement, social control, social resistance, coalitions for change, grassroots initiatives, and indirect social work.

Student interest in community organization and policy practice did not show any marked increase in most schools of social work during the decade. Clinical social work continues to attract the lion's share of students, and job openings are overwhelmingly in this area (Carter et al., 1994; Gibelman, 1995).

Nevertheless, in 1996 and 1997, *Social Work* published more articles on community intervention than before. The two centennial issues of *Social Work* reviewed the history of the profession, stressing the legacy of the two primary goals of individual practice and social reform. In the first issue

(November 1998), a few papers dealt with the integration of the two paths. Despite protestations to the effect that the two goals were reconcilable, no blueprint for their integration was forthcoming.

Two interesting examples were the articles of Swenson (1998) and Abramovitz (1998). The first paper argued that clinical social work contributed to social justice by liberating people from their private oppressions, from the consequences of their own privileged position, and from prejudices toward others. In the process of this transformation, clients are empowered. In this interaction with clients, the clinical social worker will share his or her definition of social justice and encourage the experience of mutual help. Furthermore, the clinical social worker engages in planning and advocating services for the clients, keeping in check his or her use of expertise, and works to transform the agency in a truly democratic setting.

Abramovitz's article gives a history of social work activists, covering their ambitions for structural change in the direction of an egalitarian and participatory society. The essay presents a very different definition of social justice. Abramovitz reveals how social work activism and its impact have been contained by structural tensions. One has involved the contradiction between adjustment to an unjust social order and an attempt to change that order. Another, related problem involves the demands for professional status within an unjust order. Still another impediment stems from a repressive political context that hinders mobilization for social change. While both Swenson and Abramovitz conclude with appeals for integration, they have quite different definitions of social justice. Abramovitz ends by exhorting the profession to become a site of political struggle.

Radical social workers in the 1990s were closer to Abramovitz's point of view. Their ideology did not change, but some moved closer to operational ways of affecting social policy. Already convinced that the inherent inequity of capitalism and the weakness of labor underpin most social problems, they added the conviction that the profession's devotion to clinical and therapeutic approaches makes it the handmaiden of the status quo. Martha Spinks, a social worker with the military, expressed the belief that true social work is "consciousness raising and community work, while clinical practice is a flaccid permutation of psychiatry" (quoted in Reisch & Andrews, 2001, p. 216). Ann Withorn, a University of Massachusetts faculty member and a leader of the Bertha C. Reynolds Society, views professionalism, with its hierarchical structure, career requirements, and status aspirations, as a major barrier to political and social structural change (Reisch & Andrews, 2001, p. 204).

Significantly, in 1990, the Bertha C. Reynolds Society changed its name to the Welfare Action Association. It was the only social work organization to join demonstrations against the 1996 welfare reform. However, concrete operational suggestions for reforming welfare short of wholesale structural transformation were absent.

The radical component of social work has changed, in several instances, from fighting class oppression to combating gender, race, and sexual-orientation discrimination. Activism based on identity politics has had a fragmenting effect, as happened with the integration of multiculturalism in mainstream social work. It tends to accentuate differences rather than communalities. Energies get diverted from structural approaches that encompass a variety of oppressive mechanisms.

Empowerment strategies in social work have also undergone a metamorphosis that has distanced the profession from social change. Activists borrowed the term from the radical lexicon, where it meant gaining resources for social change. Now mainstream social work uses the term to signify a psychological feeling of efficacy, potency, or self-esteem. Whatever the partial overlap between them, the two understandings are pretty distinct. Psychological empowerment might well prompt individuals to accept their own strengths and shape their lives accordingly without, however, leading them to social action or to construct avenues that foster such an engagement. Self-realization and social reform are different things (Figueira-McDonough, 2001, p. 156).

The "new" radicalism argues for a transformative dynamics of practice. These features press toward the formulation of anti-oppressive strategies, based on a dialogue and increasing consciousness among workers and clients about the causes of inequality. The beneficial side of radical social work is often credited with driving the profession to adopt liberal and humanistic directions (Fabricant & Burghardt, 1992; Van Soetz, 1992).

An alternative interpretation is that organized social work gives lip service to radical ideas, then domesticates them in light of a path it has followed for most of its history. The marginal status of radicals in social work has kept them from political discussion of policy and from having an impact on social change (Wagner, 1989). Radical social workers tend to maintain ties with grassroots organizations and other movements to promote their goals. This corresponds to a dialectical radicalism, intentionally reformist, based on power from below and strategic interventions. It does not place a premium on single, overarching solutions (Mullaly, 1997; Reisch & Andrews, 2001).

Reintegrating politics into practice, as Abramovitz (1998) advocates, implies a version of politics beyond a competition between groups within the system. It entails a struggle to change the entire political and economic structure. This not only means a visionary desire to achieve big, predefined ends, but it also requires calibrating ends by exposing injustice and by proposing alternatives that can be evaluated. It requires feedback. In sum, this type of activism depends on the translation of justice into specific policies and concrete modes of intervention (Parenti, 1988). As Titmuss (1967) proposed nearly 50 years ago, this means creating social policies that address selective needs within a universalistic framework.

There are other obstacles that blunt the impact of radicals on the profession and social policy, besides their numerical marginality. The cult of individualism and a belief in the supremacy of the American way are powerful barriers. Reform proposals that appear to deviate from, or are labeled as deviating from, these givens of national identity, swim against a very strong current. The economic success of the United States and its superpower status reflect, according to this logic, superior values and civilization. The country is simply further along the evolutionary scale. With the dissolution of the Soviet Union and the fall of communist regimes in Eastern and Central Europe, the idea that democratic capitalist societies, with the United States in the lead, represent the apotheosis of civilization appeared to be confirmed (Fukuyama, 1992). Chua (2003) traces much of the missionary zeal of the United States in exporting democracy and laissez-faire capitalism to this creed. Her research indicates, however, that some of these crusades have foundered, out of ignorance of other cultures, and have ended up consolidating oligarchies or inciting tribal disorder.

Part II: Suggestions for Exercises _____

_____ The Utility of Documentaries for Historical Analysis

"The past is another country," historians are fond of noting. In fact, history often seems distant, and it is frequently hard to grasp the impact of events on our ancestors.

As it happens, there are excellent documentaries in the field of welfare that help us make these connections. Below is a short list of videos that many professors of social policy, including myself, have found useful in bringing history alive and at the same time encouraging conceptual analysis. These are just a few examples. Many other documentary sources exist.

> PBS documentary, "The Great Depression," Part 4 in *The Emergence of Modern America*
>
> White House Central Films, *The War on Poverty, 1964–1968* (35mm, 16 reels with printed guide)
>
> Frederick Wiseman, *Welfare* (1975)
>
> Michael Moore, *Roger and Me* (1989)
>
> CBS *Face the Nation,* "Welfare Reform" (1995)

Class Discussion for Each Historical Period Reported in the Documentaries

Some possible questions related to the historical analytic framework are the following:

- What aspects of the documentary revealed unknown facts to the students?
- How were the origins of poverty or oppression presented?
- How did the subjects speak about their needs and claims?

- How did the observers (advocates, service workers and decision makers, bosses) interpret their needs and claims? Which ideologies were reflected in those interpretations?
- How did authorities react to the claims of the oppressed?
- Which programs and policies were used to respond to those experiencing the problem? Were these the most effective? Can you think about others that would make more sense? Explain why more effective ways were not adopted.
- Which groups were on the side of the most vulnerable? Which against?

Written Exams

Comparison of differences or similarities between periods concerning the following:

Dominant ideologies

The structures of welfare

Existence or nonexistence of labor and social advocacy groups

Institutional rigidities

Paper

Ask students to obtain the syllabus of an introductory social work course on Human Behavior and the Social Environment (HBSE). Two readings should be selected from the syllabus, one with greater implications for direct practice and another with greater implications for social change.

The first part of the paper should analyze each reading, making the connection between the assumptions about the nature of the problem and the outcome of the intervention. The second part should give a quick assessment of the ratio of syllabus readings relevant to direct intervention versus macro intervention. A discussion of the criteria of evaluation used should be given.

The concluding part of the paper should entail suggestions about the syllabus. Should it or should it not be changed? Justifications for one position or the other should be presented.

PART III

The Lesser Americans: Historical Legacies

It is not by denying the existence of difference that one must fight difference but by modifying our image of normal.

—Giuseppe Pontiglia (2002, p. 25)

The Story of a Limited Democracy

The history of welfare in the United States has followed an uncertain, even erratic, course. Its late start and periodic regressions reflect the influence of three powerful factors: a deeply rooted ideology of individualism, extraordinarily sticky institutional path dependence, and a federal government under centrifugal pressure from the states and business interests.

Broadly speaking, the ingredients of the dominant ideology were twofold. Values such as self-reliance nurtured by the first settlers shaped an embryonic American identity. Novel political and philosophical ideas, crafted by Enlightenment thinkers in Europe, also impacted on the experiment that gave birth to a new republic.

Modern for its time, the culture proved to be exceptionally long lasting. It was a distinctive amalgam that outlived the specific conditions in which it arose. At least until the early years of the twentieth century, the country was relatively isolated, and this insulation from Old Europe, together with breakneck rates of economic development, seemed to validate the idea of a triumphant Americanism. The American Dream persisted through times when expediency and pragmatism dictated deviations from these ideals, and it held on even among society's losers (De Grazia, 1951; McDougall, 2004). The hybrid ethos was both widely popular and durable. It took on a life of its own.

This dynamic vision meant that democracy was bound up with the demographic and political hegemony of the Americans who shaped the first new nation (Mink, 1990). In the early years, citizenship was a formal expression of autonomy. In practice, it ratified male independence. Citizenship in this sense was endowed with property ownership, the right to bear arms, and self-employment (Okin, 1989). This restricted right to participation was a borrowing from Europe, from the German philosopher Georg Wilhelm Friedrich Hegel, that quickly took root in North America. Hegel felt that since a couple united in marriage shared the same interests, the husband could act on behalf of all family members. They were his dependents, to whom he was linked, as they were to him, by love (Pateman, 1988).

The story of women's dependence in the United States starts with this limited reading of democracy. Manhood stood opposed to womanhood. It was a short step from gender ideology of this stamp to the construction of a racially demarcated citizenship. The notions of servility and dependence ascribed to women were easily transferred to ethnic males. Their servitude was a sign of inadequacy, be it of the black man, the Asian coolie, the seasonal Mexican laborer, or the Native American. All were "people who never conceived the idea of independent manhood" (Mink, 1990, p. 96). They were, like women, weak. By the nineteenth century, American democracy had taken the politics of subordination and exclusion fully on board. Segregation, cultural regulation, barriers to suffrage, and brutal suppression of unions were "just common sense."

Simply attributing discrimination and the social control foisted on women and minorities to a patriarchal inheritance can be misleading. "Patriarchy" is a term derived from the ecclesiastical world. It connotes fatherly love, family solidarity, organic community, and fixed relationships. None of these properties accurately describes the modern practice of white male supremacy. Moreover, the patriarchy label obscures significant historical change driven by the resistance of women and minorities.

Invoking "capitalism" as an exclusive predictor of discrimination against women or "women-like" men has the same problem. After all, gender discrimination has thrived in certain planned economies, and some market economies have achieved remarkable gender equality and human justice. The dynamics of capitalism, if not regulated, *do* create large inequalities, including gender and ethnic inequalities. But this differs from the claim that capitalism, or patriarchy, is the sole cause of such outcomes.

Structural arguments can be deceptively neat. Gordon (1990) points out that their schematic rigidity forces functional explanations on complex events. Whatever rationality welfare programs may appear to have is reduced to a charade played out to satisfy the interests of powerful groups. Welfare policy in the real world, she argues, is more likely to be the product of the interaction of historical circumstances and power compromises that elude single-factor explanations. It is not routinely predictable or explicable in terms of just one or another "cause of all causes." The disempowerment associated with welfare in the United States is a joint result of class, gender, and racial discrimination.

Chapters 9 and 10 examine how the welfare policies described in Chapters 4 through 8 have affected women and minorities of color.

9

Women and the Welfare State

Woman's place is home, and she must not be forbidden to dwell there. . . . For woman's work is race preservation, race improvement and who opposes her or interferes with her, simply fights nature and nature never loses her battles.

—Rheta Childe Dorr (1910)

Most social policy aimed at women has kept their roles as wives and mothers plainly in view. It has been designed particularly to benefit those dependent on them. Women exist, in effect, to benefit others. This helps explain why women have been treated as second-class citizens for so long, and why the struggle for gender equality has been so drawn out. The feminist movement and revisionist research have positioned gender at the core of policy analysis, and gender has been accepted as an analytic category.

The fixation on traditional gender roles and functions blocked women from political and economic participation. It imprisoned them in a private sphere controlled by others in the off-limits world of masculine accomplishment. How were women's needs met when they were forced out, or willingly left, or refused to enter that enclave in the first place, in the times before the growth of welfare? And what happened "after welfare"? Answering these questions turns up evidence of both entrenched discrimination and resistance.

The Preindustrial Period

The family had enormous importance in America at the time of colonization. Small clusters of newcomers had to put down roots in a strange and often inhospitable land. Trying to scratch out a living from the rocky soil of New England was particularly difficult, and rural life was not much easier in the hardscrabble lands to the south, in Maryland and Virginia.

The settlers depended for survival on family solidarity. The new world permitted quite a bit of freedom from institutional regulations, but it also fostered a strict family hierarchy. Religious custom, traditional family laws, and economic hardship conspired to open a path with men unquestionably in the lead. The man—or the ideal image of him—was a husband over his wife, a father over his children, a father figure for any other dependents, and the master of his servants. All family members were subordinate to the male head. Sacred scripture, nature, and family tradition justified the subordination of wives, who were not allowed to own property or to enter into contracts. They also ran up against legal impediments with inheritance and, in the rare cases of divorce, they faced the loss of their offspring to the father (Shapiro, 1990).

In an agricultural, work-intensive society, with high mortality rates at delivery, the reproductive role of women was literally vital. Wives were also partners in production, although the tasks allotted them were mostly "women's work." Socialization was also gender-specialized. Mothers trained daughters in domestic crafts and suitably female agricultural chores. Fathers did the same with sons, with an emphasis on hunting, plowing, the clearing of land, and carpentry (Wertheimer, 1977).

In a preindustrial environment, women without ties to a family were extremely vulnerable. Those who did not marry, or were deserted by their husbands, or had children out of wedlock, or were widowed were marginalized. To one degree or another, they did not fit.

White indentured servants, free black women, and recent immigrants were at highest risk. Once freed, indentured white women could marry. But it was often the case that they did not; economically, most of them were not good catches. At times they bore the illegitimate children of their bosses. Some entered into forbidden mixed marriages. Such women were despised. They were irredeemably undeserving, and in certain states their mixed-blood children would not escape slavery. The system of poor laws in the North treated impoverished black women and men as the lowest of the low. Often they were hired out to slave owners (Mohl, 1971).

In colonial America, as long as geographic mobility and rates of poverty were modest, communities handled paupers charitably through a variety of foster-care procedures. But by the middle of the seventeenth century, poverty increased. Landless tenant farmers and husbandless women flocked to the cities, joining the unemployed. In some towns, women comprised between one-quarter and one-third of the poor; most of them were without husbands. In Boston, it was reported that over 83 percent of widows were in need of economic relief (Nash, 1979, p. 172).

Towns kept a watchful eye on the residence requirement of the poor laws in order to avoid the expense of giving relief to strangers. Self-sufficiency and moral character were taken into account when evaluating applications for resident status. Families and able-bodied men went to the front of the line. Among husbandless women, widows were favored. Women who did not pass these checkpoints were sent back either to the towns of their husbands or to their places of origin (Kelso, 1969, p. 76). Black women, to whom family criteria were not applied at all, were viewed mostly as laborers.

There were several categories of deserving poor white women: widows, wives of the sick or disabled, wives of temporarily unproductive husbands, sick women, or those unable to work because they had to care for young children. These women often boarded with families at public expense.

By the end of the eighteenth century, indoor relief became more common. The system hinged on the principle that shelter should be provided in exchange for work. Indoor relief was the fate of the poorest of the poor, as it was for those considered undeserving. Statistics from the Boston workhouse showed that by the middle of the eighteenth century, nearly 60 percent of the adults admitted were women, and nearly one-third were husbandless mothers (Rothman, D., 1971, pp. 39–40). Workhouse children could be separated from their mothers for a series of moral reasons, unruly behavior, and the like, or simply because of destitution (Jernegan, 1931a, p. 180).

By the 1750s, the treatment of blacks, free as well as slave, had deteriorated. The liberties enjoyed by free blacks shrunk. The few social and economic rights granted to slaves were withdrawn. They were forbidden to marry. They were prohibited from inheriting property. Regardless of the father's status, the children of slave women were automatically enslaved.

Slaves resisted this inhuman treatment in a daring series of insurrections. Each insurrection was brutally quashed, and each was followed by further restrictions. Slaves were forbidden to assemble, to have weapons, to beat drums (this was a means of communication), to buy liquor, to leave their plantation without a pass, to testify in court, to serve on a jury, and so on (Abramovitz, 1996a, pp. 96–98).

Economic and Social Restructuring

Originally, "factories" were nothing more than warehouses—depots for storing all sorts of goods. Manufacturing in the modern sense (the cutting-edge industry was textiles) began to take off toward the end of the eighteenth century. The best-sellerdom of Adam Smith's *The Wealth of Nations*, promoting free market competition as the road to development, coincided with the American Revolution. Industrialization on a grand scale dominated the nineteenth century. The reconfiguration of the labor market and the urbanization that accompanied it had a huge impact on family structure.

This mammoth transformation triggered panic at the prospect of the dissolution of the family. Fixation on a single type of family as the norm lasted into the twentieth century, years after the self-sustaining family with multiple functions had disappeared. Drawing on research conducted in the 1920s and 1930s, Ogburn (1953) and Wirth (1933) dramatically portray this metamorphosis. The family lost its functions as a unit of production, and it was no longer a primary center of socialization, education, religion, or health maintenance. It was increasingly dependent on outside organizations—on factories, formal education facilities, hospitals, and Sunday schools. All this signaled the debility and eventual demise of the nuclear family. Visions of an *anomic* future—one populated by young people without moral values—threatened the socioeconomic order.

The Construction of the Nuclear Family

Rather than empowering them, the transformation of the traditional family further restricted women. Their sole functions were to reproduce and to take care of their husbands and children. This became the proper role of good women. Only the man would have to compete in the world of work, to earn a "living wage," enough to provide for his entire family while his wife stayed at home. In principle, this division of labor was supposed to amplify the role of women as supports for present and future workers. The home would be reinvented as "a haven in a heartless world." The ideal of domesticity was born, and it became a shrine for the nuclear family.

"Womanhood" was a confining model. The scope of women's responsibilities narrowed, and the power imbalance between the genders deepened. In a burgeoning consumer society, only men had access to and control over economic resources. Their wives became even more dependent on spousal goodwill than when they were partners in an agricultural economy.

The sequestration of women reflected their psychological and "natural," biological nature. Ministers, educators, advice manuals, and sentimental novels cast devotional incense around the cult of domesticity and true womanhood (Ryan, 1975, pp. 142–143). Although women did not have legal control over their own children, motherhood was the paragon of femininity, and it rested on a pedestal of perfect virtue.

Women in the Workforce: Exploitation and Resistance

In theory, the economic foundation of the nuclear family was the "living" or family wage. In practice, this was a wishful fiction, given the paltry incomes of most workers.

From the early 1800s on, many women entered the labor force. In 1816, for example, women and children made up two-thirds of the nation's cotton mill workers. In 1844, an estimated 10 percent of all women, of all ages, worked for wages, nearly half of these in manufacturing jobs. In 1855, one-fourth to one-third of married immigrant women worked outside the home, and by 1870, an estimated 15 percent of all adult females did (Jones, J., 1985; Kennedy, 1979; Kessler-Harris, 1982). In spite of the fact that men headed between 70 and 90 percent of black families, black women participated in the labor force at a rate triple that of white women. Among married black women, the percentage was six times higher (Gutman, 1983).

The idealized household was a cultural success. It became hegemonic, whatever the realities of female labor force participation. Middle class white women absorbed the soothing myth of the nuclear family. So did the small black middle class, and many poor women aspired to the norm. Since poor married women could not survive without working, they frequently chose to bring work home. They did piecework, did washing and sewing for others, and received boarders. Comparatively affluent white women made themselves into ladies of leisure, cultivating social and cultural graces, and delegating women's chores to their female domestic staff.

Sheer need, together with social conventions that demeaned female work outside the home, combined to cheapen the value of poor women's labor. They carried a double burden. Subordinate within the household, they were exploited as workers. Their wages were low and their working conditions unsavory.

Resistance to their predicament surfaced as early as 1825 in a series of strikes, work confrontations, and alliances with supportive organizations. The United Tailoresses Society in New York went on strike, demanding a wage hike. Two years later, another strike took place, this time in New Hampshire, against degrading factory conditions. Seamstresses in New York, Boston, and Philadelphia followed up these actions with strikes of their own. New England, the center of the textile industry, was a flash point for female workers. In 1833, in Massachusetts, the Female Society of Lynn and Vicinity for the Protection and Promotion of Female Industry came into being, and the Lowell Female Reform Association promoted a 10-day work stoppage to protest against pay cuts (Dublin, 1979; Kessler-Harris, 1982).

Prior to emancipation, black women in the South participated in work slowdowns and helped run the Underground Railroad. Many refused to breed slave children. They joined slave revolts in Virginia in the early 1800s, in South Carolina and, in 1822, some threw themselves into Nat Turner's insurrection. After 1865 and emancipation, black women organized a washerwomen's labor organization in Mississippi to establish a standard rate for their work (Jones, J., 1985).

From 1827 to the eve of the Civil War, blacks in the North reacted against legal impositions through a series of meetings in the cities where they had settled. Middle class black women started up a variety of mutual aid societies calling for abolition. They founded schools in their neighborhoods, and fought problems created by discrimination in work and housing (Davis, A., 1983).

Middle class white women also mobilized. They fought in state legislatures for equitable property laws for married women. The first female Anti-Slavery Society emerged in 1837 from the Convention of American Women, and the 1848 Women's Rights Convention in Seneca, in upstate New York, marked the start of the women's movement. Its platform demanded property rights for women and equal social opportunities (McGlen & O'Connor, 1983).

Cheap labor fueled industrialization. Pay was low, work irregular, unemployment frequent, and control over working conditions nonexistent. The chances of accidents were extremely high. Many workers traveled in search of jobs, leaving their families and communities. The number of widows, women with handicapped husbands, and abandoned women grew, as did the number of female paupers (Gordon, 1994).

According to the 1823 Yates survey in New York, public aid alone comprised one-fourth of the city's expenditures, covering 17 percent of the population. Fifty-two percent of all paupers were women. Twenty-five percent of these were widows or deserted wives, while 30 percent were recent immigrants. An 1820 survey in Philadelphia found that 25 percent of the paupers were wives whose husbands had deserted them. Ten years later, all the women helped by the Philadelphia Female Hospitable Society were widows or deserted wives (Matthaei, 1982; Mohl, 1971).

As need increased, policies towards the poor took on a selective and punitive edge. Relief measures reflected the conventional wisdom that character flaws and immorality were root causes of poverty. Indoor relief became less common, and there was a correspondingly greater reliance on workhouses. Derelicts, the destitute, and assorted idlers and slackers were to be rehabilitated by forcing them to work. The punitive features of indoor relief became even harsher after the Civil War. Conditions were so demeaning that it seemed their ultimate rationale was to protect the non-poor from the poor. More and more husbandless women whose records showed that they had been impoverished for a long time, entered poorhouses. Their children were often taken away and either institutionalized or forced to work in contracts that the poorhouses had with private manufacturers.

Poverty was seen as resulting from a weak work ethic and, in the case of women, from an insufficient commitment to the family ethic. This was the logic behind the appalling treatment meted out to the poor. Widows might escape censure, but women who were husbandless through desertion or divorce, or who remained single, deviated from the nuclear family norm. By definition, therefore, they were undeserving.

This stigma extended to their presumed ineptitude as mothers. Such dysfunction was felt to be the source of other problems as well—in particular, juvenile delinquency. Removal of children from toxic family settings was the indicated remedy. Private voluntary organizations, staffed by middle class white women, focused on deserving poor families, in line with the individual rehabilitative theories of the day. More effort was put into counseling families than into helping them materially. The reasoning, inspired by the Malthusian doctrine that making things easier for the poor only encouraged them in their profligate ways, seemed bizarre at times, though it made a certain sense given the fusion of religious and economic righteousness. Not giving alms to women and children to relieve their misery would motivate husbands to assume their role as providers (Putnam, M., 1887). Blaming women for economic and social failures opened a path that persisted into the twentieth century.

The First Two Decades of the Twentieth Century

The women's movement became more assertive toward the end of the nineteenth century. Women fought for mothers' pensions, the extension of suffrage, labor laws that would protect female workers, and maternal and child health programs. Together with groups of social reformers, these women professed that poverty was the result of *social* evils beyond the control of individuals, who should therefore be protected from suffering they were not responsible for bringing on themselves (Brenner, R., 1964). Many women activists eventually joined the Progressive movement.

Photo 9.1   Textile Workers

Source: From the private collection of Peter McDonough.

Photo 9.2   Workplace Clean-Up

Source: From the private collection of Peter McDonough.

Photo 9.3   A Settlement House Worker

Source: From the private collection of Peter McDonough.

Like white women, women of color had mobilized since the end of the nineteenth century. The movements shared many emancipatory goals, but the historical legacy of African Americans shaped some of their priorities and strategies differently.

Black women's groups focused on welfare and discrimination. Black male activists were almost entirely absorbed with the struggle for economic opportunity, in order to live up to their role as providers. This left the leadership of many civic organizations open mainly to black women. Their first priority was education. These civic leaders made up a privileged elite within their community and looked on the lower classes as a force in need of improvement. However, they were aware that race in the United States constituted a steeper hierarchy than class. The routine refusal of white women's organizations to allow black women to participate or cooperate with them confirmed this insight (Gordon, 1994).

Black activists supported marriage, sexual morality, and motherhood, but not maternal policies. With a history of working outside the home, they favored women's participation in the labor market, and they demanded that males do a fair share of housework. Black women of all classes lacked political power, and they faced widespread discrimination. Participants gathered strength by way of common experiences—as educated women, as community leaders, and as church members. As respect for their leadership grew and as racism softened a bit, black women joined with some southern white evangelists to create the Commission on Interracial Cooperation, and they had an important role in the establishment of the Urban League in Chicago. In association with the YWCA, they helped develop programs for young black women (Gordon, 1994).

This sort of activism was unique among minorities of color. Among Mexican Americans and Native Americans, organizing on such a scale was very uncommon. Traditionally, Mexican American women handled problems through the extended family and volunteer organizations tied to the Catholic Church. The tribal and kinship arrangements of Native Americans were not conducive to volunteer organizations. Central to their lives were the programs of the Bureau of Indian Affairs, shortsighted as their policies might have been. Because Native Americans were overwhelmingly rural, the Agricultural Extension Service, created in 1914, might have triggered social activism among women. In fact, the reverse was true. Since its initiation, the program followed gender-specific guidelines. In the process, it managed to ignore the fact that, among poor farm families, gender lines were frequently crossed, either because of cultural habits or because of a need to adapt to difficult times (Schackel, 1992).

Eventually, social policies were put in place that were cognizant of women's work in and outside the home. Protective labor laws for female workers, mothers' pensions, and, for a short time, maternal and child health programs all exemplified protective legislation that had both positive and unforeseen negative consequences. In 1908, the Supreme Court cut the legal maximum workday for women to 10 hours. State legislatures were lobbied for higher wages and safer conditions. By the end of 1917, a total of 41 states had passed laws limiting the hours of work and night work. They had also fixed limits on women lifting heavy objects. One unanticipated byproduct of the legal upsurge was to justify the barring of women from certain occupations. This segregation of labor by gender is at the root of the male–female disparity in wages and in compensation for "noncomparable" work. Women have been fighting against this asymmetry since the 1960s.

The concentration of women in certain jobs and the anti-woman and anti-black policies of the largest union, the American Federation of Labor, prompted female workers to develop their own protective leagues—notably, the Women's Trade Union League (WTUL), a federation of women's union and middle class sympathizers. When the Knights of Labor, a national organization, opened its doors to women and blacks, 5,000 signed up. In Chicago, unions organized 35,000 women in 26 trades, and several walkouts and strikes demonstrated the women's will to protect themselves. Twenty thousand shirtwaist makers in New York staged a walkout for 13 weeks. Forty thousand garment workers struck in Chicago. In 1912, textile workers in Lawrence, Massachusetts, also went on strike. Women were at the center of the action, which became known as the "bread and roses" strike (Abramovitz, 1996a; Watson, 2005; Wertheimer, 1977). The designation was inspired by a woman's sign that read, "We want bread, but we want roses, too!"

The increasing numbers of working women who were married—24 percent of all working women and 11 percent of all married women—worried policy makers. The fact that 15 percent of these women were widowed or divorced mothers especially bothered them. They feared that the employment of mothers affected children negatively. This struck at the heart of the nuclear family ideal. The purpose of mothers' pensions was to give cash aid to indigent mothers so that they could stay home and care for their children.

In sum, two criteria, both reinforcing the family ethic, kept these women within the camp of the deserving poor: First, they had belonged to a legitimate family. Second, their primary role—mothering—was in jeopardy. Poor women who failed to meet these criteria fell beyond the pale, and they were denied public support.

Between 1911 and 1921, a total of 40 states adopted the Mothers' Pension Program. However, because it was not mandatory, implementation varied greatly. In the South, black women who would have met the requirements elsewhere were for the most part denied access to the program. In other places, white widows were favored. Few divorcees or separated mothers were helped. Everywhere, cash benefits were very low. Miserly payments defeated the purpose of preventing mothers from working. As late as 1931, an estimated 96 percent of the recipients were white, most of them Anglos (Bell, 1965).

Settlement houses played an important role in helping immigrant women without much access to public programs. While some of their services echoed the gendered division of labor in the nuclear family and promoted training for gender-segregated occupations, they also ran nurseries, which poor working mothers desperately needed. Furthermore, because the leaders of some of these settlement houses had strong ties with the labor movement, they were instrumental in training working women in strategies of resistance. Black middle class women, well experienced in self-help, built various organizations and programs to assist their working sisters. The National League for Protection of Colored Women, the National Association of Colored Women, and programs coordinated by the National Urban League are the outstanding examples. These organizations offered a variety of services: employment assistance, recreation, health, nutrition, housing, and day nurseries (Abramovitz, 1996a).

The Place of Women in the New Deal _____

> The man loses his job, cannot find another, then leaves. The older children try to get money, fail and leave or are taken to community farms. The mother stays with the little children, helped by charity, until they too are sucked under by the diminishing whole and the growing terror.
>
> —Meridel LeSueur (1982),
> cited in Abramovitz (1996a, p. 220)

Progressives rethought poverty in the wake of the devastating depression at the end of the nineteenth century. Likewise, the impulse for the New Deal came out of the Great Depression of the 1930s. A historical analysis of three of the programs institutionalized by the 1935 Social Security Act shows unequal treatment of gender in relief.

Old-Age Insurance

Retirement insurance is the program that comes closest to universal coverage in the United States. From the outset, the program of old-age insurance has been regressive. FICA rates are flat, and withholding is absent entirely at the highest income tiers. In 1942, only half of the workforce was covered. Women and minority workers figured heavily among the excluded. A wide array of occupations involving domestics, government workers, workers in nonprofit organizations, and farm labor were simply not covered.

The selective impact of the exclusions stands out as soon as the areas in which women and minorities worked are pinpointed. Around this time, just under 30 (29.6) percent of female workers fell in the domestic and personal service category. Nearly two-thirds (62.5 percent) of those designated as domestics were black. Among the 8.5 percent classified as agricultural laborers—a sector that totaled 4 million workers—62.7 percent were black females and 40.7 percent were black males. The same held true for Mexican Americans, who constituted the vast majority of agricultural labor in the Southwest. Other exclusions affected 14.2 percent of professional workers, 18 percent of clerical workers, and 0.2 percent of public servants. These took in white female professions: teachers, nurses, social workers, and secretaries. Among nonprofit organizations alone, where 6 out of 10 employees were female, 1.8 million women were not entitled to Social Security (Wandersee, 1981).

Between 1932 and 1937, Section 213 of the Federal Economic Act curtailed the employment of married women by allowing only one member of the same family to work in the civil service. Conceivably, this was a fair way of distributing scarce jobs, but the provision also reflected an anxiety about working wives (Abramovitz, 1996a).

By 1930, an estimated 11 percent of all married women worked. By 1940, the figure had jumped to 15.5 percent. The trend was often blamed for aggravating the scarcity of jobs for men. Some Social Security regulations—the failure to cover mainly female occupations, and the exclusion of low-wage jobs and discontinuous work from benefits—can be understood as devices to discourage married women from entering the labor market (Wandersee, 1981).

The original Society Security Act of 1935 gave widows of entitled workers only a lump sum upon their husbands' death. A 1939 amendment provided supplementary grants to the members of a retired or deceased worker's family. This was in line with the image of women as dependent homemakers; it paid homage to the norm of the nuclear family. There was a catch, however. More and more wives were working to supplement household incomes. However, upon retirement, they had to choose between their work benefits or their dependent benefits, even if they paid into Social Security during the time they had been employed. Because of the gender gap in wages, dependent benefits were more generous, so women forfeited what they had paid into the system of old-age insurance. The message was clear: wives would be better off as homemakers than wage earners.

The "widow gap" was another example of gender bias in early legislation. It stood as an indicator of how women were valued mainly for their reproductive function. Widows were entitled to the benefits of their husbands until their youngest child reached 16 or when they themselves turned 65. This worked against younger widows, who probably would be middle-aged when their entitlement ran out. At that age, decent work would be hard to come by.

Conversely, upon the death of a working wife, the husband and the children would not be entitled to dependents' benefits. This was finally corrected in 1950. But widowers still had to pass a "support test" to establish their financial dependence on their wives. Their own contribution had to be one-quarter or less of the couple's income. Only in the 1970s, responding to vociferous demands from women activists, did the Supreme Court outlaw some of these regulations as discriminatory and allow full dual entitlement (Abramovitz, 1996a).

The right of divorced women to benefits was recognized in 1965, and retired spousal and widows' benefits were extended to divorced women. Still, eligibility tests—length of marriage, for example, and marital status at the time of application—had to be met. In 1977, the same rights were extended to divorced men. These rules were further liberalized in the 1980s for divorced couples over 62 years of age (Abramovitz, 1996a).

By 1981, over half—52 percent—of all women worked. Women made up 43 percent of the civilian labor force. The number of women receiving benefits on the basis of their own participation in the labor market grew significantly. Despite this progress, inequality among retirees actually got worse, driven by the gender and wage gaps prevalent during their years of employment. The greater likelihood that white males enjoyed public benefits supplemented by private pensions exacerbated the problem. Retirees depending exclusively on Social Security were seven times more apt to be poor than those drawing on private pensions as well. African American women received the lowest Social Security benefits, in spite of their higher and more continuous participation in the workforce, compared to white women (Flynn, E., 2002).

The eighties were marked not only by an anti-welfare administration but also by worries about what appeared to be the looming insolvency of Social Security. The budgetary catastrophe apparently just over the horizon was attributed in part to the cost-of-living adjustments (COLA) launched by Nixon, in tandem with the inexorable aging of the population.

These fears resulted in some steps backward, although the steps were not as large as they might have been, thanks to the political muscle of increasingly numerous retirees, largely represented by the American Association of Retired Persons. Nevertheless, the changes hurt both women and minorities:

- The minimum grant received by low-income and occasional workers was cut. This hit three-quarters of female beneficiaries negatively. Only 20 percent of women 65 and older had private pensions, as compared to 43 percent of men. Many women were forced to seek public assistance, where they faced both the stigma and the stinginess of such programs.
- The widow's gap was widened, affecting nearly two-thirds of poor families, 20 percent of which were black. The maximum age of the youngest child assuring a widow's benefit was rolled back 2 years, from 18 to 16.
- The maximum age for student benefits was decreased from 21 to 18.
- The timing of cost-of-living adjustments went from every 6 months to once a year, thereby restricting the COLA as a hedge against inflation.

On the positive side, coverage was at last extended to employees of federal, state, and local governments and to nonprofit organizations—all sectors employing high proportions of women (Abramovitz, 1996a).

The recent push for the privatization of retirement, a movement that gained momentum in the 1990s, includes tax-favored IRAs (Individual Retirement Accounts). The option is seductive in a period of economic growth. In principle, the policy does not discriminate directly by gender and race, but as a practical matter it leaves behind those without surplus savings to invest. Women and minorities are disproportionately in low-wage sectors where the fraction of income available for investment, over and above immediate consumption, is small.

Unemployment Insurance

Roosevelt's emergency programs were the antecedents of unemployment insurance. They were urgent responses to the disastrous loss of jobs in the Depression. The measures were an acknowledgment that workers needed some protection from the fluctuations of the market.

Evidence of discrimination against women and people of color cropped up in emergency programs. While the Federal Emergency Relief Administration (FERA) helped twice as many blacks as whites, the reverse was true in terms of the respective poor populations. Because so many blacks were poor, the proportion of blacks reached by such assistance was much lower than the corresponding proportion for whites. The difference was accentuated to the extent that the programs favored male heads of households, while women headed two-fifths of poor black households. The WPA—the Works Progress Administration—turned down black and Mexican American applicants at higher rates than it did whites, and there was an inclination to assign skilled black and Hispanic workers who were accepted to unskilled jobs.

In predominantly Mexican American and Native American areas, gender discrimination was evident. Women were typically assigned to sewing and weaving, activities that paid much lower than the work that men did, and they had their days of work reduced arbitrarily (Schackel, 1992).

By accepting local wage rates, FERA aggravated the racial wage gap, especially because most blacks lived in the South. The Civilian Conservation Corps (CCC) maintained segregated camps for young men and excluded young women altogether (Salmond, 1967). By setting high acreage totals on land that qualified as big enough to receive aid, the Agricultural Adjustment Agency (AAA) displaced large numbers of black farmers (Howard, D., 1943).

In spite of inequities due to differences in implementation across the states, unemployment insurance covered more and more jobless workers up to the mid-1970s. Coverage rose from 16 percent of the unemployed in 1939 to 85 percent in the 1970s. But when unemployment rose during the recession of the early 1980s, coverage dropped. The free fall can be tied to Reagan's policies of slicing loans to the states with excessive unemployment and imposing federal taxes on low benefits.

The model of unemployment insurance continued to be based on a full-time male worker. This flew in the face of the reality that women increasingly were part of the labor force, while bearing a disproportionate share of family responsibilities. Rules that exempted employers from participation in the program regarding part-time workers, and exclusions based on discontinuous work, significantly undercut the access of women to unemployment benefits. If women had to take time off to cope with a family crisis, this was classified as a voluntary absence from the job. Up until the passage of the 1978 Pregnancy Discrimination Act, expectant mothers could be denied or dismissed from work.

By 1973, an estimated 9 out of 10 uncovered workers fell into three occupational groups, in which women, blacks, and Mexican Americans were overrepresented: agriculture, domestic services, and state and local government. The gender and race wage gaps were tied directly to unemployment benefits. As a result, even for those employed in sectors that were covered, benefits could be quite low. The official benefit rate, set at 50 percent of gross wages, varied across states. Depressed by benefit ceilings and restrictions put in place by the Reagan administration, average wage replacement did not keep pace with inflation. In 1985, the unemployment benefit rate dropped to 35 percent of gross wage replacement.

A comparison made in 1983 between male- and female-dominated occupations shows the repercussions of the gender effect. In male-dominated sectors (e.g., mining, durable goods manufacturing, construction), unemployment coverage ranged from 51 to 67 percent. In areas dominated by women (like retail sales and professional services), the percentage covered varied between 24 and 31 percent (Abramovitz, 1996a; Pearce, 1985).

Public Assistance for Families With Dependent Children

The Social Security Act of 1935 instituted two distinct types of programs. The first, Social Security, was designed to offer some protection to steady participants in the labor force. The second was destined to help deserving non-workers. Social Security proper followed the private insurance model. On the other hand, public assistance for poor husbandless women with dependent children (Aid to Dependent Children—ADC), and for elderly or blind people without economic resources—Old-Age Assistance and Assistance to the Blind (OAA and AB, respectively)—was modeled after the poor laws or public charity. The ADC program was akin to mothers' pensions, except that it was more comprehensive and became an entitlement with federal matching support.

From the start, ADC was the most poorly endowed of the public assistance programs. By 1936, a total of 42 states had implemented OAA programs, but ADC had gotten off the ground in only 26 states. ADC also had lower benefits and federal matching. The monthly benefit in OAA was $30, with federal matching set at 50 percent. The average benefit per child in ADC was $18, and the federal contribution was set at 30 percent. A year later, the matching formula was raised for OAA and AB but not for ADC. It was only in 1950 that mothers were added as beneficiaries (AFDC), and unemployed parents were added in 1962, at the discretion of the states (AFDC-UP). Interestingly, when Nixon federalized OAA and AB under SSI, AFDC was the only public assistance program left out (Abramovitz, 1996a).

Between 1935 and 1945, there was no change in the structure of the ADC program. Mothers were to care for their children full-time. Taking the place of the father, the government had authority over recipients. It was to ensure the suitability of the home in terms of hygiene, standards of child care, and moral behavior. The mixture of surveillance and supervision allowed for various invasions of privacy and the imposition of middle class standards. In addition, because the states established benefit levels and application criteria, there was considerable variation on both counts (Boris & Bardaglio, 1983). Women of color suffered discrimination because of distinctive family traditions, especially in the South, where they had always been treated as laborers (Amott, 1990; Boris & Bardaglio, 1983). This engendered a certain independence, which, joined with their traditional links to extended-family and quasi-family networks, came to be viewed as signs of weakness based on the standard of the nuclear family.

The treatment of white women during the Second World War gives credence to the suspicion that they were seen as workers-in-reserve. Their backup status contributed to a lag in access to benefits, relative to male workers. Factories opened their gates to women when so many American men were fighting abroad, and an extensive network of nursery schools spread across the nation. Once the soldiers returned, those schools closed, and the women were encouraged to pursue a suburban family ideal–centered self-realization.

By 1960, when the number of recipients had doubled from 1945 and costs had increased seven-and-a-half times to $994 million, concern about AFDC mounted. A portion of this increase simply reflected population growth, and a good deal of it derived from labor market dislocations. However, it was the changes in family structure that caught the attention of policy makers.

Now, unwed mothers and women of color had displaced many of the eminently deserving white widows who were the poster moms of the founding days of AFDC. This worrisome imagery gave renewed life to the notion that rehabilitating the family was the way out of poverty, and a sound means of reducing AFDC rolls. "Family breakdown" became a catch phrase of the time, like "the population bomb." Nearly 60 percent of recipients were unwed mothers, and black families made up 48 percent of the rolls. The statistics fed into the characterization of such women as deviants. The theme gained further prominence in Daniel Patrick Moynihan's book (*The Negro Family*, 1965) about the dysfunctional black family. This was one of the opening salvos in the argument that AFDC was itself a cause of the deterioration in family life.

What the prevalence of black single mothers actually signified turned out to be more complex. According to the 1950 census, most black families had two parents, and only 18 percent of these families were headed solely by a woman. Amott (1990) argues that out-of-wedlock parenthood had picked up momentum some time before, in the 1940s. However, at that time, young mothers usually lived with their parents, so the incidence of single-motherhood was greatly undercounted. This meant the trend toward unwed black mothers was not as steep as Moynihan had surmised, and that the trend preceded their overrepresentation on the welfare rolls. In other words, black families had suffered from social and economic upheavals that preceded the expansion of the AFDC program. If this was the case, it was hard to see how AFDC might be a *cause* of family breakdown.

The mechanization of agriculture in the South during the forties, and the attendant loss of work in rural areas, fueled black migration just as the war opened job opportunities in the industrial cities of the North. This massive migration, like the thousands of Africans brought into slavery in the Americas a century before, severed family ties and kinship networks. These were the same bonds that had made for extended family support, including child rearing, in the harsh circumstances of the black subculture before the 1964 Civil Rights Act.

The North offered ghetto living and high unemployment, an escape from the South rather than a way into the affluence of modernity. To family separation and a chaotic day-to-day existence, Wilson (1987) adds another, demographic factor: a low male-to-female ratio. In the depressed black communities studied by Wilson, there has been a dearth of young men who can find the type of work that would allow them to provide for a family. Recent statistics support his account. Black men have a low life expectancy, and they are one-and-a-half times more likely to die from heart disease, cancer, or diabetes than white men. They are six times more likely than white men to die from homicide. They are more often victims of on-the-job accidents, and their jobless rate is twice that of their white counterparts. In addition, they are vastly overrepresented in the penal system. In contrast, black women have traditionally participated in the labor market, and black men tend to earn less. These two factors contribute to the substantial autonomy of black women in relation to black men, in contrast to the pattern that prevails among white women (Amott, 1990).

Worries about the number of single mothers on the AFDC rolls went back as far as the fifties. This concern prompted the program's efforts to collect child support from absent fathers. In most states, AFDC payments depended on the *inability* of relatives to help the family. Nevertheless, the recognition of the fathers' responsibility for their children broke with the custom of maternal welfare. Requiring recipients to give the address of their children's father as a condition of eligibility posed problems for some women who had either lost contact with them or feared reprisals. In 1951, the Jenner Amendment to the Social Security Act mandated an even more serious intrusion into the privacy of women on AFDC. The amendment allowed states to make AFDC rolls public as a way of preventing fraud (Abramovitz, 1996a, p. 323).

It was also during this period that the states cut financial support for the program. They tightened eligibility, enforced and extended residency rules, and increased oversight of home suitability. The states issued regulations on residency and application of middle class rules of household propriety that effectively excluded both black and Mexican American mothers and their children from AFDC. Only in 1968 did the Supreme Court invalidate "man-in-the-house" and "substitute-father" prohibitions and forbid the states to close cases on the basis of home unsuitability unless the care of the child was provided for (Jansson, 2001).

By the early sixties, public awareness of the huge increase in AFDC rolls, combined with a selective interpretation of the origins of this growth, led to an effort to rehabilitate poor families. The 1962 Social Service Amendments to the Social Security Act had two familiar purposes: to strengthen the family and to promote self-sufficiency. This notion of self-support was the first acknowledged departure from the rationale behind mothers' pensions. Federal backing for these services grew from 50 to 75 percent, and funds were available for social work training to staff the services. Work incentives established a new direction toward self-support, that is, to encourage mothers' work outside of the home. The program included a deduction for child care and a type of wage subsidy. The mother could keep the first $30, and one-third of her wages, up to a wage level above poverty, without losing her benefits.

This approach did nothing to reduce AFDC rolls, which expanded by 30 percent between 1960 and 1967. Total costs doubled to $2.2 billion. It was during that time that Legal Aid, a War on Poverty program, helped many women who had been denied AFDC to battle for their rights in court.

Their successes made welfare officials more cautious about procedures, and fewer women were excluded. Concurrently with civil rights victories, this made AFDC recipients—especially black recipients—ready to fight for their entitlements, and the National Welfare Rights Organization (NWRO) was born. One of its most important objectives was to claim rights of support for mothers' work—that is, for nurturing and child rearing that had traditionally gone unpaid (Amott, 1990).

Signs of retrenchment in AFDC surfaced in 1967 and accelerated in the mid-seventies. AFDC was reined in still further in the eighties, and its elimination came in the mid-nineties. The downward trend of the only national program protecting poor families began with the economic recession of the seventies. Twelve consecutive years of conservative administrations representing interests averse to public assistance and even Social Security, and favorable to the privatization of welfare, also helped to do AFDC in. Early in his political career, in a nationally televised speech in support of Barry Goldwater (October 27, 1964), Ronald Reagan noted that the chief administrators of Social Security had declared it a welfare, not an insurance, program (see Reagan, 1983).

The demographic profile of AFDC recipients remained reasonably stable during the eighties, but the numbers of the potentially eligible grew substantially. A simple statistic indicates this mismatch. In 1973, an estimated 85 percent of children living in poverty were enrolled in AFDC. By 1986 that figure number had been cut to 60 percent (Amott, 1990).

A series of myths sustained the image of poor women as deviants and exploiters of public generosity: AFDC benefits were too generous. Women on AFDC had lots of kids. Once on welfare, women kept having children and stayed in the program for a long time. The ones who *wanted* to work kicked the habit, found good jobs, and left welfare.

The reality was quite different. Half of AFDC recipients had benefits that were 50 percent below the poverty line. These mothers had slightly fewer children than the average non-welfare mother. On average, two-thirds of the women stayed on AFDC for 4 years. Four out of five women on welfare worked, but their income remained below the poverty level. Fully half of the successful exits from AFDC were by way of marriage (Berrick, 1995; Duncan, 1985).

Although the myths have been proven wrong, they have stuck in the public mind as facts. The extent to which the overrepresentation of black mothers and single mothers on the rolls played a role in the acceptance and perpetuation of this misinformation, fueled by hidden racism and gendered moral biases, remains an empirical question (Berrick, 1995).

In 1967, Congress enacted the first mandatory work program for AFDC recipients, the Work Incentive Program (WIN, first known as WIP). This clearly reversed the original policy of keeping women at home to take care of their children. The first obligation of women became to provide for their children on their own without, at the same time, neglecting their care. Only recipients with preschool-age children or who were taking care of a disabled relative were exempt from the work requirement, although they could be excused if ill or too old, or if they lacked transportation or child care. Previous work incentives—for example, allowing recipients to retain part of their wages without losing their welfare checks—were maintained, but many of the departments were unable to provide the training, child care, job search activities, and counseling services that were part of the package.

In 1974, WIN II—the Talmadge Amendment—dropped the pretense of offering training and family services and became simply a workfare program, reducing exemptions to a minimum. At that time, about 40 percent of AFDC recipients were either working, looking for work, or in school. Six percent were incapacitated, and 39.8 percent were at home caring for young children or disabled family members (Garvin, Smith, & Reid, 1978).

Even as women recipients worked more, had past work experiences, and had finished high school and even some college courses, very few escaped poverty because their wages were very low. The minimum wage, even for full-time workers, was not a living wage. It could not sustain a family above the poverty level.

By the 1980s, a new explanation of poverty was floated and began to take hold: it was not low wages that damaged the work ethic but welfare itself. The argument blamed the disintegration of the black family on AFDC dependence. AFDC was seen as both destructive and addictive. The medicine caused the illness, or made it worse, and the patient was a deviant "other" (Murray, 1984). This pair of claims made it easier to cut welfare.

The deadliest attacks on the AFDC took place on Reagan's watch. Entitlements were capped through regulation. The first restrictions on eligibility involved the use of gross rather than net income for calculating qualification thresholds. This encompassed common assets and consumer durables like cars and television receivers. Further regulations cut the needs standards set by states, postponed applications to the last month of a first pregnancy, and cut work incentives.

An estimated 400,000 AFDC families lost their benefits with the implementation of these regulations. In 1970, AFDC covered 80 percent of all poor families with children below 18 years of age. In 1982, a year of high unemployment, only 49 percent received AFDC benefits. Furthermore, because the grants were not price-indexed, their value had depreciated by 31 percent between 1970 and 1983. In at least half of the states, this corresponded to 75 percent of the official threshold of need (Piven & Cloward, 1982).

The new regulations grievously affected the South, where 45 percent of applicants, representing over 1.5 million people, were deprived of eligibility. In 1979, one black woman out of seven was raised from poverty. That figure dropped to 1 out of 14 in 1987. In the same year, 56 percent of children of poor black families lived with incomes that amounted to half of the absolute poverty level, set at $9,056 for a family of three.

The most frequent reason for denial was "failure to comply with procedures." A look at the process shows how it stood as a barrier against entitlement:

- The application form consisted of four to five pages of detailed information that take a few hours for a college graduate to complete.
- The required documentation included Social Security cards for all family members, pay stubs, letters from Social Security and state employment compensation offices and (where applicable) the Veterans Administration, bank statements, rent and utility receipts, proof of residence, children's birth certificates, and proof of absence or disability of a parent.
- Income testing, including evaluation of assets, was required.

If the applicant survives this obstacle course and is accepted, there is a waiting period of a month or more (Amott, 1990; Southern Governors' Association, 1988).

The Family Support Act of 1988 opened another chapter in the demise of AFDC. Two apparently reasonable arguments underlay the act: First, absent fathers should be responsible for the support of their children. Second, in view of the high participation of mothers in the workforce generally, there was no reason to exempt AFDC mothers from work.

Both arguments failed to address the special circumstances of poverty. First, the overwhelming majority of AFDC recipients were poor before as well as after separating from their children's father (Bane, 1986). In addition, middle class mothers were able to work because they could pay for child care. Indeed, they could afford to pay for the cheap labor of their sisters in poverty, who could not afford child care themselves. They usually lived in stable and protected neighborhoods where children are not regularly at risk. The last and probably most emphatic assumption was that paid employment would represent a ticket out of poverty. The problem was that the facts showed otherwise. One out of three black mothers and 17 percent of white mothers working for pay in 1987 lived in poverty (U.S. Census Bureau, 1987, Tables 19, 37).

These assumptions, and the conviction that women on welfare should be forced to work for their own good, prevailed. The minimum grant was dropped, and WIN II was replaced with the Jobs Opportunities and Basic Skills Programs (JOBS). AFDC recipients with children over 3 years old were required to find work or be trained for employment. AFDC departments would provide basic employment, education and training programs, one year of Medicaid, child care, and social services. As usual, states varied widely in offering these guarantees.

An evaluation study by the U.S. General Accounting Office (1987) of 45 programs showed that the reforms left women in poverty. Their average wage was either below or just at the minimum wage. Only in some areas with high economic growth (as was the case in Massachusetts at the time) were recipients placed in somewhat better jobs.

AFDC had been transformed into an unemployment program based on a contractual obligation between two extremely unequal parties: mothers in poverty and the state. The path leading to this policy can be traced back to the English poor laws and to nineteenth-century constructions of poverty as the outcome of shiftlessness and immorality that would be cured by forced labor. The entitlement status of this public assistance program was nonetheless preserved, though some states were granted waivers to experiment with procedures to expedite moving AFDC recipients into the labor market.

By 1995, the Department of Health and Human Services granted permission to 22 states to experiment with time limits and workfare programs. The Department authorized 13 child-exclusion or eugenic experiments. Recipients were given cash bonuses for the use of birth control. Florida and Ohio encouraged the use of the Norplant contraceptive. In Colorado, those who refused family planning counseling were met with penalties, and in Utah, unwed mothers who gave up their children for adoption were paid $3,000 per child. In Wisconsin, a program (Learnfare) held mothers responsible for the school attendance and performance of their children. Failure to achieve a positive outcome brought a decrease in benefits. Although reputable evaluations showed the ineffectiveness of the policy, Learnfare was reauthorized (Trattner, 1999).

In 1996, the largest public assistance program, created in 1935 as an entitlement to children at risk of poverty, was dismantled. The Temporary Assistance for Needy Families (TANF) block grant took its place, as part of the Personal Responsibility and Work Opportunity Reconciliation Act. TANF was supposed to address welfare for families in poverty. Part IV of this book takes up a critical evaluation of this legislation, and of the issues surrounding its renewal.

10 Welfare Through the Color Lens

No longer a regional embarrassment, racial inequality became a national malady.

—Jill Quadagno (1994, p. 4)

Like Native Americans and Mexican Americans, African Americans were a conquered people, exploited through genocide, slavery, or confiscation of their land, then reluctantly given second-class citizenship.

African Americans

As noted in the introduction to Part II, "exceptionalism" is the omnibus term for several related theories about why public welfare emerged so late in the United States and why, in comparison to other industrialized democracies, it has been so meager. The puzzle can be stated simply: If the full development of democracy includes the universal distribution of civil, political, and social rights, why does the world's first democracy measure up so poorly, specifically with regard to entitlements?

Quadagno (1994) points out that the United States has been slow to develop a fully integrated democracy. The Founding Fathers declared all men equal, but some were evidently more equal than others. They permitted the enslavement of blacks, "that peculiar institution," to continue. Political rights also developed slowly, though limited suffrage for literate and otherwise qualified white men was granted earlier than in Europe. It was only after the Civil War that all males got the vote, and it was not until 1920 that suffrage was extended to women.

Even after the Civil War, democracy was an uneven reality. The solidly Democratic South was a one-party oligarchy. The rights of blacks—to vote, to assemble, to attend school, and the like—were observed more often in the breach than as a rule.

The New Deal represented the first serious commitment to social rights nationwide. The primary purpose of Social Security was to protect workers in times of unemployment and in old age and, secondarily, to offer protection to deserving non-workers, but these were hardly universal programs. Certain workers were excluded, and non-protected occupations employed very large proportions of people of color and women.

How did this happen? Southern Democrats dominated the Congress. They went mostly unchallenged in their one-party districts and states and stayed on for a long time, accumulating seniority. The "colonels" controlled major committees, and their support was necessary for the passage of Social Security. They exacted their price and managed to preserve a stratified South (Cates, 1983). The fledgling welfare state failed to protect African Americans and Mexican Americans.

Other programs of the time, especially housing and labor, also ignored African Americans and Mexican Americans. The National Labor Relations Act of 1935 legalized unions and gave workers the right to bargain, yet the government allowed the American Federation of Labor (AFL), the largest union, to discriminate against minorities of color for the next two decades. The National Housing Act of 1934 allowed for lower down payments, extended loan periods, and regulated mortgage rates, in order to facilitate home ownership for working families. The Federal Home Loan Agency insured lending institutions against default by selecting economically sound mortgages. This led to "redlining"—that is, depriving non-whites of home loans and thus reserving white neighborhoods for whites. Certain areas were classified as risky and therefore uninsurable. In practice, the indicators of risk were racial as well as economic, leaving most black families ineligible and trapped in the ghetto. The Housing Act of 1937 looked like a step forward. It allowed local housing authorities to use tax-free bonds to build public housing projects and to subsidize rents for poor tenants. However, tenants were selected by race, and no dent was made in segregation (Quadagno, 1994). Even postwar programs like the celebrated GI Bill are now known to have benefited white to the detriment of black veterans (Katznelson, 2005).

Movements toward racial and ethnic integration made little progress until the 1960s. Neubeck and Casenave (2001) cite the following three incidents that exemplify how the race card was played to divert reform energies. All of those examples put African Americans' entitlement to AFDC in question.

Undeserving Black Mothers

The first example comes from Louisiana. The 1954 Supreme Court decision in *Brown v. Board of Education* in Topeka, Kansas, rendered school segregation illegal. The landmark ruling provoked violent resistance in many southern states, including Louisiana, one-third of whose population was African American. "States' rights" was the rallying cry against federal intervention.

Photo 10.1   Segregation in New Deal Work Programs

Source: From the private collection of Peter McDonough.

Photo 10.2   Agricultural Laborer Excluded From New Deal Protection

Source: From the private collection of Peter McDonough.

Nevertheless, the government in Washington stood fast about integrating the schools, so local politicians moved the battle to another ground: the AFDC. The Louisiana legislature passed a series of bills sharpening the criteria that define a suitable home for applicants and recipients of AFDC. Women who had more than one child out of wedlock, as well as common-law couples, became ineligible. Statements to the effect that tax money should not be used to encourage promiscuous behavior or promote illegitimate "breeding" resonated among whites. The campaign resulted in the loss of eligibility for 6,000 families and 22,500 children, 95 percent of whom were African American.

Attacks like these were not confined to the South. What occurred in New York State serves as a second illustration of the persistence of racism. The course taken by efforts to reform AFDC in Newburgh, New York, generated national news. Nestled on the west bank of the Hudson River a few hours' drive north of New York City, Newburgh had once been a prosperous town, with a history going back to Revolutionary War days. (General George Washington had slept there several times). By the end of the 1950s, however, the city was going through an economic crisis. The landscape was transfigured into a classic rust-belt scenario. Railroads and trucking had cut into Newburgh's importance as a port. Work on President Eisenhower's pet project, the interstate highway system, was going full speed ahead. As industries and workers moved out, factories closed, leaving behind a crumbling downtown. Some African Americans who had migrated north settled into old family houses that were transformed into multiple-family apartments.

George F. McKnealy, a Republican city council member, responded to a skirmish between white and black high school students by targeting AFDC and African Americans with draconian measures. "I am not anti-Negro," he insisted in one speech, "I am anti-knifing. I am not anti-Negro, I am anti-delinquent. I am not anti-Negro, I am anti-welfare chiselers." "The people who live in the slums," he went on to say in another speech, "created them, the slum dwellers are Negroes; therefore, keep the Negroes from moving into the city" (Rollins & Lefkowitz, 1961, p. 158).

In 1960, McKnealy threw his support for city manager behind Joseph McDowell Mitchell, a kindred spirit. Mitchell implemented a 13-point program that barred "the usual suspects" from AFDC and that cut out anyone applying for or receiving assistance from the city welfare department. Help in kind replaced cash payments. The period of assistance was limited to 3 months a year. Single mothers who had a child while in the program were dropped. Home suitability criteria were rigorously enforced.

In tones reminiscent of his southern counterparts, Mitchell justified the new restrictions by fulminating against "the right of social parasites to breed illegitimate children at the taxpayer's expense." AFDC amounted to a disincentive "to a *naturally* lazy people to work if they can exist without working" ("McKnealy Offers Rebuttal," 1959, emphasis original). Toward the end of 1960, the New York Supreme Court handed down a permanent injunction against 12 of the 13 rules. However, the case had attracted enormous media attention, and the damage had already been done. The uproar surrounding the Newburgh case helped frame AFDC as a racial issue.

The third case discussed by Neubeck and Casenave (2001) has a similar profile, this time unfolding at the service of political aspirations. Membership in the committees and subcommittees overseeing the District of Columbia was a plum for ambitious members of Congress. Robert Byrd, senator from Virginia and one-time associate of the Ku Klux Klan, chaired the Senate Subcommittee on Appropriations for the District of Columbia. In 1963, the subcommittee conducted hearings on alleged welfare fraud. Alarm at the growth of AFDC cases was the apparent motivation. During the postwar years, African Americans had become the majority population of the nation's capital. Consternation at this trend took the form of hostility against public assistance.

Senator Byrd saw his mission to be a search for shiftless, dishonest, and irresponsible African American men who were involved in predatory relationships with immoral, sexually promiscuous African American women. His was a crusade against the "breeding" of future citizens with no concept of law and order (Rawick, 1972, p. 143). According to Senator Byrd, indolent and depraved people took advantage of welfare. Since 85 percent of recipients were African American, these characteristics applied to the race as a whole. Byrd was fond of recounting how he had been raised in a poor but upstanding family, imbued with American ideals, in an atmosphere that was the opposite of the noxious dissipation in which welfare recipients were sunk.

The Byrd hearings had two results: First, 40 percent of the applications to AFDC in the District of Columbia were denied. Second, extensive media coverage amplified still further the unsavory connection between public assistance and unworthy African Americans.

The Great Society and White Backlash

As the diaspora of African Americans from the South spread across the nation, the leverage exercised by southern members of Congress on welfare policy diminished. Muted for more than a century, northern support for the civil rights movement finally brought to fruition, in 1964, legislation that could be enforced. The Civil Rights Act became law. The thin majority that had elected President Kennedy included an overwhelming majority of the black vote, and this constituency became central to the Democratic Party.

Lyndon Johnson's agenda for the War on Poverty and the Office of Economic Opportunity (OEO) was to eradicate poverty. The means were to be government services aiming to increase opportunities.

Community Action was one of the administration's most creative ventures. The program bypassed state and city governments and gave grants directly to poor communities. Fomenting local participation was a way to get programs to respond to grassroots needs. "Poor communities" in the cities were often African American, and many Community Action initiatives functioned as testing grounds for a variety of ideas and demands from the black movement and eventually led to the emergence of African American political actors into national prominence (Fisher, R., 1984; Wellstone, 1978).

Problems arose right away. The funds allocated to the OEO were skimpy, and city officials dug their heels in about the way these funds, modest as they were, were channeled through Community Action leaders. Feuding escalated over a small pie. Expectations had been raised, then quashed.

Frustrated once again, African Americans took to the streets. Riots erupted in 1967, the largest in Detroit and Los Angeles. Flames lit the night skies. Many whites saw the War on Poverty as a sop to African Americans. The outbreaks of collective violence in the inner cities, with high concentrations of blacks, branded these programs as an utter waste in the eyes of the silent majority.

Legal Aid, another program of the War on Poverty, turned out to be extremely effective in helping poor women gain access to AFDC. Success on this front, helped along by a generally more assertive civil rights movement, blossomed into the National Welfare Rights Organization (NWRO). With a mostly African American membership, the NWRO aggressively pushed AFDC entitlements in the late sixties and early seventies. The claims and tactics of the NWRO got under the skin of many conservatives.

When it became clear that the unions were barring African American graduates of the job-training programs, affirmative action measures gained ground. To many members of the white working class, affirmative action, coming on top of the War on Poverty, felt like a one-two punch. It all boiled down, so they felt, to undeserved preferential treatment for blacks—in short, to pandering. An irate working class, sensing themselves disdained, their views evidently scorned by the government, turned against public assistance. It looked like a sellout to blacks.

White backlash was a gift to the Republican Party. Republicans who regularly denounced waste in government redoubled their criticisms of the profligacy and unfairness of a liberal Democratic administration. Two traditionally Democratic constituencies—southern whites, whose racial hierarchy had been overturned by anti-discriminatory legislation, and working class whites offended by what they saw as reverse discrimination in public programs—changed party allegiance. The electoral realignment was of historic proportions. The solidly Democratic South was no longer solid (and was to become solidly Republican), and many blue collar inheritors of New Deal largesse abandoned the Democratic fold (Isserman & Kazin, 1989).

Some Republicans took advantage of this massive discontent by stressing the link between race and public assistance—even though there were as many white as black AFDC recipients. The connection, already latent, became etched in the minds of many Americans during the seventies and the eighties.

Ronald Reagan put the race–welfare nexus in graphic terms. He talked frequently about the black "welfare queen." "She has," Reagan insisted, "80 names, 30 addresses, 12 Social Security cards, and is collecting veterans' benefits on four non-existing deceased husbands. . . . She's collecting Social

Security on her cards, she's got Medicaid, getting food stamps, and she is collecting welfare under each of her names. Her tax-free cash alone is over $150" (Waller, 2006). A later Republican presidential candidate, George H. W. Bush, built his successful campaign around the laxity of Massachusetts' prison system. He spotlighted Willie Horton, a black prisoner, who had committed murder on a weekend furlough.

The image, propagated by an obliging media, was of a poverty-stricken black subculture, deviant, without moral principles, embroiled in a dangerously criminal underworld. Myths about laziness, reproductive excesses, and the exploitation of AFDC were immune to factual correction. Stories and images about poverty, AFDC, and crime focused on African Americans. The identification of black poverty with public assistance stuck with the general public.

Gillens (1999) analyzed the coverage of three national magazines: *Time, Newsweek*, and *U.S. News and World Report*. From 1964, the beginning of the War on Poverty, to 1967, the period of the riots, there is a startling spurt in stories and images about poverty with a racial content. In 1964, a total of 29 percent of stories mentioned blacks and 27 percent depicted blacks among poor people. In 1967, these percentages had shot up to 64 percent and 72 percent, respectively.

In prime time news broadcasts by NBC, ABC, and CBS during 1968, the portrayal of poverty as black was present in 95 percent of the stories, and it remained at comparably high levels during the period of 1988 to 1992. Data from the National Election Study indicated that in 1986, a belief that blacks lacked a work ethic was significantly correlated with negative feelings toward welfare recipients and positively associated with support for cuts in welfare programs (Gillens, 1999, p. 70). In a 1994 CBS/*New York Times* poll, 64 percent of respondents who thought most recipients of public assistance were black were of the opinion that people were on welfare not because of need but because they did not apply themselves and did not want to work. These negative opinions were reversed for those who thought that the majority of public assistance recipients were white (Gillens, 1999). Table 10.1 shows some of these results.

Neubeck and Casenave's (2001) thesis is that the racialization of AFDC is at the root of the cuts in the program, the tightening of eligibility, the impulse to eliminate dependence with workfare, and ultimately the collapse of AFDC itself. As the racial stereotypes about AFDC mothers spread, so did attitudes against welfare dependence (Gillens, 1999). The Reagan reforms that eliminated 400,000 families from AFDC met with little resistance. Both parties backed a Family Support Act that incorporated strong work requirements. It was a Democratic president, Bill Clinton, who gave the coup de grace to AFDC. The 1996 Welfare Reform Act put an end to national entitlements established generations earlier by the New Deal.

The focus of policy makers had shifted from overcoming poverty to cutting public assistance rolls. This shift helps account for the opportunities that closed in the faces of many black ghetto dwellers, living where unemployment

Table 10.1   Opinions on Welfare by Perceptions of Recipients

	Thinks Most Recipients Are Black	*Thinks Most Recipients Are White*
In your opinion, what is more to blame when people are on welfare?		
Lack of effort on their part	63%	40%
Circumstances beyond their control	26	50
Do most people on welfare want to work?		
Yes	31	55
No	69	45
Do most people really need it?		
Yes	36	50
No	64	50

Source: CBS/*New York Times* poll (1994, December).

is three or four times higher than elsewhere, and where schools are understaffed and run down (Jargowski, 1997; Massey & Denton, 1993). Some researchers nonetheless justified white backlash by claiming that the plight of African Americans was self-inflicted, reflecting a reluctance to work. The recommendation was that they be forced to do so (Mead, 1986). Murray (1984) pointed to other pathologies: for example, an insufficiency of entrepreneurial spirit and marital instability traceable to addiction to the dole.

The equation of race with welfare spilled over toward non-black recipients. Black "welfare mothers" so saturated the media that it was easy to envision *all* recipients as "others." This iconography thrived on the penchant, long-standing in American culture, to blame not the economic system but individuals for their fate. Character deficiencies, loose morals, and a generally irresponsible lifestyle cried out, so it seemed, for the imposition of restrictive interventions that respectable citizens escaped. Survey after survey picked up on this way of thinking and the support it gave to retrenchment (Gillens, 1999).

Two features of this backlash are particularly intriguing. Recall, first, that punitive measures for rehabilitating the poor come with rules that are not imposed on others. Hard-earned tax dollars go to welfare recipients, and it seems only natural that they should behave according to American norms. Notice, however, that homeowners get help, in the form of tax write-offs (the mortgage allowance) that cost the government billions annually. Yet no moral and behavioral uprightness is demanded in return; the transaction involves no talk of home suitability, limits on childbearing, adherence to monogamy, and the like.

Table 10.2   Public Support for Work Requirements for Welfare Recipients

	Percent Supporting Work Requirements
Do you think the government should create work programs for people on welfare and require people to participate in them or not?	92
Do you favor or oppose this proposal: Require welfare recipients to work in exchange for their benefits	97
Work requirements should apply to . . . single parents with drug and alcohol problems	71
Any family for whom the government cannot find a job and provide child care	63
Any family that cannot find a job where jobs are hard to find	60
Any family where the parent has a significant physical or mental disability	37
Do you think that women with young children who receive welfare should be required to work, or should they stay at home and take care of their young children?	74
Single mothers should be excused from working if child is	
Younger than 5 years old	22
Younger than 3 years old	40
Younger than 1 year old	57
Younger than 3 months old	68
A single mother on welfare should have to work regardless of whether she has a young child at home	32

Source: Adapted from Gillens (1999, p. 186, Table 8.1). Data obtained from five national telephone surveys between 1993 and 1997 by CBS/*New York Times*, NBC/*Wall Street Journal*, *U.S. News and World Report*, and the Associated Press.

The second oddity concerns the visibility accorded public assistance. The media attention is justified as a way of accounting to taxpayers for government expenditures. This sounds fair enough, but Table 10.3 shows that the rule of thumb goes very wide of the mark.

AFDC and general welfare amount to only 3 percent of all social expenditures. The relatively modest sums involved mean that high-powered efforts to save taxpayers money in these areas are out of proportion with whatever waste occurs. The disproportion between the impulse for exposing welfare scandals (and the real costs of such surveillance) and what actually goes on suggests a strategy of deflecting attention from larger, more serious problems, or perhaps a reflex way of affirming old values during times of confusing change.

Divorce, single motherhood, cohabitation, unemployment, teen sexuality, abortion, and homosexual marriages are spreading alarm through society. The control of what many see as symptoms of the decay of civilization

Table 10.3   Spending by Category as Percentages of Welfare Expenditures

(All Levels of Government)	
Education	24%
Social Security	22
Medicare	11
Medicaid	9
Public Employees' Retirement	8
Medical research	5
Worker Compensation	3
Unemployment Insurance	3
Veterans' Programs	3
Public Assistance, AFDC	3
Miscellaneous	3
SSI	2
Food Stamps	2
Housing	1

Source: U.S. Census Bureau, Statistical Abstract (1997, p. 323).

among public assistance recipients may have the same symbolic value as the prayers required by the Salvation Army when handing out meals to the hungry. In both cases, enforcement targets the powerless. With public assistance, goals get displaced. Reforms are designed more to decrease welfare rolls than to decrease poverty and economic injustice.

Mexican Americans

Outsiders in Their Own Land

The United States provoked and won the Mexican American War, a conflict in which many junior officers, like Ulysses Grant, who were to become field commanders in the Civil War, earned their combat spurs. The Treaty of Guadalupe Hidalgo, signed on February 2, 1848, conceded to the United States land that corresponds roughly to one-third of the present national area: Arizona, California, New Mexico, Utah, Texas, and part of Colorado (Meier & Rivera, 1972). The treaty also specified the rights of Mexicans, about 75 percent of whom wished to remain on their land. They could keep their farms, receive American citizenship, and preserve their culture and language (Estrada, Garcia, Macias, & Maldonado, 1988).

The treaty conditions were quickly broken. Through a series of development schemes and discriminatory taxation, most Mexicans lost their land and were forced into agricultural labor. They were denied access to schools, jobs, and housing. The ability to read and write in English was a prerequisite for voting, so most were effectively disenfranchised, while Mexican American children were forbidden to speak Spanish in school. The difference between conquered and conquerors was accentuated by color (mestizos versus whites) and religion (Catholics versus Protestants) (Alvarez, 1976; Estrada et al., 1988). Mexican Americans were no longer farmers and ranchers. They became handymen and seasonal laborers for the agricultural and cattle-raising enterprises of the new Southwest, and they lived in extreme poverty. Barred from mainstream institutions, Mexican Americans relied on traditional mutual aid societies, which helped members with low interest loans and funeral and insurance benefits (Nava, 1973).

The frontier between Mexico and the Southwest was porous. The process of drawing the border had followed a political as much as a geographical rationale, with the result that families were often split between the two countries. Mexicans served as an agrarian labor force in reserve. Depending on the season, they came to work across the Rio Grande, then went back home. They were called "sojourners," forerunners of the *braceros* who would enter into written contractual arrangements to ensure a modicum of predictability in the workforce. Some temporary workers stayed in the area. Both Mexican American families and migrant newcomers lived predominantly in barracks, without health care or schooling.

The Depression was devastating for Mexican Americans and the nearly 2 million Mexicans who resided in this country. The farming sector was already in bad straits before the stock market crash. Unemployment was rampant, and Mexican Americans became scapegoats of welfare administrators facing an onslaught of impoverished petitioners. Local officials demanded that Hispanics be repatriated to Mexico. In 1929, nearly half a million families were in fact returned to Mexico, half of whom were Mexican Americans. The disruption of families and communities was tremendous.

Mexican American women who were allowed to stay got little help from the emergency programs of the New Deal, which favored male heads of households. The WPA opened a few sewing and weaving programs. The pay was a fraction of what the men received, and enrollment, hours, and workdays were often arbitrarily cut by local officials (Schackel, 1992).

Discrimination Under the New Deal

Since Social Security did not cover farm workers, Mexican Americans, like African Americans, were particularly hard hit during the 1930s. Another blow was that the 1936 Wagner Act did not protect the right of farm laborers to organize. Employers violently suppressed any such efforts on the part of farm workers. Mexican Americans were on their own, treated to long hours and low wages (Estrada et al., 1988).

The demand for manpower set off by World War II worked to the advantage of Mexican Americans who moved to the cities and found work in the factories of the Midwest. However, they also ran up against the same conditions as black migrants did: segregated housing, bad schools, lower wages, poor work protection, union ineligibility, and police discrimination.

The need for agricultural workers in the burgeoning agribusinesses of the Southwest led to the *bracero* program, which was periodically extended up until 1964. On paper, contractual conditions for seasonal workers introduced a degree of rationality into their lives: equitable treatment, a minimum wage, and transportation from and to Mexico. The problem was that there was no mechanism for enforcing the contracts, so the conditions were rarely met.

The *bracero* program was also supposed to control the illegal immigration of seasonal workers. A steady flow of undocumented Mexicans infiltrated the Southwest anyway, and periodic roundups sent them back to Mexico. There was little interest on the side of agribusinesses in tightening up controls, since undocumented labor benefited productivity and profits. Therefore, undocumented workers remained without protection under American law. They labored under any conditions, at the bottom of the pay scale.

Resistance

The Chicano movement took off in the 1960s, signaling the start of militancy bent on organizing Mexican immigrants and Mexican Americans to improve their economic conditions. The charismatic leadership of César Chavez provided the breakthrough. Chavez put together the United Farm Workers Organizing Committee, leading a march to Sacramento, the capital of California, to press for the rights of farm workers. Community Action and Legal Aid programs supported his efforts, and Chavez successfully orchestrated grape and lettuce boycotts among consumers that brought enormous pressures on agribusinesses to concede the right to organize. He also used a variety of political stratagems to get farm laborers protections afforded other workers under the Wagner Act. Chavez quickly learned the importance of political coalitions. He became fast friends with Bobby Kennedy, and he networked among Hollywood sympathizers to boost the cause of the farm workers.

With the support of the Ford Foundation, the Mexican American Legal Defense and Education Fund fought to extend the provisions of the Voting Rights Act of 1965 to Mexican Americans and other Hispanics. The Fund also investigated cases of job discrimination while pushing hard for voter registration and the protection of civil rights. California, with a high concentration of Mexican Americans, was a hot spot for activist organizations: the Mexican American Political Association, the Southwest Council of La Raza (a coalition of community interest groups), and the United Neighborhood Organization by Parishes, led by Ernesto Cortes, an Alinsky-style community organizer.

Activism among Chicana women followed a few years later with the emergence of such organizations as the Comisión Femenil Mexicana

Nacional, founded in California in 1970; the Chicana Service Action Center, another California operation; and the Mexican American National Association founded in 1976 in Washington, DC (Curiel, 1995; Hernandez, 1970).

Gains and Losses

The Bilingual Education Act of 1968 (Title VII of the 1965 Elementary and Secondary Education Act) was reauthorized in 1974, 1978, 1984, 1988, and 1992. It provided for educational services to school-age students of limited English proficiency. The purpose was to help them learn English, so that they could function in mainstream schools (Curiel, 1995; Hernandez, 1970).

Formal recognition that children from Spanish-speaking families, living in Spanish-speaking *barrios*, might need services to help them in the transition to another language represents an effort to equalize learning opportunity. There are conflicting views about how the program works out in practice. Serious evaluative research on the effectiveness of different formats is required to sort out the validity of the positive and negative opinions the program has elicited (Meier, M., 1990).

Another piece of legislation that affected the Mexican community involved Ronald Reagan's amnesty for aliens. This was the Immigration Reform and Control Act of 1986. To benefit from the amnesty, undocumented immigrants had to prove that they had lived in the country since January 1982, or that they had worked for 90 days between May 1985 and May 1986. The application process prior to citizenship had three stages: temporary legal status, permanent legal status, and eligibility for citizenship. The government received over 2 million applications (Curiel, 1995).

The 1996 Personal Responsibility and Work Opportunity Reconciliation Act (PRWORA) had profound implications for both legal and illegal immigrants (see Title IV of the Act). It took away the entitlement to food stamps, AFDC, and SSI from most legal immigrants. The only immigrants to keep their benefits were those who had become citizens or who had worked in the United States and paid Social Security taxes for at least 10 years, as well as non-citizens who were military veterans. States also had the option to deny Medicaid benefits to immigrants. In Texas, for example, the prediction was that 187,000 people would lose Food Stamps, 22,000 would be deprived of AFDC benefits, and 55,000 would be dropped from SSI. Congress eventually softened these rules, but the message was clear. Regardless of legal status, access to public assistance on the part of Hispanic immigrants was uncertain.

The next congressional action came a few months later, and it seemed to target immigrants from Mexico specifically. The size of the border patrol was doubled, and the penalties for false documents and the smuggling of immigrants were stiffened. As it happened, in 1996, the largest number of illegal immigrants were Poles, Philippinos, Italians, and Canadians. They accounted for about half of all immigrants, compared to about 18 percent for Mexicans

(U.S. Department of Justice, 1997). So the suspicion that the border patrol measures had Mexicans in their sights does not seem far-fetched.

A series of difficulties plague efforts to pinpoint the socioeconomic status of immigrants of Mexican origin in the United States (Hayes-Bautista, 1996). One problem is that the label "Hispanic" used in most national and state statistics takes in Cubans, Puerto Ricans, and people from various regions of Central and South America, all with different histories vis-à-vis the United States.

A second problem stands in the way of attempts to set historical baselines against which to assess present-day indicators on the status of Mexican Americans. On the whole, in contrast to African Americans and Native Americans, Mexicans have entered the United States at very different times. Among respondents identifying their ethnic background as Mexican, there will be some who are American citizens, others who are descendents of long-time Mexican Americans, and others who are undocumented immigrants. Under the generic rubric of "Hispanic," we will get averages biased by the relatively high status of Cubans and the urban poverty of Puerto Ricans.

In many instances, it is possible to isolate people of Mexican origin, and more recent census enumerations sometimes use this category. Differentiation by time of arrival, however, is more difficult. With these reservations in mind, Table 10.4 lays out a few important indicators of how people of Mexican background are faring in the United States.

Table 10.4   Poverty, Education, and Health Insurance Coverage

	By Race and Ethnicity (in percentages)		
	White	Black	Hispanic
Poverty			
Avg. 2001–2003	10.1%	23.6%	21.9%
High school grads			
(25 y.+)			
2000	84.9	78.5	57.0
2003	85.1	80.0	57.0
College grads			
2003	27.6	17.3	11.4
No health coverage (age 25y.+)			
2002	10.7	20.2	32.4

Education statistics: National Center of Education, *Digest of Education Statistics 2000–2003,* (Table A-2).

Health statistics: U.S. Census Bureau 2003. *Income, Poverty, and Health Insurance Coverage in the U.S.* (Table 5).

Poverty statistics: *Ibid.* (Table 4).

Native Americans

Genocide, Manifest Destiny, and Contradictory Federal Policy

North America had a population estimated at about 10 million, dispersed from coast to coast, in 1490 (Potter, 1984, p. 133). Three hundred years later, the number of Native Americans had collapsed to about 2 million. The demographic cataclysm testifies to the scale of injustice and suffering imposed by conquerors who, acting against the religious beliefs they espoused, satisfied their greed for land (Carrillo, 1998).

The Treaty Era

Under the English, Native Americans were accorded the status of independent nations, even if the definition of "nation" was imprecise (Kickingbird, Kickingbird, Chinitty, & Berkey, 1996). Decisions ratified between colonizers and the tribes took the form of treaties. Diplomatic niceties were upheld in part because throughout colonial times, the British found themselves in a fierce rivalry with the French for control of the North American continent. Cultivating cordial relations with the tribes and snatching coalitional partners away from the French made strategic sense.

By 1778, in the midst of the Revolutionary War, George Washington as commander in chief declared a policy of coexistence with the tribes. Court decisions and the Northwest Ordinance of 1787 upheld the rights of Native Americans to keep their lands.

All this notwithstanding, newcomers took their belief in the superiority of whites as a mandate to control and civilize the continent. Presidents from the earliest days of the republic gave tacit approval to the invasion of Native American lands. Even before then, the proclamation line of 1763 was an attempt to bar the settlers from tribal lands. However, feuding among inland tribes opened up the area for incursions by white settlers. Indigenous traditional modes of survival broke down, and new diseases, to which Native Americans had no immunity, spread through contact with the newcomers (Wunder, 1996c).

The Removal Era

The Bureau of Indian Affairs (BIA) was created in 1824 under the War Department. Treaties were negotiated and broken. Native Americans first had to give up lands east of the Mississippi. In 1828, President Andrew Jackson, hero of the Battle of New Orleans during the War of 1812 against the British, encouraged the states to fight court rulings that protected Native Americans. In 1830, he had engineered the passage of the Indian Removal Act. Over the next 10 years, "Old Hickory" ordered almost all eastern

Native Americans to move to lands west of the Mississippi. Some left voluntarily but many were forced to leave. In 1836, the Cherokee nation was given 2 years to leave their lands voluntarily. Only 2,000 left, but 16,000 remained. In 1838, U.S. troops forcibly removed them. The route they followed to the West became known as the "Trail of Tears" as an estimated 4,000 Cherokee died along the way. Several nations of the Southeast were crowded into Oklahoma, areas of which became like a vast concentration camp. All told, an estimated 70,000 people were forced to move. Between 1840 and 1860, a quarter of a million white settlers migrated westward, as Native Americans were settled on reservations (Feagin, 1985).

The Allotment and Assimilation Era

In exchange for their land, the government agreed to supply certain services to the tribes. The effect was not only to alter a traditional way of life but also to curtail the autonomy of Native Americans. The situation deteriorated with the Dawes Act of 1897. For the sake of assimilation, tribes on reservations could now be broken up (Taylor, 1984). At the beginning of the twentieth century, Native American activism grew up in the face of repression from the BIA. Founded in 1900, the Society of American Indians promoted cultural pride, leadership, and education. The Native American Church was recognized, and the use of peyote, a cactus-derived hallucinogen, in its religious ceremonies was protected (Wunder, 1996c).

The first three decades of the 1900s witnessed significant interference by the BIA in the daily lives of the tribes. Every aspect of Indian life was monitored in order to regulate or eliminate vestiges of native culture. Indian boarding schools signed on to the assimilation project. Children were removed from their families and tribes so they could be more efficiently taught "white" language and manners and receive training in menial trades. Grants of some fishing, hunting, and water rights to Native Americans were the only silver lining during this period.

The 1921 Snyder Act made the BIA responsible for bringing education, welfare, and health care to the reservations. Native Americans gained citizenship in 1924. In 1928, the practice of keeping Indian children in boarding schools slowed as the federal government gave aid to the states to create day schools (Wunder, 1996c).

The Indian Reorganization Era

Conditions on the reservations during the 1930s were so desperate that the government was embarrassed by a report from the Brookings Institution on *The Problem of Indian Administration* (Meriam, Brown, Cloud, & Everett, 1928). The "Indian New Deal" was incorporated into the Indian Reorganization Act of 1934. Now, tribal government had to be based on representative selection and economic development committees. The measure also reversed the provisions of the Dawes Act, and thus put an end to the loss of tribal lands.

The Termination Era

In the aftermath of World War II, the Indian Claims Commission Act of 1946 raised hopes that land restitution would occur, but only a few wrongs were rectified.

During the 1950s, federal laws and programs were introduced with the intent of undermining the Native American way of life. The first part of the policy—termination—ended all federal–tribes ties. It abolished the Indian land base, the reservations, and tribal assets. The goal was complete assimilation. The tribes resisted by appealing unsuccessfully to higher courts.

The second part—relocation—offered incentives to encourage young Indians to leave the reservations and move to cities. On top of this, Public Law 280 took away the ability of Indian governments to regulate reservations, and it withdrew civil and criminal jurisdiction over reservations from tribal courts. In 1955, the Supreme Court handed down a ruling in a dispute involving the Department of Agriculture. The Department wanted to cut timber without compensation from lands belonging to Alaskan Indians, and the court sided with the Department. The direction of the Indian Claims Commission was set, as was the withdrawal of federal authority over Indian policy in favor of the states (Wunder, 1996a).

The Era of Evolving Self-Determination

Government policy swung the other way during the period of the Great Society. Packaged with the Civil Rights Act of 1968 was the Indian Bill of Rights. These provisions did not extend all of the rights granted by the Act to Native Americans, and this omission became the grounds for successive suits (Wunder, 1996b).

Nevertheless, federal authorities supported the cultural and tribal functions of the reservations, and funds from the War on Poverty were directed to improve housing, education, and local economies on Native American lands. A 1968 Supreme Court decision reaffirmed the fishing rights of Native Indians. Activism gained force on the reservations. Tribes demanded compensation for the lands that had been taken from them and joined forces with Mexican Americans on this issue.

It was only in 1979, with the Supreme Court decision in *St Clare Pueblo v. Martinez*, that rights, in terms of forms of redress, were interpreted as part of the Indian Bill of Rights. The 1971 Alaska Native Claims Settlement Act gave tribes greater control of their lands and conceded limited means to protect tribal interests in negotiating with oil companies.

The 1975 Indian Settlement and Education Act, supported by Nixon, amounted to both official recognition of the existence of tribes and the establishment of a restoration process for tribes that had been terminated by the legislation of the 1950s. Tribes were allowed to buy lands, and they could be reimbursed for those that had been taken from them. Nixon's legislation reaffirmed the responsibility of the federal government at the same time that it ceded more autonomy to the tribes to administer programs of the Departments of Interior as well as of Health, Education, and Welfare.

The 1975 Indian Self-Determination Act strengthened tribal self-government and the independence of health, education, and welfare services administration. These reforms addressed Indian resources, allocations, and protections. The Indian Child Welfare Act of 1978 returned to tribes their most precious resources—their children. Tribal jurisdiction was reinstated, and referrals made off reservation went to tribal courts. Likewise, reservation social services were recognized (Barsh, 1996).

These moves by the federal government were in step with the reinvigoration of racial and ethnic cultures. The call for cultural preservation was especially powerful among Native Americans. An extraordinarily high proportion of Native American offspring had been separated from their parents. In 1970, this figure stood at about 1 in 4—more than 20 times the corresponding rate of parent–child separation among non-Indians.

Nevertheless, the Indian Child Welfare Act was controversial even among social workers, who believed that the best interest of the children was not necessarily tied to tribal integration (Barsh, 1996). A representative supporter of the legislation, John Red Horse (1980), argued that the care of children should encompass cultural and spiritual as well as physical and psychological maintenance. Children learn what is expected of them through oral tradition and the teachings of relatives and elders. Fischler (1980) defended the opposite position, contending that culture should not restrict the universal rights of children.

Recently, reservations have been in a position to protect their environment. Tribal governments have passed zoning laws, and they can charge fees to outsiders who use resources like lakes and rivers. When the nuclear power industry expressed an interest in dumping radioactive waste on reservation lands, the Nuclear Waste Policy Act of 1982 made Native Americans partners in the decision making.

With enormous tax revenues at stake, gambling has become an increasingly contentious issue between reservations and state governments. The Indian Gaming Regulatory Act of 1989 favored the rights of reservations. Native Americans also won recognition for their claims to exercise sovereignty over funerary and sacred objects. The Native American Graves Protection and Repatriation Act of 1990 marked another step in the slow evolution to self-determination (Carrillo, 1998; Wunder, 1996d).

There is little knowledge about the role of Native American women in tribal governance, in part because researchers are accustomed to social categories that are alien to tribal life. For example, Native American flexibility in allowing for third and fourth categories in classifying female and male gender traits has been reconstructed "on the outside" in terms of gay and lesbian categories.

Sifting through an accumulation of narrative data, Rayna Green (1980) shows the central influence of women in tribal governance. External surveillance, efforts at assimilation, and habits of cultural repression have impacted these structures negatively. But Green and, more recently, Woodsum (1998) have reviewed studies, conducted mostly by insiders, that have uncovered women's roles and power attached to them. Among these hard-to-detect dynamics are the resilient intra-tribal and pan-Indian networks sustained by women. One of the foci of these networks is on health issues and the fusion between indigenous practices and modern medicine. Female leadership has a surprisingly long tradition. It is one that includes women telling male members of the American Indian Movement what to do when planning militant actions.

The era of self-determination has witnessed important moves toward the consolidation of tribes as sovereign nations. However, pendulum swings have marked the history of federal Indian law. The "one step forward, two steps back" pattern requires vigilance on the part of Native Americans. Just under 1 million Native Americans—62 percent of the entire native population—live on reservations. Unemployment on "the res" is three times what it is for the rest of the population. More than one-third of reservation residents live below the poverty level. The median income is $20,000, and 16 percent of houses are without electricity. Maternal mortality is 20 percent above the national average, and average life expectancy is 10 years lower (*American Indian Census Facts,* 2000; U.S. Census Bureau, 2002).

Part III: Suggestions for Exercises

Exercise A

1. Students select a book in one of the following areas. The topics can vary as suggested below.
   - *Women*: employment, family/work, single mothers, employment insurance, old-age poverty, health
   - *African Americans*: employment, middle class, ghettoization, poverty, health, family
   - *Hispanics*: education, employment, diversity, language, cultural traditions
   - *Native Americans*: tribal links, reservation versus living outside, cultural traditions, state–tribe relations

2. Summarize the book chosen and relate it to the relevant content in Part III of this text. Discuss extensions, corroborations, and criticisms.

3. Use case examples or statistics that validate the conclusions in (2).

Exercise B

1. Students select one social work professional group focusing on the advancement of any of the four populations listed in Exercise A (e.g., NASW Women's Commission).

2. Contact the group and find out about its goals and activities.

3. Analyze and evaluate the possible contribution of (2) to problems that the group faces.

4. Propose changes that might make the group's efforts more effective.

PART IV

Contemporary Directions of the Liberal Welfare State

Assessments of program outcomes form one powerful determinant of welfare policies. The other factor shaping policy derives from the importance of prevalent ideological assumptions for constructing a better society. Sometimes these preconceptions have a life of their own, sustained more by values and norms than experience or evidence.

We need to identify the directions that welfare policy is poised to take at the beginning of the new millennium. TANF, Medicare, Social Security, and private occupational—that is, shadow—welfare policies have to be evaluated in light of both research and ideological fashions. Chapters 11 and 12 address TANF regulations, outcomes, and evaluations, while Chapter 13 discusses recent medical insurance reforms and proposals for privatization of retirement insurance.

11 Temporary Assistance for Needy Families—I

When there is suffering, there is duty. Americans in need are not strangers. They are citizens. Not problems, but priorities.

—Inaugural address of George W. Bush, 2001

The Welfare Reform Act of 1996 grew out of alarm spurred by the growth of AFDC cases (there were 5 million in 1995). Policy makers and policy wonks worried that the system encouraged recipients not to work. The fear was that it led to long-term dependence. The threefold goal of the new legislation was to make recipients *work*, to have them achieve *self-sufficiency*, and to *decrease the caseload*.

Temporary Assistance for Needy Families (TANF), unlike AFDC, is not a federal entitlement. Federal contributions were transformed into block grants to the states. Grants were calculated as a function of welfare costs to each state in 1995. The legislation stipulated the percentage decrease of cases expected for each year in every state, and put teeth in this stipulation with sanctions and rewards.

To end dependence, *time limits* for assistance were fixed. Recipients would max out at 2 consecutive years or at 5 years over a lifetime. Program implementation became the sole responsibility of the states. Criteria of admission, benefits, strategies of moving recipients from assistance to work, sanctions, follow-ups, what counted as work—all these issues were up to state governments. Administrative devolution was the key response to local diversity, and it took in both the definition of problems and the deployment of resources. Decentralization extended to recognized Native American tribes as well as to the states.

Another goal of TANF was less explicitly worked out. This had to do with the implementation of family policies for *promoting marriage, decreasing single motherhood, and preventing out-of-wedlock births while reducing abortions.*

Congress was scheduled to reauthorize the law in 2002. In preparation for this, several studies of the TANF experiment were carried out.

Positive Outcomes, Concerns, and Questions

Favorable Outcomes

The TANF experiment succeeded handsomely in meeting some of its goals:

- Between 1994 and 2000, caseloads decreased by more than half, from 5 million to 2.2 million.
- Fully 60 percent of recipients who have left welfare are working.
- Employment rates among single mothers have increased.
- Child poverty has decreased (Sawhill, 2002).

Concerns

Serious concerns remain, however:

- Nearly 30 percent of the caseloads remain on the rolls because they face serious barriers to work: poor education, no prior work experience, physical and mental health problems, the need to care for disabled family members, lack of transportation, substance abuse, domestic violence, etc.

- The reduction in caseloads is spread unevenly. Smaller decreases occurred in cities, which continued to be plagued by lack of jobs and an underclass environment (Katz, B., & Allen, 2001).

- The wages of those who find work average $6.60 an hour. This cannot raise them to self-sufficiency. According to one study, about 700,000 families were significantly worse off in 1999 than in 1995 (Downey, 2001).

- The lack of follow-up studies on people who left welfare without work, because of sanctions or time limits, hinders evaluation of the program's impact.

- There is little evidence regarding concerted effort or results in the promotion of marriage, in the reduction of teen pregnancy, or the lowering of out-of-wedlock births (Horn, 2001).

Further Questions

TANF got underway during boom times, and it was accompanied by the growth of other programs such as the earned income tax credit. This makes it hard to pinpoint the employment outcomes directly attributable to TANF.

Defenders of the program argue that a comparison of caseloads and employment with the 1980s, another period of economic expansion, shows that the late 1990s had many more recipients working and fewer caseloads (Haskins, 2001). This claim has been challenged on three grounds. First, critics point out the comparison is invalid because economic expansion was not uniform throughout the 1980s, occurring only after 1985. In the second place, there is evidence that many single women on welfare in the late 1980s worked off the books to make ends meet (Edin & Lein, 1997; Jencks, 2002). Finally, comparison of outcomes between the late 1990s and the years after 2001, when the country entered into a recession and unemployment rose, suggests that welfare policies need to be interpreted in the context of economic cycles. In short, more definitive analysis of TANF requires evaluation of the contributions and deficiencies distinctively identified with the experiment, including what happened after 2001.

Devolution: Unaccountability, Creativity, and State Budgets Crisis

TANF block grants were set at the level of AFDC spending in 1994–1995. Each state had to meet a Maintenance of Effort (MOE) obligation. This meant that spending for low-income benefits would have to be 75 to 80 percent of the state's previous spending. Around the country, block grants came to $16.5 billion a year, plus 10 to 11 billion from MOE. As cash assistance declined, states were allowed to redirect funds to help low-income families (Greenberg, M., 2001).

The states followed various strategies in implementing TANF. Some—Minnesota, Michigan, and Kansas—emphasized work engagement; others, like Wisconsin and Texas, gave priority to caseload reduction. Still others turned to in-kind assistance, minimizing cash benefits. Strategies varied considerably.

Minnesota favored financial incentives to work. The state gave cash assistance even to families well over the poverty level by offering generous benefits and wage disregards. It supplemented earnings with state earned income tax credits and provided substantial work supports, including child care for many working families. The purpose was to increase total income as a major incentive to work participation.

In Michigan, cutting the number of non-working families on welfare was the chief goal. The state used a wide range of training, employment, and educational programs to move people into work and keep them there. It eliminated time limits and committed state funds to help families who were past the 5-year limit. Kansas also adopted a service approach, one that was specifically geared to recipients with multiple barriers to work. Wisconsin was mainly interested in reducing caseloads, linking cash with work hours and requiring copayments for other benefits (Nathan & Gais, 2001). In addition, many states contracted out services and employment programs to private for-profit entities, such as Lockheed Martin, or to nonprofit community organizations with political ties (Bennett, 2003; Marwell, 2004).

Some states have shown versatility, creativity, and strategic coherence, but there is still a large margin of unaccountability regarding program implementation and outcomes. State reports are generally limited. There have been few efforts to generate comparable measures that would permit rigorous comparison of outcomes across the states. Systematic evaluation of this type would be essential for generating and sharing meaningful information, for assessing the relative impact of different strategies, and for smoothing out the mutual learning curve (Greenberg, M., 2001; Nathan & Gais, 2001).

The flexibility given states to implement TANF has been accompanied by greater litigation. Courts have been instrumental in determining individual rights to benefits, as defined by state and local welfare statutes, and in ensuring that state welfare regulations are in accordance with federal due process, equal protection, employment rights, and civil rights protections.

For example, Los Angeles County reached a civil rights settlement regarding access to services by Limited English Proficiency (LEP) welfare families. A Michigan circuit court upheld an injunction against a private contractor's requirement of drug testing for eligibility. Also in Michigan, the district court issued an order preventing the state from discontinuing Medicaid coverage of individuals who care for children receiving government assistance, if they qualify under other categories of Medicaid eligibility. In Missouri, the Supreme Court ordered the state to provide coverage to approximately 20,000 people who had lost their Medicaid benefits because of a legislative decision to lower the income cap. However, only some groups will have resources to pursue litigation. Similar issues without legal oversight might go unchecked (Welfare Information Network, 2004).

Some commentators worry that an economic downturn could swell welfare caseloads and strain state budgets, forcing cuts in benefits (Sawhill, 2001). Data from the Center on Budget and Policy Priorities confirm this fear. In 2003, in the midst of the most severe budget crisis in memory, states adopted measures to close their budget shortfalls. For the 2004 fiscal year, those downward adjustments totaled $78 billion. Data more recent than 2001 are still scarce, but there are already indicators of the impact these cuts have on the health coverage of low-income families. Around 1.5 million have been cut from Medicaid, SCHIP, and other state health insurance programs in 36 states. About half of those who have lost health insurance are children (Ku & Nimalendran, 2003).

Several tactics for implementing these cuts come into play. Income thresholds for eligibility may be lowered. Hurdles against enrollment such as burdensome applications and requirements of frequent reapplications can be introduced. Monthly premiums can be increased, or coverage may be dropped entirely if two consecutive payments are missed. Enrollments can be capped or frozen, forcing eligible individuals onto long waiting lists.

Federal matching funds set aside to help alleviate the budget squeeze in the states were scheduled to expire in July of 2004. The estimate is that, as

Table 11.1 Estimates of Medicaid, SCHIP, and Other Health Care Reductions Based on Approved Policies

State Fiscal Year 2003–2004			
National total		1.2 to 1.6 million	
State	Number Cut	State	Number Cut
Alabama	3,000–4,000	Montana	no estimate*
Alaska	1,600	Nebraska	28,700
Arizona	no estimate	Nevada	2,900
Arkansas	no estimate	New Jersey	1,900
California	250,000–500,000	North Carolina	no estimate
Colorado	16,300	North Dakota	2,600
Connecticut	20,500	Oklahoma	8,300
Florida	74,000	Oregon	40,000
Indiana	32,000–40,000	Rhode Island	1,200
Iowa	no estimate	South Carolina	7,000
Kansas	no estimate	Tennessee	150,000*
Kentucky	3,000	Texas	344,000–494,000
Louisiana	no estimate	Utah	no estimate*
Maryland	no estimate*	Vermont	10,000
Massachusetts	13,000	Virginia	no estimate
Minnesota	35,000	Washington	116,000
Missouri	32,000–42,000	Wisconsin	1,600

These estimates are generally conservative because of the lack of data about the number of people who would lose coverage in a number of the states. For states marked "no estimate," we lack an estimate; for other states, only partial information is available concerning some of the cuts. States marked with an asterisk (*) froze or capped children's enrollments in their SCHIP or Medicaid waiver programs.

Source: Center on Budget and Policy Priorities.

of 2004, the states face about a $50 billion budgetary shortfall. The expectation is that they will return to the same cutbacks regarding health and other services, even those matched by the federal government.

The governors of most states reacted very strongly against President Bush's budget plan for 2006. The proposal presented to the Congress in February 2005 outlined over $200 billion in cuts in discretionary domestic programs, including Medicaid, Food Stamps, and low-income housing. The decline in contributions from the federal government meant that the states, already contending with large revenue shortfalls, were increasingly backed into a corner.

In some areas, devolution has brought greater responsiveness to the diversity of state needs and has fomented programmatic ingenuity and creativity.

Enrollment Barriers Are Cut

Most states have made major strides over the past several years in streamlining the enrollment of children and families in Medicaid and SCHIP. The states have also helped those already enrolled to maintain coverage. This they have done by making it easier to enroll by mail or phone, simplifying applications, reducing paperwork, or offering 12 months of continuous eligibility. These measures have resulted in improved access for low-income working families.

Large numbers of eligible low-income children were in fact going without insurance because their families were not aware of the programs or found it too complicated to enroll. Efforts to facilitate procedures have increased the enrollment of eligible people without any significant jump in participation by ineligible people (Ross & Cox, 2003).

Keeping enrolled was a challenge for many. Almost half of the families whose children's enrollments had lapsed said that it was too difficult to obtain the documents required to complete the process. This was the outcome of frequent redeterminations of eligibility (Riley, Pernice, Perry, & Kannel, 2002).

Due to budget pressures, some states have rescinded their simplification efforts and reinstated policies that make enrollment more difficult. Many policy officials consider this strategy less harsh than direct eligibility cuts. However, to the extent that these barriers entail a loss of health insurance for eligible children, the harm done is the same.

However, it also has the potential to endanger the rights of recipients. Accountability is weak to nonexistent. There are no cross-state procedures for collecting data that would make comparative evaluation and development feasible. These difficulties, in combination with severe pressures on state budgets, encourage expedient, makeshift cuts that exclude low-income families from basic services.

Promoting the Work Ethic and Self-Sufficiency _____

The Move From Welfare to Work

The Administration for Children and Families (ACF) and the Office of Planning Research and Evaluation (OPRE) contracted with Manpower Demonstration Research Corporation (MDRC) and Child Trends to compare programs that emphasize short-term job search for quick employment and those that emphasize human capital development through education and skill building. The study covered seven locations but reported most extensively on five—Atlanta, GA; Grand Rapids, MI; Oklahoma City, OK; Portland, OR; and Riverside, CA—and over 40,000 participants. An in-depth study of young children was added in three of the sites (Atlanta, Grand Rapids, and Riverside).

The results were rather disappointing:

- Neither strategy increased the financial well-being of parents, nor did either have any effect on the well-being of children. The quick approach did succeed in moving recipients more rapidly into jobs.
- Both programs helped single parents work for longer periods and earn more than the non-program participants (members of the control group), but family income failed to improve, since increased earnings were offset by reduced welfare cash assistance.
- A mixed program, combining quick work search with human capital development, turned out to be the most successful.

The overall conclusion was that making a recipient work, regardless of strategy, did not produce the expected benefits to the family.

Job Instability and Poverty

The average earnings of TANF recipients—$6.60 per hour—clearly cannot lead to self-sufficiency. Supporters of TANF insist that the intent of the program is not to erase poverty but to decrease dependence. The argument sounds far-fetched. The poverty standard is set at access to the minimum resources for survival, and those falling below that standard cannot be considered self-sufficient. From this perspective, the decline in the welfare caseload and the increase in the number of recipients working cannot be the only criteria of programmatic success.

There is little evidence of self-sufficiency among welfare leavers.

A study conducted in 2000 by Johns Hopkins University revealed that two-thirds of welfare leavers had incomes lower than when they were on welfare. An Economic Policy Institute study of 1999 found that 44 percent of the families that had left TANF went without food, shelter, and medical care as compared with 33 percent of those who remained on the rolls, and that 1 out of 7 leavers had returned to welfare (Gourevitch, 2002).

A study by the Urban Institute on recipients who had left public assistance found that two-thirds of those working had incomes below the poverty level (Loprest, 2002). The Joyce Foundation examined the same issue in seven Midwestern cities. Of those who had transitioned to jobs, less than half had steady work and half of those became unemployed within 2 years. Only 17 percent of this group had worked continuously for the same employer. What's more, many had lost Food Stamps and Medicaid, even when their earnings qualified them for these programs, due to misinformation among case workers and confusing application procedures (Nox, 2002). Between 1996 and 2000, the poverty rate of working single mothers increased slightly—a remarkable fact in a booming economy (Bhargava, 2002). A comparison between AFDC welfare leavers between 1993 and 1995 and TANF leavers between 1997 and 1999 showed that the first group fared better than the second (Ozawa & Yoon, 2005).

Making Work Pay: The Role of Income Supplements

Findings from three projects—the New Hope project in Milwaukee, the Canadian Self-Sufficient Project, and the Minnesota Family Investment Program—show that positive results in children's behavior and school performance are associated with increases in *work and in income* (Nox, 2002).

Making work pay is clearly tied to the goal of self-sufficiency. The core argument should focus on raising the minimum wage and extending work benefits, but both reforms lack enough political support. Providing access to education and job training could improve the prospects of those leaving welfare for work, but the costs and unproven effectiveness of this approach make it unlikely to be adopted on a large scale (Jencks, 1995).

A 1995 analysis of the demographics of AFDC recipients prior to the passage of TANF's work requirements concluded that no self-sufficiency could be achieved with jobs paying less than $15 an hour. Considering the level of education, skills, and prior work experience of AFDC recipients, the conclusion meant that only a small minority of the AFDC caseload could achieve self-sufficiency in the labor market. In view of the qualifications of the remaining caseload and the very low minimum wage in the country, self-sufficiency would be impossible without income supplements (Jencks, 1995).

The goal of self-sufficiency inscribed in the TANF legislation has allowed some states to extend both income and service supplements that help raise the incomes of those entering the ranks of the working poor. The Minnesota Family Investment Program followed this road by giving an income supplement to those who worked full time for 1 year while on assistance, and the state allowed recipients to keep part of their welfare cash while working. Other states, such as Alaska, Florida, Illinois, Mississippi, and New Jersey, have also used earning supplements and income disregards to ease the transition from welfare to work (Welfare Information Network, 2001). These policies operate both as work incentives and as strategies for overcoming poverty. Research has confirmed the positive results. Labor force participation has gone up among adults, and the well-being of children has taken a turn for the better (Colleen, Werschkul, & Rao, 2003; Nox, 2002).

The Earned Income Tax Credit (EITC) is the most effective of all these measures. It is paid in full to the working poor whether they earn enough to pay taxes or not. In 2001, a total of 16 million low-income families with children received $30 billion under this federal program. For example, a single mother of two, earning minimum wage, receives 40 cents for each dollar earned up to $10,350 in wages; this boosts her income to $14,000. The program has raised 500,000 children out of poverty (Bhargava, 2002).

The 2003 Self-Sufficiency Standard report for California found the following to be true in Los Angeles County:

A single adult with no children would need to earn $9.83 per hour (or an annual salary of $20,751) to be able to meet his or her basic needs (housing = $807; food = $182; health care = $72; miscellaneous = $130; taxes = $295).

One adult with one preschooler and one school-age child would need to earn $20.07 an hour or an annual salary of $42,392)* to be able to meet basic needs (housing = $1,021; child care = $1,056; food = $411; transportation = $248; health care = $238; miscellaneous = $297; taxes = $534 with some tax credits). *With some public assistance such as housing, child care, and Healthy Families, the adult still has to earn $20,207 a year (which would essentially disqualify the family from cash aid and food stamps).*

Two adults, with one preschooler and one school-age child, would need to earn $11.50 per hour each (or a combined annual salary of $48,590) to be able to meet their basic needs (housing = $1,021; child care $1,056; food = $565; transportation = $475; health care = $276; miscellaneous = $339; taxes = $583 with some tax credits).

***Note:** Minimum wage in California = $6.75 per hour (full-time = $14,040 annually).

U.S. federal poverty level for a family of three is $15,260.

While the EITC is plainly the best income supplement for all working poor and, to this date, the strongest work incentive, the rules of eligibility are mind numbing. The forms are longer and the instructions more complex than those for the alternative minimum tax that middle-income citizens confront. Complexity makes for a high error rate. This often works against beneficiaries who do not get all the credits they qualify for (Greenstein, 2002).

The Need for and Promise of Child Care

As TANF took the place of AFDC, the obligation of adult recipients to work became unavoidable. This crucial change triggered a corollary need for child care and raised, in turn, the importance of the government's role in providing it through the program. The 1996 welfare reform combined federal programs of child care subsidies under the Child Care Development Fund (CCDF). In accordance with the move toward devolution, states could exercise considerable discretion regarding eligibility and benefits. They could use TANF money for child care, either directly or by transferring up to 30 percent of TANF money to CCDF, and they could add their own funds as well (Adams & Rohacek, 2002).

Child care subsidies burgeoned rapidly from 1996 to 2000, and state TANF funds grew to exceed the primary CCDF funding. The number of children receiving subsidies nearly doubled during this period, reaching 1.9 million (Schumacher, Greenberg, & Duffy, 2001). The subsidies are generally provided through vouchers set at 75 percent of child care costs in the community of the recipient. The guidelines for the voucher program are parental choice, work requirement, and the priority given to families leaving welfare for work. Copayments, income eligibility, and reimbursements vary from state to state.

Despite the increase in funding, a large proportion of low-income working families are not getting subsidies. In 13 of the 16 states studied by Colleen et al. (2003), 30 percent or more of eligible children were not getting subsidies. Because the funds were insufficient to meet demand, states rationed services in several ways. In an expanded countrywide assessment, it was found that nearly all (47) states, eligibility levels were lowered. More than half (35) of the states excluded low-income working parents who were not receiving welfare. Thirteen states required a minimum of work hours for eligibility. All states limited outreach efforts, leaving many low-income working parents in the dark about the subsidies.

To these problems, a number of the usual bureaucratic obstacles were added. Intakes were frozen and waiting lists created. Priorities were set so that only certain categories of applicants were served. Applications were made very complex, requiring lengthy paperwork and office visits, forcing parents to take time from work (Adams, Snyder, & Sandfort, 2002; Meyers et al., 2002; Schulman, Blank, & Ewen, 2001).

Other barriers stem from the inadequacy of child care centers in the areas where low-income families live and the high fees charged by these centers, relative to family budgets. Table 11.2 shows that as income declines, the proportion of child care costs goes up. Forty-two percent of families who left welfare for low-skilled, low-wage jobs paid an average of $232 a month for child care in 1999 (Colleen et al., 2003). Another hindrance is that the tight schedules that many low-income women encounter at work reduce their child care options.

Table 11.2   Percent of Monthly Incomes Spent on Child Care by Employed Mothers of Children Under 14

Income	
Less than $1,500	28.54%
$1,500 to $2,900	14.7
$3,000 to $4,499	8.06
$4,500 and over	4.97

Source: U.S. Census Bureau (2000, PPL Table 6, from a Survey of Income and Program Participation, 1999 Panel, Wave 10). See www.census.gov/population/socdemo/child/ppl-168/tab6.pdf.

This mismatch between child care funding and demand worsened in 2001, when many states entered budget crises. By then, the states served 18 percent—1 in 7—of federally eligible children (Mezey, Greenberg, & Schumacher, 2002). The situation has deteriorated further, as 13 states decreased their investment in child care assistance in 2002 (Ewen & Hart, 2003). In one of these states, California, over 200,000 eligible children are on the waiting list. The costs of services and restrictions on these services seriously jeopardize poor working women trying to keep up their work commitments, and lack of access to quality child care compounds the problem.

Parents who get child care subsidies in the amount calculated for services in their neighborhood are faced with hard choices. Nearly all live in poor neighborhoods, with limited choices, where child care services may be unable to adapt to the mothers' work schedules (Fullers & Strah, 2001). Faced with these hassles, almost 30 percent of parents with subsidies have recoursed to unregulated child care.

Regulated group care and child centers have to meet health and safety standards even if they cannot provide quality care. The states might devote some of their child care money to improve these services, but there is no evidence that they have engaged in interventions, recommended by child care experts, such as lower child–adult ratios and improved staff training.

Two considerations make the deficiency of child care under TANF the big failure of the program. The first concerns the sheer number of children in need of this service. According to 2001 TANF statistics, half of the parents receiving assistance have children under 6 years of age. Second, good child

---

Vitoria, a previous welfare recipient, the mother of three, used to be an officer in the Parent Teacher Association of her children's school. Now that she is working full-time, and often overtime, she seldom goes there and spends very little time with her children. At the end of the workday, Vitoria commutes from her office on Wall Street to her mother-in-law's home in Harlem to pick up her kids. Then she takes a subway to Queens with her kids in tow. Whenever overtime is required at the office, she accepts it because she wants to solidify her position and needs extra money for rent.

Time pressure has led Vitoria to press her oldest, a 10-year-old girl, to take more responsibility for the two younger boys, and this has caused some resentment on the part of the little girl. Vitoria knows that her elderly mother-in-law, who cannot read English, cannot supervise the children's homework and has a hard time controlling them. The two oldest are failing in school and the 2-year-old's speech development is hampered. Vitoria likes her work but is struggling with her diminished ability to monitor the children. While she is increasing her human capital for a stable job, Vitoria is concerned that the high-stakes testing of the No Child Left Behind program might set her children back.

care offers the best chance to break the intergenerational cycle of poverty. A growing number of studies indicate that the initial years of life are critical for children's long-run social, emotional, and cognitive development. Intervention in early childhood can help overcome obstacles created by poverty (Campbell, Ramey, Pungello, Sparling, & Miller-Johnson, 2002; Skonkoff & Phillips, 2002; Zigler & Styfco, 2001).

Evidence from the Perry School in Ypsilanti, Michigan, the North Carolina Abecedarian Project, and the Chicago Child–Parent Program confirm this. All three programs developed preschool programs for children living in poverty. By age 20, those who had been enrolled in any of these experiments had significantly higher rates of secondary school completion and lower rates of juvenile delinquency than the control groups. The Chicago Program calculated that good public child care would result in a return to society of $7 for every dollar spent on the program, calculating both tax revenues from future economic activity and savings in remedial education and crime control costs. In sum, good child care might in fact be an effective tool in breaking the generational cycle of poverty (Figueira-McDonough, in press; Wolfe & Vandell, 2002).

Other research shows a strong connection between the availability of child care and the participation of mothers in the workforce. Child care subsidies increase the duration of employment, both for welfare recipients and those off welfare. Forty percent of those receiving this type of assistance were more likely to stay employed for at least 2 years than were those without. The impact goes still higher (60 percent) for former welfare recipients, and the benefits show up in the quality and stability of child care (Colleen et al., 2003).

We know, then, that child care has two important effects: It makes it easier for low-income women to work in a sustained manner, and it helps give their children a better future.

Some commentators point out that, at least for low-income workers, child care should not be left to the market, which by definition responds to competitive pressures and profit. Many OECD (Organization for Economic Cooperation and Development) countries—Denmark, England, Finland, New Zealand, Scotland, Spain, and Sweden—have made the care of preschool children a universal right. The delay of the United States in responding to the balance of benefits/costs in child care may reflect an unresolved schizophrenia. Two ideals—the self-sufficiency/work ethic and the traditional nuclear family ethic, with its gendered functions—pull against each other.

Toward a Nuclear Family State

Marriage as a Cure for Poverty

Preoccupation with family breakdown has a long history. We can see the issue simmering as early as the late 1800s, when the metamorphosis of the extended family into the nuclear family was already well underway. The problem stayed on the front burner with the increase in divorce in the 1920s and later again in the 1940s, and boiled over with the sexual revolution and spread of cohabitation in the 1960s. Demographic, economic, and technological transformations—the entrance of women into the workforce, the spread of higher education, advances in reproductive control modifying sexual behavior—powered these cultural changes. At each juncture, as family structures shifted in sync with broader trends, predictions about the breakdown of the family and alarm over social disaster proliferated (Coontz, 1992; Figueira-McDonough, 1994a).

With the passage of the Welfare Reform Act of 1996, the government decided to take an active role in the promotion of marriage. The law exhorts states to encourage the formation and maintenance of two-parent families.

The connection between marriage and welfare owes much of its inspiration to conservative thinkers like Charles Murray (1984), who linked the enforcement of marriage to the end of welfare, and William Bennett, who asserted that serious social problems originated in family breakdown. "Most of our social pathologies," Bennett (1999) argued, "—crime, imprisonment, welfare, alcoholism, drug abuse, sexually transmitted diseases—are manifestations, direct or indirect, of the crack up of the modern American family." Robert Hector of the Heritage Foundation took the same view, and proposed a solution: Give women at risk of giving birth out of wedlock $5,000 to marry and stay married for 2 years (Horn, 2001, p. 42).

Promoting marriage in this way targets welfare recipients exclusively. The strategy is based on evidence that the overwhelming majority of recipients are single mothers of *out-of-wedlock children*. The inference seems obvious: marriage is a shield against poverty. Research showing the benefits of marriage for both adults and children seems to validate the inference. Adults appear to be more productive on the job, earn more, save more, have better mental and physical health, and live longer (Waite & Gallagher, 2000). While conceding that stable married couples might represent a selection of better adjusted people, the researchers stress how their findings substantiate the causal role of marriage in promoting other good things.

Children living with single mothers are five times more likely to be poor than those in two-parent families. In addition, growing up in a single-parent family doubles the risk of children dropping out of school, having trouble getting a job, and becoming teen parents (McLanahan & Teitler, 1999). Some family experts argue that these findings underplay the importance of economics. Their criticism is that advocates like Murray have reversed the role of marriage in the causal chain involving economic well-being. "It is not just the case," Ooms (2002b) points out, "that single mothers find themselves poor because they are unmarried, but they find themselves unmarried because they are poor. Economic hardship and other problems associated with poverty can wreak havoc on a couple's relationship" (p. 25).

Occasional crises, such as divorce, can drive previously non-poor women, who are overwhelmingly the custodians of their children, to welfare. But these same women are among those found to leave welfare within 2 years

(Duncan, 1985). It is also the case that poor women who separated from their husbands were just as poor before as after the split (Bane, 1986). Wilson's (1987) analysis of poor African American neighborhoods with high rates of single motherhood shows that available young men with provider capacities are very scarce in these areas. Even if male providers are more abundant in other communities, mothers with children, divorced or single, have a hard time finding husbands.

Table 11.3 underscores the limits of the mystique of marriage as a cure for poverty. Other family formats do as well as those based on marriage in avoiding situations of extreme need. As might be expected, a single mother with no adult companion is more vulnerable to such a predicament.

Remarkably, although the incidence of non-married families and single motherhood is as high in other developed countries as in the United States, their rates of poverty are much lower (Christopher, 2002). What accounts for the difference? It is employment and children's benefits that raise mothers and their children above the poverty level (see Table 11.4).

The marriage-promoting features of the 1996 welfare reform are controversial because they are embedded in two disparate traditions. One is a conservative, religious tradition that defines the family restrictively. This is at least in partial conflict with another tradition of resistance against government involvement in private decisions. To marry and to have children are private decisions, and hints of government coercion in these areas infringe on American values of individual autonomy. The attempt to enforce marriage as a higher form of family formation might have other unintended

---

Two, Three, Many Husbands

[T]he fact that many black female-headed families . . . are poor is taken as prima facie evidence that a mother is not enough. . . . That plus the wisdom of 7,000 years of patriarchy, 70 years of Freudian psychology, and 40 years of Parsonsian sociology, establishes conclusively that the black family is short one person, and that person should be an adult male. But can we assume that adding a husband will solve the problem?

It takes a few simple calculations to reveal the inadequacy of the two-parent black family. First we observe that the median black male income is $9,448, which is approximately $1,000 less than the poverty level for a family of four. So adding a median-type black male to a preformed family unit consisting of a mother and two children leaves us with a black family that still has a problem, namely, poverty. Adding two black males is still not much of an improvement: only by adding three can we hope to clear the median U.S. family income, which is $26,433. If our hypothetical black family is to enter the middle class mainstream, which means home ownership, it will need at least $34,596—or four husbands.

Source: Ehrenreich (July/August, 1986, p. 8).

Table 11.3   Experience of Selected Material Hardships Among the Poor, by
                  Marital and Household Status, 1998

Family Type	% Who Missed Meals for Economic Reasons	% Unable to Pay Utilities, Rent, Mortgage
Married couple, two biological or adoptive parents	22.8	31.0
Married couple, one biological or adoptive parent (step-families)	25.7	30.5
Cohabiting couple, two biological or adoptive parents	22.1	35.2
Cohabiting couple, one biological or adoptive parent	27.5	38.9
Single parent, another adult present	25.6	29.1
Single parent, no other adult present	32.7	38.9

Source: Lerman, R. (2002b, Table 9). Reprinted with permission from the Urban Institute.

Table 11.4   Poverty Rates for Working Women in Industrialized Nations

	All Women	Single Mothers
Australia	22%	26%
Canada	37	37
France	32	38
Germany	22	36
Netherlands	12	33
Sweden	16	11
United Kingdom	8	10
United States	33	42

Source: Luxembourg Income Study (2000).

consequences. The policy tends to belittle single mothers who stand by their
children in spite of extremely trying conditions, and it encourages women to
submit to any marital conditions, ignoring (for example) domestic violence
(Ooms, 2002a).

In fact, few states have been involved in promoting marriage and reducing adult non-marital child bearing, and this probably reflects a recognition
of what has been called the futility of family policy (Steiner, G., 1981). As of
1999, a total of 14 states encouraged sexual abstinence, but only 3 states
offered programs to encourage marriage among unmarried couples expect-
ing a child. Twenty-three states have imposed family caps preventing
mothers who got pregnant while on welfare from receiving additional
TANF payments, but there is no evidence of a drop in extramarital births

(Lerman, R., 2002a; U.S. General Accounting Office, 2001). In 2000, the number of children in single-parent households grew by 3.1% (O'Hare, 2003).

Set up to encourage work by increasing incentives, the Minnesota Family Investment Program (MFIP) used a similar strategy to remove penalties that had become financial obstacles to marrying and staying married. Work requirements were lowered and low-income couples were allowed to earn more money before losing benefits. A 3-year comparison of marriage stability in this and other more traditional programs showed MFIP with a 20-percent advantage. Sixty-eight percent of couples in the MFIP remained married, as compared to 48 percent in the matching groups. Furthermore, the MFIP had more single mothers who married in the same period: 11 percent as compared to 7 percent (Horn, 2001).

These successes validate some proposals for protecting fragile families from added economic stress. Reduction of tax and EITC penalties, lower TANF work requirements for couples, additional economic work incentives, and making education available for those getting married are promising ideas. So are measures such as the development of healthy relationships through stress management and access to marriage counseling, as well as developing work policies that are family-friendly, like Employee Assistance Benefit Programs (Dizard & Gadlin, 1990; Ooms, 2002a). The purpose of these strategies is to reward marriage rather than impose it.

Teen Sexuality and Poor Single Motherhood

The design of the 1996 welfare reform tied the reduction of teen motherhood—of "kids having kids"—to a reduction in the dependence of mothers on assistance. Thirty percent of all out-of-wedlock births are to teens, and half the single mothers had their first baby before the age of 20 (Sawhill, 2002). Low-income teen mothers tend to drop out of school, go on welfare, and have more children in their twenties without marrying. So, although the problem of poor single motherhood is not confined to teens, it often starts with them.

Part of the TANF budget in 30 states is targeted at teen pregnancy prevention and family planning. Strategies include media campaigns to discourage teen pregnancy and contracts with private agencies offering programs to prevent teen sexual activity (Lerman, R., 2002a). The tendency in many of these programs, particularly those run by religious agencies, is to focus on abstinence. A national evaluation of programs addressing teenage sexual activities indicates that the most effective interventions incorporated youth development and reproductive health components (Glei, 1994; Kirby, D., 2001). The claims of success for TANF in this area are greatly overstated, as Figure 11.1 demonstrates. Teenage births started to drop well before the implementation of the 1996 reform.

Explanations of the downward trend are still speculative. Although teenage pregnancy peaked at the same time that AIDS awareness was very

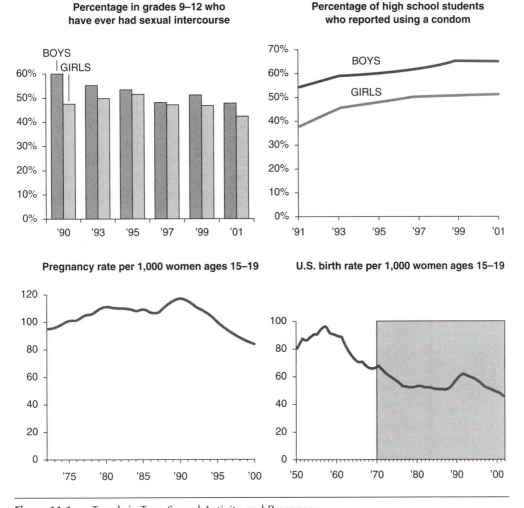

Percentage in grades 9–12 who have ever had sexual intercourse

Percentage of high school students who reported using a condom

Pregnancy rate per 1,000 women ages 15–19

U.S. birth rate per 1,000 women ages 15–19

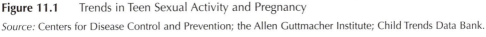

Figure 11.1   Trends in Teen Sexual Activity and Pregnancy

Source: Centers for Disease Control and Prevention; the Allen Guttmacher Institute; Child Trends Data Bank.

high, some observers believe that the drop might be a response to the AIDS scare. Others attribute the drop to greater access to contraceptives. Still other explanations link the downturn to media campaigns or to a plethora of sex education programs in schools and volunteer organizations.

Frank Furstenberg, a University of Pennsylvania sociologist with extensive research experience on the subject, offers an alternative theory. The previous increase in teen parenthood could be attributed to "poor teenagers adapting to the growing gap between the typical onset of sexual activity and viable economic adulthood" (quoted in Bernstein, 2004). This view was bolstered by a study by the Children's Defense Fund (1987), which established the relationship between declining earnings of young men, especially African Americans, and marriage rates in low-income areas. The opportunity for marriage in this population declined with the drop in blue collar job opportunities for young workers, with or without a high school education. Starting in the late seventies, early marriage, the oldest answer to unintended pregnancies, nearly vanished as an option (Grant Foundation, 1988).

Exactly why the decline in teenage parenthood gained speed in the early nineties remains unclear. It appears that as the economy improved, young adults had better economic prospects than before. The data also indicate that the drop reflected some postponement of sexual activity among teenagers and greater use of contraceptives, but not marriage growth. Qualitative evidence suggests that both males and females began to realize how their relatives and friends have experienced the deleterious consequences of precocious sex and "premature" parenthood (Bernstein, 2004; Figueira-McDonough, 1998a).

Experiential learning along these lines will be more efficient if teenagers have positive goals they think are achievable (Brewster, Billy, & Grady, 1993; Butler, 1992). Equally important for preventive intervention is the finding that a large percentage of the fathers of children born to teenage girls, especially in depressed neighborhoods, are adults (Figueira-McDonough, 1997; Glei, 1994).

The present time offers a good climate in which to work for the prevention of teenage parenthood. Preventive education that appeals to positive aspirations of teenagers, the encouragement of self-protection, avoidance of health and emotional risks, awareness of self-development, and reflection on the consequences of unplanned sexual activity could accelerate the positive trends. As a defensive strategy, diligently prosecuting statutory rape might be an effective tool to protect vulnerable younger girls (Figueira-McDonough, 1998a; Glei, 1994).

Enforcing the Responsibility of Fathers

Two family-related policies explicitly refer to fathers' responsibility: promoting fathers' marriage to the mothers of their children and enforcing child support.

Fathers who forgo their economic obligation plainly contribute to their children's poverty. The Child Support Enforcement Program was established in 1975 as a strategy to recoup the welfare costs of non-support. Child support money obtained in this way went to AFDC coffers to pay for the benefits received by abandoned mothers. Only in the late 1980s did legislation require states to provide services to *all* families who made applications for child support services. The new performance-based incentives of TANF, mandated by the Child Support Performance and Incentive Act, strengthened implementation on behalf of children on public assistance.

Congress made enforcement a component of PRWORA. The law aims to improve collection in several ways. First, states are to ensure paternity verification by reducing welfare benefits to families who do not cooperate in establishing paternity and obtaining child support orders. Second, states

High school students in very poor neighborhoods in a large city were interviewed in focus groups about a variety of issues of direct interest to them.

Here are some of their comments on sexual behavior and early parenthood:

Boys

- If you're going to have sex it is your prerogative. Can't nobody tell you not to do it because if there are two willing people, then it's going to happen . . . you cannot keep them from being together . . . they are going to be alone at some time. So if you are going to have sex you should protect yourself.
- Regardless, people are going to have sex anyway. I feel that you should wait until you are married because there are many diseases and a condom is not 100% effective.
- Sex is, that's true, to bring another life into the world, but also sex is for pleasure. Considering nowadays teenagers, I think if they protect themselves and have protected sex, then have maybe one partner, make sure is one on one, I think is fine, you know.
- I would say [it is OK to have a child] whenever you get a job and can support the child. If you cannot support yourself, how are you going to support another person? I don't care. . . . I don't think nobody is ready at the age of 14. Even if you were a millionaire you will not be ready emotionally. You might want to go out to clubs but [if] you have a child you can't.

Girls

- I wouldn't have sex if. . . . I see people do it because, um, to get back to their mom or dad somethin' that they do. And think to get revenge back or try to get popular or somethin'. But that don't make you popular. I never did it but . . . as long as you have a strong mind and you're in touch with your feelings and everything, it is your business.
- A lot of people, it don't matter. Some people they just have sex because they want to. Older boys talk younger girls into having sex. A lot of people . . . I think it's bad to have sex because you could get pregnant. You could get pregnant, and the last thing I want is some kids now.
- Girls will always be tricked into having sex, because boys are always going to pull that thing, well, you know, if you love me, and girls are much more emotional than boys so, I mean it's a shame, and I think girls should wait off because sex is a big responsibility. And sex comes with a lot of attachments and you could get attached to one boy and most of the time boys are going to be like, yah, so what? So I think that girls should abstain until later age.
- I think that a lot of teens that are having kids now . . . although you may say that . . . you're going to support them and be their friend and everything . . . you tend to flee away from them. I personally have friends that have children, and I try to be the same around them but it is a little different because they can't go like they used to because they got to get somebody to watch the baby, and you got to wait.

Source: Figueira-McDonough (1996).

failing to comply with this requirement get hit with financial penalties. Third, states are required to enact specific procedures for compliance—for example, revoking licenses and imposing work requirements on the delinquent non-custodial parent of children receiving TANF benefits. Finally, states have to pay the federal government their share of child support amounts collected for TANF recipients.

The problem for the states is how to carry out the law cost-effectively (Yates, 1997). Increased collections do not translate into substantially reduced welfare expenses. Many low-income, non-custodial parents cannot afford to pay full child support. Besides, the administrative costs of enforcing the orders (especially when children in the same family have different parents), of collecting arrears and making sure that the payments of those leaving welfare revert to TANF to cover the cost of prior assistance, all cut into the gains derived from the sums collected. Nonetheless, between 1995 and 2000, child support collection increased. The downside is that the amounts are modest. Acknowledging the connection between the ability to pay child support and employment, the Senate has proposed adding services for employment and training for non-custodial parents (Ganow, 2000).

An experiment conducted in Wisconsin offers insights regarding alternative ways to handle the collection of child support for TANF recipients. The experiment was done under the Wisconsin waiver and therefore not yet under the new legislation. Randomly selected recipients were compared in two conditions: receiving full child support and receiving half child support. The results suggest that Wisconsin's policy of passing all child support to TANF recipients and disregarding it in the calculation of TANF benefits was a success. More low-income mothers received more child support, many fathers were more likely to pay (and pay more), and more children had their paternity established.

Along with these accomplishments, the welfare administration was streamlined. Wisconsin, a state that had adopted a very strict stance about moving recipients into the labor market, lowered its welfare caseload by 90 percent (De Parle, 1999). The willingness to experiment with passing full child support to the recipients was based on the philosophy that recipients should be treated like other families in the labor force. Fathers cooperate more with the child support system when it is of direct benefit to their children. This investment might represent an avenue for the rapprochement between non-custodial fathers and children.

Child support for poor families comes to about 26 percent of their average income, so the Wisconsin experiment had the same positive effects on children that were found in other evaluations regarding income supplements in states like Minnesota. Wisconsin disregarded child support in determining eligibility and subsidies for child care assistance. The evaluators concluded that disregards for SCHIP, Food Stamps, and medical assistance would contribute still more to the welfare of children (Meyer & Cancian, 2003).

Current legislation uses child support as compensation to the states and the federal government for TANF's expenditures on benefits. The system runs contrary to the spirit of the Wisconsin experiment. Unless it is changed in the next reauthorization, the system will decrease income for many recipients, and this is known to hurt poor children on welfare. In addition, it will likely weaken the involvement of fathers with their children.

Some proponents of passing support directly to the children also propose that EITC eligibility should disregard child support. Wisconsin's ability to move in this direction was made possible because it functioned under a waiver. Most other states would meet strong impediments against following suit because they have to pay the federal government's share of child support money.

Child Support and Family Formation Among Low-Income African Americans

In 2001, an estimated 35 percent of single mothers in TANF were African American (Administration for Families and Children, 2001).

Directly tied to this situation is the chronically high rate of unemployment among young African Americans. Over the years, unemployment rates for whites and Hispanics have been consistently lower, as Figure 11.2 shows. Strikingly, the gap between African Americans and other groups did not decrease during the economic expansion of the late nineties. In fact, by 2000, young blacks were 23 to 25 points behind other groups in rates of employment (Fig. 11.2). Several non–mutually exclusive hypotheses have been advanced to account for this gap.

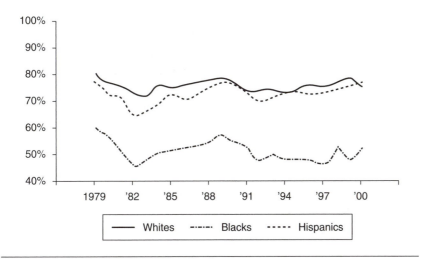

Figure 11.2   Employment/Population Rates for Men, 1979–2000

Source: Current Population Surveys, Outgoing Rotation Groups (samples include men aged 16–24 who are not enrolled in school).

• *Discrimination.* An exhaustive study of employers in Chicago discovered considerable resistance against hiring young black males. The standard expectation envisioned traits such as bad attitude, resistance to authority, and lack of discipline. Most expectations were not based on direct experience. They were stereotypes generalized to all young black males (Wilson, 1996).

- *Retrenchment.* Most young blacks live in urban industrial centers that have suffered a loss of manufacturing jobs. Economic restructuring probably affects these men disproportionately.

- *Segregation.* In the large cities where most African Americans grow up, schools are poor, jobs scarce, and connections to the outside weak. This environment breeds defeatism among young people (Figueira-McDonough, 1998a; Jargowski, 1997; Massey & Denton, 1993).

- *Incarceration.* As crime has declined, the number of people behind bars has topped 2 million, and African Americans are overrepresented in the prison population by a factor of 3.5 to 1. The thousands of prisoners released each year face employment prospects that are very poor indeed (Butterfield, 2000; Chaiken, 2000; Davis, A., 1998; Tonry, 1995; Yglesias, 2003).

- *Child support.* For men affected by any of the hindrances just listed, and therefore with low expectations for a decent job, demands for child support might weaken incentives to search for a regular job (Offner & Holzer, 2002).

A major employment initiative directed at young men, especially African American men, seems to be a necessary condition for increasing child support and father–child rapprochement. This would include work-oriented programs that integrate academic and occupational skills, and targeted training linked to local employers, supplemented by community jobs that emphasize skill acquisition and certification (Mincy, 1994).

Marriage-promotion policies have also to consider the experiences of African Americans. How the painful history of race relations in the United States contributed to desertions and victimization tends to be forgotten. The frequent rape of women and the discouragement of marriage prior to the Civil War, the separations of couples searching for work during the flight from the South, the breakup of communities and families in the migration to the northern cities, continuous poverty and male unemployment—all these pressures have gone into shaping a different form of family, with an extended support network, centered on women, but often with men assuming fatherly roles for children other than their own (De Parle, 2004; Jarrett, R., 1994). This family type is an adaptive survival mechanism under terrible circumstances (McAdoo, 2002).

Implementing the marriage goal must take the historical and present experiences of this group into realistic consideration and view it as the culmination of a series of steps. Unwed parents have four options: They can abandon their children, they can maintain some contact with the children, they can cohabitate, or they can marry. The options can be looked on as progressive steps, each one considered as an improvement over the previous one, with benefits for the children even if the final goal of marriage is not achieved. The approach sets progressive, incremental goals that may be more constructive than the $100 that some states set aside for recipients who get married.

Sociologist Robin L. Jarrett (1994) conducted focus groups with single black women regarding their beliefs about marriage, their reasons for not having married, the network they counted on for help, and the role of the fathers of their children in their lives. The following are excerpts from their comments.

Even though he don't have a job, sometimes what counts is the time he spends with his child. That child will think about that: "Well, my father's here when my mother's not here." The child will have someone to turn to. And the father say: "Well, I ain't got no job. I ain't going to be around a child." That's not all of it.

I got three kids all by him and he try to help out when he can. He is not working now but he did try to help. And . . . he be going out for a job. I don't try to pressure. [Men] care about their kids. They wanna help.

If he ain't out there trying to find a job doing anything . . . he can be there with that baby, holding the baby, changing that baby's Pampers and let that mommy rest or let her go out there and do what she have to do to support the baby.

It's not what you do, it is how you do it. I don't expect him to buy my baby snowsuits and boots. . . . It's just the thought. When Keith's (my son's) birthday came around, (his father) ain't got to give him a quarter, he ain't got to give him a card. You could pick up a phone and wish him a happy birthday.

It's not a father, but a male image. . . . My daughter will mind my brother better than she do me. I will tell her to sit down, whereas I would probably tell her four or five times, whereas my brother will come in with that manly image and will say sit down one time and she be sitting down.

It don't have to be blood to be like a father to somebody. . . . You can meet a man that will be a better father to your child than the natural father and that is nothing wrong with that.

The guy I am with is not my daughter's father; but he accepts my daughter. With him accepting and helping me out with her, that's all right. Most men they not going to do much except maybe like buy a little something, play with her and call it a day. But he accepts my daughter. And seeing that it is not his, I think that is a big responsibility. Because if I ask him for something for my daughter, he'll give it to me. So I figure that right there is a man.

Source: From Jarret, R. L., Living poor: Living life among single parent, African-American women, *Social Problems, 41*(1), 1994. Reprinted with permission of the University of California Press.

12 Temporary Assistance for Needy Families—II

Barriers and Exclusions

Among those affected by the TANF legislation, two groups deserve special attention. One includes families suffering from multiple problems that constitute severe barriers to work. The other is made up of families without benefits, despite their extreme poverty, together with legal immigrants who find themselves barred from certain programs.

Barriers

Families With Multiple Barriers to Work

According to the National Survey of America's Families (Urban Institute, 1999), half of the people who left welfare between 1997 and 1999 were working at the time of their interview. The statistic, while impressive, reflects the boom times of the late nineties.

Data from the *Fifth Annual Report to Congress* (TANF, 2003), covering 2001–2002, a period of recession, highlight the relatively modest and complex characteristics of TANF leavers. Only 19.4 percent were employed, and 31 percent either left because they were sanctioned or simply dropped out. The latter group is sizable, yet we know little about their economic situation, nor do we know much about the reasons that led 22 percent of former beneficiaries to return to TANF or why others—those who stayed on welfare for 2 years or more—took so long to leave. After early successes in moving recipients from welfare to work, attention has turned to cases that cannot live up to the "quick job" scenario—the immediate employment placement of recipients—especially during times of high unemployment when the job hunt, which is never easy, becomes truly daunting.

Living in poverty generates a variety of barriers against getting out of poverty. Table 12.1 documents the significant differences between those who are working and all the other groups (long-term recipients; welfare recidivists; and the disconnected, voluntarily or otherwise).

Table 12.1   Comparison of Barriers

	Working	Long-Term	Returning	Disconnected
Poor physical/ mental health	30%	39%	46%	50%
Less than high school education	7	50	38	38
Child younger than one year	11	6	19	8
Child SSI	5	6	7	19

Source: National Survey of America's Families (1999). Data organized by Pamela J. Loprest (2002, pp. 26, 27).

Recipients who do not move quickly into jobs are considered the "hard to serve." As Table 12.1 suggests, and as caseworkers figured out once the rush to lower caseloads was over, these recipients face multiple barriers that make the move to work extremely difficult or short-lived (Burt, 2002). A study of welfare recipients in Michigan during the late 1990s, when unemployment was very low (3.4 percent), permits an estimate of labor supply conditions while demand is high (Danziger et al., 2002). The results show that the number of barriers was strongly and negatively associated with employment status.

TANF Responses to Barriers

For recipients with multiple barriers, the move toward work requires complex strategies. A variety of services are needed, and this entails a significant investment of time and resources.

The barriers are likely to be interrelated. Social handicaps might be connected to depression, or lack of proficiency in English with lack of education and limited work experience. Mental health problems are often linked to domestic abuse and drug addiction.

Since TANF is unlikely to have expertise in all these fields, states opting to work with the "hard to serve" must contract out for the needed services. Outsourcing of the delivery of human services demands coordination and the capacity to monitor performance (Bandoh, 2003). De Parle's account (2004) of the poor families he followed highlights the inefficiency of this approach. Another concern is the challenge of identifying recipients who need extra help. Will an assessment at the time of TANF application lead to early identification of barriers? Or will referral after failures—those sanctioned, those reaching time limits, or those who return to welfare—result in more efficient decision points?

As happens with any aspect of TANF, states respond to hard-to-serve clients in a variety of ways. Some states allow them to fail, enforce sanctions on them, or wait for time limits to drop them out of TANF. Others have invoked criteria of failure before referring recipients to outside services. Still others try to identify multiple problems earlier in the process.

Even states that have actively contracted out for services to deal with hard-to-serve clients acknowledge a difficulty built into this strategy. The process of applying to different services, under different administrative domains, is confusing and overwhelming for many clients. Furthermore, those with multiple barriers often find themselves with no options. Certain mental health clinics exclude people with addictions, and organizations dealing with addictions do not accept people with mental problems. The Catch-22 is particularly vicious because these conditions often occur together (Burt, 2002).

A sprawling labyrinth of nongovernmental organizations (NGOs) and public departments is onerous for some states and all the more so for families handicapped by multiple challenges. The system tends to suffocate from its own weight and complexity. For some time now, professionals who work with multi-problem families have favored a model of multi-service community centers. This is very similar to the proposal formulated by Specht and Courtney (1994) reviewed in Chapter 1.

Experiments with such models have produced mixed results. In the late fifties and sixties, the Ford Foundation sponsored the Gray Areas Projects and Mobilization for Youth, and the Casey Foundation backed the New Futures Initiatives. These programs tried to provide integrated services to poor communities. Two factors worked against this goal: One was competition among the different service organizations themselves. The other was mistrust among those whom the organizations were supposed to serve. More recently, the Community Building Initiative of Maryland became hostage to a large number of contributors with different agendas.

Several inter-organizational studies of service delivery have offered a few guidelines for improvement: the development of trust among agencies, agreement about the overall goal to be achieved, negotiation of parameters of involvement and institutionalization of cross-agency alliances, and active involvement of the community in the planning and running of the centers (Figueira-McDonough, 2001, pp. 115–160). Reaching some formula along these lines, founded on multitasking centers, to integrate services for welfare recipients with multiple barriers would be a great improvement over the counterproductive system of forcing clients to navigate their way through dispersed agencies (Orland & Foley, 1996).

Outsiders

Families facing extraordinary problems—the homeless, for example, and those headed by ex-felons—have to deal with a variety of organizations—with the Department of Housing and Urban Development (HUD), the

Departments of Justice, the Department of Health and Human Services—all with different regulations that usually get in the way of progress toward self-sufficiency. A homeless family has to search for housing, and at the same time acquire work skills and find employment.

According to one study (Homes for the Homeless and the Institute for Children and Poverty, 1998; Mulroy & Lane, 1992), 68 percent of homeless parents over 25 had not finished high school, and 80 percent were unemployed and had become homeless for the second time. Their loss of housing was often preceded by traumatic experiences: eviction, break with extended family or friends with whom they lived, domestic violence, or mental disturbances.

Homelessness is mostly traceable to a lack of low-income housing. Scarcity drives up rents, which often consume more than half the earnings of low-income families. Quite a few pilot programs, implemented by volunteer organizations and supported by a handful of counties, have shown great success in developing provisional housing, but the number of such ventures does not keep up with the need (Mullenix, 1999). The problem is likely to get worse. In September 2004, the Bush administration proposed cuts in rent subsidies (Section 8 housing) for families residing in large cities where the problem is most acute. The size of the homeless population will go up as a result, and poor urban families will be placed at undue risk.

Another sector at high risk are mothers with criminal records. The 1996 Personal Responsibility and Work Opportunity Reconciliation Act (PRWORA) permanently barred individuals with drug-related felony convictions or probation or parole violations from federal TANF and Food Stamps (Mumola, 2000). In 1999, an estimated 146,000 women were incarcerated in the United States (Beck, 2002). Sixty-five percent were in state, and 59 percent in federal, prisons. Almost all are low-income, and the majority of them have minor children. The women typically have little education and work experience. Many have suffered from domestic violence, sexual abuse, and physical and mental health problems (Brown, 2000; Mumola, 2000). As of 2000, a total of 28 states deny welfare cash assistance to mothers with drug-related criminal histories. Drug-related offenses comprise a very large part of the crimes committed by women: 72 percent of federal offenses and 34 percent of state offenses (U.S. Department of Justice, 1999).

The Adoption and Safe Families Act of 1997 stepped up the pressure to terminate parental rights regarding children placed in foster homes while mothers are in prison. When they are released, mothers are often denied housing help. Women with criminal records find it difficult to qualify for either public housing or rent assistance through Section 8. Moreover, the stigma of a criminal record makes it hard for these women to get a job.

So their situation is extreme. In many states, women released from prison cannot receive assistance. They have to reenter the community and rejoin their children, but their schooling and work experience is quite limited, and shelter is unpredictable. The obstacles against reintegration seem insurmountable (O'Brien & Harm, 2002). The odds are stacked against them.

Jennifer Gonnerman (2003) describes the experiences of a young mother caught in the excessive rules of the new War on Drugs:

Elaine Bartlett was sent to prison for a first drug offense and received a sentence of 20 to life. Her children at the time were 10, 6, 3, and 1. As told by a reviewer of the book, the most heartbreaking scenes in *Life on the Outside* depict Elaine huddled with her children in prison visiting rooms. The family gathered every weekend and posed for pictures taken by the visiting room photographer. As the children grew up, the common problems of each stage were compounded by the trauma of separation from their mother. Prisoners' children spend holidays and birthdays behind bars. The author has Elaine's mother recounting these problems, and the letters sent to Elaine by their children reveal the pain of her absence. The book ends at the time Elaine is pardoned. Her mother, who had taken care of Elaine's children, has died and her extended family has come apart. Elaine had to create a life for herself and her younger children after 14 years behind bars: find a job, a place to live, and reconnect to her damaged family. She realizes that she has exchanged the prison behind bars for the prison that awaits ex-offenders who try to make it in the real world.

Source: Gonnerman (2003).

In recognition of the dire predicaments of ex-cons, the Departments of Justice, Labor, and Health and Human Services developed the Reentry Initiative Partnership in 2000. Eight states are running pilot programs. On the job front, applicants can earn certificates of good conduct to be handed to prospective employers. In addition, employers can be given Welfare to Work tax credits, or the Department of Labor (DOL) Work Opportunity Tax Credit, or simply a free bond from the DOL in the amount of $5,000 to protect against losses potentially incurred by employing workers with criminal records (Brown, 2000; Haberkern, 2003).

The Excluded

The Removal of Immigrants From Federal Assistance

The United States is a nation of immigrants, but public policies on immigration are at odds with this reality and the rhetoric surrounding it. They continue to reflect a schizophrenia between the need for labor and nativist impulses directed against foreigners.

The 1986 Immigration and Reform Control Act is a clear example of this conflicted mindset. It gave amnesty to many undocumented immigrants but, at the same time, required employers to certify that their employees were properly documented. There was no stipulation about establishing the validity of the documents, so the production of fraudulent papers became a cottage industry.

Why the double message? The demand for workers in menial, low-paying jobs in agribusiness, construction, landscaping, restaurants, and hotels provides a good part of the answer. Consigning immigrants to a vulnerable status benefited businesses. Non-protected workers increased profits, and cheap services in construction, gardening, house cleaning, and the like made the comforts of respectability available to the middle class (Jencks, 2001; Portes & Rumbaut, 2001).

The new rules of PRWORA in 1996, spelled out in Title IV of the Act, were much more punitive. They put virtually all federal, state, and local non-universal programs out of the reach of most immigrants. The 1996 Illegal Immigration Reform and Immigrant Responsibility Act raised the barriers to benefits still higher, by limiting the rights of non-residents to judicial appeal.

The legislation had a threefold rationale:

- Welfare benefits attract immigrants to the United States, thereby driving up the dependent population. The new rules were designed to deactivate "the welfare magnet."
- To seal off pathways to importing poverty, greater requirements and responsibilities were put on the sponsors of immigrants. In order to qualify as sponsors, their income has to be 125% above the poverty level. Sponsors must sign an affidavit of responsibility for the entrant up to naturalization or for 10 working years, and they are liable for reimbursing public agencies for any benefits during that period.
- The law authorized (but did not require) states to offer their own food, cash, and health benefit programs as substitutes for lost federal benefits. In fact, almost all states extended Medicaid, SCHIP, and TANF to pre-enactment immigrants but were more reluctant to extend these benefits to post-enactment immigrants.

The promise of lowering assistance costs was the major attraction of these measures. Savings were estimated at $54 billion—on the assumption that caseloads would be cut by 40 percent.

There is in fact no evidence that the "welfare magnet" brings immigrants to the United States in the first place. A Brookings Institution study showed, on the contrary, that between 1995 and 2000, the strongest growth in immigration occurred in the states with the least generous welfare provisions. Likewise, other research has contested the idea that immigrants are prone to be dependent and to draw down a disproportionate share of benefits (Borjas & Hilton, 1995; Duleep & Regets, 1994; Fix & Passel, 1994; Van Hook, Glick, & Bean, 1999).

If immigrants are not attracted by welfare benefits, why do they keep coming? They come to work. Immigrant males 16 or older have slightly higher labor force participation than native males: 79 versus 74 percent.

Table 12.2   Categories of Immigrants and Benefits Under PRWORA, 1996

Undocumented	Legal prior to 1996	Naturalized after 1996
Emergency medical	Optional for states	All means-tested federal programs
Immunization	TANF	TANF
School lunch	Medicaid	SSI
School breakfast	SCHIP	Food stamps
Populations exempt:	Refugees (first 5–7 years) Immigrants with 40 quarters of work history Non-citizens serving/having served in the military	
Changes affecting legal immigrants:	All elderly and disabled are eligible for SSI and Medicaid Food Stamps benefits for all children, elderly, and disabled	

Source: Balanced Budget Act of 1997 (pp. 105–133).

Among low-income workers, foreigners have a 73 percent employment rate as compared to 64 percent and 58 percent of natives in Los Angeles and New York, respectively. These estimates of engagement in the labor force are consistent with the conclusion of the National Academy of Sciences that the United States nets a $50 billion surplus from taxes paid by immigrants to all levels of government (Porter, 2005; Thrupkaew, 2002).

Table 12.2 shows that the barriers in means-tested programs follow a detailed categorization of immigrants. By 1997, some reforms had eased the PRWORA restrictions. Access to SSI and Medicaid was reinstated for immigrants in those programs before the 1996 legislation, and to all others who would become eligible in the future (Balanced Budget Act of 1997). The Food Stamps program was extended to all legal immigrant children, the elderly, and disabled persons (Agricultural Research, Extension, and Education Reform Act of 1998). However, 75 percent of the pre–welfare enactment legal immigrants were left out, together with all legal immigrants who entered the United States after 1996 (Fix & Passel, 2002).

Consequences

Table 12.3 lays out the reduction in TANF benefits according to immigration status. Legal non-citizens and refugees lost the most, probably because of misinformation about the cuts in benefits and also because of the "chilling effect"—the fear that their status would be questioned. In less

Table 12.3 Number of Families Receiving TANF, by Citizenship of Head and Spouse, 1994 and 1999

Status of Family Head/Spouse	Families		Change (%)	Distribution (%)			
				All Families		Foreign-Born	
	1984 (000s)	1999 (000s)		1994	1999	1994	1999
Citizen	3,502	1,607	-54	87	88	N/A	N/A
U.S.-born	3,450	1,531	-56	85	83	N/A	N/A
Naturalized	52	76	45	1	4	9	25
Non-citizen	411	197	-52	10	11	70	65
Legal	347	132	-62	9	7	59	43
Undocumented	60	66	4	2	4	11	22
Refugee alien	127	30	-76	3	2	21	10
Total	4,041	1,835	-55	100	100	100	100

Note: "Refugee alien" represents persons admitted as refugees since 1980 and who have not become naturalized citizens, regardless of current status. "Legal" includes all persons who are not citizens and who were admitted as legal permanent residents (LPRs), except those admitted as refugees. "Legal non-immigrants" or "legal temporary residents" are persons with valid entry visas who are considered U.S. residents, such as foreign students, intracompany transfers, or H-1 B "high-tech" guest workers.

Source: Urban Institute, tabulations from March 1995 and 2000 Current Population Surveys. Immigration status imputed with methods based on Passel and Clark (1998).

generous states, the fall-off reached 73 percent. Overall decreases in family Medicaid and SCHIP were smaller (Fix & Passel, 2002).

Nonetheless, the percentage of children under 18 without health insurance is of great concern. More than half (54.6 percent) of non-citizen children of undocumented parents have no health insurance. The same goes for over one-third of the offspring of legal immigrants (38.7 percent) and refugees (35 percent). Still more amazing is that so many citizen children of legal immigrants and of undocumented immigrants—39.3 percent—lack health insurance (Fix & Passel, 2002). This is particularly worrisome because citizen children of immigrants constitute 80 percent of all immigrant children. Among the chief preoccupations of immigrant advocates are the serious consequences of health care deprivation for the development of these young citizens (Fix & Passel, 2002; Portes & Rumbaut, 2001).

An in-depth study conducted by the Urban Institute in 2002 in New York and Los Angeles—the cities with the largest immigrant populations—found that about 30 percent were "food-insecure" and that over 20 percent were "home-insecure." They could not get enough food and at the same time pay rent. Families unable or barely able to speak English fared the worst (Capps, Ku, & Fix, 2002).

There are some basic contradictions between the goals of PRWORA and the exclusionary policies of Title IV. The intent of the legislation is to promote work and the family ethic among those dependent on welfare. The program developed a system of work supports: for example, transportation, child care, and skills development (English proficiency). Prior to the legislation, immigrants made up only 15 percent of the caseload, and their work rates, among those in low-income jobs, were higher than that of citizens. Why not then extend the work supports to a group already committed to the work ethic? Furthermore, among poor children, immigrants live up better to the TANF family goal. Forty-four percent have two parents as compared to 22 percent of native recipients (U.S. Census Bureau, 1998).

The limitations on access to Food Stamps raise questions regarding workers' rights and human rights. Labor force participation is very high among immigrants, so their inability to provide for basic goods is often traceable to sub-minimum wages. This amounts to sanctioning the exploitation of labor.

The restrictions on health coverage—Medicaid and SCHIP—are equally senseless from the perspective of human as well as citizenship rights. Immigrants have entered the United States for centuries, and their relatively low-cost labor has worked to the advantage of the economy in the aggregate. For this reason, refusing immigrants access to health services is irresponsible, even without taking into account the fact that these services would protect the health of legal residents as well. Then, too, depriving anyone within the borders of the United States of basic health services is tantamount to infringing on human rights. Recent policy regarding the sponsorship of immigrants is poisoned by the same pious hypocrisy. It circumvents the law of reciprocity— that is, the duty to provide minimal protections to a workforce brought to the United States for the benefit of American businesses (Fix & Passel, 2002).

TANF Reauthorization

Authorization for the 1996 TANF ended in the fall of 2002. Since then, the program has operated on short-term extensions. The most recent extension took place on September 30 of 2004 and expired on March 31, 2005. For the program to continue, Congress must eventually pass legislation reauthorizing the program. Work on new legislation began in earnest in 2004.

The program has been the object of extensive evaluation. These evaluations form the basis of many recommendations to improve it. The political back-and-forth between the president and Congress also stirs the pot. As is the case with much legislation, the president sends a proposal to the House and Senate, and each house comes up with its own revisions, both of which then go to a conference committee to reconcile the differences. The process has been more drawn out than usual. The House, with a strong Republican majority, tends to favor the White House version, while the Senate—Republican but less overwhelmingly so—has been divided.

How have assessments of the program affected the tortuous trail of reauthorization? Put bluntly, what has been the weight of research versus political interests and ideology? The House approved a reauthorization bill in 2003. The Senate has continued to debate a variety of issues and concerns. Table 12.4 compares key elements of legislation already on the books with the House bill and the Senate finance bill.

Table 12.4   Comparison of Key Provisions of Current Law to Pending TANF Bills

	Current Law	House-Passed Bill	Senate Finance Bill
Participation Rate Standards	50% in FY2004 and thereafter.	55% in 2005; increases by 5 percentage points each year until reaching 70% in 2008. Credit given toward rate for caseload reduction.	55% in 2005; increases by 5 percentage points each year until reaching 70% in 2008. Credit given toward rate for employed welfare leavers.
Hours of Work Required for Single Parents to Count Toward Participation Rate	Single parent with a child under age 6: 20 hours. Other single parents: 30 hours per week. No "partial credit" for parents engaged in work activities for fewer than required number of hours.	40 hours, regardless of age of child. Monthly rate determined using a 4-week month. Partial credit for adults who participate at least 24 hours in specified work activities.	Single parent with child under age 6: 24 hours. Other single parents: 34 hours. Monthly rate determined using a 4-week month. Partial credit for single parents who participate for at least 20 hours.

(Continued)

Table 12.4 (Continued)

	Current Law	House-Passed Bill	Senate Finance Bill
Education and Training	Vocational education training allowed as a full-time activity that counts toward participation rates for up to 12 months.	Allowed as a countable activity: 1) if recipient is working 24 hours a week; and 2) during 3-month period discussed under "Services for Individuals with Barriers."	Retains current law and provides state option to count postsecondary or vocational education as a work activity for more than 12 months (capped at 10% of caseload).
Services for Individuals With Barriers to Work	Not a countable activity.	Allowed under a provision that gives states the discretion to count state-defined work activities for 3 months.	Allowed for 6 months; months 4–6 must be combined with work or job-readiness activities.
Sanctions	Sanction amount left to state.	Mandates "full-family" sanction.	Current law.
Child Care Funding	Mandatory: Frozen at $2.7 billion per year. Discretionary: $2.1 billion appropriated in FY2003.	$1 increase in mandatory funding over 5 years; increased discretionary authorization level.	$7 billion increase in mandatory funding over 5 years.
Funding for "Marriage Promotion Activities"	State can use TANF funds for marriage-promotion activities, but no funding is earmarked for this purpose.	Earmarks up to $1.7 billion over 5 years for marriage promotion.	Earmarks up to $1.5 billion over 5 years for marriage promotion.
Superwaiver	No "superwaiver" authority in current law, but extensive authority exists to align and coordinate programs.	Superwaiver includes Food Stamps, public housing, child care, and other programs.	10-state demonstration limited to child care, TANF, and social services block grant.
Legal Immigrant Eligibility for TANF and Medicaid	Legal immigrants ineligible during first 5 years in U.S., except for refugees and certain humanitarian immigrants.	Current law.	Current law.

Source: Center on Budget and Policy Priorities, Executive Summary (May 12, 2004).

The following comments summarize differences and similarities among both bills and the present law. They underscore inconsistencies as well as the disregard for the body of information collected about the program over the past 6 years.

1. Both bills increase the participation-level standards. While the House proposes to tie credits to caseload reduction, the Senate gives states credit for *employed* leavers.

2. The difference in hours required of single parents is important. The House version requires 40 hours of work from all single parents. The Senate lowers the hours for mothers of preschool children and other single parents. Even so, the new requirements are more stringent than those of the current law. The Senate's proposal of partial credit also gives more leeway to the states in meeting the participation standards. The Senate bill is more in tune with the realities of single motherhood, especially for women with preschool children, and it is more realistic in terms of the access to work of people in transition from welfare.

3. The law as it stands allows vocational training to count for up to 12 months of work. The House not only limits the time period but also requires half-time work. The Senate would maintain the present criteria and add a longer period for secondary education, for up to 10 percent of the caseload. In this instance, the Senate proposal would better contribute to the chances of finding work and keeping a job, in addition to assuring some mobility.

4. The present law does not stipulate special conditions for recipients with multiple barriers to work. Some states contract with a variety of services to help these recipients, and exempt them from time limitations. Others simply use time limits or sanctions to push these clients out of TANF. Both House and Senate bills acknowledge the presence of these recipients. Changes envisioned in the House version seem unduly optimistic or disingenuous. They allow only 3 months of services to count as work for these clients. The Senate proposal is only a touch more realistic: 6 months of services are allowed, but the last 2 months must be combined with work or job-readiness activities. Studies of the complexity of providing services to clients with multiple barriers, and how hard it is to overcome them, show definitive time predictions to be of doubtful utility. A close look at the states with experience in this area, and their evaluations, shows the depth and clustering of multiple barriers. In many cases, time limits are simply infeasible. The danger is that those unable to meet the proposed schedule will, voluntarily or through sanctions, leave TANF with little or no hope of other economic support. Data from 2001 suggest that this number is quite high: 30 percent of the caseload (TANF, 2003).

Under the current law, states have discretionary power over the application of sanctions. The Senate proposal would not change that, but the House wants all sanctions to be family sanctions. In other words, if adults do not or cannot follow TANF rules, their children would be sanctioned as well. This can be construed as a breach of human rights.

5. The current law freezes child care funding at $2.7 billion. However, in 2003, a total of $2.1 billion in discretionary funds was appropriated. The House proposes an increase of $1 billion over 5 years, together with an increase in the level of discretionary authorizations. The bill pending in the Senate, as of this writing, increases mandatory funding over the same 5 years by $7 billion.

Because of increased work requirements and the decrease in TANF funds diverted to child care, the House proposal would leave more than 500,000 eligible children without child care assistance. In 2000, only an estimated 1 in 7 children eligible for child care subsidies received them (Ewen & Hart, 2003; Mezey et al., 2002). The Senate version may not be enough to increase the quality of care, which experts on early education consider essential to breaking the cycle of poverty.

6. While currently no funding is earmarked for marriage promotion (although states can use TANF money for that purpose) both bills in Congress propose to allot between $1.5 and $1.7 billion. This is a lot of money for narrowly defined programs whose effectiveness has yet to be proven. Most research links marriage with economic conditions—single motherhood among the poor is more a function of economics than morality. Therefore, it would make more sense to invest in raising employment in impoverished neighborhoods and opening opportunities for teenagers, so that they have an investment in their future. In the face of this evidence, these proposals reaffirm the myth that marriage is a cure for poverty (Ooms, Buchet, & Parke, 2004; Seefeldt & Smock, 2004).

7. The House would allow sweeping super-waivers affecting more than a dozen low-income programs. It would allow the executive branch to modify programs, effectively overriding congressional decisions about the level of resources devoted to specific programs and purposes (Fremstad & Parrott, 2004). Coordination exists in the present law and in the Senate proposal. Demonstration grants are limited to TANF, child care, and social services.

8. Neither of the two bills alters rules for immigrant eligibility. This may be their most disheartening feature. Most children of low-income immigrants live in working, married settings. These families meet the goals set by TANF. Giving the states the option to provide TANF and

Medicaid to all legal immigrants would extend the same safety net and work support that are now provided to citizens. The proposal on guest workers does not signal an improvement for immigrants. Instead, it retools the old *bracero* program, geared to respond to the needs of business for cheap labor (National Immigration Law Center [NILC], 1994). Some observers call it indentured servitude (Sanchez, 2004).

The Senate bill includes some important amendments. It would extend Transitional Medical Assistance that provides temporary Medicaid coverage to families moving from welfare to work through 2008. It would help states to implement changes, so that all child support collected reverts to the children. It would revamp the contingency fund to help states going through recessions so they can deal with rising caseloads without cutting services. This would address budgetary shortfalls evident in many states since the 9/11 trauma of 2001 (Fremstad & Parrott, 2004).

In April 2004, the Senate set aside the bill to reauthorize TANF after Republicans failed to muster enough votes to limit debate on the legislation. The disagreement centered on an amendment to increase the minimum wage from $5.15 to $7.00 an hour. Senators in favor of the increase argued that the income generated by a person working full time, at the current minimum wage, would put him or her and the person's family below the poverty line. For a mother with two children, this would amount to a gap of nearly $5,000: earnings of $10,712 versus a poverty level of $15,670. Senator Barbara Boxer of California noted that boosting the minimum wage was a logical corollary of the welfare bill. "We want to get people off welfare," Boxer stressed. "That's the underlying point of the bill. Let's get them into work that pays" (Pear, 2004e, p. A12).

On the whole, while the Senate bill does not speak directly to all the suggestions coming from the evaluations of TANF, it appears to be more in tune with this body of research. The House version seems to be heavily influenced by the givens embedded in the Contract with America. The learning curve looks pretty flat. Little attention is paid to the real-world knowledge that has been gained from over 6 years of experience with the program.

In February of 2006, Congress reauthorized TANF as a part of the Deficit Reduction Act of 2005. Caseload reduction requirements were increased. Activities counting as work were limited, and sanctioned cases were considered as part of active caseloads. The difficulties in meeting these stricter requirements mean that federal block grants to states will shrink. This, in turn, will lead to further cuts in services for TANF recipients (Herald, 2006).

13

Social Insurance and the Push Toward Privatization

To hear critics of the welfare state tell it, public social programs have become opulent ocean liners comfortably conveying Americans past the routine eddies of modern life. Surveyed from a longer distance that a wider canvas provides us, they look more like waterlogged lifeboats in a rolling sea of inequality.

—Jacob S. Hacker (2002, p. 333)

According to the 2005 Annual Report of the Social Security and Medicare Board of Trustees, the financial outlook of Part A of Medicare (hospital care) has deteriorated dramatically since the turn of the century. The projection is that reserves will be exhausted by 2020. On the other hand, Part B (doctors' office visits) and the new Part D (prescription benefits) will always be able to cover costs since general revenue transfers and beneficiaries' premiums are automatically adjusted each year. It is against this background that the effectiveness of the Medicare prescription reform has to be evaluated.

The Medicare Prescription Drug Improvement and Modernization Act of 2003

Major Components

Drug expenditures in the United States doubled between 1993 and 2002 (Confessore, 2002, p. 18). During the same period, seniors spent more on pills than on doctors' bills. Anecdotes about older citizens having to choose between groceries and blood pressure medicine ring true for many retirees. So it is understandable that when Debbie Stabenow called for price controls on prescription drugs during her bid for a Michigan senate seat, support for her campaign skyrocketed. She won the election.

However, sympathetic political leaders have been unable to make the pharmaceutical industry budge. Backed by their allies in Congress, drug companies claim that prices for their products reflect the cost of proprietary research and development. Congress has regularly defeated proposals for closing the patent loopholes that discourage the production of cheaper generic drugs, and it has refused to grant Medicare the power to bargain directly with pharmaceutical companies for lower prices.

The rationale given for this intransigence is that government interference would inhibit private research and hurt the prospects of improving the health of the country in the long term. In 2001, spokespeople claimed that the industry spent over $800 million on research and development (Confessore, 2002). On the other hand, Families USA (2002) reported that the drug corporation making 50 of the best-selling drugs spent twice as much on advertising as on R & D.

In the face of surveys documenting increasing distrust of the pharmaceutical companies, the industry-friendly Medicare Prescription Drug Improvement and Modernization Act was approved in 2003. The endorsement of the American Association of Retired Persons' (AARP's) chief executive officer, Bill Novelli, was decisive in moving the bill along. At the time, AARP had 35 million members. The majority of members had not been consulted, and 60,000 dropped their membership soon after the Act became law. Later, it became known that Novelli was an admirer and friend of Newt Gingrich, a leading ideologue of private insurance (Dreyfuss, 2004).

President Bush signed the legislation on December 8, 2003. Speaking at the ceremony, the president explained that he was giving older Americans better choices, and more control over their health care. He stressed several aspects of the Act:

- Insurance premiums cost about $35 a month on Medicare. After a deductible of $250, the plan covers 75 percent of the cost of prescription drugs up to $2,250 a year. It also covers 95 percent of drug costs after patients have spent $3,600 out of pocket.
- More health choices are made available to Medicare beneficiaries. They can choose to drop out of the conventional Medicare program and join private HMOs subsidized by the government.
- Medicare coverage of routine physical examinations will become available.
- Tax-free health savings accounts will allow Americans to buy high-deductible health insurance and set money aside to meet medical expenses not covered by their insurance.
- As coverage starts in 2006, Medicare beneficiaries can buy discount cards from several insurance companies that reduce some of their pharmaceutical expenses.

What is missing from this picture? The kick-off speech overlooked a few important details:

- There is a gap in coverage. Once a patient has spent $2,500 on drugs in a year, including $750 in out-of-pocket expenditures, Medicare coverage stops until the patient runs up a $3,600 out-of-pocket tab on medications.
- The law restricts the importation of drugs from Canada and other countries.
- Beneficiaries are prohibited from buying supplemental insurance to meet the cost of drugs not covered by Medicare.
- The government—that is, Medicare—is not allowed to negotiate drug prices with manufacturers.
- Coverage is reduced for some poor people whose drug costs are now paid by Medicaid.

For the first time since Medicare's inception, private insurers have a much bigger role and receive great incentives. In effect, private insurers are given favored treatment over the traditional fee-for-service Medicare system.

The Effectiveness of the Law: Costs, Benefits, and Consequences

Present and Future Costs

The most widespread criticism of the drug legislation is its cost. The low estimate is that the program will cost $350 billion in the first 10 years and over $1 trillion per decade after that. This aggravates an already sizeable budgetary deficit and adds to the national debt.

Some policy experts point out that even before this legislation, Medicare was facing dire fiscal problems in anticipation of the retirement of baby boomers. The budget surplus of the Clinton administration had been exhausted. The anticipated costs of the new initiative are likely to put the entire Medicare program at risk. The added incentives given to HMOs further strain Medicare's capacity to deliver basic benefits.

The policy does not address the major problem, which is the ever-rising costs of medical care in general and of prescription drugs in particular. By refusing to impose price controls, and by forbidding Medicare to use its purchasing power to bargain with drug companies, the law does nothing to inhibit prescription drug inflation (Greenstein, 2004; Starr, 2004).

Medicare is funded by a combination of payroll taxes and general revenues. Prior legislation stipulates that a "crisis" has to be declared when more than 45 percent of Medicare funding is projected to be drawn from general revenues over the next 7 years. Two choices are possible to avoid triggering the crisis: shift financing into payroll taxes—a regressive strategy—or adopt progressive income taxes. The new hike of 17.4 percent in the FICA withholding indicates the preference of the administration for the regressive option (Skocpol, 2004).

Who Benefits?

The new legislation specifies inordinately complicated coverage, replete with gaps. At the same time, it provides billions of dollars in subsidies to HMOs and other managed care operations, paying them considerably more than what it costs Medicare to provide the same services.

More to the point, the promise of greater choice is an illusion. HMO beneficiaries cannot choose doctors, unless they pay higher premiums—to PPOs (preferred provider organizations), for example. Allowable drugs are limited, and beneficiaries cannot purchase supplemental coverage to help fill the holes in the drug benefit. Past experience with HMOs has not been promising. In 1999, HMOs simply dropped 2.4 million Medicare beneficiaries on the grounds that government payments had been delayed.

President George W. Bush's plan calls for an increase of those presently in private managed care, from 11 percent to 35 percent. In order to attract private health organizations to play a larger role, the increase of 2 percent in payments that was on the books went up to 10.2 percent in January 2004 (Jost, 2003; Pear, 2004c). Private insurers and health plans under contract with the government will manage the drug benefit program. The legislation sets forth entitlements to drug benefits, but insurers can modify them.

About 14 million low-income Americans, 35 percent of all Medicare beneficiaries, will qualify for extra subsidies. However, to achieve this, an enormous enrollment effort will be needed, with resources yet to be identified. The 2003 Medicare Act also affects beneficiaries near or below the poverty level who used to be able to enroll in Medicaid and get their drugs free. Now, a modest copayment is required, but, given the meteoric inflation in drug prices, copayments are likely to go up. This adds another hardship for those who live on minimal fixed incomes (Park, Nathanson, Greenstein, & Springer, 2003).

Anticipated Consequences

Some aspects of the reform—private plans, health savings accounts, and prescription discount cards—have received considerable attention. What are likely to be the consequences of these measures for the most vulnerable Medicare beneficiaries?

- *Private plans.* Medicare already reimburses private managed plans at rates that are 19 percent higher than traditional Medicare paying directly to providers. The new legislation exacerbates this disparity by privileging private managed plans. Without price controls on drugs and medical services, the likelihood is that premiums as well as copayments will increase. Wealthier clients will be better able to cope, and healthier clients will be given preference. Medicare will be left with the less well-off and sicker beneficiaries, who enroll on a pay-as-you-go, fee-for-service basis, and therefore accrue higher average health costs.

- *Health savings accounts.* Tax-advantaged savings accounts will be available to people with high-deductible health insurance policies. These accounts set up a lucrative tax shelter favorable to those well off enough to have high-deductible health plans in the first place and who are in fairly good health. This group would also represent a threat for employer-based comprehensive plans. As more and more healthy workers move to these profitable accounts, the premiums for the less healthy in comprehensive plans would more than double (Greenstein & Orszag, 2004; Jost, 2003; Park et al., 2003).

- *Discount cards* went into effect on July 1, 2004. They offer an opportunity to save on the price of prescription drugs before the law is implemented in 2006. The cards are a stopgap measure to provide discounts of 10 to 25 percent for Medicare participants who have no prescription drug coverage. Each card costs up to $30 a year. With the approval of Medicare, various companies and organizations offer the cards. The initial reaction among retirees across different income groups was incomprehension. They found 73 competing cards, each providing different savings on different drugs, with prices subject to change. Each participant can choose only one card. The complexity of choice keeps many people away from the program (Lelland, 2004).

John Lelland (2004), a *New York Times* journalist, approached some elderly people to assess their reaction to the Medicare drug reform. Two examples highlight a rather typical reaction.

"I'm 85, do I have to go through this nonsense?" asked Florence Daniels, a retired engineer who said she received less than $1,000 a month from Social Security, of which she paid $179 a month for supplemental medical insurance. She gets drugs through a New York State program, which provides any prescription for $20 or less. To make ends meet and afford her drugs, she said she bought used clothing and put off buying new glasses. Some of her friends travel by bus to Canada to buy drugs; others do without.

Another elderly lady expressed a feeling of confusion because of the amount of information required to make the right decision. The choice among the variety of cards and the drugs they cover would require paying other people to make sense of it all. She would much prefer if there was a single card administered by Medicare.

Ms. Daniels did not use the government Web site to compare drug cards, in part because she cannot afford a computer. "I'm trying to absorb all the information, but it is ridiculous," she said. "If there was a single card and it was administered by Medicare, and it got the cost of drugs down—wonderful, marvelous. But with these cards, the only thing we know is that we'll have to pay money to other people to administer what we can and can't get."

Source: From an interview reported by John Lelland in the *New York Times* (May 12, 2004, p. A17).

A battle has already ensued between insurance and pharmaceutical companies. Insurers want to limit the types and number of drugs offered in their plans. The drug companies are pushing for the inclusion of as many drugs as possible.

The public's reception of the drug law has not been favorable. According to a survey covering over 1,000 Medicare beneficiaries, released in the summer of 2004 by the Kaiser Foundation and the Harvard School of Public Health, nearly half—47 percent—of the beneficiaries had an unfavorable view of the new law, as against 27 percent who favored it. (The remainder had no opinion.) Eighty percent favored changes that would permit the importation of low-cost drugs from Canada and allow the government to negotiate for lower prices. Even the AARP executive director, aware of the unpopularity of the law he had supported, sent out letters to the membership promoting changes to allow for the importation of drugs and the strengthening of traditional Medicaid (Pear, 2004d, 2004f).

In addition, the governors of some states have accused Washington of trying to cut its share of Medicaid contributions. Insurers themselves object to a provision requiring companies to cover regions that include more than one state. The origin of the regional coverage policy was twofold: it was designed to cover rural areas often neglected by private insurers and to foster greater competition. Insurers felt that developing networks of doctors and hospitals in areas unfamiliar to them was too expensive. Besides, they argued, the variation in health resources among states made a larger, one-size-fits-all plan nonsensical (Pear, 2004b, 2004g).

Seen from a broader perspective, the patchwork nature of the 2003 reform may stem from more than just the usual problems of planning, which could be tweaked and eventually ironed out. Its tortuous unwieldiness may also reflect a political strategy to weaken public health insurance and have private insurance take its place (Jost, 2003).

Social Insurance Financing and Alternative Proposals

The Search for Correct Information

Social Security was the crowning achievement of the New Deal. It was the largest and most popular program ever devised by the federal government, and it attained untouchable status. For more than 60 years, Social Security has helped millions of Americans to avoid poverty when they reach old age, when they become disabled, or after the death of a family breadwinner. It has offered basic protections against the vicissitudes of losing the capacity to work.

The way the system works presently, employers and employees are both assessed a payroll tax of 6.2 percent on wages up to $90,000 a year. This money is used to pay a monthly average of $900 to 47 million beneficiaries,

75 percent of whom are retirees and their dependents, and the remainder to survivors and disabled people. Each succeeding generation pays for the retirement of the previous one.

As life expectancy grows and the population ages, the number of retirees inexorably goes up faster than the number of workers. Benefits will increase by 2 percent of the GDP over the next 30 years, and creep up slowly thereafter. Assorted predictions about the vulnerability of the program have proliferated, and a plethora of solutions have been proposed.

The 2005 report of the Social Security and Medicare Board of Trustees indicates that the financial outlook of Social Security has improved since 2000. A cash flow deficit in Old Age, Survivors and Disability Insurance (OASDI) is likely to occur in 2017. The Board projects that the assets of the trust fund will be exhausted by 2041. Redeeming treasury bonds will cut into the ability to underwrite other programs because the government has routinely relied on Social Security taxes to cover a variety of expenditures. Even if these predictions are less alarming than those of many popular reports, the costs of Social Security are expected to reach 6.4 percent of the GDP by the mid-seventies of the present century. The basic problem is that the number of beneficiaries will surpass the number of contributors. Alternative scenarios for solving the problem offer varying levels of equity.

Proposals to Restore Social Security

Private Accounts

One component of President Bush's ideal of an "ownership society" is the transformation of Social Security from a public program into private holdings. The plan would start by allowing younger workers to divert some of their payroll (FICA) taxes into personal accounts. The message was a refrain throughout his 2004 electoral campaign: "Younger workers ought to be able to take some of their taxes and set up a personal savings account, an account that they can call their own, an account that the government cannot take away and an account that they can pass from one generation to the other" (Toner & Rosenbaum, 2004).

Yet even in the president's 2005 State of the Union address, the specifics of the plan remained vague. There was no statement of how much the plan would cost, no mention of the magnitude of reductions in Social Security checks for those investing in private accounts, and no discussion of how much the government would retain from these accounts.

Some responsible analysts have set the price of the Social Security reform at $2 trillion over 10 years (Diamond & Orszag, 2004). Advocates for the elderly—AARP's policy director among them—fear that, unless unacceptably drastic cuts are made in guaranteed benefits, such costs would severely endanger the fiscal health of Social Security. Defenders of private accounts argue that returns from the individual accounts would make up for these losses.

Exhibit 13.1   Alan Greenspan on Social Security

Source: Copyright © Tom Tomorrow. Reprinted with permission.

Others see still more serious problems with the administration's program:

• It will cost trillions to move from a system run entirely by the government to one that is partly a private pension. During the transition, the government is obligated to continue paying retirees their benefits. However, concurrently, revenues to pay for those benefits will shrink, as FICA taxes that would have gone to Social Security are diverted into personal accounts.

• Personal accounts are risky. Retirees could do well, or poorly, depending on their investment savvy and the dynamics of financial markets. Since guaranteed Social Security benefits are the only source of income for 20 percent of Americans 65 and older and account for half the income of 75 percent of the rest, the consequences of that risk could be disastrous (Aaron & Reischauer, 2001; Diamond & Orszag, 2004; Toner & Rosenbaum, 2004).

One hypothetical plan for Social Security private accounts would divert 2 percentage points of the taxes workers now pay into the accounts and reduce the workers' promised retirement benefits to take account of their lower contributions. The lost tax revenue would exceed the reduced benefits for the next 45 years.

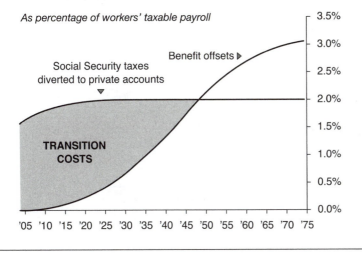

Figure 13.1   Costs of Transition of Proposed Privatization of Social Security

Source: Peter R. Orszag, Brookings Institution, 2004. Reprinted with permission of the author.

Tax Reform

Various proposals to alleviate shortfalls in Social Security concentrate on tax reform.

Social Security payroll earnings cap. The cap on income liable to the Social Security payroll tax was set at $87,900 for 2004. Income beyond this level is simply not taxed. From 1983 to 2002, the percent of earnings above that limit grew from 10 to 15 percent, with the result that FICA withholding became more regressive. Furthermore, people with higher education and earnings tend to live longer than those without. The upshot is that high earners collect more benefits for longer periods, after paying proportionately less taxes. Raising the cap would not only be more equitable. It would also ease Social Security financing (Diamond & Orszag, 2004).

Estate tax reform. The revenue that could be secured from a specific change in the 2001 tax cut could help the Social Security reform effort. Prior to the 2001 estate tax cut, estates worth less than $675,000 for an individual and $1.5 million for a couple were exempt. The heirs of about 98 percent of Americans were exempt from "the death tax."

The alternative proposal recommends reforming rather than repealing, by 2009, the estate tax cut of 2001. It would keep the exemption for estates worth less than $3.5 million for an individual and $7 million for a couple.

Table 13.1 The Size of the Bush Tax Cuts and the Actuarial Imbalance in the Social Security Trust Fund

	% of GDP	Year trust fund will be unable to pay full benefits
Social Security trust fund 75-year actuarial imbalance:		
March 2004 Trustees' report	0.7%	2042
June 2004 CBO report	0.4%	2052
75-year cost of 2001–2003 tax cuts, if extended as proposed by the President:		
Total cost of tax cuts	2.0%	
Tax cuts for top 1 percent	0.6%	

Source: Congressional Budget Office (CBO) and Joint Committee on Taxation.

According to this formula, 99.7 percent of Americans would escape the death tax. The estates of the other 0.3 percent—in short, the wealthiest—would be subject to taxes. If this estate tax were dedicated to Social Security, 40 percent of the shortfall projected by the Congressional Budget Office would be eliminated by 2009 (Greenstein, 2004; Greenstein, Orszag, & Kogan, 2004).

Keeping the 2001 and 2003 tax cuts from becoming permanent. If the 2001 and 2003 tax cuts are made permanent, as the administration has proposed, their cost to the Treasury over 75 years will amount to more than five times the Social Security shortfall forecast for the same period. In graphic terms, the tax cuts just for the 1 percent of households with average yearly incomes of about $1 million, exceed the entire 75-year Social Security shortfall projected by the Congressional Budget Office. Sunsetting these tax breaks rather than making them permanent would resolve the financial problems of Social Security, as Table 13.1 indicates (Greenstein et al., 2004).

Restructuring Social Security

Progressive proponents of remaking Social Security start by locating the causes of long-term deficits, and focus on three key factors. First and foremost is rising life expectancy. Long-lived beneficiaries collect benefits over longer periods. Second, the income cap on payroll taxes seems both costly and unfair. Finally, there is the legacy debt. Benefits paid to almost all current and past beneficiaries exceed what would have been financed by their contributions, including interest. Future generations would carry the burden of this debt.

How might these issues be dealt with? A multi-level response emerges.

The life expectancy issue cannot in fairness be handled simply by decreasing benefits. A balanced approach would be one in which half of the life expectancy adjustment occurs through a reduction in benefits and the other half through an increase in payroll taxes.

A combination of revenue and benefit adjustments might also be applied to the issue of earnings inequality. First, the maximum taxable earnings base would be raised until the share of earnings above the base does not surpass 10 percent. Second, the FICA would become more progressive to offset the difference in life expectancy between high and low earners. This would lead to benefit reductions affecting only relatively high earners—about 15 percent of beneficiaries.

The cost of lightening the "legacy debt" has to be distributed fairly by attempting to stabilize the ratio of this debt from one generation to the next. (This is the ratio of benefits for the elderly relative to taxes paid into the system by workers.) Three steps could achieve this:

All state and local government workers would be covered under Social Security. Currently, 4 million of them are not. This would ensure that all workers bear their share of the generosity shown to earlier generations.

A legacy charge would be imposed on earnings above the maximum taxable base starting at 3 percent.

A universal legacy charge on future workers and beneficiaries would come in two parts: half as a benefit reduction and the other half as a very modest increase in the FICA.

This restructuring of Social Security would produce a balance between present cohorts and generations to come, between lower and higher earners, and between workers presently covered by the program and those who are not. The reforms would ensure the long-term solvency of Social Security over the next 75 years and produce a modestly growing ratio of the trust fund to annual costs at the end of that period.

A more ambitious agenda envisions enhancing benefits for three particularly vulnerable groups: long-term minimum-wage workers, elderly survivors/disabled workers, and young survivors of deceased workers (Aaron & Reischauer, 2001; Diamond & Orszag, 2004). The alternatives that AARP has proposed are consistent with this type of restructuring (Calmes, 2005).

Shadow (Private) Welfare

Occupational Health Benefits

Public health programs cover the elderly and disabled, under Medicare, and individuals and families below or slightly above the poverty line, under Medicaid. Everyone else must obtain private coverage, typically by way of health care benefits granted through work contracts.

The government encourages these arrangements through incentives and tax deductions, and the programs are loosely regulated. In 2000, employment-based health plans covered 170 million Americans, roughly two-thirds of the population. Fewer than 70 million had government coverage. Private health expenditures represent 55 percent of total health costs in the United States. While occupational pensions cover less than half of the workforce, in 2000 their cost exceeded the old-age and survivors benefits awarded by Social Security: $460 billion versus $353 billion (Mills, 2000; Social Security Administration [SSA], 2002; U. S. Department of Commerce, 2001). A significant percentage of the workforce is not covered at all. Forty-five million Americans have no health insurance (U.S. Census Bureau, 2003a).

For more than two decades, the private side of the American system of social benefits has been eroding as corporations eliminate and restructure benefits to cut costs and encourage self-reliance. Coverage under workplace programs has dropped, benefits have grown more unequal, and recipients have faced more restrictions and assumed more of the risks that plans used to cover.

In practice, the system is a hybrid rather than being strictly private—in Gottschalk's (2000) metaphorical terminology, it is a shadow welfare system. Voluntary, lightly regulated occupational welfare receives tax breaks as incentives from the government. These incentives have become instruments of social and economic policy, a spending program in disguise. The arrangement allows for new spending without subjecting it to the kind of scrutiny that traditionally accompanies such outlays on public programs. Incentives, in the form of deductions, to employers' health insurance contributions top the tax breaks; they are projected to amount to $106.7 billion for 2005 (Vieth, 2004).

In the meantime, health costs have been going up at five times the rate of wage increases. According to a survey of large corporations conducted by the Kaiser Family Foundation, the cost of employee health insurance had increased by 59 percent over 4 years (Vrana, 2004).

Responses for coping with these increases have all proved costly for workers. Slow job growth has been linked to the unwillingness of employers to assume the health costs of new full-time employees when they can hire temporary workers. Other strategies involve increasing the employee share in premiums, eliminating the coverage of dependents, freezing wages to make up for health benefits, hiring young people to decrease premiums, or canceling health plans altogether (Porter, 2004b).

Organized labor has battled these adaptations, as the 5-month strike against California supermarkets in 2003 indicates. But the settlement was not a success for the unions. They wound up conceding that new hires would pay higher premiums and get lower wages (AFL-CIO, 2004b; Cleeland, 2003).

The upsurge in the number of the uninsured has reached middle class families. Some have found themselves unable to pay for hikes in their premiums. In other cases, where plans were canceled or never existed, some could not afford to pay for private insurance. The annual family premium averages $9,950. Without employer or government help, this is a chunk of money that even those with incomes of $50,000 are hard-pressed to pay out. This explains why 21 million of the uninsured are steady, full-time workers (Freudenheim, 2004b; Porter, 2004b).

Retirees are the other group jeopardized by the increase in health costs and their employers' response to it. Some companies, especially those with large numbers of retirees, decided that keeping their health plans was excessively burdensome. The Kaiser Hewitt Survey reported the changes, shown in Figure 13.2, that the large companies were more likely to consider implementing (Freudenheim, 2004a; Vrana & Kemper, 2004).

The Equal Employment Opportunity Commission (EEOC) greenlighted such cuts when it ruled that the reduction or elimination of health benefits for retirees was permissible when they became eligible for Medicare. This created an exemption to the Age Discrimination in Employment Act of 1967, and it set off alarms among the 12 million retirees who used employer-sponsored health plans to pay medical expenses not covered by Medicare (Pear, 2004a). A survey of women workers identified health care as the single most important issue that unions need to address (AFL-CIO, 2004a). Twenty-six percent of working women have no health benefits.

Percentage of companies that said the following changes were very likely or somewhat likely in the next three years

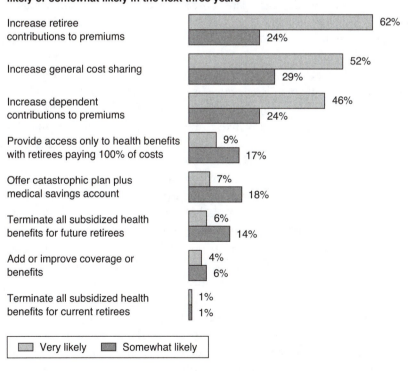

Figure 13.2   Changes Planned by Companies in Private Welfare

Source: Findings from the Kaiser/Hewitt 2004 Survey on Retiree Health Benefits #7194. This information was reprinted with permission of the Henry J. Kaiser Family Foundation, a nonprofit, independent national health care philanthropy and is not associated with Kaiser Permanente or Kaiser Industries.

The private health care model, developed early in the history of welfare in the United States, appears to be disintegrating. A combination of retrenchment on the part of employers, regardless of government incentives, and the explosion of medical costs have put tremendous pressure on the system. Ironically, as happened with the legislation that prevents Medicare from negotiating the price of drugs, there has been no effort to control costs. The consolidation of the insurance industry, and the political clout this entails, contribute to the excessive climb in premiums more than doctors' fees and hospital care costs (Freudenheim, 2004c).

Spending on health accounted for 15 percent of the GDP in 2003. This translates into $1.5 trillion dollars, or $5,446 per person. No matter how they are calibrated (relative to the GDP, on a per capita basis, and so forth), health expenditures are higher than in other OECD countries, where public spending covers about twice as many citizens as in the United States (Clinton, 2004; Pear, 2004a).

Pensions

A favorite analogy for retirement security is the comparison to a three-legged stool: Social Security, employer-provided pensions, and personal savings. Over the past decades, pensions have been viewed as supplementary to Social Security. In some instances, "supplementary to" can morph into "integrated with." Social Security contributions might be partially or fully discounted from employer-supported pensions.

Labor unions actively promoted pensions as work benefits. Pension plans, though not officially mandated, came in for increased regulation in the 1974 Employee Retirement Income Security Act (ERISA) legislation. The collapse of Studebaker, once an innovative if not major automobile manufacturer, left 10,000 workers without pensions. The ERISA measures were in part a reaction to this catastrophe (Hacker, 2002).

Traditional pensions are *defined-benefit* plans, funded by employers, workers, or both. They provide a guaranteed benefit—a predetermined amount at fixed intervals until the end of life. Complex formulas link earnings and length of job tenure to determine eventual benefits (Sass, 1997). Workers retain the promised benefits only if they work for the same organization for a certain number of years. If they leave the organization before the established period, they lose the pension.

These types of pensions are *redistributive*. Employees contribute a percentage of their earnings and receive benefits according to the same formula, pooling the risks. The plans are professionally managed and federally guaranteed.

Defined-benefit pensions have become significantly less common over the past 15 years. In 1979, nearly two-fifths—37 percent—of private sector workers were covered under traditional pensions. Today, defined-benefit plans protect only 1 in 5 (21 percent) (Hacker, 2002).

However, pensions based on defined contributions have increased over the same period, from 7 to 27 percent. *Defined-contribution* plans do not

Table 13.2 Share of Workers Participating
in 401(k) Pension Plans

Income Level	Percentage
Less than $10,000	4.5
$10–20,000	10.5
$20–30,000	18.3
$30–40,000	26.2
$40–50,000	31.9
$50–75,000	39.4
$75,000 +	41.3

Source: Adapted from Poterba (1997, p. 182).

embody the promise of predetermined periodic benefits upon retirement, nor are they federally insured. They are a form of organized retirement savings that depends on how much is contributed, by the worker alone or together with the employer. These plans are funded mostly by employee contributions to 401(k)-type individual accounts (AFL-CIO, 2004c). The bull market of the mid- to late nineties made them very attractive. The problem is that they overwhelmingly favor employees who earn comparatively well, since they are the ones most able to invest over and above what they consume for food, housing, and other necessities. Table 13.2 shows the share of workers participating in 401(k) pension plans by income in 1991.

If workers had been eligible to contribute equally to 401(k) plans, those earning below $15,000 would have accounted for 15 percent of the total contribution, as compared to the 0.7 percent of those with income above $75,000, based on the number of full-time workers at each wage level.

Companies benefit from defined-contribution plans. The programs reduce their own obligations to contribute, and they shift investment risk and responsibility to individual workers. The good news is that these plans are transportable from job to job. The bad news is that benefits from these plans have been highly inflated by including the gains of high-income private accounts into the average gains of workers entering retirement. These gains for the decade of the nineties, using median-income accounts, are modest and even negative. Both systems depend on tax deductions. Employer contributors to pension plans cost the Treasury $59.4 billion in 2000, while 401(k) plans cost $56.7 billion in tax exemptions (Gale, Shoven, & Warshowsky, 2004; Hacker, 2002; Walsh, 2004a).

Three factors might dampen the rush towards individual 401(k) accounts as an alternative to defined-benefit pensions. The first is the uncertainty of outcomes, together with the complexity of managing them. Some human service institutions, such as the United Methodist Church, have returned to traditional defined-benefit pensions in response to these problems. They have also done so to ensure greater equity.

The United Methodist Church, with 25,000 employees, is in the same league as other big pension plan sponsors, such as Bank of America and Dow Chemical. More than two-thirds of the Fortune 500 companies still run this type of plan, while they press more and more for a relaxation of regulations. In addition, a series of small plans, mostly covering service organizations, appear to be returning to the defined-benefits model. Conceivably, human service organizations operate within a fairly stable labor market that suits defined-benefit plans (Walsh, 2004b).

A second factor is the instability of companies themselves. The spectacular implosion of Enron in 2001 drew attention to the potential for massive damage to employees when pension accounts are invested in stocks of the employers sponsoring the plan. Enron had more than 60 percent of its 401(k) portfolio in company stocks. This came about because Enron matched employee contributions with company shares. These plans are not federally insured, and when the company failed, thousands of employees lost their retirement savings along with their jobs.

In half of the defined-contribution plans, 10 percent or more of employer contributions are from stocks of the company and nearly one-fifth of these plans have half of the holdings in company stocks (Crenshaw, 2001). Whether the Enron debacle will lead to more federal regulation of such accounts is a matter of speculation.

The last factor concerns age discrimination. A 1995 ruling by the Internal Revenue Service made cash-balance plans, a type of defined-contribution pension, permissible. One out of five large companies have converted their traditional defined-benefits plans to cash-balance plans. Cash-balance plans appeal to companies because they allow them to shrink long-term pension debt and reap accounting gains, while still providing benefits to employees. These plans set aside a specific sum for each worker and guarantee a minimum interest rate. However, because of the compounding of interest, they favor younger workers. Besides privileging younger workers, the switch from the traditional to cash-balance plans has caused older workers to lose a portion of their benefits.

A class action suit was filed with the federal court in Illinois on behalf of 130,000 former and present IBM employees who claimed that the company had discriminated against older workers when it switched from a traditional pension to a cash-balance plan. The company has been trying to settle, as the judge was about to rule in favor of the plaintiffs. Whatever the outcome, the case raises questions for all companies that have adopted cash-balance plans (Johnson, 2004).

Further Thoughts About Privatization

The United States is approaching another crossroads in the protracted debate over public and private benefits. Opponents of the status quo get behind remedies that are premised on the weakness of public social programs. In part, the position is based on a historical path that considers government intervention as a threat to individual freedom and private solutions as more efficient than public.

The same reservations were heard during the original debate over Social Security in the 1930s. Many business groups attacked the program as a socialist ploy. Besides, it was supposed to undermine the economy, invalidate voluntary arrangements, aggravate price inflation, lead to wage cuts, and worse (Gottschalk, 2000).

As a practical matter, the privatization of social policy comes down to four priorities. The first is to scale back direct government intervention. The idea is to encourage thrift and self-reliance. TANF follows this rationale. The second priority is to expand subsidies for private insurance, savings, and charitable activities. The shadow welfare of health and pension plans accords with this model. The third mechanism is to get the government to contract for services with voluntary organizations and for-profit service providers, as TANF programs do. Finally, vouchers and similar devices play an important role. They allow, or require, recipients to opt out of public programs, like Medicare and Social Security, to obtain benefits from private organizations instead.

In reality, neither contracting nor opting out of public provision reduces government intervention. What takes place is a shift of emphasis from direct government action to public management and oversight of private actors, operating within a new framework of regulatory authority (Hacker, 2002; Majone, 1996). More important, the major beneficiaries of these changes are private, for-profit organizations rather than recipients themselves. Thus far, private welfare has resulted in the fragmentation of health insurance and a shift from defined-benefits to defined-contribution pension plans, and from compulsory to voluntary plans. This has exacerbated inequality across workers and sectors by undermining risk pooling and the redistribution of benefits.

Private and public insurance benefits are more and more likely to flow toward the winners of America's postindustrial economy, and to become ever more elusive and costly to those lower down the social ladder. For more than two decades, the shift toward private benefits has mirrored the concentration of economic rewards in favor of the better off. These changes rely on tax breaks for those who are already doing very well. In this way, the new directions in welfare reform subsidize inequality. Furthermore, tax concessions and the privatization of insurance, heavily tilted toward the affluent, threaten to increase the fiscal strain that public programs will face in coming decades (Congressional Budget Office [CBO], 2001a, 2001b).

The justification for preferential treatment of the wealthy—tax-exempt savings accounts, tax-favored retirement accounts, tax-free dividends, accelerated income tax cuts, and an end to inheritance taxes—is that all these gimmicks are incentives to create jobs for American workers. Robert B. Reich, Secretary of Labor in the Clinton administration, estimates that the hoped-for trickle-down effect will become a *trickle-out* effect. Guided more by profit maximization than patriotism, those who can will, in all likelihood, invest outside the country. By Reich's account, the actual trickle-down effect is one of pain. The financial crunch generated by this largesse to the rich will lead to severe cuts in social services. Virtually no states have the constitutional authority to run deficits. Yet severe cuts are already visible at the state level, since it is the states that run most of the programs that serve the working and poor families: Medicaid, special education, homeless shelters, mental health services, and the like. The irony is that while welfare states were set up to reduce the inequality that is the natural outcome of market systems, the system in the United States is being transformed in such a way that it augments inequality (Reich, 2002).

Regardless of whether you agree or disagree with Reich's argument, it is worth looking at the outcome of another experiment in privatization of social insurance. Chile's privatization reform has figured in many of President Bush's speeches as an example of a brave and successful venture that deserves to be emulated by the United States. Putting aside for a moment the fact that the country implemented its overhaul of social security at a time of budget surplus—quite different from the growing deficits in the United States—and under the auspices of a military dictatorship, consider what is happening in Chile. Without doubt, private accounts set aside a large amount of accumulated savings that were invested in the economy, allowing capital markets to modernize, promoting cheaper credit for businesses, and serving as a barrier to deficits (Ferrara, Goodman, & Matthews Jr., 1995; Rodriguez, 1999). However, the privatized system has an Achilles' heel. It has not succeeded in insuring a dignified retirement for the elderly, and the government has been forced to respond to this shortcoming.

The reform got underway in the early eighties, under the aegis of General Augusto Pinochet. Now, the first workers to participate in the new system are retiring. Comparisons between workers who entered the private accounts in 1981 and those who were under the public system prior to that date show substantial differences in retirement income, after controlling for type of work and pay. With 20 years of contributions behind them, retirees under the new system wind up getting less than half the benefits as retirees under the old public system. Furthermore, with the private accounts, retirement income is limited to 24 years, while for those under the public plan it is for life. "It is absolutely impossible to think," Ricardo Scolari, the Chilean Minister of Labor and Social Security, commented, "that a system of this nature is going to resolve the income needs of Chileans when they reach old age" (quoted in Rohter, 2005, p. C1).

The Chilean outcome is sobering. In spite of the shift that occurred a quarter century ago, the government still spends 26 percent of its budget on providing income for its elderly population, as compared to 19 percent in the United States (Ehrlich, 2002; Lazarus, 2005; Rohter, 2005). Privatization of Social Security in the United States might avoid the problems encountered in

Chile, but workers need much more detail about plans for reform and the protections they are supposed to be granted, beyond ideologically grounded promises of success. Accountability to working America presupposes a transparent sharing of the specifics of a program that can guarantee a dignified old age for all.

Other cross-national comparisons—with European countries such as Sweden, for example—can be misleading. In that country, private accounts involve only 2.5 percent of the taxes collected for social insurance, and various protections abound. A guaranteed minimum pension, for example, is available to anyone in need, and there are adjustments according to the age of workers. In addition, Sweden makes health care, nursing homes, child care, and the like available to all citizens (Norman & Mitchell, 2000).

Part IV: Suggestions for Exercises _____

The three chapters covered in Part IV of the text address recent or proposed legislation in welfare policy and will become dated as new proposals and information emerge. The intent of the following exercise is to keep students updated and involved in ongoing welfare issues.

1. Students may choose to focus on TANF, Medicaid, Social Security, or Medicare.

2. Search for recent information on the topic selected in the national press and from organizations such as the Social Security Administration, Welfare Information Network, Finance Project Information, Center for Budget and Policy Priorities, Center for Law and Social Policy, Institute for Women's Policy Research, the U.S. Census Bureau: Current Population Reports, Department of Housing and Urban Development, Department of Agriculture, Brookings Institution, Urban Institute, the Casey Foundation, and the Fannie Mae Foundation. To get to the Web sites for these organizations, go to google.com and type the name of the organization you want to access. Follow the links to access the topics of interest.

3. Update the information given in Chapters 10, 11, and 12, and rectify or elaborate upon the interpretations given in the text on the status of the program chosen.

PART V

Contemporary Directions of Welfare States in Developed Nations

Chapter 14 compares priorities and concrete outcomes across different types of welfare states. Chapter 15 addresses the key social problems common to postindustrial societies in the twenty-first century and the reform proposals that are emerging to cope with them.

14

Types of Welfare States, Different Outcomes, and Future Needs

The distribution of income and wealth in a democratic country goes to the heart of its political ethic.

—Thomas Byrne Edsall (1984, p. 18)

Welfare states developed at different times, in distinctive cultural settings, across industrial societies, and they have produced markedly different outcomes. The variety of programs and the range of results they have produced represent a series of historical experiments. We can compare and evaluate what has worked, and what has not worked, in the light of national priorities.

Different Logics of Welfare States

In 1994, led by Britain's Labor Party, the Commission on Social Justice issued a report listing the values expressed by all welfare states in advanced market economies. To a greater or lesser extent, all of the countries were committed to a variety of good things: fostering economic efficiency, social equality, social stability, social integration and inclusion, and reducing poverty. It is the promise to move toward these goals that is the source of the political legitimacy on which capitalist welfare regimes depend (Habermas, 1975; Offe, 1984).

Clearly, however, the priorities assigned to each goal vary from country to country, and these rankings reflect value hierarchies that produce notably different types of welfare regimes.

Promoting Economic Efficiency

Welfare expenses are sometimes considered a drag on economic growth. A belief that has gained popularity in the United States since the 1980s is that welfare adds to the cost of doing business, and thereby diminishes productivity. From this point of view, there is a harsh trade-off between equity and efficiency.

Furthermore, when welfare policies intrude on the operations of the market, the fear is that they risk upsetting instruments and institutions that are working to promote the greater economic good. They undermine incentives to work, for example, and to save. On the other hand, welfare policies may be viewed as remedies for market failures. This was the major rationale behind the New Deal in the United States. Still a third perspective assumes a symbiotic interdependence: markets promote welfare as welfare promotes markets (Arrow & Hahn, 1971).

If we are trying to achieve welfare, it is plainly better to do so efficiently. Efficiency itself, however, is an instrumental rather than an ultimate value. It is a means whose merits depend on the attainment of other goals.

Reducing Poverty

Poverty simply means having inadequate resources to meet one's needs. However, "needs" have to be defined, as does what constitutes "adequate." Strategies for reducing poverty will vary according to how the key terms are understood.

A minimalist or *absolute* definition of poverty construes needs in terms of physical survival. Adequate resources are limited to food, in the sense of minimal caloric intake; shelter; and clothing. *Relative* poverty defines needs and resources relative to the social and economic context. The idea goes well beyond basic necessities to encompass a range of instrumental goods necessary to secure basic ones. These involve resources that allow people to participate in the ordinary life of the community (for example, television, picnics in the park, local associations, and so on) (Townsend, 1979).

Promoting Social Equality

During the heady days following World War II, the English scholar T. H. Marshall (1950) predicted that democracy would continue to evolve and expand. What had started in the late eighteenth century as a breakthrough of civil rights, like freedom of assembly, and had later expanded to political rights like the extension of the franchise, would eventually grant social rights to all citizens as a means to improve equality. The achievement of social rights goes beyond access to equal opportunity; it moves toward equal outcomes. In the realm of welfare policy, this typically translates into access to equal resources (Dworkin, 1981).

The notion of "specific equality" (Tobin, 1970) adheres to more operational criteria. It envisions a distribution of different sorts of goods according to different rules. The distribution of basic resources such as food, housing, child benefits, education, and health should be universal, while some variation in income is permitted. From this perspective, the provision of many goods in strictly egalitarian fashion goes with equal demands imposed by civic duties—taxation, jury duty, voting, service in the armed forces, and the like. These goods, therefore, are rights of social citizenship, just as paying taxes is part of civic obligation. The goods also include decent levels of work-related items such as unemployment benefits, old-age pensions, and the right to work (Elster, 1988; Therborn, 1986).

Promoting Social Integration and Avoiding Exclusion

The ideal of an organic society—a harmonious, functionally interdependent system—places a premium on integration. Workable societies are based on family-like reciprocity. Mutual-aid groups start with kin and expand to the community—to churches, volunteer and occupational associations, and productive corporations—to create what Robert Putnam (1993) and others call social capital. Such capital grows rather than depreciates with use, and it constitutes the infrastructure of civil society.

Where does the state fit in? The role of the government is to facilitate the mutually supporting interactions that build up civil society, complementing and strengthening them. The overarching purpose is social inclusion. In a nutshell, poverty results from exclusion from supportive networks. Exclusion leads to cumulative disadvantages in ever-widening sectors of social life—education, health, housing, occupational skills, jobs. In other words, poverty expresses social marginalization.

Promoting Social Stability

Social security comes closest to the idea of "stability." Offering social security—insurance for unemployment, disability, and old age—to all helps counteract the tendency for earnings and the returns on earnings to favor those who are already better off. To compensate for inequalities, social security benefits should follow a flat or progressive rate of distribution. While the differences in earnings remain untouched, the social benefits would be the same for everyone, or perhaps favor those lower on the income hierarchy. Some commentators (e.g., Goodin, 1990) believe that an equalizing system would boost social and political participation across the board.

Promoting Autonomy

"Freedom" is what autonomy means to many people. Still, there are competing understandings of freedom. One reading equates it with self-reliance, which often means shifting from dependence on welfare to dependence on the market. Tied to this view is the notion of negative freedom. Since compulsory taxation finances public assistance, the state is viewed as infringing on the freedom of taxpayers (Goodin, 1998).

A rival argument contends that great inequality leads to subservience and, at the end of the day, to a lack of freedom. The problem is how to avoid another infringement: the unwarranted manipulation of the most vulnerable members of society. The answer is that assistance should come from the government as an entitlement rather than as charity handed out in a discretionary fashion (Goodin, 1985). A basic income should be paid to all who are in need, as a right. Soss (2000) claims that, in spite of some of its unreasonable regulations, the old AFDC in the United States contributed to a degree of independence and autonomy for poor women.

Alternative Institutional Designs

Welfare states have internal logics that go back to their distinctive histories and that reflect certain worldviews. Their dynamics are inscribed in past policy responses that limit, through path dependence, institutional options in the present and future. Moral preferences and social goals are important guides with a universal ring, but it is their embodiment in institutional policies and practices that distinguishes one welfare state from another. Each welfare regime carries its characteristic cultural and historical baggage.

To characterize welfare regimes, we need to identity (a) their dominant values, (b) the strategies used in developing welfare, (c) policies for responding to social failures, and (d) the construction of goals and their evaluation. Each type of welfare regime has a distinctive political, economic, and social profile.

In 1990, Gøsta Esping-Andersen introduced a three-part classification of welfare regimes: liberal, social-democratic, and corporatist.

Liberal Welfare States

Liberal welfare states attach supreme importance to *economic efficiency* and *individual autonomy*. Individuals have primary responsibility for their own welfare, and the state assumes a correspondingly passive role. This is consistent with the market premise favoring free exchanges, with minimal government intervention. Freedom of choice entails responsibility for consequences.

Liberal systems recognize the imperfections of the market. They allow for government interference as a regrettable but necessary means to correct these flaws. Inclusion in the productive process is the priority, and jobholders are to be rewarded according to their individual contributions. The vagaries of the market are also acknowledged, so that the state offers some type of security against forces beyond the control of individuals. Since the primary commitment is to capitalism and open competition, the system values the accumulation of capital, protects high incomes, and favors low taxes.

Chronic poverty in the liberal welfare state reflects an inability to participate in productive work among the deserving poor, or an unwillingness to do so on the part of the undeserving poor. Humanitarian considerations dictate that the government allow the distribution of basic benefits to the first group, adjusted for individual assets and contingent on approved behavior (Wagner, 2000).

Five countries—Switzerland, Japan, the United States, and, to a lesser degree, Canada and Australia—have liberal welfare regimes (Esping-Andersen, 1990).

Social-Democratic Regimes

Social-democratic regimes put *equality* at the top of their agenda. Class politics, regulated economies, and redistributive social policies characterize their operations. Public policies express a direct reaction to the consequences of laissez-faire markets. While the state plays a major role, accounting for a larger share of the GDP than in liberal welfare systems, social-democratic regimes are based on market economies that guarantee property rights and free competition. The difference is that the accent is on *social* democracy. They try to ensure a fair distribution of gains to guarantee equal access to economic and political participation.

Social-democratic regimes seek to transform political equality into social equity. They approximate Marshall's (1950) vision of a progressively evolving democracy, implementing social rights as well as protecting political and civil liberties. Citizenship means participation in community life, validating the worth of all citizens (Townsend, 1979).

The equalizing bent of social-democratic regimes involves curtailing the power of capital through regulation and strengthening the power of labor organizations. The relative power of capital and labor is subject to compulsory arbitration. Nationwide wage bargaining takes place, and full-employment policies are encouraged.

"Decommodification" is a major characteristic of social-democratic regimes. The distribution of certain goods and services does not occur through the market. Rather, the state makes universal goods—health services, child care, elderly care, and the like—available to all citizens. These services are supported by progressive taxes; the higher the income, the higher the tax rate. The expectation is that since everyone has access to universal welfare, *solidarity* will increase, and so will equalization. In turn, equalization will decrease relative *poverty*.

This regime—the Scandinavian model—covers social democracies in Denmark, Norway, Sweden, and the Netherlands (Esping-Andersen, 1990).

Corporatist Welfare Regimes

Corporatist welfare regimes give priority to *integration* followed by *stability*. Since maintaining functional interdependence within and among groups is the means toward an integrated society, compromise is the favored political style.

The economy is often marked by "communitarian socialism." Cooperation and collaboration, rather than outright competition, are supposed to generate wealth. The system recognizes the advantages of a division of labor, but not cutthroat competition. What matters is the smooth interplay of sectional interests through consultation among key leaders of capital and labor. This greases the gears in the direction of consensual or quasi-consensual solutions as, for example, in the case of bargaining over wages (Lehmbruch, 1984), and toward setting productivity goals.

Social policies reflect mutuality. Their purpose is to support the integration of groups so that they take care of their members. "Subsidiarity" becomes a crucial principle here. It boils down to the rule of thumb that serious efforts should be made to sort problems out at the local level before they are kicked upstairs. Thus, responsibility falls first on those closest to individuals—family members, then the local church, volunteer organizations, professional and occupational associations, and so on to municipalities. Duties are assigned to corporate identities, represented in professional and occupational associations. Mutual aid is akin to mutual insurance.

The big risk in such societies is to be unaffiliated. The state either encourages loners to enter groups or offers charity-like forms of help. The maintenance of social order counts for more than individualism. Great inequalities among groups are also undesirable, because they threaten stability.

The constitutive organizations of corporate welfare regimes—the labor unions, for example—have their origins in the guilds of the Middle Ages. The Catholic Church has encouraged this model as an adaptation to the social pressures of modernity. (In fact, the concept of "subsidiarity" surfaced in a papal encyclical of the 1930s.) The authoritarian trappings that characterized some of these regimes in their earlier days have since given way to "societal corporatism"—that is, to periodic bargaining among economic interests, within electoral democracies.

The countries that approach this model, according to Esping-Andersen (1990), are Austria, Belgium, France, Germany, and Italy.

Comparing Welfare Types

In setting out to evaluate the strengths and weaknesses of the three regimes, Goodin, Heady, Muffels, and Dirven (1999) selected three countries that fit the ideal types delineated by Esping-Andersen. The United States represents the liberal model, the Netherlands exemplifies the social-democratic variant of welfare regimes, and Germany stands for the corporatist model.

Goodin and his colleagues draw on panel data from the Luxembourg Income Study (LIS) that provides information comparable across the three countries. Some of their findings are discussed later in this section. The purpose now is to assess how each regime meets the six goals of efficiency, poverty reduction, social equality, social integration, social stability, and autonomy.

Historical Synopses

The United States

Until the start of the New Deal, the rugged individualism of laissez-faire and liberal notions of self-help dominated social policy in the United States. The tradition of the English Poor Laws, combined with private charities, shaped relief to the old and the destitute. This heritage remained powerful for two or three generations after the time that most other industrialized countries had enacted old-age pensions (Katz, 1986).

The Social Security Act of 1935 created old-age, survivors, and disability insurance, and these programs eventually covered a substantial number of citizens. The level of benefits was quite low for the first 40 years, so that many recipients also had to rely on means-tested public assistance. Alone among developed nations, the United States does not provide universal family insurance or national health coverage. Instead, the government has offered means-tested benefits through AFDC and Medicaid. Health insurance and retirement portfolios, tied to work, are contributory and contractual. Public assistance is residual and linked to multiple tests of need and worthiness (Pierson, 1994).

Throughout the 1980s and early 1990s, total federal spending on these programs hovered around 12 percent of the GNP. The biggest chunk went to Social Security, with about one-fifth for means-tested programs. By 1996, welfare for poor families was no longer an entitlement. TANF (Temporary Assistance for Needy Families) replaced AFDC. TANF retained means-testing, to which work requirements were added, as well as time limits on the duration of assistance.

The Netherlands

The United Provinces of the Netherlands was among the first republics in Europe, and it has operated for centuries with a system of "sovereignty from below." Decision-making authority was decentralized among multiple local interests and religious groups. In the absence of any strong central power, collaboration was the watchword (Bloom, 1995). Religious conflict eventually shifted power from regions to confessional—that is, Catholic and Protestant—parties. Each of these "pillars" took over responsibility for the welfare of its constituents. The system became known as "consociationalism." By 1960, with secularization, trade unions superseded the fading confessional parties, and alliances and programs became organized along national lines.

The National Assistance Act was enacted in 1963 and implemented in 1965. The government assumed primary responsibility for welfare. Poor relief became an entitlement—a citizen's right. Poverty was defined at 50 percent below median earnings. Generous universal programs followed: children's allowances, old-age pensions, pensions for invalids, long-term medical benefits. All of these measures were traceable to Dutch traditions of mutual solidarity (Therborn, 1989).

The Netherlands was affected, like other countries, by the oil shocks and economic crisis of the 1970s. Unemployment rose, as did the national debt. The generosity of the welfare state was hard to maintain. A series of reforms, implemented in 1987, tightened some eligibility rules for unemployment and disability, and reduced selected benefits. However, because replacement benefits were very high, running at 80 percent of wages, lowering them to 70 percent still kept unemployment compensation well above the level of most other developed countries. Abuses in some programs also came in for closer inspection. Finally, in 1996, workfare requirements were put in place, and the social minimum payment was slightly reduced—remaining, however, well above the standards in liberal regimes (Stephens, 1996).

Germany

Industrialization began to take off in Germany in the mid-1800s, several decades after the British forged their breakthrough toward modernization. Manufacturing, especially heavy industry, developed rapidly, but it did so with a smaller middle class, and without as strong a legacy of liberal ideas in England. The guilds and mutual aid societies of preindustrial times, with their paternalistic ethic and corporatist organization, provided something of a template for responding to the social challenges of the industrial era (Esping-Andersen, 1987).

During the second half of the nineteenth century, Prime Minister Otto von Bismarck, the "Iron Chancellor," unified Prussia and the German provinces into a single nation under a central bureaucracy and powerful military machine. His social insurance initiatives cast the state as the protector of the emerging working class. However, the older corporate bodies and guilds, representing occupations and trades, managed to insinuate themselves into the management of social insurance. The objective of social protection was to promote solidarity among employers and workers within the same industry. The upshot was a crazy quilt of insurance programs based on the profiles of separate occupational categories. Each group shared the same "risk pool" and developed its own type of insurance. Benefits were tagged to occupational membership. The General Federation of Trade Unions successfully opposed efforts to universalize insurance programs (Esping-Andersen, 1987).

This legacy suited the philosophy of the Christian Democratic Party that assumed power immediately following World War II. The government developed a compact with the trade unions that combined social and market principles. The idea was to achieve finely tuned, more or less consensual decisions through participatory works councils in every factory (Dahrendorf, 1990).

The corporatist approach to industrial relations was a cornerstone of the postwar economic "miracle" in Germany. The premise was that nearly everyone in industrial society is at risk, so protection should not be confined to those presently in distress. Corporatist insurance protection has redistributive goals, up to a point. Thus, whenever the earnings of workers are interrupted through unemployment or sickness, their earnings are replaced at the previous earning level. In other words, those who were laid out continued to receive their normal wage.

The German system is modeled, metaphorically, on the reciprocal obligations of the traditional family. Neo-corporatism has privileged the role of the male as head of the household, and its policies have reinforced the supportive status of women (Esping-Andersen, 1990). Full employment of heads of households is the major goal, and social insurance is the core of the welfare regime. A very small, residual public assistance program is reserved for individuals detached from families or labor organizations.

Germany, too, was hit hard by the economic crisis of the seventies and the globalization that gathered momentum in succeeding decades. Unemployment rose sharply and stayed high through the eighties and nineties. The government made a few modest adjustments that did not significantly alter the structure of the system. A delay in benefits, a reduction in sickness and health expenditures, and an adjustment linking pensions to net rather than gross earnings were the key measures. More recently, the very generous length of paid vacations has been trimmed, and the standard weekly work hours—the lowest in Europe—were raised. These reforms were modest, especially if we take into account the costs of reunifying the two Germanys. This was a task that required investment in retooling a sizable workforce and in rebuilding the infrastructure of the East. The impact of welfare reductions was greatest on guest workers (Offe, 1998). Up until the end of the nineties, the social policies of the German government remained fairly intact.

Achievements of the Welfare Regimes

The definition of poverty that Goodin and his colleagues go by differs from that used in the United States. Goodin et al. concentrate on *relative* poverty, operationalized as incomes that are 50 percent below the median income in a society. The United States uses an *absolute* poverty criterion, described in Chapter 5, and this results in a lower count of those living in poverty.

Liberal Welfare in the United States

The goal of *efficiency* assumes an inverse relationship between welfare costs and economic growth: the higher the expenditures on welfare, the slower the pace of economic expansion is supposed to be. A crucial tenet of beliefs about public assistance in the United States is that welfare acts as a drag on the economy; social spending curtails economic growth. The upshot is that higher welfare expense should be associated with slower growth.

Table 14.1   Welfare Expenditures as Percent of GDP

	1985	1993
Netherlands	23.11	23.44
Germany	19.12	18.63
USA	8.83	9.79

Source: OECD (1996, Occasional Paper 17).

Table 14.1 shows the percentage of GDP spent on welfare by each country in 1985 and 1993. The United States spends less than half of what Germany does and nearly one-third less than the Netherlands. In fact, data from OECD countries demonstrate that, of the 18 wealthiest member nations, the United States and Japan spend the least on welfare.

Yet economic growth, adjusted for inflation, did not differ significantly across the three countries. The German economy grew by 26.7 percent, the Dutch by 26.5 percent, and the United States by 27.8 percent during the same period. If expenditures on welfare impeded growth, the economy of the United States, where welfare budgets are smaller, should have grown faster. Growth in real GDP per capita, measured in terms of median income, also disconfirms the proposition that welfare costs jeopardize the economy. Median income grew 19.1 percent in the Netherlands, 17.4 percent in Germany, and 17.2 percent in the United States.

The second argument on efficiency relates to *administrative* targeting. Managerial oversight is supposed to ensure an exhaustive investigation of need in order to prevent an excessive distribution of benefits. The idea, in short, is to curb cheating. However, another appropriate measure of administrative inefficiency is the number of poor who wind up being excluded from the benefits for which they qualify. The cross-national contrast is striking. In the United States, 39 percent of the poor were not covered in this way. The corresponding figure in Germany is 24 percent. *All* of the poor were covered in the Netherlands.

Economic efficiency, for the liberal regime, means meeting needs through the market. Participation in the labor force serves as an indicator of this type of efficiency. Table 14.2 shows that the United States has considerably higher rates of employment than the other two countries.

Table 14.2   Employment Rates

	USA	Germany	Netherlands
1987	70.4	57.3	47.6
1992	72.2	46.8	47.8

Source: Derived from Goodin et al. (1999, Appendix, Table A-1: EFF).

Liberal welfare regimes are similarly intent on promoting *individual autonomy*. Adults are supposed to be economically self-sufficient. To measure autonomy, Goodin et al. (1999, pp. 225–236) constructed a cumulative measure: income from individual labor, derived from the labor market; household equivalent income—that is, pooled family income; and post-government household equivalent income—in other words, government benefits. The results reported in Table 14.3 refer to working heads of households for the period of 1985–1994.

The United States falls behind in the comparison, not because the income of individual workers is lower, but because family contributions are smaller and the government's contribution is very modest indeed. Reliance on individual market resources leaves a high proportion of households below the poverty level in all three countries and at both at the pre- and post-government contribution periods. Pooling family resources significantly improves the autonomy of households. The Netherlands is ahead of the other two countries on this score. Both Germany and the Netherlands are far ahead of the United States when it comes to the government's investment in raising heads of households above the poverty level. Both raise the economic autonomy of 16 percent of the households with a working head, while the American contribution helps only 4 percent of working households.

In conclusion, the liberal presumption that welfare costs hinder economic growth is not borne out by the LIS data. Both Germany and the Netherlands spend a considerably greater proportion of their GDP on welfare than the United States. Yet, in the period studied, their economic growth was at about the same level as that of the United States, and so was the median income in both countries.

Administrative efficiency was assessed in terms of the percentage of the poor not covered by the welfare systems. Again, the Netherlands takes the

Table 14.3   Measuring Autonomy

	Netherlands	Germany	USA
Individual labor income	43.6	34.5	40.2
Household equivalent income	84.8	71.2	66.9
Household post-government	97.0	86.6	70.9

Source: Adapted from Goodin et al. (1999, Appendix, Table A6, Aut. C).

lead, covering all its poor at the end of the decade. Germany is far behind, and the United States takes up the rear, with 39 percent of the poor not covered. Promoting labor market efficiency is another goal of liberal welfare states. On this dimension, the United States takes the lead, far ahead of the other two countries. The economy of the United States generates proportionately higher employment.

Lastly, the income generated by the heads of household, taken alone, leaves a considerable percentage of the population in poverty in all three countries. The incidence of poverty declines as household incomes are pooled, and as government benefits are forthcoming. The results vary systematically across the three countries. In the Netherlands, only 3 percent of households are below the poverty line, as compared to 13.4 percent in Germany and nearly 30 percent in the United States.

The Social-Democratic Welfare Regime in the Netherlands

Reducing poverty is the top priority of social-democratic welfare systems. By this standard, we would expect the Netherlands to come out ahead of Germany and the United States. To be sure, all three countries have market economies. Indeed, the incidence of poverty directly generated by the operations of the market is similar—about 20 percent in all three cases. However, after government transfers are taken into account, levels of poverty vary considerably. Markets alone, then, are not particularly effective mechanisms of distribution, and the type of welfare state really does make a difference in reducing poverty.

The over-time data make for relatively precise temporal and cross-national comparisons. On an annual basis, government transfers reduce poverty by 2 percent (from 20 to 18 percent) in the United States, by more than half (to 9 percent) in Germany, and by nearly 75 percent in the Netherlands (to 6 percent). In the subsequent 5 years, the United States managed to cut poverty within the same cohort to nearly 15 percent. Germany did better, cutting it to 7.6 percent. The Netherlands is the success story, with a poverty rate of 3 percent. After 10 years, the poverty rate in the original cohort came down to 13 percent in the United States and dropped to 5.8 percent in Germany. At 0.5 percent, poverty virtually disappeared in the Netherlands.

Prior to government transfers, people in *deep poverty* (defined as those with 30 percent or less of the median income) stand at about 10 percent in the three countries. The effect of government transfers is particularly visible among these very poor. After 10 years, the Netherlands succeeded in raising 94.8 percent of the poorest of the poor out of poverty. Germany's rate of success was 72.6 percent. The United States comes in last at 23.1 percent.

Promoting equality is another priority of social-democratic regimes, besides reducing poverty. The Gini Index is a widely used measure of inequality that varies from zero—a perfectly equal distribution of material resources—to 1.00, signifying that one person controls all resources.

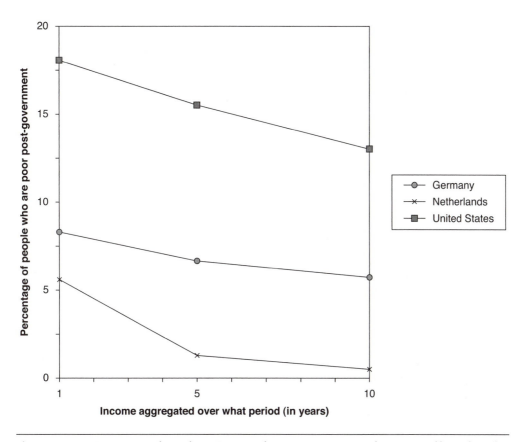

Figure 14.1   Percentage of People in Poverty After Government Transfers (First, Fifth, and Tenth
                    Year)

Source: Goodin et al., 1999: 155.

Naturally, inequality before government transfers is higher than after public
transfers and taxation. Still, in both circumstances, the cross-country differences are significant, although not as glaring as they are in the case of poverty.

The social-democratic regime in the Netherlands is the most effective in
reducing inequality generated by the market. Germany's corporatist regime is
somewhat less effective, and the liberal model represented by the United
States comes in last by a wide margin. The same results emerge when we look
at deep poverty. Although market-generated economic inequality stands at
similar levels across the country, after state intervention the Netherlands
shows a much lower level of inequality, followed by Germany, with the
United States once again taking up the rear among the OECD countries.

Thus, the social-democratic welfare regime of the Netherlands is more
effective in pursuing the goal of equalization and reducing poverty than
corporatist Germany. The performance of the liberal welfare regime of the
United States puts it in last place on this dimension (see Table 14.4).

Table 14.4   Index of Inequality

	USA	Germany	Netherlands
Pre-Government Gini Index	.43	.43	.41
Post-Government Gini Index year 1	.37	.27	.27
Post-Government Gini Index year 10	.32	.22	.19

Source: Derived from Goodin et al. (1999, Appendix Tables 3.1a, 3.1b).

Corporatist Welfare in Germany

The paramount values of Germany's welfare system are *integration* and *stability*. Close-knit groups depend on stability to maintain their continuity. Disruptive changes go against the culture of corporatism.

The family as the archetypal unit of reciprocity and mutual help anchors the corporatist regime symbolically and functionally. More than in other regimes, family traumas like divorce are likely to be viewed as a blow to the integrative nexus of the social order. Divorce rates in the United States tend to be more than double that of the two European countries. While Germany has the lowest rate, the difference is small when compared to the Netherlands. In 1994, an estimated 2.04 percent of German marriages and 2.35 percent of Dutch marriages ended in divorce, as compared to 4.67 percent in the United States (United Nations, 1997, Table 25).

The attachment of citizens to the workforce is central to the corporatist system. Dense networks of occupational and professional associations structure employment and tie people to the economy. Rates of unionization are high. In all three countries, over 90 percent of heads of households of prime working age are employed full-time at least 1 year out of 10. The more telling statistic is that the proportion of heads of households who are employed full-time during the decade drops off in varying degrees. Contrary to expectations, the drop is highest in Germany, which has the lowest job stability for heads of households.

While corporatist systems are committed to growth, sudden changes in the hierarchical ensemble of economic interests send tremors through their institutional architecture. Collective economic mobility is desirable, individual mobility less so. In the first case, everyone benefits without shocks to the hierarchical structure, but high rates of personal mobility might disrupt the collectivity.

Table 14.5   Heads of Households' Full Employment

	Germany	Netherlands	USA
One-year period	94.8	91.5	96.6
Ten-year period	41.6	64.0	57.6

Source: Data derived from Goodin et al. (1999, Appendix A-4, 2a, p. 297).

Table 14.6   Percentage of People Who Moved Upward in Income Quintile
              Over 10 Years

	Germany	Netherlands	USA
Pre-Government	12.3%	13.3%	8.8%
Post-Government	11.9	15.2	8.6

Source: Derived from Goodin et al. (1999, Appendix, Table A5).

All in all, then, rates of individual mobility should be lower in Germany than in the other countries. Table 14.6 shows the proportion of individuals who, during the decade under study, moved to a higher quintile (that is, jumped to the next level or higher) in the income rankings.

The results are perplexing. A reasonable expectation is that liberal regimes like that of the United States, with open competition and being relatively unencumbered by regulation, should have the highest mobility, and that social-democratic regimes, which prize redistribution, should have the least. The data tell a different story. Even prior to government transfers, the United States shows the lowest mobility. Germany has slightly lower mobility than the Netherlands, and there is some indication that this is furthered by government intervention (from 12.3 to 11.9 percent).

Figure 14.2 tracks *economic stability,* indexed by the median coefficient of variation in incomes over 10 years for households headed by a person of

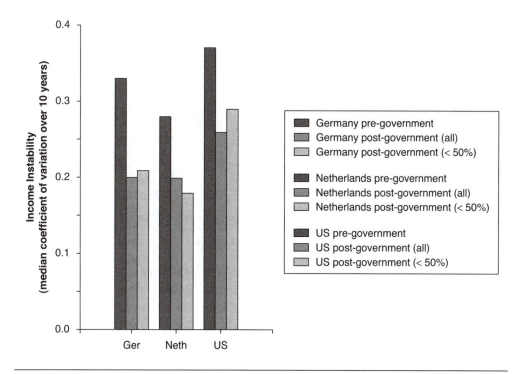

Figure 14.2   Income Instability Pre- and Post-Government Contribution

Source: Based on data from Appendix table A5, Stab 3A in Goodin et al., 1999.

working age. Incomes prior to taxation and transfers are very unstable in the three countries, with those in the United States being the least stable. With government transfers, some stability is restored. The increase in income stability is one-quarter larger in the European countries than in the United States.

On the whole, considering the priorities of each welfare type, the Netherlands comes out as the most consistent system. The outcomes produced by the liberal system in the United States contradict its own values regarding efficiency. However, the comparatively high levels of employment in the United States live up, at least partially, to its commitment to autonomy. As regards income stability, the German corporatist welfare state performs slightly better than the social-democratic Netherlands, while the United States ranks the lowest.

15 The Future of Welfare in Postindustrial Societies

Our society can extend guarantees against lifelong entrapment.

—Gøsta Esping-Andersen (2002, p. 13)

Globalization is taking the place of fate as the origin, uncontrollable and mysterious, of social change. The attribution of a multiplicity of problems to exogenous forces fuels a certain pessimism. Assigning irresistible consequences to the complex dynamics of globalization discourages the imagination and analytic precision necessary for adaptation and reform.

Welfare states have learned to adjust before. The regimes now in place in OECD countries took shape during the industrial era and expanded and consolidated themselves after the Second World War. Manufacturing reigned, and most blue collar workers, even those with few or basic skills, were in demand. Secure employment, progressive wage increases, and the achievement of something close to middle class affluence for most blue collar workers were, if not taken for granted, at least plausible aspirations. Unions were able to negotiate solid contracts, and the life course of workers offered the prospect of reasonable stability.

Path dependence resembles Yogi Berra's principle of "it's déjà vu, all over again." As nations entered the postindustrial era, welfare states tinkered with and tweaked institutional structures and strategies inherited from a successful past. When the oil shocks of the seventies changed the economic gestalt for the worse, the first reaction was usually to cut expenditures without much structural adjustment.

However, as stagflation persisted through the eighties, some countries—the United States, Great Britain, and New Zealand—pursued supply-side strategies, blaming big government, regulatory overload, and welfare for economic decline. The protracted downturn became the justification for a draconian retrenchment in welfare (Pierson, 1994). An amalgamated model, dubbed the Third Way, gained momentum in the nineties, with Bill Clinton in the United States and Tony Blair in England taking the lead. The Third Way tried for a fusion between the most popular aspects of neoliberalism—in particular, its accent on individual responsibility and a more competitive system of rewards—and concomitant standards of public responsibility.

What was lacking in these maneuvers was a trenchant analysis of the socioeconomic transformations brought about by postindustrialism and how these changes altered the policy horizons of welfare states in OECD countries (Esping-Andersen, Gallie, Hemrijck, & Miles, 2002d; Reich, 2002b). The most salient shifts are demographic and economic. These forces undercut traditional family stability and expanded the demand for services.

A pair of related conclusions follows. First, the status quo is extremely difficult to maintain in the face of demographic and economic sea changes that undermine the foundations on which entrenched welfare states were built. Second, "golden age" welfare states are increasingly out of date and ill-suited to confront future challenges. Left as they are, systems of social protection may hinder rather than promote employment growth, suffocate the knowledge base for intensively competitive economies, and be unable to respond to new social risks and needs.

Demographic and Economic Shifts _____

The OECD countries are aging. The elderly take up a larger proportion of the total population as a result of welfare state protections and improvements in medical science. The senior population is not only growing, but living longer as well. At the same time, fertility is declining. In combination, these changes create a troubling imbalance between workers and dependent sectors of the population.

The nearly full employment that characterized the high point of the industrial era has disappeared. The idea that the emigration of manufacturing jobs to developing countries is the culprit provides only a partial explanation. In 2004, a Labor Department report showed that in the first quarter of the year, only 2.5 percent of the long-term job losses in the United States were due to outsourcing (Porter, 2004a). More decisive factors are global economic competition and technological advances. Employment opportunities favor highly skilled workers, because the edge in international competition depends on their productivity. In the long run, progress in the economic well-being of OECD countries depends on the continuing, quality education of their workers.

More employment, however, cannot solve the demographic age imbalance, nor can the economic future of families rest on the traditional nuclear family. The feminist movement, rising levels of education among women, and the rough economic times that resulted in lost family income—all have propelled the massive entry of women into the paid workforce, at what is now approaching the same rate as males. The growing financial independence of women plays a role in the breakup of families and, more importantly, in taking child care and elderly care off the menu of free family services. The entrance of women into the labor market on a large scale has contributed to economic growth, but it also requires the creation of services previously "donated" by homemakers.

Low fertility in OECD countries remains a concern, especially for the European members. Immigration adds new workers, but not enough to counter the growth of the elderly population. Europe now has 3 workers for every 1 retiree, and in the United States the ratio is 5 to 1.

Traditional modes of policy making, parceled out into specialized domains and based on static diagnoses, are not equipped to cope with these new circumstances. An analysis of postindustrial scenarios and their antici-pated long-term consequences is urgently needed.

For Esping-Andersen, the core issue for welfare is not how many people are ill-paid or shabbily housed at a given moment but how many are likely to live in these circumstances through the course of their lives. "The foremost challenge we face," Esping-Andersen (2002c) argues, "is to avert that social ills become permanent, that citizens become entrapped in exclusion or infe-rior opportunities in such a way that their life chances are affected" (p. 6).

Welfare policies have to adopt a life-course perspective. The problems that welfare measures are designed to meet are often consequences of prior con-ditions, and these problems continue, in turn, to condition prospects later in life. Recognition of this dynamic aids both preventive interventions and pre-dictive planning, and it helps us distinguish between momentary hardship and lasting hardship.

We know, for example, that young people without a secondary education and skills will be locked into the low end of the labor market. Their future is likely to be one with low pay and frequent unemployment. With demographic pressures mounting on pensions, it is also likely that these cohorts will not have accumulated savings to lift them from poverty in old age. Indeed, youths without a high school education are likely to come from poor families in the first place, growing up in poor neighborhoods with depleted schools.

How do remedial and preventive interventions come into play within the life-course framework? Their objective is to meet the fundamental criteria of a social contract that precludes social exclusion. Solidarity should be rein-forced precisely at a time when society is in flux and citizens feel insecure. This high-risk context is evocative of Rawls's veil of ignorance—an unknown world that requires joint effort for survival.

The Three Pillars of Welfare

The interdependence of the market, the family, and government takes on increasing salience in postindustrial settings. Welfare efforts need to target the interactions between these pillars by repairing failures at each level to improve social justice. Within the postindustrial gestalt of OECD countries, interactions between the pillars have to complement and reinforce one another, and move toward fair human investment in child welfare, gender equality, and reciprocity between active workers and the elderly (Esping-Andersen et al., 2002; Reich, 2002a).

Child-Centered Social Investment

The overall economy and individual well-being improve with the skills brought to bear at work. Policies should pay close attention to programs that enhance the skills of young people entering the labor market and that promote retooling for those already working. It makes sense, in the face of ongoing technological advances, for businesses to get involved in periodically upgrading the skills of employees. Denmark has dealt successfully with unemployment among young workers by extending their coverage and simultaneously requiring an 18-month period of paid training, sheltered work, and placement.

Measures to improve learning and school retention rates among children in deprived contexts involve the availability of afterschool programs and parental benefits that depend on their children's attendance. Wisconsin tried something like this, but the program was implemented differently from its counterparts in Northern Europe. In Wisconsin, punishment—the withdrawal of welfare benefits—was used to obtain compliance, but such policy turned out to be ineffective (Trattner, 1999). In Northern Europe, rewards were the instrument, and the results were positive (Diamond & Orszag, 2004; Esping-Andersen, 1996; Stephens, 1996).

The most productive approaches are preventive, not rehabilitative. There is clear evidence that a social inheritance process operates between parents' education and the economic prospects of children (Erikson & Goldthorpe, 1992; Shavit & Blossfeld, 1993). Many countries in Northern Europe have invested in universal child care and preschooling. It is impossible to eradicate poverty in the new economic environment without highly skilled workers because they are indispensable to the productivity of competitive postindustrial markets (Esping-Anderson, 2002a). Thus, investment in education and the social resources surrounding it (e.g., child care) looks like a win–win situation.

The United States can boast of having several cutting-edge institutions of educational achievement, but 20 percent of the country's population is rated as cognitively dysfunctional. We have what Reich (2004) calls "islands of excellence in a sea of ignorance." These educational disparities are likely to dull whatever competitive edge the country maintains in the future, in both human and economic terms.

Means-tested assistance for families with children is not the answer to this challenge. Welfare of this sort does not generally lift the poor out of poverty. On the contrary, it results for the most part in life-long entrapment in poverty (Edin & Lein, 1997; Jencks, 1995).

Table 15.1 The Cost of Eliminating Child Poverty: National Accounts Estimates, 1990*

	Number of poor children in HH (relative measure, in thousands)	Poverty gap (1995 US $)	Extra cost as percentage of GDP
Denmark (1992)	19	3,952	0.01
Sweden (1995)	25	3,403	0.01
France (1994)	< 315	1,460	0.08
Italy (1995)	1,033	2,497	0.29
Spain (1990)	531	1,319	0.16
UK (1995)	1,210	1,927	0.26
USA (1997)	6,665	3,481	0.30

*Estimates are based on the objective of bringing poor child families above 50 percent of the median adjusted disposable income line.

HH = Households

Source: LIS databases and OECD national accounts reported in Esping-Andersen (2002d, p. 60).

Job strategies make more sense if earnings are life-sustaining or if there are adequate supplements. It matters, too, that the work not be too stressful (especially in the case of single mothers) and that good-quality child care is available. This view is consistent with evaluations of the effect on children of the work requirements implemented by TANF, outlined in Chapter 10. There is no evidence, however, that proposals for the reauthorization of TANF take available research seriously.

The costs of child-centered social investments are heavier for countries with higher rates of poverty. The good news, shown in Table 15.1, is that the expenditures are, on the whole, modest. Upgrading and equalizing educational opportunities converge with the goal of national prosperity in the postindustrial world (Figueira-McDonough, in press).

A New Gender Contract

Driven by calls for independence, by the need to supplement household incomes, and by the growth of the service sector, paid work by women has come to play a major role in postindustrial society. Working women have become the lynchpins between households and the economy. Their participation in the labor market has nearly doubled the size of the workforce in an aging society. Conversely, women are the key to social reproduction. The quality of postindustrial life revolves around how their demands on men, the welfare state, and society at large are met (Block, 1990; Clement & Myles, 1994; Gershuny, 2000).

Women have diverse preferences about their social roles. Family-centered women see the value of devoting themselves to the care of children and the elderly and of volunteering in the community. On the other side are career-centered women who put their work above other activities. According to research in OECD countries, the first group is quickly vanishing, while the second accounts for about 15 percent of respondents. The vast majority opts for dual roles: lifetime employment without sacrificing motherhood. It is for this huge segment that women-friendly policies have to be devised (Bernhardt, 2000; Hakim, 1996).

Nordic countries are far ahead in two types of policies crucial for working mothers: public child care and paid child leave. The United States ranks lowest among OECD countries on both counts. Half of the children up to 3 years of age of employed mothers are in private day care of very uneven quality. Standards of quality are directly related to costs. Only one-quarter of these facilities are licensed; in other words, 75 percent may not meet minimum standards (Gornick & Meyers, 2003).

Sweden provides an example that is close to representative of other Scandinavian countries. Most women are employed in personal services like education, health, and welfare. The pay is above average, and part-time work includes benefits. Job tenure is very high. The only downside is the gender segregation of these career lines, as compared to Britain and the United States. On the other hand, the earnings of women with low education show less gender discrepancy in Sweden. There, these women make about 77 percent of what their male counterparts earn, as compared to 45 percent in the United Kingdom and 52 percent in the United States (Esping-Andersen et al., 2002d, p. 81).

Other policies common in Northern Europe are paid leaves, for both fathers and mothers, for pregnancy and childbirth. In 1990, fathers' use of family leaves grew by 32 percent in Denmark, by 69 percent in Finland, and 45 percent in Sweden. Provision for absence from work in cases of child sickness also applies to both genders. Matching parents' work schedules with the hours of child care and schools makes employment for families with children easier.

Evening out the division of domestic work between husbands and wives is more difficult. Swedish fathers pitch in with about the same number of hours (21) as mothers. The contribution of men in countries like Denmark and the United States, though smaller, is increasing. It stands at about 13 to 15 hours a week (Esping-Andersen, 2002b).

A New Social Contract for an Aging Society

One of the triumphs of affluent societies in the twentieth century was secure retirement. Before the 1950s, most rank-and-file workers in the

United States retired because they were laid off or because of poor health—in other words, because they were economically dispensable. Thirty years later, most left work voluntarily (Burtless & Quinn, 2001). The rapid drop in old-age poverty testifies to the success of the nearly universal coverage provided by Social Security. Other OECD countries registered equally or even more successful outcomes.

By now, however, the aging of postindustrial societies has put the financing of these systems under enormous stress. As noted earlier, increases in life expectancy and rates of fertility that barely meet replacement levels have thrown pay-as-you-go systems of retirement out of balance. The number of workers whose payroll taxes help pay for retirees' benefits is getting smaller, just as the number of retirees keeps growing. Compounding the problem is the falling age of retirement plus the cost of services for the very old and disabled.

In the old days, family support mechanisms—that is, women—absorbed some of these costs, but with more and more women in the labor market, this caretaker option decreased greatly. Forecasts of economic growth in OECD countries indicate that these demographic changes will not be disastrous (Turner, Giorno, DeSerres, Vourc'h, & Richardson, 1998). Alarmist projections of the demise of retirement coverage are not justified, even though consideration of alternative reforms is needed, given the pressures on the public budget.

The core questions for democratic countries are these: Which proposals might lead to socioeconomic polarization? Which might foster greater fairness?

Intergenerational distributive justice—the issue of fairness between generations—concerns the balance between the contributions of workers and the benefits of the retired. Handing the solution for the demographic unbalance in postmodern societies over to the market contradicts intergenerational justice (Diamond & Orszag, 2004). The rationale of social security systems has been to protect workers from the vagaries of markets and extreme inequality. The historical inertia built into path dependence is likely to make a radical overhaul of pension systems either short-lived or politically infeasible in OECD countries (Myles & Pierson, 1997; Pierson, 2004).

Two options in typical pay-as-you-go retirement systems would bias the costs of aging demographic pyramids either against the elderly or against the workers. With a fixed replacement rate (FRR), retirees are entitled to a portion of their earnings as benefits, plus an adjustment factor reflecting productivity gains and higher earnings of the upcoming generation of workers. When the ratio of retirees to workers goes up, taxes on contributors go up, too. Therefore, all costs fall on the workers and their dependents.

An alternative system—the fixed contributor rate (FCR)—would have the reverse effect. The working population is required to contribute a fixed rate to retirees. Any increase in the ratio of retirees to workers would result in reduced benefits for retirees.

A third model, the fixed ratio position (FRP), requires an adjustment for both generations. Contributions and benefits are set to hold constant the ratio of per capita earnings of the workers (net of contributions) to per capita benefits of retirees (net of taxes). The result is an equal distribution of the costs of demographic change (Musgrave, 1986).

Increasing the age of retirement as a way to contain costs for both generations is a proposal that has been given special attention. The problem is that this requires countering a hidden culture anxious for early retirement, as well as the opening of new pathways for continued employment. Promoting continued employment is likely to have modest results. The initiative has to face intra-generational distributive inequalities. Low-wage workers receive the biggest share of their retirement from Social Security, while higher-income employees have access to private, employer-administered benefits, and their ability to generate personal savings is greater, because their discretionary income is higher. Furthermore, since health and wealth are positively correlated, better-off employers tend to live longer. Any reform in public benefits under Social Security is unlikely to affect the decisions of these favored employees regarding early retirement. Delaying the age of retirement would require coordination among public plans, employer plans, and savings plans.

Some OECD social security systems—notably, the one in the United States—are set up in such a way that they generate intra-generational inequities. The FICA payroll tax is flat, with a wage ceiling that makes it doubly regressive. It also lacks any exemptions for family size, so that low-wage workers with young families pay a disproportionate share. Longer terms of work for full retirement that fail to take into account family interruptions in women's work are another source of inequality. In addition, some cohorts of workers may be caught in periods of high unemployment. Finally, formulas based on recent wage periods benefit higher-level employees in upwardly mobile career tracks rather than rank-and-file workers.

These sources of inequality have been changed in some countries. Canada and Sweden are among the most successful in this respect, as Table 15.2 shows. Both provide guaranteed minimum benefits that raise the vast majority of their citizens above the poverty level.

Table 15.2   Poverty Rates Among Those 65 Years of Age and Older, 1990s

<5%	5–9%	10–14%	15–19%	>20%
Canada	Finland	Austria		Australia
Sweden	France	Belgium		USA
	Germany	Denmark		
	Luxembourg	Italy		
	Netherlands	Norway		
	Switzerland	Spain		
		UK		

Source: LIS key figures, Luxembourg Income Study, 2001.

Focusing on OECD countries has the advantage of establishing the broad context within which welfare reforms play out. On the one hand, the perspective recognizes that all welfare states show strong traces of path dependence. Their institutional legacies are distinctive, and they cannot be reformed overnight. On the other hand, the problems of postindustrialism are common to all these societies. Welfare reform in the early decades of the twenty-first century will increasingly involve a combination of domestic learning, learning from and with others, and—it is hoped—learning ahead of failure (Hemerijck, 2002).

Part V: Suggestions for Exercises _____

1. Select one of the areas of inequality discussed in Chapter 13 (e.g., housing, health, education).

2. Compare the level of inequality between the United States and another OECD country.

3. Examine the policies between the two countries and explain how they account for the different outcomes.

4. Discuss the advantages or disadvantages of each system. Suggest changes that might improve outcomes in the United States.

PART VI

Locating and Counteracting Sources of Injustice

The new politics define equality as inclusion and inequality as exclusion. . . . Inclusion refers in its broadest sense to citizenship, to civil and political rights and obligations that all members of society should have. . . . It also refers to opportunity and involvement in the public sphere.

—Anthony Giddens (1998, pp. 102–103)

Where does the profession of social work stand today with regard to its commitment to social justice? To what extent does the profession live up to the standards of justice discussed in Part I of this book?

In answering questions like these, it helps to situate the aspirations of the profession within a specific context, that of the liberal democracies within which the field evolved and in which concrete practices are implemented. Likewise, we need to keep in mind how historical conditions have shaped the tasks that social workers set for themselves.

Action toward social justice cannot afford to ignore political and historical contexts if the goal is to develop targeted, effective methodologies of intervention. This is the task of policy practice in social work. Chapter 16 highlights the contemporary attention given by social workers to policy practice in tune with the profession's commitment to social justice. Chapter 17 gives an overview of types and methods of policy practice available to professionals.

16 Framing Policy Practice

Social Work's Commitment to Justice for the Twenty-First Century

The life stories of social workers reported by Craig LeCroy (2002) corroborate Gil's (1998) depiction of social workers as grasping intuitively and emotionally the significance of demeaning experiences and their impulse to get involved with victims of injustice. My own experience of teaching in social work and social science departments for over three decades confirms the same thing. Social work students tend to respond to issues of injustice more vigorously than do students in other fields. They also show strong support for policies that promote social justice, regardless of their intended practice specialization.

Cross-national research confirms the pro-justice proclivities of social workers. Interviews with BSW (Bachelor of Social Work) students show that they attribute poverty more to social than to individual causes and that they favor extending welfare state programs as the appropriate response. Students in the United States give equal weight to the promotion of social justice and individual well-being of their clients as professional goals (Weiss, 2005). At the same time, two impediments against pursuing a practice that is squarely consistent with the ideals of the profession crop up in the United States. One is a perceived lack of jobs linked to policy practice in social work. The other is a lack of course offerings on policy practice in most schools of social work.

Concerns about social injustice are very much alive in the recent social work literature (Abramovitz, 1998; Mullaly, 1997; Reisch & Andrews, 2001). Two edited volumes laying out possible directions for social work in the twenty-first century testify to this commitment (Hopps & Morris, 2000; Reisch & Gambrill, 1997). Although policy practice rarely appears in the indexes of these publications, concerns about policy change abound.

Several authors worry about the consequences of demographic trends for Social Security in the United States, about the impact of economic restructuring on unemployment and wages, and about growing inequality and anti-welfare government policies (Iatridies, 2000; Korr & Brieland, 2000; Morris, 2000; Ozawa, 1997; Reisch, 1997; Rose, 1997). Others look at trends in health and housing that undercut access to these basic goods (Cuttler, 1997; Gorin & Moniz, 1997; Mulroy, 2002).

When they consider how social work might counter these developments, most observers point to the structural causes of inequality. They see entrapment in poverty as a crucial antecedent of the problems social workers deal with. They also express impatience that so much effort goes into fixing symptoms that are likely to recur if underlying causes are not addressed. Suggestions about how to promote the needed structural changes vary. Longres (1997) complains that petty identity conflicts obscure the shared experience of oppression and divert attention from fighting inequality. Stern (2005) laments unawareness of the damage that a biased economic system inflicts on the middle class, the working class, and the poor alike.

Disappointment with lost opportunities for a movement mobilized behind the achievement of a more egalitarian society is a common refrain. The most prominent avenue for confronting injustice is probably community power built up through grassroots organizing and coalitions with local public and private organizations (Cnann, 1997; Coulton, 2000; Hochman, 1997; Wenocur & Soifer, 1997). However, when it comes to dealing with specific problems such as access to health services, the power of judicial policy gets special attention.

The National Association of Social Workers (NASW) appeared, in the chapters of this book devoted to the history of social work, as an organization given more to the pursuit of professional status than to leading the fight for social justice. However, professionalization need not be associated with ideological neutrality. On the contrary, Reeser and Epstein (1990) found active involvement in professional associations to be positively correlated with political participation in other areas.

In light of some of the organization's recent activities and policy statements, the initial judgment needs to be tempered. For example, the association has declared its support of, and encouraged its members toward, active involvement in efforts to elect political candidates with a social justice agenda. Establishing the Political Action for Candidate Election (PACE) committee reflects this commitment. Directly relevant to the issues discussed in this book is the section called "Poverty and Social Justice," which keeps members apprised of issues and activities such as the Poor People's Economic Campaign, criticisms of swollen military budgets, and challenges to the structure of TANF.

Similarly, the sixth edition of the NASW Policy Statements (NASW, 2003) underscores declarations that address issues of inequality, and encourages professional action consistent with the promotion of a just social order. This stance is most emphatic in recommendations that concern access to health, housing, immigration, peace and justice, and voter participation. The statement on "the Role of Government, Social Policy, and Social Work," partially transcribed below, is probably the most inclusive:

> It is the position of NASW that federal, state and local governments must have a role in developing policies and programs that expand opportunities, address social and economic justice, improve the quality of life of all people in this country, and enhance the social conditions in this nation's communities. NASW reaffirms its commitment to the promotion of the positive role of the federal, state and local governments as serving as guarantors of the social safety net and as mechanisms by which people through their elected representatives can ensure equitable and accountable policies to address:
> - entitlements to assistance in the elimination of poverty
> - access to universal comprehensive healthcare
> - standards for public service
> - enabling citizen participation in the development and implementation of social programs
> - taxation that is balanced and fair
> - an income floor for the working poor through earned income tax credits and other mechanisms
> - adequate federal minimum wage laws
> - standards and laws for the protection of workers in the work place
> - standards and laws for the protection of vulnerable populations
> - product safety standards
> - access to legal services
> - commitment to full employment
> - adequate and affordable housing
> - assurance of adequate public education and educational standards for all schools
> - a justice system rooted in law and administered impartially (NASW, 2003, pp. 296–297)

The stress on the government's responsibility for the well-being of citizens, together with the list of mechanisms considered necessary to achieve this end, constitutes a fairly clear policy direction. Discussion of how these mechanisms relate to one another, forming an ensemble of interlocking strategies, would have added a useful dimension for policy practitioners.

How Do Professional Statements Fit With Social Work Theories of Justice?

A review of social work theories of justice discussed in the first chapter of this book serves as a background to evaluate the degree of fitness between professional statements mentioned above and the theories of justice of social work authors.

Gil (1998) as well as Piven and Cloward (1971) give primacy to structural transformation as a key to implementing social justice. From their perspective, restructuring of this magnitude would entail replacing the present political arrangement with a socialist-style government. At the same time, they concede that progress can be achieved through reform or by disruption during times of political realignment. The professional statements just summarized speak against the increasing domination of conservatives in government and the growing inequality produced by anti-welfare policies—but the call is for reform, not revolution.

Both Gil and Piven and Cloward agree with social workers that the impetus to counteract inequities in the policy-making apparatus has to come from below, from civil society. Gilbert (1995), on the other hand, is concerned with maintaining a safety net, and in this sense he is closer to the orientation of the present government. The first mechanism listed in the NASW proposal—"entitlements to assistance in the elimination of poverty"—overlaps somewhat with Gilbert's agenda. This can be construed as a minimal requirement of social justice in any welfare state. In attacking "wealthfare," Gilbert makes common cause with critics of economic inequality that is aggravated by official policy.

Wakefield (1988a, 1988b) and Jordan (1990) address the implementations of justice at any level of social work practice. Wakefield argues that a commitment to social justice constitutes the core of social work and that any type of practice dedicated to this end is appropriate. Since social injustice takes a toll on individuals who experience it, practice geared to redressing such consequences is, by definition, pursuing social justice. Therefore, direct practice can be at the same level as policy practice. It is a method that can enhance justice.

Jordan adopts a similar approach. He urges social workers to take advantage of their positions as enactors of social policies. Since policies are general and open to interpretation about how to achieve operational goals, social workers have leeway to affect their practical consequences. Some confirmation of this tactic comes from the programs implemented under TANF (see Chapters 7 and 8 in this volume). Jordan's is a proposal for change from within. Implementers are like second-level regulators. They can advance reform from inside agencies through their ongoing work in social services. It is a valuable model for the majority of social workers who operate in human services agencies.

In sum, evaluations of the status of social justice from within the profession do not contradict theories in the field. The neoconservative orientation of governments since the eighties, growing economic inequality, the failure of the democratic process—these are the culprits. They underlie poverty, restricted opportunity, and the psychological consequences that accompany such obstacles. (See Chapter 1 in this volume for a review of these positions.)

What Do Social Justice Theories Add?

Chapter 2 gave an overview of selected conceptualizations of social justice within a liberal-democratic setting. The idea was to approach social justice not in abstract or generic terms but rather with reference to a specific context: the political economy of liberal democracies. Contrary to Gil's and Piven and Cloward's position, theorists like Rawls and Phillips do not posit the overthrow of an entire system. Instead, they explore how justice might be optimized by giving priority to freedom or to democracy.

Theories that prize democracy over freedom resonate with social work professionals nowadays, and they are in line with most of the social work philosophies of justice. Gilbert and Wakefield, who take a mixed approach, are exceptions to the mainstream.

Zucker (2001) and Dahl (1998) argue that the overwhelming dominance of liberal market values makes for excessive economic freedom. This has two consequences. First, society becomes increasingly unequal, and second, an extremely unequal society cannot be truly democratic. When social workers criticize economic inequality and poverty, they contend in the same breath that these conditions lead to political powerlessness. Economic inequality underpins political inequality, and this in turn violates the principle of equal democratic participation.

Murray Edelman (2001) and Herbert Gans (2003) develop this theme by showing how the manifold connections between economic and political influence affect the policy paths of particular institutions. For example, the relentless growth of the military budget, presented as necessary to national defense, becomes self-justifying. Whatever its desirability, the option of *not* spending more on defense seems less and less viable. Expansion of the military budget means favorable contracts to many corporations who come to depend, as if addicted, on the geometric growth of the defense industry. Corporate contractors, in turn, support growth in defense spending. The feedback loop is unbroken.

Elites oppose changes that might cut into their power and financial resources. A good deal of decision making that has profound consequences appears to be technical and receives little publicity—regulatory rulings for industry, for example, actions of corporations regarding personnel matters, taxation and production, and so on. While these regulatory measures affect the treatment of workers, they tend to be viewed as private matters and therefore receive little scrutiny. For the most part, they remain outside the public spotlight.

The contrast in public awareness carries over into different "attention spans" for issues of public and private welfare. The latter has a hidden side, as Hacker (2002, p. 35) indicates:

Public	Private
Lesser role for intermediaries	Greater role for intermediaries
More likely to be compulsory	More likely to be voluntary
More visible and traceable	Less visible and traceable
More progressive distribution	Less progressive distribution

Those who gain the support of economic interests by defending inequality dominate both the legislature and top executive positions. Toward the end of the twentieth century, the sway of these elites grew in part because electoral campaigns depended on generous financial support from affluent groups. Both parties elected and appointed officials who were unenthusiastic about reform.

The distribution of wealth became increasingly concentrated. Comparing the income gain for the middle class to that of the wealthiest 1 percent of the population, over the last two decades of the twentieth century, confirms this trend. The income growth was calculated at 9 percent for the middle class and 140 percent for the richest 1 percent (Krugman, 2002; Wolff, 2000).

Policies and strategies that created larger and more powerful corporations and less security for workers accompanied the concentration of wealth. In 1999, for example, 9,634 corporate mergers or takeovers took place, up from 1,719 in 1985 (U.S. Census Bureau, 2000). During the same period, employers' obligations to workers, such as health benefits and pensions, were cut.

Rebecca Blank (1997), a member of the Council of Economic Advisors in the Clinton administration, concluded that economic growth during the eighties and especially the nineties failed to benefit workers. On the whole, wages were stagnant, and minimum wage and temporary work grew. For the first time in American history, the economy expanded without any improvement for workers. Blank's vision of the future is pessimistic. The prospects of the unskilled and semi-skilled, she forecasts, will deteriorate, making a workfare solution for welfare recipients untenable.

It is no secret that a small sector benefits from policies that enhance their economic power. In 1999, there were 4,000 lobbying firms in Washington. These organizations employed 12,000 lobbyists, spending $1.5 billion (Gans, 2003). Although some of them represent professional associations, most work for corporations. Many lobbyists are former government officials who enjoy privileged access to old colleagues and have inside knowledge about channels of influence. The promise of campaign funds can be a strong incentive to favor certain policies over others.

The alliance between political and economic power is reflected in voting behavior (Jacobs & Shapiro, 2000; Teixeira, 1992). According to the U.S. Census Bureau (1997), the richest 20 percent of the population supplies 50 percent of the votes in presidential elections. The other half comes from the remaining 80 percent of voters at lower income levels. Moderate-income and poor citizens compose the largest number of nonvoters. This stands as an indicator of the political disaffection that has occurred over the past 20 years (Gans, 2003).

In short, great economic inequality produces and reinforces political inequality. The economically weak become less visible and relevant to their political representatives. Policies continue to benefit the economically advantaged while neglecting workers and the poor. A cumulative sense of powerlessness distances them further from politics. The upshot is a make-believe democracy that does not meet the standard of a government of the people, by the people, and for the people.

Overall, considering the functioning and outcomes of the liberal-democratic system in the United States, two conclusions stand out. To begin with, a workable democracy requires a degree of economic equalization. Secondly, the politically marginalized have to be informed, motivated, and united to create channels that foster participation in policies that affect them. The United States has a long way to go on both counts.

What Guidelines Can Be Derived From the Historical Analysis?

The framework we have used to analyze the history of the welfare state has four components: ideology, path dependence in the evolution of policy, the degree of centralization in policy implementation, and the variable strength of labor organizations. The combinations of conservative vs. liberal ideology with government decentralization/centralization, on the one hand, and the autonomy/control or cooptation of workers' organizations on the other characterize distinctive historical periods.

Ideology

American ideology may lack internal consistency (Ellwood, 1988; Heclo, 1986; Swidler, 1986) in a strictly logical sense, but emphasizing certain values over others is a good tip-off to characteristically conservative or progressive belief systems. Insisting on individual responsibility while ignoring social circumstances appears to be a conservative stance. Conversely, believing in social causation and insisting on equal opportunity reflects a progressive view. General mindsets are reasonably clear even if detailed policy preferences are not.

Efforts to derive support for or opposition to a variety of specific policies from the commitment to one or another of the core components of American ideology have met with limited success. Particular policies succeed or fail on something more than their merits alone. George Lakoff, a cognitive scientist at Berkeley, has diagnosed the inner logic of the Contract with America, the sweeping package of policy changes laid out by conservative Republicans during the Clinton administration. Eventually, Lakoff (2002) came up with some plausible cognitive models. Cognitive modeling emphasizes the power of conceptual metaphors that pull together a wide and possibly disparate range of phenomena. In the case of the Contract with America, Lakoff wanted to account for how certain beliefs or preferences stuck together in clusters—in other words, how they reflected larger, underlying worldviews.

Lakoff (2002) identifies two basic models: the "strict father" and the "nurturant parent" family. He points out that such models originate from firsthand experience in making sense of the world, and that early experiences within the family shape later views. In addition, there is plenty of evidence that family metaphors are linked to the construct of the nation. References to the nation as a family are staples of political speeches. We frequently talk of the Founding Fathers and Uncle Sam, of the fatherland (more commonly, the homeland), of heroic sons lost in wars, and we compare federal budget decisions with household budgeting. Family metaphors are everyday analogies that link up with the imagery of a government that has the responsibilities of a parent to protect citizens (its children) from harm and guide them to prosperity.

Table 16.1 lays out the characteristics of the "strict father" family and the worldview associated with it.

The Contract with America, which might initially appear to be an incoherent hodgepodge, fits this cognitive framework: rejection of abortion, opposition to environmental regulation and affirmative action, support for traditional family values and gun control, strict control of welfare, and enthusiasm for flat taxes.

As Table 16.2 shows, the nurturant parent family mindset grows out of a different set of values. It is practically the flip side of the strict father worldview, and it projects quite different meanings about what constitutes a good society.

Lakoff's formulation clarifies how preferences are bundled under distinct interpretations of policy issues. His approach is also instructive about the difficulty of communication between the frameworks. The two models do *not* constitute a smooth continuum from left to right, with a moderate center in between. Though pragmatic adaptations can occur, the tendency is for individuals to adhere to one or the other cluster of ideas rather than break ranks and go over to the other side. By and large, these clusters form separate universes of discourse. They are like magnetic poles. There need be no "natural," gravitational pull toward the center, no incremental gradient between extremes.

Nevertheless, for those engaging in social change, it is crucial to understand that there is considerable de facto give within these diametrically opposed conservative and progressive worldviews, specifically with regard to how they get translated into action. Conviction in the rightness of a cognitive framework, a set of values, forms the basis for action in the idealized world of true believers. However, some who share the same vision might put

Table 16.1

The Strict Father Family

- World is viewed as a dangerous and difficult place.
- To stand up to evil people, he has to be strong and disciplined.
- The father's job is to protect and support the family.
- Therefore, he has authority over family members.
- He controls women and reproduction.
- He uses physical discipline to correct evil tendencies in children.
- By punishing and rewarding children, he inculcates internal discipline.
- Self-discipline is the key to success.

Derived Cognitive Model of Politics

- The purpose of government is to maximize overall wealth (success) and guarantee security.
- Therefore, rewarding the successful is justified.
- Taxing the successful is an immoral punishment.
- Social programs encourage dependence and reward a lack of discipline.
- Control and punishment will encourage self-discipline among the unsuccessful.
- Girls who get involved in illicit sex should suffer the consequences.
- Environmental regulations are unwarranted obstacles to the pursuit of the self-interest of citizens and their achievements.
- Guns are appropriate weapons for good citizens to defend themselves within a dangerous world.
- A strong military is necessary to protect the nation against enemies and outsiders.

---

their self-interest in first place, even though they rationalize their actions in terms of the overall model. These pragmatic adaptations can clear the ground for compromise.

Recently, for example, Green Party activists have joined the opposition to the expansion of Wal-Mart in certain localities. The corporation decided to give a generous grant to a local environmental project. This does not mean that Wal-Mart will push for environmentally friendly policies in Washington. By the same token, many progressives saw Bill Clinton's signing of the PRWORA bill as a move to win reelection—that is, as unabashed self-interest. Simultaneously, however, Clinton resisted cuts in Medicaid, and he expanded health care for children.

In practice, the moral focus can shift within the same broad agenda. Some issues might gain priority over others. For black progressives, issues of racial equality might trump class issues. For conservative feminists, the demand for

Table 16.2

The Nurturant Parent Family

- The world is viewed as a nurturant place.
- The role of parents is to nurture the child.
- This means that to be responsible requires empathy, and protection.
- Social connection with others is part of education.
- Empathy requires freedom, fairness, and communication.
- Cooperation is more effective than competition.
- So are ethics of care rather than specific rules.
- The goal is a fulfilled life.

Derived Cognitive Model of Politics

- Government is charged with taking care of and protecting citizens, especially the vulnerable.
- Democracy is guaranteed by sharing power with the citizens.
- Its goal is to promote well-being by investing in public goods.
- Ensuring fairness to all means access to basic goods (food, health, living wages).
- Civil freedom includes motherhood choice, sexual choice, and free communication.
- Safety means safe neighborhoods and safe schools, requiring the control of guns.
- The economy is a means to achieve these goals.
- Art and education are moral necessities for self-fulfillment.
- Nature should be respected as an extension of the nurturant ethic.

equal pay for equal work might override qualms about regulating business. Agendas tend to be composed of rank-ordered preferences that are subject to adjustment.

In addition, some individuals compartmentalize. They adhere to different models in different areas of their lives. A common example in the academic world is progressive politics alongside conservatism in the professional sphere. Many academics are committed to greater rights for welfare recipients at the same time that they favor greater control over student discipline and want to base rewards exclusively on the competitive performance of students.

While variations due to self-interest, shifts in moral focus, or compartmentalization might open the door to occasional compromise, wholesale conversions are rare. Cases of extremism that occur within each worldview also pose problems for mediation. Gun-toting citizens who patrol the southern borders of Arizona on the lookout for illegal migrants exemplify a type of conservative vigilantism. The organic movement for unpolluted food or New Age adepts might be counted as equivalents on the progressive side.

Communication theory provides a more dynamic take on policy differences with the potential for bridging polarized worldviews. Americans may indeed select those elements of the national ideological heritage they feel most at home with and settle in one or the other, "strict" or "nurturant" camp, but they rarely reject other aspects of the ideology out of hand. For progressive change to gain traction, policy recommendations must be presented in a way that takes the values of target publics clearly into account (Lens, 2005). How empirical evidence is brought to bear in the struggle for public opinion requires a feel for words, metaphors, and examples that avoid reinforcing negative stereotypes. In addition, the connections that are drawn between evidence and the policies under consideration have to show how these measures will enhance the value commitments of the groups whose views progressives are trying to sway.

Issues of child welfare illustrate how a sophisticated understanding of values can work to the advantage of reformers. The welfare of children is essential to the future well-being of the nation. This is a claim that enjoys nearly sacred, consensual status. What's more, it has solid evidential backing. Two-thirds of the children of working mothers lack adequate child care, and good child care predicts superior school achievement and better behavior among teenagers, as well as productive habits in adulthood. These two components—what Toulmin (1958) calls "warrants"—compose a plausible chain of rationales. Together, they make a persuasive case that providing good child care to working mothers is a sound investment in the well-being and economic growth of the country as a whole.

Policy Decision Making

Although the cognitive frameworks identified by Lakoff and Lens have important implications for organizing movements and taking advantage of opportunities for alliances, the models themselves do not take into consideration how power affects the perception of deservedness. Social divisions tempt decision makers to attribute either favorable or pejorative characteristics to groups. These stereotypes lead them to treat some groups with lenience and others more punitively for morally equivalent behavior.

Critiques of unfair and unsuccessful policies often blame failures on policy design. It is common to cite the disinclination of policy makers to pay sufficient attention to experts on the issues. An alternative explanation is that policy makers tend be selectively attentive to influential groups who might be affected by the policies under consideration. The temptation is to cherry-pick rationales from accommodating experts. Decision makers calculate the political costs of the distribution of burdens and benefits, and these estimates go into the mix alongside considerations of the suitability of policies on technical grounds.

According to Schneider and Ingram (1993), such estimates involve an assessment of the power and the public standing of the groups being affected. "Public standing" means the images constructed about policy recipients. These images, frequently stereotypical, are shaped in part by the worldviews just discussed, and they are reinforced through socialization and the media. They become generalized even among progressives and internalized among the groups damaged by such caricatures.

By way of example, take the notion of a culture of poverty and single motherhood as the root causes of poverty. This construct ran through the writings, speeches, and political behavior of the generally progressive Daniel Patrick Moynihan. Acceptance of the negative traits attributed to single mothers on welfare is not uncommon among recipients themselves, even if the judgment does not square with their own experience (e.g., Luna, 2005). The power and pervasiveness of such constructions are remarkable.

This is what Antonio Gramsci (1985) meant by "hegemony." His fundamental insight is that the powerful, with their dominance of the means of communication and socialization, are in a position to propagate images that support their power. The strategy is to deactivate resistance or revolt from below. Hegemonic control works through the inculcation of values rather than by coercion, framing the terms of discussion. Although the resources of the groups affected can have an impact on policy making, Schneider and Ingram (1993) point out that how these groups become defined in public consciousness by selective constructions matters at least as much.

Table 16.3 arrays four groups that vary in power and in the positive or negative images attached to them. The "advantaged" groups with great power vis-à-vis policy makers have a generally favorable image enhanced by a well-publicized contribution to the economy. Their success is attributed to hard work, initiative, creativity, and responsibility. Policies that affect them tend to reduce burdens (e.g., lower taxes) and increase benefits (incentives, relaxed regulations, government contracts). They have access to policy makers and are often consulted. They are in the loop. Indeed, some policies simply do not get enacted without their participation. The off-the-record meetings of Vice President Cheney with representatives of the major energy firms prior to the formulation of energy policy during the first term of the Bush administration illustrate the syndrome forcefully.

The largesse that flows from closed-circuit decision making of this sort is either justified as essential to the good of the nation, via the trickle-down effect, or mixed with policies, like President Bush's tax cuts, that benefit other groups only marginally. If favorable policies come with a downside (for example, decreasing mercury emissions), compliance is voluntary, or accompanied by incentives (e.g., private occupational welfare). Above all, the privileged group is supposed to consist of upright citizens who can be trusted to do the right thing. Transgressions are likely to be handled through protracted investigations, usually leading to symbolic punishments largely disproportional to the material damage caused. The case of Enron might stand as an example.

Table 16.3 Social Constructions and Political Power: Different Impacts on Target Populations

Advantaged Groups

Powerful groups with positive image (corporate leaders: financial, industrial, agricultural, media, etc.) Access to political leaders: consultation, lobbies Group seen as essential to the well-being of society Leaders portrayed as good citizens committed to act honestly	Large benefits Few burdens Little or no control

Contender Groups

Powerful groups with negative/ambivalent public image (the ostentatiously rich, insurance companies, pharmaceutical industry, weapons industry, etc.) Lobbies, hidden access to public decision makers, political donors Few public references to these groups	Invisible benefits Symbolic burdens Occasional public control

Dependent Groups

Powerless groups with sympathetic image (the disabled, poor with children, elderly without support, etc.) No participation in policy decisions Response to need based on humanitarian values, not citizens' rights Protection as dependence Need close supervision and strict rules	Low benefits High burdens Strict regulation

Deviants

Powerless individuals Public image as society's enemies (street criminals, drug addicts, communists, illegal immigrants) Have to be controlled and punished Inherently dangerous: expulsion or isolation as remedies Civil rights curtailed	Minimal benefits Human rights protections Heavy burdens

Other powerful groups have access and lobbyists at high levels of decision making, but their public image is less positive. This would include the ostentatiously wealthy, some professional associations, insurance companies, and the like. Whatever benefits they manage to extract tend to have low visibility. Recent prescription drug legislation did not help the drug industry directly. Still, the provision, written into the law, forbidding Medicare to negotiate prices for bulk purchases of drugs certainly did so. By the same token, burdens might be more symbolic than real. Health insurance companies have been required to cover whole regions. The purpose was to ensure the availability of insurance to rural residents. When insurance companies balked because of the investment that the requirement entailed, compromises were made that diluted the original goal.

The shaping of policies that affect less powerful groups does not call for their participation even if their image is positive (e.g., people with handicaps or poor families with children). To use the old terminology, these are worthy people who deserve protective policies. They are "dependent." Their dependence places them in the general category of children who need direction and control for their own good. Although deserving, these groups are not seen as equipped to decide what is best for themselves. Protection hinges on humanitarian duty, not rights. The policies that are handed down tend to have inflexible rules requiring close supervision. Dependence assures submission.

The association of powerlessness with a negative popular image characterizes "deviant" groups. These include people viewed as enemies of society because they engage in criminal behavior (e.g., drug addicts, gang members) or because their beliefs or habits are taken as unpatriotic (communists, illegal immigrants, and the like). Control is the standard response. By and large, the damage that deviants are thought to inflict justifies the removal of citizens' rights and punishment without much rehabilitation. Their status as outsiders means that even after their debt to society is supposedly paid, deviants remain objects of surveillance. Rights such as voting or access to welfare are often curtailed. To a large extent, this group is branded for life. Many deviants are prevented from reentering society. With few alternatives, defeatism, anger, and recidivism set in. From this perspective, it is no surprise that the United States has the highest rate of incarceration among the world's democracies.

In the 1950s, communists and other political radicals were the targets of witch hunts, barred from many jobs and certainly from political careers. Illegal immigrants are another group who, despite their contribution to the wealth and well-being of the nation, are cut off from benefits. Their contribution to Social Security taxes is calculated to have reached $56 billion in 2002, but they will receive no benefits in old age (Porter, 2005). Even legal immigrants have been deprived of federal assistance. Their outsider status renders them the least visible of repressed groups.

Policy processes that aggravate inequality are not self-correcting (Edelman, 1988). They can be manipulated to support an increasingly uneven allocation of benefits and burdens. However, public officials calculate how the public and media will react, and there is a possibility that significant sectors of the public can be aroused by injustices. Scandals surrounding exorbitant payouts to advantaged groups or the wildly excessive punishment of powerless groups have served to rectify the social constructions of certain groups. The preferential contracts to Halliburton provide one such example. Hate crimes against homosexuals are another. Independent media (Gans, 2003) and an informed public, together with the removal of institutional impediments to participation, are crucial to this dynamic. Much of the policy to secure the rights of powerless, negatively perceived groups has been achieved through court actions and court mandates (Schneider & Ingram, 1993).

Summary

This review has covered a lot of ground. We have highlighted recent policy stands taken by the social work profession, within the context of different historical circumstances and contending theoretical positions. We have sketched in various diagnoses of injustice and suggested routes toward social justice. Table 16.4 gives a panoramic view of the major approaches.

It is against this background that the following chapter suggests guides to policy practice.

Table 16.4 Sources of Social Injustice and Directions for Redress: an Overview of the Literature

	Sources of injustice	*Countering injustice*
NASW and Social Work in the 21st Century	High inequality Poverty Barriers to basic services Unfair policies	Uniting the oppressed Professional policy influence Political activism Community organization Organizational coalitions Judicial interventions
Social Work Theories of Social Justice	Unjust socioeconomic system Inefficient welfare system Inadequate policy implementation Goals displaced by techniques	Replace the system Raise awareness of the oppressed Social upheavals Professional discretion Safety nets Combat wealthfare All social work practice geared to justice
Philosophies of Social Justice		
Freedom	Inequality not a problem Extreme inequality	Access to charity Access to basic goods Equal opportunity

(Continued)

Table 16.4 (Continued)

	Sources of injustice	Countering injustice
Democracy	Distorted democracy	Universal suffrage Informed electorate
	Economic interests	Fair distribution of rewards
	Control policies	Citizens' participation in economic policies Decommodification of essential goods
Historical Analysis Ideology		
Individually centered	Individual free to choose	Progress depends on right choices
	Responsible for bad outcomes	Learn to be self-reliant
Socially centered	Social causation of social problems	Change social conditions
Conservative	Lack of discipline causes problems	Reward the successful
	Lack of traditional values causes social disorganization	Control the unsuccessful
Progressive	Lack of support causes problems	Development of supports
	Intolerance of different cultures underlies repression	Intercultural openness
Policy Decisions	Low public image and lack of power	Break stereotypes Experiential awareness Accurate news Judicial intervention

17

Policy Practice

The unique nature of the social services area [that addresses] forms of overlapping market failures provides an opportunity for effective government involvement.

—Rebecca Blank (2004, p. 41)

Two sets of deficiencies dominate the sources of injustice listed at the end of the previous chapter, in Table 16.4. Economic inequality and the poverty that goes with it make up one cluster. The other is a system of government that is low in participation. This is a political arrangement that is bound to produce biased policy decisions.

Proposals for correcting injustice also fall into a few major groups. They take in, first, the empowerment of the oppressed to demand their rights; second, advocacy in the process of policy making and implementation to favor the powerless; and third, the pursuit of rights through the courts.

While interest in policy has been apparent throughout the history of social work, "policy practice" in the sense of a formalized area of responsibility in the profession is only now reaching maturity. The subfield came alive in the eighties (Dear & Patti, 1981; Mahaffey & Hanks, 1982). It burgeoned in the nineties (e.g., Figueira-McDonough, 1993; Flynn, J. P., 1982; Hefferman, 1992) and became more systematic with the beginning of this century, offering guidelines about the skills needed for diverse interventions (Jansson, 2003; Jansson, Dempsey, McCroskey, & Schneider, 2005).

As Wakefield insists (see Chapters 1 and 16 of this volume), what distinguishes policy practice in social work is not so much its methodology as its adherence to the goal of justice. Clearly, not all social work is policy practice. Yet clinical social work can have justice components. It can meet the needs of clients, support their self-awareness, and eventually empower them socially.

The purpose of policy practice is to change an unjust social system. Even empowerment has a social connotation: the ability of clients to gain access to civil and social rights as participant members of a democracy. Progress in that direction, as Gil and Piven and Cloward argue, is translated into structural change and is measured by outcomes that enhance social equality. According to Le Grand (1982), this involves the redistribution of services.

Diagnosing the mechanisms of exclusion and their ramifications is a first step in calculating the efficacy of methods and activities designed to foster justice goals. Analysis of this sort can also throw light on the wider potential for economic and political participation that the methods open up (Jordan, 2000).

The ideas about strategies for policy practice proposed here grew out of the material presented in Chapter 16. Four key strategies can be identified: (1) building influence from the bottom up; (2) using and strengthening available channels of policy influence; (3) active influence in policy implementation; and (4) rectification of unfair policies through the courts. While each of these methods of policy practice has different targets and develops strategies accordingly, they may also be interdependent.

Building Influence From the Bottom Up

Inequitable policies result from a skewed distribution of power and the attribution of positive or negative characteristics to the policy targets (Schneider & Ingram, 1993). The objective of from-the-bottom-up models of policy practice is to empower groups that enjoy few benefits and suffer large disadvantages. The main strategies involve reconstructing negative public images and amplifying power through numbers. Political action movements and community-rooted organizations come under this type of policy practice. Though their specific tactics may vary, at the heart of both is the goal of social empowerment of non-participant or marginally participant groups (Mondros, 2005).

Social Movements

Purpose and Characteristics

For social movements to gain momentum, a handful of core elements need to come into play: (1) an incident plainly recognizable as a case of social injustice; (2) close interaction among the population hurt by the injustice; (3) the emergence of a leader respected by the group; (4) identification of the source of the injustice; and (5) proposals to address the source of injustice (Gamson, 1995).

The liftoff of the civil rights movement in the 1960s met all these conditions. Blatant discrimination—notably, back-of-the-bus seating regulations—came on top of pervasive social exclusion inflicted on black servicemen returning from World War II. Large numbers of African Americans had migrated from rural areas to urban centers in the South as well as the North.

Housing discrimination intensified their interaction. Martin Luther King, the son of a Baptist minister and a minister himself, emerged as an eloquent leader. King identified the source of discrimination endured by his people as a lack of equal opportunity. Pushing for equality of opportunity—a cherished American value—required the equalization of civil rights.

During the 1960s, many radicals and conservatives alike saw the War on Poverty undercut, and they witnessed the subsequent explosion of civic disorder as entire neighborhoods in Detroit, Los Angeles, and Newark erupted in rioting. The waning of the War on Poverty and the rise of collective violence in the cities seemed to indicate that participation by the have-nots was a failure. Close inspection of the inheritance of the civil rights movement and of the War on Poverty reveals that they led to an irreversible trend legitimizing demands for a variety of rights. The seventies saw an explosion of advocacy groups and movements (Minkoff, 1995; Quadagno, 1994). While these advocacy groups did not provide the drama of street confrontations, they did build networks that came to constitute a solid infrastructure for social participation and change. Groups such as the National People's Action, Labor/Community Strategy Center, Acorn, and Grassroots Leadership exemplify movements with extensive local branches.

Development

In order to deliver tangible social justice gains to their constituents, political action movements depend on developing four factors (Porta & Diani, 1999).

1. *The study of the systemic bases of conflicts, including a clear identification of justice problems, their origins and visible consequences.* The task involves linking experienced inequality to its sources. The welfare rights movement, for example, was built on infractions of rights to privacy and unaccountability in services, joined with the devaluation of motherhood.

2. *Production of shared beliefs and collective identities.* To a large extent, this depends on the skillful use of information linking the consequences of policies across a plurality of groups. It also requires an active challenge to images of inferiority and powerlessness that underpin a chronic fatalism.

The Green Movement employed the second strategy to draw groups with diverse commitments (education, housing, health, etc.) to join their ranks. The second task of reasserting the self-esteem and activating marginalized groups to pursue their interests is generally more time-consuming. Informal occasions of interaction, such as those afforded in focus groups, are known to be successful in sharing lived experiences, and felt injustices, and forging resistance among welfare recipients (e.g., Luna, 2005; Tretheway, 1997). Such resistance is conducive to group activism.

3. *Organizational collaboration.* Inter-organizational linkages are necessary to uphold a movement's objectives and sustain the commitment of followers. By themselves, highly specialized organizations concentrating on a single problem of the have-nots will almost certainly be unable to command the size of constituency required to make themselves heard. Successful organizations depend crucially on inter-organizational links, and the mobilization of resources is necessary to maintain the networks of groups and organizations. For example, cooperation between organizations has a lot to do with how they see each other, in competitive or complementary terms (Porta & Diani, 1999). The possible interaction of these dimensions, shown in Table 17.1, helps predict what type of organizational response to expect, even from groups sharing the same goals.

Table 17.1   Conditions of Inter-Organizational Cooperation

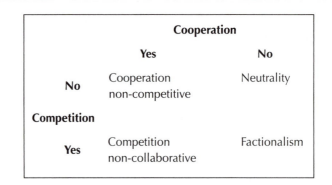

Cooperation can best be assured if organizations do not view themselves as competitors and share the same goal. Even if one views itself as competitive and the other as cooperative, a competitive cooperation is possible. At certain junctures, they will stick together while going their own way at different times. If neither views the other as having cooperative potential—for example, if they support very different goals—interaction is likely to be nonexistent. On the other hand, if both compete for the same resources, this is likely to lead to conflict. Each organization will lose some support, or one will take the lead and minimize the other's capacity for action.

The following examples illustrate each of these inter-organizational conditions. Facilitative cooperation often takes place in alliances between groups primarily dedicated to health improvement and environmental protection of impoverished people living in environmentally degraded areas. On the other hand, although civil rights associations and anti-discrimination lobbies serve the same population from slightly different perspectives, they have not joined forces in pressing their demands on the government. In spite of their early contribution to the movement for the abolition of slavery, white women's groups that pioneered women's emancipation were not terribly responsive to the black women's movement (Gordon, 1994). In addition, during the late sixties, many black women often faced a mutually exclusive choice between supporting women's rights and supporting race rights (Davis, A., 1975). Identity politics defined the goals of each movement as competitive, the obvious advantages of collaboration notwithstanding. Longres (1997) complains that such rivalries often weaken efforts to address broad social justice issues.

A full-time nucleus with the capacity to define targets of action, to keep communication flowing, and to plan specific actions is essential to activate the coalition that forms social movements. The central apparatus has to be able to lead while promoting participation.

4. *Repertoires of influence attuned to political circumstances.* The political context and culture, types of political institutions, and the array of opponents shape the choice of strategy. Demonstrations involving large numbers of participants, for example, might transmit the discontent of large parts of the citizenry. Anti-war protests in Manhattan during the Republican national convention of 2004, however, had little or no impact. Spotty coverage from the media and restrictive rules set by the city had a good deal to do with this. The magnitude of the protest was not transmitted visually, nor was there much public opportunity for protesters to express their concerns and motivations for joining the demonstrations or how they felt about the costs of the war to Americans like themselves. This "embargo" stands in sharp contrast to the role that the media played in revealing the hardships that civil rights marchers suffered in the South.

According to Piven and Cloward (1974), the only real option for poor people's movements involves surges of highly disruptive protests that can succeed in times of political weakness on the part of the government. However, the historical record gives no support for exclusive reliance on this strategy (Gamson & Schmeidler, 1984). In practice, the choice of bottom-up strategies of influence depends on how trustworthy decision makers are perceived to be. Table 17.2 shows how perceptions of authorities as trustworthy or not condition the type of strategy favored (Gamson, 1990).

If movement leaders believe that the authorities sympathize with their goals, they are more likely to use persuasion to get them on their side. This could entail collecting signatures in support of a favorable decision or presenting collected information that backs one decision over another. For example, a mayor might be presented with two budget alternatives: to increase the school bus fleet and improve racial balance in the schools, or hire more teachers and reduce class size in poor districts. Presenting evidence that minority parents

Table 17.2   Strategies of Influence From Below

	Authorities perceived as		
	Opposed	Supportive	Indifferent
Preferred strategies of influence	Persuasion	Negotiation	Coercion

favor the second course, together with evaluations—for example, performance scores—for bused students as compared to students in smaller classes might be a powerful strategy for influencing authorities who have already demonstrated concern with educational outcomes in poorer schools.

Conversely, if the same issue was going to be decided at the state level by a special committee made up of members who have not shown any particular commitment to education in poorer communities, the assumption might be that the authorities are more or less neutral. In effect, they might choose an alternative that, in their estimation, works to their political advantage. A strategy that offers members of the committee some political benefit could provide a counterweight to whatever advantages the "bus lobby" might offer. Here the size of the constituency that supports hiring more teachers matters. As potentially active voters, they can have an impact in future elections. Furthermore, declarations of concerned parents about where they stand, if publicized through the media, make it more costly for committee members to oppose the movement. Finally, the dissemination of research findings might result in bringing voters with no prior commitment on board.

Conceivably, a key decision maker may adopt the line that the problems of minorities derive from bad cultural values and inept socialization. His or her position is that the best chance for minority children living in poor neighborhoods is to expose them to white values. Concretely, their best chance is to leave their neighborhoods and undergo white middle class education.

In this instance, the movement faces an authority who not only denigrates minorities but has already stated what his or her decision is going to be. The decision maker cannot be influenced by self-interest or evidence. That person is an adversary, and the only course is confrontation and coercion. Under these circumstances, the movement may have little to lose by opting for disruptive strategies that will be costly to the authority. This would mean well-planned protests; amply covered by the media, well-publicized quotes from the decision maker against minorities; interviews with minority leaders and educators disapproving the hidden discrimination; and so on. Whether the authority will change his or her decision remains uncertain, but to the extent that their political reputation suffers, decision makers ignore the preferences of those affected by their decisions at their peril.

Research conducted on the tactics of environmentalists in Europe shows that the most common strategy of the movement was getting the attention of the media, followed by formal and informal contacts with national or local authorities and administrators. Demonstrations were the strategies used least often by the European green movement (Dalton, 1994). It would be interesting to have a similar study done in the United States regarding contemporary poor people's movements. According to Gans (2003), two circumstances are of concern for social/political movements: first, growing corporate spin and political control over public opinion; and second, an air of even-handedness, cultivated by media professionals, that can convey detachment from or indifference to social issues.

The Roles of Social Workers

Probably the most relevant skill in keeping social movements going is coalition building and forming alliances to fight injustice. While numerous groups advocate missions consistent with a justice goal, many have highly restricted interests or address issues affecting only a narrow identity clientele. In building coalitions that combat specific forms of oppression, it is essential to recognize that the powerless suffer from a variety of interrelated injustices.

Whether they come about through incremental reform or a larger, systemic restructuring, meaningful transformations involve altering the prevalent order at some level. They can affect policies, the allocation of rights, or norms of behavior. Such changes have to decrease inequality, which will impact blacks, women, the elderly, and homosexuals (Galper, 1980; Moreau, 1990; Sills, 1991). Solidarity among the least powerful groups has a multiplier effect. Single-issue changes have little staying power. What's more, they promote division among activist groups, weakening all by a divide-and-conquer process (Biklen, 1983; Dluhy & Kravitz, 1990; Wineman, 1984). Social workers are familiar with the benefits of solidarity for rallying social movements, and they have firsthand knowledge of the interrelated offenses against the rights of their clients in everyday life. Social service agencies often contact other organizations as they go about helping their clients, and social workers routinely attend inter-professional meetings on issues of common interest. Through such multitasking, they have accumulated a rich store of "best practices" and operational wisdom. In short, social workers have an important role to play in building the groundwork for solidarity and reciprocity among single-issue and otherwise exclusive identity groups.

Local Grassroots Organizations

The key difference between the two approaches to building influence from the bottom up—political action movements and local grassroots organizations—is the priority given to the neighborhood in the second approach as a context that facilitates informal interaction and solidarity and that puts people in touch with nearby organizations. The primacy of neighborhoods has been the basis for community organization practice. The strategy draws on preexisting forms of social capital that facilitate mobilization.

Purpose and Characteristics

In the face of high rates of mobility and the onrush of globalization, some observers have concluded that community has lost its strength and function (Christenson, 1979; Reisman, 1950; Warren, R., 1978). While most communities do not have the self-sustaining characteristics of isolated rural settings of the past, locale of residence nevertheless has an important impact on the worldviews, interests, and behavior of individuals (Brooks-Gunn, Duncan, Cato, & Sealand, 1993; Figueira-McDonough, 2001; Jargowski, 1997; Jencks & Peterson, 1991; Warren, D., 1981).

Several analysts and practitioners have contributed to models that try to pin down which dimensions of community are pertinent to empowerment, and these assessments have informed the choice of strategies aimed at promoting local activism and solidarity.

Development

1. *Dimensions of community.* There is some agreement that the degree of informal interaction, the extent of local organizations, and links to external sources of power are fundamental characteristics of communities (e.g., Figueira-McDonough, 2001; Warren & Warren, 1980). Community solidarity depends on the first two dimensions; the ability to mobilize resources and use influence hinges on the last one.

A community ranking high on all these dimensions no doubt enjoys the ideal conditions for having its needs communicated and responded to. Yet research on a variety of communities has isolated certain demographic variables as crucial to communities in building down-up policy influence: poverty and mobility.

Figure 17.1 shows the relationship between these demographic variables on the three dimensions. For example, although poor communities might have strong informal ties, they usually lack resources to maintain local organizations or to cultivate powerful links to the outside. Conversely, neighborhoods with high mobility will have difficulty in forming strong interpersonal bonds but are more likely to maintain external links (see Figueira-McDonough, 2001, for a review of this research). Table 17.3 gives a simple typology of these relationships.

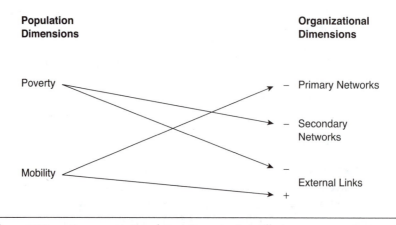

Figure 17.1   Community Population-Organization Effects

Source: Figueira-McDonough (2001): 35.

Table 17.3

	Community Ideal Types	
	Mobile	*Stable*
Non-poor	*Stepping-stone*	*Established*
	Low informal networks	High informal networks
	High formal networks	High formal networks
	High external links	Low external links
Poor	*Disorganized*	*Parochial*
	Low informal networks	High informal networks
	Low formal networks	Low formal networks
	Low external links	Low external links

2. *Assessment of poor communities.* Because grassroots policy practice is supposed to empower communities, the idea is to figure out where in the continuum between cells 3 and 4 the target communities stand. These are the poor neighborhoods with varying degrees of mobility that are associated with different levels of informal organization. Such estimates will guide the practitioner in gauging where to initiate the empowerment strategy. The process is analogous to what goes on among clinical practitioners when they assess the strengths and weaknesses of individual clients before planning intervention. So, if the strength of a community lies in its informal networks, this would be the starting point. If, however, informal ties are weak in a deprived neighborhood, external links have to be forged to sustain existing or create local organizations, which in turn could develop activities to help the formation of informal groups, if they are nonexistent. Some poor neighborhoods with high residential mobility exhibit just this syndrome.

3. *Internal resources and solidarity: women and multiculturalism.* Studies of collective action have consistently found that women are an often invisible but resilient force in grassroots activism. According to Weil, Gamble, and Williams (1998) and Smith (1990), depictions of community action that focus on vocal leaders rather than on the sustained work of "foot soldiers" account for much of this neglect. A careful look at the dynamics of grassroots work reveals that the desire of women to protect their families and promote their children's welfare translates into powerful activism in poor communities (Abramovitz, 1996b; Heskins, 1991; Levitt & Saegert, 1990; Naples, 1998; Seitz, 1995; Stoutland, 1997).

Increasingly, bottom-rung poor communities are made up of minorities from different ethnic and racial backgrounds (Jargowski, 1997). It makes sense, given the growing prominence of cultural over class identity, for community practitioners to address this massive demographic trend (Gutierrez et al., 2005; Longres, 1997). The danger is that cultural identity might override community solidarity, hampering effective communal action. To manage multiculturalism, organizers have to become acquainted with the customs—the "silent language"—of communities before attempting to bring them together. This knowledge will help to formulate and transmit common goals and organize joint participation (Gamson, 1995). Linda Stout (1996), founder of the Piedmont Peace Project, suggests practical procedures to enhance cooperation—for example, setting up working teams with representatives from every cultural group with close interests, rotating leadership, and free exchange of different views regarding action plans.

> 4. *Establishing links between grassroots groups and formal service organizations.* Failure to make this connection severely restricts empowerment. Case studies in community organization offer many leads for encouraging collaboration between informal associations and formal agencies (Balsanek, 1997; Mulroy & Shay, 1997; Scannapieco & Jackson, 1996). One of the most intriguing suggestions flows from acceptance of the mutual advantages of collaboration. The trust and rapid responsiveness of close informal groups and the expertise and greater formality of social service agencies would, if synchronized, increase effectiveness in dealing with social problems (Litwak, 1985; Warren, D., 1981).

As an example, assume that a community is afflicted with child abuse. Universal child care, by reducing exposure to abuse, is likely to decrease the incidence of this behavior. Counseling services could help the abuser to gain some insight into his or her anger and learn other means of expressing it, and a support group could respond quickly to the call of a parent whose stress might lead to abuse against the child. Table 17.4 summarizes the conditions affecting organization–grassroots collaboration.

Table 17.4   Conditions Affecting Organization-Grassroots Collaboration

Organizational Preconditions

- Definitions of the problem as requiring professional and grassroots expertise
- Assessment of advantages or disadvantages of integrating both kinds of expertise or of working separately but simultaneously

Grassroots Motivation

- Relevance of the problem to everyday grassroots life
- Level of trust in the organizations
- Degree of participatory influence in grassroots-organizational linkages

5. *Public and private resources in community empowerment.* The War
   on Poverty has been misrepresented as a failed experiment in organizing poor communities. In fact, the growth of participation among
   poor residents in Community Action Programs was a significant
   achievement, as were public enthusiasm and involvement in the
   administration, planning, and staffing of local programs. The abrupt
   cut in resources, due in part to the budget squeeze brought on by the
   Vietnam War as well as by congressional uneasiness with grassroots
   demands for economic and political participation, not only put an end
   to the program but also angered many of the participants who had
   believed in its promise and whose expectations had been raised
   (Quadagno, 1994; Warren, D., 1975).

Later experiments have centered on the rehabilitation of selected neighborhoods, and they have involved outside and local businesses working
with service organizations. Some were top-down projects (for example, the
Enterprise Zones promoted by Bill Clinton). Others, like the Community
Development Corporations, were more community-centered. In both cases,
the goals of development adapted to economic interests at the cost of
participation at the bottom, and the fundamental goal of empowerment
receded. In one instance—the Comprehensive Community Revitalization
Program in the Bronx—some equilibrium was achieved, and community
control was preserved (Halpern, 1995; Schorr, 1997).

Poor communities need to reach out for resources they cannot generate
on their own. These experiments constitute a process of trial-and-error
learning in how to grow such resources while empowering the community at
the same time:

- Comprehensive, single-community, grassroots initiatives require a
  stable source of public funding to pursue their objectives.
- The initiatives without sufficient public funding will run the risk of
  being dominated by business interests that sidetrack the comprehensive
  goals of the community.
- Partnerships with private and government entities can preserve
  community goals if grassroots entities come to be viewed as true partners and have equal say in decision making and implementation.

The first and last solutions are conducive to community empowerment,
while other suggestions accentuate different alternatives to empowerment.
These involve forms of coordination among marginalized communities.
Building coalitions of poor communities behind common goals or in support
of reciprocity is a tactic that has been proposed since the 1990s (Halpern,
1995; Korsching & Borich, 1997). The basic idea is to accumulate power
through mechanisms similar to the networking that is common among social
movements. Coalitions like these are more likely to exert influence at the
state and federal levels.

A seminal study by Gilbert (1979) and an account of community planning by Checkway (1995) suggest avenues of interaction between neighborhoods and city governments. Because they have very limited resources, councils cannot satisfy the needs of all neighborhoods evenhandedly. Decision-making styles depend, according to Gilbert, on the structure of government. He identifies three types of representative structures:

> *Type One* provides for direct, systematic lines of communication between neighborhood and city councils. Neighborhood councils have access to planning support services, and each neighborhood submits proposals for improvements in its area. The neighborhood proposals compete with one another. The expectation is that neighborhoods with greater political leverage will grab more resources than the others.

> In *Type Two,* each community sends representatives to a central body. This body reviews all proposals, and the one forwarded to the city council is the one on which the coalition of representatives finally agrees.

> *Type Three* has also a central representative unit but with an advisory function only. It is the city council that makes the final decision based on technical planning criteria.

Type One is the least beneficial to poor communities; their resource deficit works against them in open competition. Type Three is chancy inasmuch as efficiency rather than need is the standard. Type Two at least guarantees equal participation among communities. In order to have a shot at competing successfully under the first type of governance, impoverished communities must line up external political backers. They must also rely on the ability to generate external/private economic resources to be successful at the third type of decision making.

Imagine, for example, that a poor community desperately needs a child care center located close by after the implementation of TANF. Under a Type One decision structure, communities with greater resources would more likely get the center located where they wanted it to be. Only full-scale demonstrations from the poor communities, media visibility of their plight compared to the situation of other communities, and the pull of child advocacy organizations could move the center closer to the community in need. To achieve the same end under a Type Three governance format, a foundation contribution to build the center in the community in need might convince the city to opt for this least costly alternative.

The Roles of Social Workers

Social workers have hands-on experience with community interventions, and they have participated in many of the experiments just outlined. The general misconception, it has been noted, was that the "failure" of the War on Poverty confirmed the weakness and incompetence of grassroots organizations.

In fact, it was the poverty program that failed the grassroots movement, not the other way around. Popular perceptions of the disappearance of grassroots activism are mostly the result of poor reporting (Anner, 1996; Flacks, 1995).

The new modes of advocacy that emerged during these years created a sound structure for participation and change. Donor institutions continue to fund local experiments and demonstrations, often in partnership with colleges and universities. Even when such experiments are not sustained in the long run, they contribute to strengthening advocacy groups, and they provide learning opportunities to solidify political bridges to local and state governments (Anner, 1996; Clotferter & Ehrlich, 1998; Flacks, 1995; *The Foundation Directory*, 1999; Padilla & Sherraden, 2005).

The grassroots approach customarily refers to local communities with some political and economic bridges to the outside. These links have to be extended if reforms are to carry over at state and national levels and if they are to foster structural transformations. Two strategies take on importance in promoting multiplier effects:

To begin with, a political procedure attuned to the weakness of economically vulnerable organizations would require (a) mapping organizations and groups outside the community concerned with the same problems that the community is concerned with, and (b) developing associations around the commonality of these goals. These associations might be truncated and ephemeral or more holistic and long-lived. In any event, their coordination would give the community a chance of being heard at different levels of decision making.

An alternative strategy to develop local political power would be to coordinate marginalized communities in order to leverage their demand capacity and increase response to their claims. Halpern (1995) links the growing unresponsiveness of the War on Poverty to local needs with the failure to establish a wide-ranging network of this type. The idea of coordination among poor communities has already caught on in social work (Korsching & Borich, 1997).

Influence in Policy Making

This is probably the type of policy practice, often referred to as legislative advocacy, that receives the most attention in the social work literature nowadays. Its immediate goal is to influence policy in the making or to propose new policy consistent with social justice goals. It represents an effort to have the concerns of the less powerful carry weight among policy makers.

Purpose and Characteristics

To turn decision making in a direction that benefits the deprived populations that the profession represents is the purpose of policy makers in social work (e.g., Mahaffey & Hanks, 1982). This can involve introducing new proposals, supporting favorable policies advanced by other groups, or opposing policies that have detrimental consequences for the well-being of the groups of concern.

Although advocacy and lobbying have received most of the attention, two other tasks are just as important in shaping policy. The argument by Schneider and Ingram (1993), discussed in Chapter 16, underscores the significance of constructed public images that condition the legitimacy of benefits and costs in legislatively enacted policies. Refurbishing such popular images is a prerequisite for political influence.

Learning about the political operations of legislative and bureaucratic institutions needs to be part of the training that social workers receive about the policy-making process. Successful promotion of policies depends on organizational clout. Edelman (1988) and Gans (2003) have demonstrated how powerful interest groups cultivate access to decision makers. Sophisticated organizations lobby in the corridors of state and national power. Any attempt to counterbalance their influence requires the development of inter-organizational linkages and the careful building of coalitions that represent the less powerful.

Development

Legislative advocacy by social workers who represent the interests of groups with, by definition, little or no power in the political arena requires planning to overcome negative perceptions of intended beneficiaries, the comparative weakness of the organizations representing their interests, and the newness of the practice itself. Such practice involves a three-pronged approach:

(1) Legislative practice

Early attempts at legislative advocacy followed standard lobbying procedures. The National Association of Social Workers and the Council of Social Work Education moved their headquarters to the Washington area to protect their interests at the national level and collaborate with each other. These organizations have joined others in support of human rights, but their work has benefited the profession more than it has the poor.

Currently, a major effort goes into developing advocacy skills. For example, the text written by Jansson (2003) offers detailed guidelines regarding the practical methods necessary for the exercise of advocacy, and the book gives useful examples of intervention at county, state, and national levels of policy decision making.

An important first step entails analysis of policies with an emphasis on consequences for economically marginal populations. The research of Sandra Danziger and her colleagues (Danziger, Danziger, Corcoran,

Tolman, & Kalil, 1999) on workfare in TANF helped unveil the impact of the program on the women involved in it. They challenged generalizations about the success of the program.

Beyond the study of the effects of existing policies, the capacity to lay out alternatives for improving policy is crucial. In the absence of such alternatives, the scanty power of the populations affected practically guarantees that the status quo will prevail. Proposals for new policies, or for correcting those in place, might have to start at a modest and not-too-expensive level, allowing for adaptations that enhance protection for target populations (Dear & Patti, 1981).

Whether the intent is to propose new policy or to amend policies on the books, knowledge of legislative rules and institutional customs has to precede intervention. For example, legislatures are always overloaded, so early introduction of initiatives is a must.

The selection of credible sponsors follows a series of steps: reviewing representatives' voting patterns, their positions in various committees, and their core interests. Information of this sort is also useful in formulating ways to approach political actors, in shaping the presentation of proposals, and in choosing team members likely to relate well to potential sponsors.

Added to this, a simple presentation of the projected consequences of the changes can be of use, along with straightforward statistics relevant to the issue at hand. Depicting the problem to be addressed in human terms and the availability of expert witnesses can also strengthen the hand of supporters as they make their case.

Kleinkauf (1989) stresses the importance of anticipating different types of opposition. Resistance might arise from erroneous or incomplete information, or it might be rooted in a rigid worldview of the sort described by Lakoff (see Chapter 16). Dissemination of information could work in the first instance but have little effect in the second. However, recognition that worldviews might be swayed by self-interest or moral priorities could suggest strategies to neutralize sectors of the opposition. Structuring legislation so that it can be broken down or safely amended in such a way that its fundamental purpose stays undamaged can be an important tactic in gaining support.

So, for example, the proposal to grant public child care to all mothers incited considerable opposition on ideological as well as pragmatic grounds. In the eyes of many legislators, the approach was un-American, and for most the costs were forbidding. As the proposal changed to apply exclusively to poor workingwomen, it gained support, especially from representatives whose opposition was budget-driven. But many remained hesitant; they still took the negative stereotypes of welfare recipients for granted. Another amendment creating child care credits for non-poor working mothers doubled the acceptability of the plan by emphasizing work rather than welfare. Though legislators with a punitively "strict father" tradition were not converted, there was enough support for the policy to pass.

(2) Redressing negative images of dependence and deviance

The foregoing example highlights how legislative policy practice needs to address disempowerment aggravated by the dissemination of negative images (Brodkin, 1993; Schneider & Ingram, 1993; Schram, 1995). Along with efforts to improve the lives of the dispossessed by legislative action, it is necessary to challenge the stereotypes that pass as everyday wisdom about the poor. Gring-Pemble's report (2003) on the legislative debate surrounding the passage of TANF testifies to the resilience of these caricatures and the crippling presuppositions that accompany them. Gans (2003) contends that the media play a crucial role here. Their damaging influence comes across in biased depictions of African Americans (Entman & Rojecki, 2000). On the other hand, some journalists have written insightfully about the entrapment of the disenfranchised in underclass neighborhoods, the limitations of welfare reform, and the resilience of black families (e.g., Auletta, 1982; De Parle, 2004), the suffering of children in poverty, the lack of services, and the inhumanity of social institutions (e.g., the documentaries of Frederick Wiseman and the books of Jonathan Kozol).

Building linkages with opinion makers in the media and groups with a social conscience has been underutilized in rectifying stereotypes of the poor. Gans (2003) argues that correcting these misperceptions can pay off if such efforts produce a better-informed and sympathetic audience. Countercultural journalism and its variants help provide alternative perspectives (Grimes, 1991; Merritt, 1995; Rosen, 1996). Integrating news and fiction is an avenue toward achieving the same end, and humor is another vehicle for undermining prejudices disguised as common sense. The "fake news" delivered on the Comedy Channel's *Daily Show* is perhaps the most successful venture along these lines.

In sum, policy practitioners in the legislative arena have to strengthen their ties with socially concerned journalists and other media influentials. At the end of the day, the idea is to fight preconceptions that profile the usual suspects. The counter-strategy relies on ampler information and balanced images.

NASW's California branch has an active legislative team in Sacramento that is exemplary in following some of these guidelines. Every year, the team puts together a Legislative Forum for between 600 and 800 social workers and social work students. Participants learn to identify political allies, and they become familiar with the ins and outs of lobbying and the techniques of organizing demonstrations (Annual Legislative Lobby Day, NASW-CA, 2006).

(3) Building an organizational base

Legislative advocacy depends on building coalitions that carry organizational weight. Advocacy and legislative practice are not individual operations. Students trained in the variety of skills needed to gain credibility in the policy field soon recognize that the complexity of policy making goes beyond what a single practitioner can dominate. Assembling organizational linkages starts with research on overlapping interests across multiple groups. The inter-organizational ties that emerge act to counter the well-financed lobbying activities of businesses and corporations (Schneider & Ingram, 1993).

Inter-organizational know-how, then, is a must for legislative practice. Jane Addams set an example of how to augment political power through this strategy, and it was a strategy followed by radical social workers that came after her (Reisch & Andrews, 2001). The outreach involved in the promotion of insurance coverage for mental health is a case of one such coalition. Nevertheless, large-scale reform coalitions at the state and national levels are still the exception rather than the rule.

With the devolution of many aspects of social policy to the states, new opportunities to affect legislation have cropped up (Jansson, Dempsey, McCroskey, & Schneider, 2005; Schneider, 2002). The competition for public goods is often thought to be more manageable at the state than the national level, and this has almost certainly heightened expectations for implementation of progressive policies.

However, the evaluations of TANF as it has worked in the states, reviewed in Chapters 10 and 11, show so much diversity that generalizations about the ease or difficulty of implementation are precarious. What the variety of outcomes documents above all is how entrenched local political cultures can be. The enactment of TANF programs in a progressive fashion occurred in states with histories of generous welfare programs. Stingier, more punitive actions typified states that had favored policies of exclusion for a long time. Thus, the decentralizing thrust of TANF worked to the advantage of some recipients in some locations, but elsewhere others lost ground. There is no one-size-fits-all solution. If, as Hoefer's (2005) research indicates, no single model of interest group advocacy satisfactorily accounts for the variation in outcomes across a small handful (four) of states, the conclusion must be that site-specific path dependence is a powerful force in shaping policy decisions.

Another limitation imposed by the devolution of social programs is inherent to the budgetary realities of the states, which are prohibited from running deficits. Once the federal government shuts down channels of support (as happened with TANF), states in financial distress are hard put to respond to added social needs regardless of political culture. Access to policy influence varies widely across the states.

Table 17.5 gives a positive example of legislative activity at the state level.

The table describes a summit conference devoted to health and child care policies held prior to the opening of the 2005 legislative session in Sacramento, California. The conference brought together about 60 agencies and commissions with interests and oversight in these areas. These organizations shared research, developed proposals, and hashed out strategies. The state senators and representatives who were present gave their views about the feasibility of specific proposals and suggested ways to increase the chances of favorable legislative treatment for these measures.

Table 17.5   The California Working Families Policy Summit

Sacramento Convention Center, January 7, 2005

Hosted by: California Center for Research on Women and Families

Sponsors: California Commission on the Status of Women
California Legislative Women's Caucus
Asian Pacific Islander Legislative Caucus
California Legislative Black Caucus
Latino Legislative Caucus

Cosponsors: Fifty agencies representing local communities or addressing special concerns (e.g., health, education, youth, homeless, domestic abuse, children's rights, welfare). Among these was the California chapter of the National Association of Social Workers.

Funding: California Endowment; The Stuart Foundation; California Nutrition Network for Healthy, Active Families; Public Health Institute.

Purpose: Bring together legislative and administration staff, nonprofit leaders, and others to identify and discuss public policy, strategies, and financing for the upcoming legislative session.

Themes for 2005: Health, welfare, and child care.

Format

Speakers: Three state senators and three representatives who have worked for and support legislation toward social justice. They focused on legislative strategies.

Directors or members of agencies working on the 2005 themes. They discussed the strategic implications of past successes, partial successes, and failures. Recent studies in the thematic areas were discussed, as were statistics on the range of the problem and new approaches. Alternative budget proposals in support of policies consistent with the new approaches were evaluated. Each speaker prepared a summary for distribution.

Provocateurs: These were people assigned to call attention to possible contradictions in the proposals and to potential barriers to implementation.

Discussion: After each presentation, there was extensive commentary from the participants. Comments ran from questions about the studies to support policy changes, to strategy proposals, to sharing experiences, and to going over the implications of the topics for specific initiatives. It was clear that many of the participants were acquainted with and took into account one another's work.

Networking: Nearly half the day was given to networking in a comfortable room with tables, seating corners, and inexpensive munchies.

The forum was open to all who wanted to come and was free. Because of space constraints, participants were asked to register ahead of time. At least 500 persons took part.

The Roles of Social Workers

Policy advocacy has given a significant boost to justice practice in social work. Professional knowledge of what goes into the exercise of legislative clout, sharpened by training in both grunt work and systematic analysis, is comparable to internships for physicians: the experience makes decisive contributions to social work policy practice. Other crucial skills include acquaintance with methods of inter-organizational coordination and the ability to diagnose routes toward social justice from different angles and for different constituencies (in education, environment, mental health, health care, and other issue areas), so as to establish both long- and short-term coalitions. Equally important is the demolition of negative images—dependence, laziness, moral weakness, deviance—ascribed to the poor or near poor. A certain media savvy is increasingly essential for countering such stereotypes.

Implicit in the engagement of social workers in legislative practice is the understanding that such activity involves interdisciplinary and inter-professional teamwork. The complexity of the legislative process rules out a generalized amateurism. As with all practice, much of the learning occurs in place, in a team setting, where individual knowledge, experience, and abilities result in some specialization of roles. Under these circumstances, concrete knowledge about the conditions of disenfranchised populations and evaluation of the on-the-ground consequences of legislation might be the most valuable assets that social workers bring to policy practice.

Shaping Policy Implementation

Policy practice in the course of legislative bargaining encompasses joint activities with other disciplines and professionals, to which social workers contribute their own expertise. Influencing policies as they are implemented in social services is tied more directly to the role of social workers.

Purpose and Characteristics

Social policies presume political decisions that have the well-being of citizens in mind. For the most part, they express desirable purposes and formulate regulations to achieve these goals. The rules are general and standardized, while actual circumstances are complex and idiosyncratic, so regulations cannot be implemented automatically by clerks. Social workers, as professionals trained to address a variety of situations and problems, are chosen to put social policies into practice. Their role is to close the gap between the general policy and the specifics of the case to which it applies, relying on their expertise. The social worker is in a position not only of control but of responsibility, with an obligation to ensure that the spirit of the policy is met (Jordan, 2000; Mullaly, 1997).

Development

The hiring of social workers to carry out services gives them power over clients. By the same token, it gives them discretion to apply the rules based on their professional judgment. A social worker in charge of a youth program may or may not send a teenager back to an institution if he or she violates a curfew stipulation, regardless of the general rule mandating that course of action when an infraction of probation occurs. The professional might decide that the purpose of the rule does not apply in light of the particular circumstances that led to breaking the curfew. Or, taking into consideration the family context of a minor who keeps running away, the social worker might decide against a rule that the child should always be returned home. The professional must, of course, justify decisions like these on a case-by-case basis.

The premise, then, is that professionals are supposed to tailor standardized rules to the idiosyncratic reality of complex cases. However, some services are organized into bureaucratic agencies, where going by the book gets top priority. Social workers can respond to this predicament in three ways: They can submit to the bureaucratic culture, they can work toward relaxing the rigid rules, or they can oppose the procedures as deviations from the intent of policy.

The last pair of options constitutes policy implementation practice.

Since the legitimacy of policy derives from the goals it seeks to achieve, the social worker can argue that blindly applying standardized regulations to specific cases contradicts the policy goals.

Another instance of rule "translation" might arise if the procedures adopted by the service wind up frustrating their purpose, while general guidelines are followed to the letter. For example, in child protective services, the welfare of children is paramount. The policy outlines certain principles of parental rehabilitation to mitigate the trauma of family separation for the child. The social worker has two tasks: family rehabilitation and supervision, on the one hand, and child protection on the other, so as to prevent new abuse and repair the damage of previous abuse.

All this involves a wide range of activities. The social worker has to enroll the parents in programs of anger management, in addition to arranging for the following: psychological treatment that isolates the sources of abusive behavior, support from Parents Anonymous, psychological assessment of the child, other services needed by the child, school evaluations, and so on. Follow-up on the involvement of parents and children in these services; evaluation of the outcomes; frequent visits to assess the risk to the child; and contacts with the schools, teachers, local police, and neighbors are also part of the job. These multiple remedies are in accord with current knowledge about how to rehabilitate the family and protect the child.

Staying on top of this array of interventions is difficult in the best of times. In practice, most agencies are set up so that the average load of social workers is 50 cases, sometimes as high as 200. Studies have indicated that, to follow policy directives as laid down, loads should be limited to about 13 to 15 cases.

Thus, the gap between goals and service regulations is egregious, and this discrepancy presents an opportunity for implementation practice. Social workers could legitimately blow the whistle on the blatant contradiction between policy proposals and the capacity to implement them. Alliances with child advocacy groups could add to the chances of having the service regulations changed.

Other lines of implementation practice grow out of infringement on the civil or human rights of clients. Policies that permitted midnight raids on the homes of welfare recipients to check if there was a man present; the sterilization of poor teenagers who were sexually active; the recent imposition of birth control on welfare recipients; putting abortion under Medicaid out of reach of these same recipients; the exclusion of children resulting from impregnation of the mother after receipt of welfare benefits; the imposition of waiting periods for eligible recipients who have changed their state of residence—all of these constitute civil rights infractions.

The Roles of Social Workers

In any service operation, besides whatever professional–client confrontations may occur, it is incumbent on social workers to empower clients by making them aware of the social origin of some of their problems. Rather than being reflections of their own incapacities, their problems may often be linked to the structure of society. Dealing in a group setting with clients who have similar problems might not only develop solidarity and mutual support but also encourage an awareness of the social obstacles they face. This consciousness-raising can lead, in turn, to the formulation of collective demands. The social worker can then direct clients to advocacy groups able to channel their demands.

Many writers (Gambrill, 1990; Hasenfeld, 1987; Longres & Mcleod, 1987; Moreau & Leonard, 1989; Pinderhues, 1983; Withorn, 1984) second Jordan's view of the importance of professional implementation in social policies. Together, their proposals can be classified under three directives: In direct social work, this involves modified types of professional–client relationships. Democratization of service organizations is central as an organizational strategy, and redressing social policies is the core of policy practice.

Strategies of Direct Social Work

The most sophisticated strategies address the interaction between social workers and clients. There is abundant evidence that clients on public assistance frequently postpone asking for help with services because "begging" is humiliating. Their reaction reflects the internalization of the undesirable traits—laziness, moral laxity, and the like—typically ascribed to "dependents." Therefore, it is crucial that their interaction with social workers does not add to the disempowerment of those already on the brink. The following are suggestions for increasing the likelihood that clients will be empowered:

As a counter-measure, social workers can set up a collaborative exchange that

- Accepts the experiential knowledge of clients and their analysis of the problem
- Treats the interaction as a process of mutual learning that avoids the professional/client hierarchy
- Informs the client about the procedures most helpful to the solution of the problem, including strategies that help speed the process and avenues to access other services for further assistance
- Shares clients' files with them, opening them to corrections or explanations

Social workers can also initiate a process of redefinition, normalization, and activism that moves toward an understanding of the social causation of problems. This can involve

- Joint analysis of historical and social causes of the problem and examples of similar cases
- Organizing groups of clients with similar experiences, for mutual support and further reflection about shared social contexts
- Referring clients to organizations interested in removing some of the social barriers

Organizational Strategies

Social work is an organizational profession. Most of its activity takes place within service agencies. Inevitably, some of those in charge of these services may develop regulations that jeopardize the well-being of clients and reduce the capacity of professionals to help them out. Social workers do not belong to a very powerful profession, partly because of the disenfranchisement of their clientele. Innovative strategies are called for to check organizational missteps.

Democratizing the management of services is one such route. The purpose is to reformat strict hierarchies or redirect them toward a system of peer supervision. The rationale is to establish a collaborative environment that encourages solidarity and the participation that raises incentives for creative solutions. Exchange among professionals regarding regulations not only brings up common experiences, but the dialogue also spurs group action for change. For obvious reasons, it is hard for a single social worker to contest organizational regulations. While it takes time, a collective approach that places a premium on organizational restructuring is usually more realistic.

Redressing Social Policies

Other actions can also help in reforming counterproductive regulations: (1) gathering evidence of the damage caused by such rules, (2) proposing alternatives, and (3) demonstrating how innovations turn out to be more in line with the purposes of policy.

Challenging a social policy on the grounds that it infringes on citizen rights or actually violates human rights requires a broader support base, not only from colleagues but also from clients, as well as the professional association and other activist organizations.

Judicial Policy Making

Over the past three decades, the number of test cases adjudicated in federal courts has increased significantly. Issues involving environmental regulations, employment practices, prison administration, educational policies and funding, welfare standards, and treatment of the mentally ill have been decided in these venues (Feeley & Rubin, 1998; Figueira-McDonough, 1993; Mnookin, 1985; Provine, 2005; Scheingold, 2004). Judges have also assumed an oversight role in the implementation of court-ordered standards (Feeley & Rubin, 1998; Moss, 1984; Provine, 2005).

Purpose and Characteristics

Since the groundbreaking decision of *Brown v. Board of Education of Topeka* on school desegregation in 1954, the courts have grown in importance as an arena for policy reform (Thelen, 2003). For this reason, they are a vital component of policy practice in social work. By and large, however, the social work literature has given scant attention to the role of the courts in policy practice (Figueira-McDonough, 1993).

The policy role of courts has its roots in common-law forms of adjudication fundamental to the Anglo American tradition. The legal system in the United States has functioned as a forum for working out the application of ambiguous precedents to unforeseen circumstances, and from the start of the republic, the courts were considered a safeguard of constitutional rights.

Nonetheless, critics have been at work to circumscribe the autonomy of the courts. Congressman Tom DeLay has vociferously attacked the use of judicial powers as undemocratic; the religious right has declared court decisions as disrespectful of the moral beliefs of the American people; libertarians have complained about the passivity of the courts in accepting government regulation; and corporations and the medical profession lament the unfairness of the courts regarding the compensation imposed for the injuries caused to others.

On the opposite side are citizens who depend on the courts to safeguard constitutionally based rights of equality, free speech, and due process in an unequal society (Frymer, 2003). Groups working against what they perceive to be the out-of-control "activism" of the courts have tried to curtail their power through legislative curbs on habeas corpus petitions, sentencing guidelines that include mandatory minimums, three-strikes laws, mandated alternative dispute resolution programs, caps on punitive damages, and so on (Zemans, 1998). Some of these initiatives have cut into the legal options of the poor. Automatic penalties; assignment to adult courts of juveniles charged with certain crimes; eviction of families charged with drug offenses from public housing; mandatory expulsion or suspension of students for certain behaviors; and automatic deportation of immigrants for minor offenses are all measures that have made inroads against the rights of the marginalized (Provine, 2005).

Contrary to popular belief, civil and tort litigation has actually decreased in the United States since the late eighties. The ire of opponents seems directed at the types of decisions rather than their frequency (Provine, 2005). Under a pluralist political system in which consciousness of rights is widespread, the courts have assumed their policy-making role in response to emerging social realities. By so doing, they guarantee another level of democratic accountability (Frymer, 2003; Peretti, 1999).

Protecting individual rights in accord with state and federal constitutions is the role assigned to the courts. For example, decisions made by the courts that require equalizing financial support for education within school districts and states ratify the principle of equal opportunity, even if these decisions have not been submitted to the popular vote.

The ascent of the courts as policy makers derives as well from the expansion of rights legislation that took off in the sixties. Legislatures are prone to respond to organized public interest constituencies by creating unfunded mandates. Specifications about how to reach legislative goals are prescribed, but the follow-through on actual funding remains with the states or counties. The courts have required states to implement legislation according to federal mandates. Many times this puts state and local governments in the position of having to reallocate funds already earmarked for other programs. Though it may not be to the liking of local notables, this type of redistribution often works to the benefit of the vulnerable. The quasi-administrative function of the courts becomes part of the implementation of new legislative rights. Requiring health services in prisons is one prominent (and controversial) example. The access of immigrant children to health services and equal funding for public schools are two others.

Development

It makes sense for activists to use litigation to advance their causes. Even if litigation is defeated, the effort itself can raise consciousness and develop support for new rights claims. This has been the course followed for issues like comparable worth, disability rights, school financing equalization, and freedom from sexual harassment (McCann, 1999; Provine, 2005; Scheingold, 2004).

Public interest litigation is of special interest for social workers. It took modern form in the sixties and seventies through the activities of Legal Aid, a program of the War on Poverty. Launched with the purpose of providing legal recourse to the poor, the program argued successfully that the rights of welfare recipients and disabled persons to benefits deserve the same protection as property rights. This strategy extended to the rights of individuals in prisons, mental institutions, and schools.

Public interest litigation has some features of particular relevance to structural reform:

- It deals with numerous individuals and groups at once.
- Litigation is forward-looking. The purpose is to shape policy, not to compensate for past violations.
- Court decisions do not end with litigation; they mark the beginning of efforts at institutional reform.
- Remedies have policy implications.
- Judges, not plaintiffs or other interested parties, control litigation because of the impact of the issues on the public at large (Chaynes, 1976; Sandler & Schoenbrod, 2003, p. 115).

The type of policy that evolves from the judicial process would not necessarily develop through elections, which favor majority preferences. Judicial policy making can respond to the claims of minorities. Some legal scholars point out that the Constitution introduced an explicit check on the will of the majority, and that the courts, as nonrepresentative bodies, have the power to protect citizens against the excesses of the majority by policing encroachments on individual rights (Black, C. L., 1960; Ely, 1980).

Judicial policy making, then, has proved instrumental in redressing problems affecting minorities. The record concerning rights of African Americans, prisoners, welfare recipients, and mentally ill people attests to this conclusion.

However, litigation is no panacea. Decisions might bring up conflicts between rights with apparently equal claims to a favorable ruling. A decision on a case might not represent the diversity of the group affected by the decision. There may well be unanticipated consequences. The legal process can be drawn out, and in the end the courts themselves often lack the resources to monitor implementation (Figueira-McDonough, 1993).

The 1977 decision in *Smith v. Offer* on a foster care case provides a classic example of unintended consequences within the field of social work practice. The due process clause of the Constitution was interpreted to require a hearing before a child could be removed from a foster care home, if the child had lived there for over a year. The decision helped prevent constant moves that are known to damage the emotional stability of children, but it also dampened the incentives of social workers to remove children from inadequate homes.

The Roles of Social Workers

The importance of judicial decision making for social sectors with little power or political representation is hard to overestimate. For social workers serving these groups, the judicial system offers a very important venue for changing the status of outsiders. Social workers can play a role in the process.

Effective involvement in judicial policy making plainly requires collaboration with legal experts—with organizations concerned with civil rights and with the rights of the poor to legal resources like the Civil Liberties Union, the Legal Defense Fund, Legal Aid, and a variety of other issue-focused advocacy organizations. Within this social–legal partnership, the role of the social worker can be extensive. Social workers can

- Develop a sense for which cases have strong legal validity
- Assess the suitability of cases as representative of the group to be affected by court decisions
- Collect and interpret evidence
- Organize public support for the issues at stake
- Establish mechanisms for accountability and the implementation of decisions
- Evaluate outcomes

While the list sounds like a heavy load, the fact is that all these activities are closely tied to the tasks for which social workers have been trained and those in which they tend to be involved anyway. Social workers have direct contact on a daily basis with clients who run up against obstacles to their citizenship or human rights. They have concrete experience with the variety of such infractions and how they reflect specific cases of exclusion. This face-to-face contact, training, and experience give social workers a leg up in evaluating evidence. Furthermore, the community and organizing aspects of their work depend on identifying advocacy organizations, both local and national, that are likely to support issues to be decided in the courts and that are adept at making issues visible. Keeping an eye on the judicial process is a critical and powerful tool for correcting distortions in the implementation of policies.

Interdependence Among Types of Policy Practice _____

Policy practices are inter-linked. To take one example, legislative advocacy gains momentum with the growth of social movements. Since the logic of change from below is the empowerment of great numbers of people, the success of social movements reinforces legislative advocacy. Grassroots development is also related to the capacity to reach out to organizations as well as across communities. Development of this sort is reciprocal, depending on and contributing to social movements. Its success can be crucial for legislative advocacy at city, county, and state levels.

Linkages of social work associations to other professions with overlapping objectives—in health or education, for example—can help in implementing policy practice. When policy implementation practice throws a spotlight on civil and human rights infractions and draws attention to mechanistic regulations, judicial policy practice can come into play as the ultimate and most effective recourse. Implementation practice can be thought of as an extension of legislative advocacy.

Conclusion

All of us in the economically developed West live within the parameters of two supreme values: freedom and equality. These principles are at the core of liberal democracy. However, their optimal combination, as we saw in Chapter 2, is a source of enormous contention. Should liberty take precedence, or should democracy have priority? The institutional context of American political culture gives the nod to freedom, though not without qualification.

The basic principles of social work reflect this duality of values. The professional goals of enhancing individual autonomy and promoting social justice correspond to the values of freedom and equal rights. Mullaly (1997) is representative of a school of thought claiming that social work curricula stress techniques that facilitate personal autonomy while neglecting the practice of social justice. The historical track record of the profession confirms this bias, as does the evolution of welfare policy in the United States. Both stories reflect an inclination to favor competitive dimensions of freedom over the rights of equal participation that are inherent in substantive democracy.

For Wakefield (1988a, 1988b), the commitment to social justice is central to the profession. This is what distinguishes social work from other professions. Methods are secondary because they are changeable. Their efficacy for professional goals varies with the development of knowledge and specific circumstances. In addition, these methods, far from being distinctive, are shared with other people-oriented professions. Since methods are tangential to professional identification, all approaches that address social justice are appropriate. While the policy practices discussed here concentrate on structural approaches, individual methods targeted to justice ends are equally valid. Some strategies proposed under policy implementation emphasize individual as well as group approaches in the pursuit of social justice.

A key question remains: How can social workers be trained to uphold the goal of social justice and avoid becoming remedial workers or handmaidens of control (Piven & Cloward, 1971; Reisch & Wenocur, 1986)? Gil (1998) contends that social workers share a sense of justice and that they are vocationally attracted to the profession by a genuine concern and empathy with the victims of injustice. What is at issue, however, is not the motivation of professionals but their socialization and training. Schools of social work need to prepare students to

- Analyze the contradictions of liberal democracies. This requires a capacity to gauge the rationales and outcomes of the dominance of freedom over democracy and of democracy over freedom.
- Identify how each orientation takes institutional form and analyze the worldviews that sustain them.
- Assess the ideological and institutional frameworks of different welfare states and compare their outcomes in terms of social justice.
- Learn methods for evaluating the social and individual roots of social problems.
- Identify the policies and the justifications that link them to the maintenance of unjust systems. Spell out the connections of these policies with the problems that are the domain of professional activity in social work.
- Prepare professionals for political involvement as a condition for promoting social justice.

Robert Morris (2000) urges professional schools to expand the horizons of social workers. He argues against limiting training to intra-professional, in-house knowledge. Social professions have to take advantage of the theoretical and basic research produced by the social sciences. However, their real contribution lies in transforming this knowledge into workable programs of change, in evaluating and refining them through demonstrations. Some demonstrations in which social workers are involved have tremendous potential for legislative advocacy (e.g., Padilla & Sherraden, 2005).

Innovation in practice requires ongoing updates about what the disciplines have generated, most especially as social work enters new areas of practice. Similarly, it requires learning successful strategies from other professions. This should not threaten our professional identity. That identity is given by the goal—social justice—toward which we use any methodology. If structural change involves a challenge to prevailing systems, it cannot be reached—though it can certainly be promoted—by isolated individuals. For social workers, solidarity among colleagues is fundamental, as is the strong support of the professional association. Yet, although such backing is necessary, it is not in most cases sufficient.

Actions that advance policy strategies depend on interdisciplinary and inter-professional links, exchanges, and teamwork. They also need a degree of empowerment beyond what can be generated from within the profession alone. Strategic alliances with other groups, sharing similar goals, are almost always a necessity. Jane Addams and her followers understood how politically important such ties were.

Part VI: Suggestions for Exercises

Have students do the following:

1. Choose an aspect of national social policy, whether implemented in centralized or decentralized fashion (e.g., TANF, Medicare, Social Security, Medicaid, or any other).

2. Review evaluation from reliable sources.

3. Highlight conclusions of the evaluation that could serve as a basis for policy change.

4. Identify groups, organizations, and associations with an interest in improving policy.

5. Identify groups that might oppose the projected change.

6. Choose a policy practice on the basis of its potential effectiveness for promoting the policy change. Justify your choice.

7. Describe the strategies to be followed within the policy practice chosen.

8. Identify the most relevant roles for social workers in the implementation of such strategies.

Note: Centralized policies call for intervention at the federal level, while decentralized policies operate at the state or county level.

References

Aaron, H., & Reischauer, R. (2001). *Countdown to reform: The great social security debate*. New York: Century Foundation.

Abel, N., & McDonnell, J. R. (1990). Preparing for practice: Motivations, expectations, and aspirations of the MSW class of 1990. *Journal of Social Work Education, 26,* 57–64.

Abramovitz, M. (1996a). *Regulating the lives of women: American social policy from colonial times to the present* (2nd ed.). Boston: South End Press.

Abramovitz, M. (1996b). *Under attack and fighting back*. New York: Monthly Review Press.

Abramovitz, M. (1998). Social work and social reform: An arena of struggle. *Social Work, 43*(6), 512–526.

Adams, G., & Rohacek, M. (2002). Child care and welfare reform. In A. Weil & K. Finegold (Eds.), *Welfare reform: The next act* (pp. 121–142). Washington, DC: Urban Institute.

Adams, G., Snyder, K., & Sandfort, J. (2002). *Getting and retaining child care assistance: How policy and practice influence parents' experiences*. (Assessing New Federalism, occasional paper number 55). Washington, DC: Urban Institute.

Addams, J. (1910). *Twenty years at Hull House*. New York: Macmillan.

Administration for Families and Children. (2001). *TANF statistics*. Washington, DC: Department of Health and Human Services. Available: www.acf.dhhs.gov/news/stats/tanf.htm

AFL-CIO. (2004a). Employer-provided health insurance coverage falls as employers refuse to pay their fair share. *Curing America's health care*. Available: http://www.aflcio.org/familyfunresources/healthcarehelp

AFL-CIO. (2004b). Ask a working woman. *Survey report*. Available: http://www.aflcio.org

AFL-CIO. (2004c). Pensions. *Pensions and savings*. Available: http://www.aflcio/issuespolitics/pensionsavings

Alinsky, S. (1946). *Reveille for radicals*. New York: Random House.

Alvarez, R. (1976). The psycho-historical and socioeconomic development of the Chicano community in the United States. In C. Hernandez, M. J. Haug, & N. N. Wagner (Eds.), *Chicanos: Social and psychological perspectives* (pp. 38–54). St. Louis, MO: C. V. Mosby.

American Indian Census Facts. (2000). Albuquerque, NM: American Indian Graduate Center. Available: http:www.aig.com/articles/ai-census-facts.html

Amidei, N. (1982, September). How to be an advocate in bad times. *Public Welfare*, pp. 37–41.

Amott, T. L. (1990). Black women and AFDC: Making entitlement out of necessity. In Linda Gordon (Ed.), *Women, the state, and welfare* (pp. 280–300). Madison: University of Wisconsin Press.

Anderson, M. (1978). *Welfare: The political economy of welfare reform in the United States.* Stanford, CA: Hoover Institute.

Anner, J. (1996). Introduction. In J. Anner (Ed.), *Beyond identity politics: Emerging social justice movements in communities* (pp. 5–13). Boston: South End Press.

Arrow, K. J., & Hahn, F. (1971). *General competitive analysis.* San Francisco: Holden Day.

Auletta, K. (1982). *The underclass.* New York: Random House.

Bailey, S. (1950). *Congress makes a law.* New York: Columbia University Press.

Balsanek, J. (1997). Addressing at-risk women's issues through community and grass roots. *Health and Social Work, 22,* 63–69.

Bandoh, E. (2003, October). Outsourcing the delivery of human services. *Welfare Information Network 7,* 12.

Bane, M. J. (1986). Household composition and poverty: Which comes first? In S. Danziger & D. Wein (Eds.), *Fighting poverty, what works and what doesn't* (pp. 209–230). Cambridge, MA: Harvard University Press.

Bane, M. J., & Ellwood, D. T. (1994). *Welfare realities: From rhetoric to reform.* Cambridge, MA: Harvard University Press.

Banfield, E. (1970). *The unheavenly city revisited.* Boston: Little, Brown.

Bar-Cohen, L. (2002). *Housing wage.* Unpublished paper, Community Scholars, National Low Income Housing Coalition. Available: http://www.NLIHC.org

Barker, R. L. (2003). Milestones in the development of social work and social Welfare. In R. L. Barker (Ed.), *The social work dictionary* (5th ed., pp. 473–493). Washington, DC: NASW Press.

Barlett, D., & Steele, J. B. (2002). *The great American tax dodge.* Boston: Little, Brown.

Barsh, R. L. (1996). The Indian Child Welfare Act of 1978: A critical analysis. In J. R. Wunder (Ed.), *Recent legal issues, 1968 to the present* (pp. 219–265). New York: Garland.

Bates, R. (Ed.). (1988). *Towards a political economy of development: A rational choice perspective.* Berkeley: University of California Press.

Beard, C. (1965). *An economic interpretation of the constitutional convention.* New York: Free Press.

Beck, A. (2002). Prison and jail inmates at midyear 1999. *(Report NJC # 18163).* Washington, DC: U.S. Department of Justice, Office of Justice Programs.

Beer, A. L. (Ed.). (1969). *Herbert Spencer.* London: Collier-Macmillan.

Beers, C. (1909). *A mind that found itself.* New York: Longman, Green.

Bell, W. (1965). *Aid to dependent children.* New York: Columbia University Press.

Bellah, R., Madsen, R., Sullivan, W., Swidler, A., & Tipton, S. (1985). *Habits of the heart.* Berkeley: University of California Press.

Bellingham, B. (1986). Institution and family: An alternative view of nineteenth century childsaving. *Social Problems, 33*(6), 33–57.

Bennett, D. (2003, November). Head cases. *American Prospect, 14,* 10.

Bennett, W. J. (1999). *The index of leading social indicators.* New York: Broadway Trade Paperback.

Berkowitz, E. D. (1991). *America's welfare state: From Roosevelt to Reagan.* Baltimore: Johns Hopkins University Press.

Bernhardt, E. M. (2000, September 15–16). *Female careers between employment and children*. Paper presented at The Observatory on Family Matters, Seville.

Bernstein, N. (2004, March 7). Behind fall in pregnancy, a new teenage culture of restraint. *New York Times*, 1, 22–23.

Berrick, J. D. (1995). *Faces of poverty*. Oxford, UK: Oxford University Press.

Bhargava, D. (2002, Summer). Why not a new war on poverty? *American Prospect*, pp. 33–35.

Biklen, D. P. (1983). *Community organizing: Theory and practice*. Englewood Cliffs, NJ: Prentice Hall.

Bilingual Education Act of 1968. Pl. 90-247, 81 Stat. 816.

Billingsley, A. (1992). *Climbing Jacob's ladder: The enduring legacy of African-American families*. New York: Simon & Schuster.

Black, C. L. (1960). *The people and the court: Judicial review in a bureaucracy*. Englewood Cliffs, NJ: Prentice Hall.

Black, W., Jr. (1991). Social work in World War I: A method lost. *Social Service Review, 65*, 340–379.

Blackburn, R. (2002). *Banking on death or investing in life: The history and future of pensions*. London: Verso.

Blanchard, E. L., & Barsh, R. L. (1980). What is best for tribal children: A response to Fischler. *Social Work, 25*, 350–357.

Blank, R. M. (1997). *It takes a nation: A new agenda to fight poverty*. Princeton, NJ: Princeton University Press.

Blank, R. M. (2004). *Is the market moral? A dialogue on religion, economics, and justice*. Washington, DC: Brookings Institution.

Block, F. L. (1990). *Postindustrial possibilities*. Berkeley: University of California Press.

Bloom, H. H. (1995). Citizens and the ideology of citizenship in the Dutch republic. *Yearbook of European Studies, 8*, 151–184.

Blum, J. M. (1963). *The national experience*. New York: Harcourt Brace.

Booth, C., et al. (1970). *Life and labor of the people of London: Poverty*. New York: AMS Press. (Original work published 1902–1904)

Boris, E., & Bardaglio, P. (1983). The transformation of patriarchy: The historic role of the state. In I. Diamond (Ed.), *Families, politics and public policy: A feminist dialogue on women and the state* (pp. 70–93). New York: Longman.

Borjas, G., & Hilton, L. (1995). *Immigration and the welfare state: Immigrant participation in means-tested entitlement programs*. Cambridge, MA: National Bureau of Economic Research.

Bowles, S., & Gintis, H. (1986). *Democracy and capitalism: Property, community and the contradictions of human thought*. London: Routledge and Kegan Paul.

Bowring, J. (1843). *The works of Jeremy Bentham*. London: Tate.

Boyer, P. (1978). *The urban masses and moral order in America, 1820–1920*. Cambridge, MA: Harvard University Press.

Brace, C. L. (1872). *The dangerous classes in New York and twenty years of work among them*. New York: Wynkoop and Hallenbeck.

Brager, G. (1999). Agency under attack: The risks, demands and rewards of community activism. In J. Rothman (Ed.), *Reflections on community organization: Enduring themes and critical* issues (pp. 57–74). Itasca, IL: F. E. Peacock.

Brake, M., & Bailey, R. (Eds.). (1980). *Radical social work and practice*. Beverly Hills, CA: Sage.

Brenden, M. E. (1993). Mary van Kleeck: Social worker and leader. In J. Andrews (Ed.), *From vision to action: Social workers of the second generation* (pp. 75–88). St. Paul, MN: St. Thomas University.

Brenner, J. (1956, June). Scientific charity 1873–93. *Social Service Review, 30,* 168–173.

Brenner, R. H. (1964). *From the depths: The discovery of poverty in the United States.* New York: New York University Press.

Brest, P. (1975). *Process of constitutional decision-making: Cases and materials.* Boston: Little, Brown.

Brewster, K. L., Billy, J. O. G., & Grady, W. R. (1993). Social context and adolescent behavior. *Social Forces, 71*(3), 713–740.

Bricker-Jennings, M., & Hooyman, N. (1986). *Not for women only: Feminist practice for a feminist future.* Silver Spring, MD: NASW Press.

Brinkley, A. (1995). *The end of reform: New Deal liberalism in recession and war.* New York: Vintage Books.

Brodkin, E. (1993). The making of an enemy: How welfare policies construct the poor. *Law and Social Enquiry, 18*(3), 647–670.

Brommel, B. J. (1978). *Eugene V. Debs: A spokesman for labor and socialism.* Chicago: C. H. Kerr.

Brooks-Gunn, J., Duncan, G., Cato, P., & Sealand, N. (1993). Do neighborhoods influence child and youth behavior? *American Journal of Sociology, 99,* 353–393.

Brown, R. (2000, December). Helping low-income mothers with criminal records achieve self-sufficiency. *Welfare Information Network, Issue Notes, 4,* 13.

Buchanan, P. J. (1973). *The new majority: President Nixon at mid-passage.* Philadelphia: Girard Bank.

Burt, M. R. (1991). Homeless families, singles and others. *Housing Policy Debate, 12,* 4, 37–78. Washington, DC: Fannie Mae Foundation.

Burt, M. R. (2002). The hard-to-serve: Definitions and implications. In A. Weil & K. Finegold (Eds.), *Welfare reform: The next act* (pp. 163–178). Washington, DC: Urban Institute.

Burtless, G., & Quinn, J. (2001). Retirement trends and policies to encourage work among older Americans. In P. Budetti, J. Gregory, & H. Allen Hunt (Eds.), *Ensuring health and income security for the older workforce.* Kalamazoo, MI: Upjohn Institute.

Butler, A. (1992). The changing economic consequences of teenage child bearing. *Social Service Review, 66*(1), 131–142.

Butterfield, F. (2000, November 11). Often parole is one way stop back to prison. *New York Times,* pp. A1, A28.

Byler, W. (1977). The destruction of American Indian families. In S. Hunger (Ed.), *The destruction of American Indian families.* New York: Association of American Indian Affairs.

California State Self-Sufficiency Standards. (2003). Family Economic Self-Sufficiency State Organization. Available: www.ci.la.ca.us

Calmes, J. (2005, January 24). On Social Security: It's Bush vs. AARP. *Wall Street Journal,* p. A4.

Cameron, D. (1982, October). *Social democracy, corporatism, and labor quiescence: The representation of economic interests in advanced capitalist societies.* Paper presented at the conference on Representation and the State: Problems of Governability and Legitimacy in Western European Democracies. Stanford University, Stanford, CA.

Campbell, F. A., Ramey, C. T., Pungello, E., Sparling, J., & Miller-Johnson, S. (2002). Early childhood education: Young adult outcomes from the Abecedarian Project. *Applied Developmental Science, 6*(1), 42–57.

Capps, R., Ku, L., & Fix, M. (2002, March). *How are immigrants faring after welfare reform: Preliminary evidence from Los Angeles and New York City.* Final report submitted to the Office of the Assistant Secretary for Planning and Evaluation, Department of Health and Human Services.

Carrillo, J. (1998). Tribal governance. In J. Carrillo (Ed.), *Readings in American Indian law: Recalling the rhythm of survival* (pp. 205–214). Philadelphia: Temple University Press.

Carter, C., Coudroglou, A., Figueira-McDonough, J., Lie, G. H., MacEachron, A. E., Netting, E., et al. (1994). Integrating women's content in the social work curriculum: A proposal. *Journal of Social Work Education, 30*(2), 200–216.

Castrovinci, J. (1976, March). Prelude to welfare capitalism: The role of business in the enactment of workmen's compensation legislation in Illinois, 1905–12. *Social Service Review, 30,* 80–102.

Cates, J. R. (1983). *Insuring inequality: Administrative leadership in Social Security, 1935–1954.* Ann Arbor: University of Michigan Press.

Caute, D. (1978). *The great fear: The anti-communism purge under Truman and Eisenhower.* New York: Simon & Schuster.

Center for Law and Social Policy. (2004). Key provisions in TANF reauthorization bills passed by the Senate Finance Committee and the House. *Center on Budget and Policy Priorities.* Available: www.cbpp.org/9-9-03tanf.htm

Chace, J. (2004). *1912, Wilson, Roosevelt, Taft and Debs: The election that changed the country.* New York: Simon & Schuster.

Chaiken, J. (2000, January). Crunching numbers: Crime and incarceration at the end of the millennium. *National Institute of Justice Journal, 242,* 10–17.

Chapin, R. C. (1970). *Standards of living among workingmen's families.* New York: Arno Press. (Original work published 1909)

Chaynes, A. (1976). The role of the judge in public law litigation. *Harvard Law Review, 89,* 1281–1316.

Checkway, B. (1995). Two types of planning in neighborhoods. In J. Rothman et al. (Eds.), *Strategies of community intervention* (pp. 314–326). Itasca, IL: F.E. Peacock.

Chen, D. (2004, September 22). U.S. seeking cuts in rent subsidies for poor people. *New York Times,* pp. A1, A24.

Children's Defense Fund. (1987). *Declining earnings of young men: Their relation to poverty, teen pregnancy and family formation.* Washington, DC: Adolescent Prevention Clearing House.

Christenson, J. (1979). Urbanism and community sentiment: Extending Wirth's model. *Social Science Quarterly, 60,* 387–400.

Christopher, K. (2002). Family friendly Europe. *American Prospect, 13,* 59–61.

Chua, A. (2003). *The world on fire: How exporting free market democracy breeds ethnic hatred and global instability.* New York: Anchor Books.

Citizens for Tax Justice. (1999). *Analysis of capital gains tax plans report.* Washington, DC: Author.

Clark, J. B., & Higgins, F. H. (1973). *Economics and social justice.* New York: Arno Press.

Cleeland, N. (2003, December 9). No end in sight for store strike. *Los Angeles Times,* pp. A1, A23.

Clement, W., & Myles, J. (1994). *Relations of ruling.* Montreal, Quebec, Canada: MacGill-Queens University Press.

Clinton, H. R. (2004, April). Now can we talk about health care: The crisis that never went away has become more complicated. *New York Times Magazine,* pp. 26–31, 55–56.

Clotferter, C., & Ehrlich, T. (Eds.). (1998). *Philanthropy and the nonprofit sector in a changing America.* Bloomington: Indiana University Press.

Cloward, R. A., & Epstein, I. (1965). *Private social work's disengagement from the poor: The case of family adjustment agencies.* Buffalo: State University of New York, School of Social Work.

Cloward, R. A., & Ohlin, L. E. (1960). *Delinquency and opportunity; a theory of delinquent gangs.* Glencoe, IL: Free Press.

Cloward, R. A., & Piven, F. F. (1974). The professional bureaucracies: Benefit systems and influence systems. In R. A. Cloward & F. F. Piven (Eds.), *The politics of turmoil* (pp. 3–14). New York: Pantheon.

Cloward, R. A., & Piven, F. F. (1975). Notes toward a radical social work. In A. Bailey & M. Brake (Eds.), *Radical social work* (pp. vii–xvii). New York: Pantheon.

Cnann, R. A. (1997). Recognizing the role of religious congregations and denominations in social service provision. In M. Reisch & E. Gambrill (Eds.), *Social work in the 21st century* (pp. 271–284). Thousand Oaks, CA: Pine Forge Press.

Cochran, T. (1961). *The age of enterprise: A social history of industrial America.* New York: Harper & Row.

Colleen, H., Werschkul, M., & Rao, M. C. (2003). *Childcare subsidies promote mothers' employment and children's development.* Institute of Women's Policy Research #G714. Available: http://www.iwpr.org

Collins, C., & Yeskel, F. (2000). *Economic apartheid in America.* New York: New Press.

Commission on Social Justice, UK Labor Party. (1994). *Social justice strategies for national renewal.* London: Vintage/Random House.

Confessore, N. (2002, July 15). This is your party on drugs. *American Prospect,* pp. 18–19.

Congressional Budget Office. (2001a). *An analysis of the president's budgetary proposals for fiscal year 2002.* Washington, DC: Author.

Congressional Budget Office. (2001b). *Historical effective tax rates: 1979–1997.* Washington, DC: Author.

Coontz, S. (1992). *The way we never were: American families and the nostalgia trap.* New York: Basic Books.

Corday, D., & Piton, G. M. (1991). Critical issues in counting homeless persons. *Homeless documents.* Washington, DC: Fannie Mae Foundation. Available: http://www.fanniemaefoundation.org

Corporate welfare runs amok. (2005, January 30). *New York Times,* p. A14.

Corrigan, R. (1983, April 30). Private sector on the spot as it prepares to take over job training. *National Journal, 15,* 894–897.

Coulton, C. J. (2000). Restoring communities within the context of the metropolis: Neighborhood revitalization at the millennium. In J. G. Hopps & R. Morris (Eds.), *Social work at the millennium* (pp. 175–206). New York: Free Press.

Council on Social Work Education. (1980). *Annual Reports, 1974–1980.* Arlington, VA: Author.

Council on Social Work Education. (1994). *Curriculum policy statement.* Arlington, VA: Author.

Cray, R. E. (1988). *Pauper and poor relief in New York City and its rural environs, 1700–1830*. Philadelphia: Temple University Press.

Crenshaw, A. (2001, December 20). A 401(k) post-mortem: After Enron, emphasis on company stock draws scrutiny. *New York Times*, p. H1.

Curiel, H. (1995). Hispanics: Mexican-Americans. *Encyclopedia of Social Work* (19th ed., vol. 2, pp. 1233–1244). Washington, DC: NASW Press.

Cuttler, N. E. (1997). The financial gerontology birthdays of 1995–1996: Social security at 60 and the baby boom at 50. In M. Reisch & E. Gambrill (Eds.), *Social work in the 21st century* (pp. 143–152). Thousand Oaks, CA: Pine Forge Press.

Dahl, R. A. (1985). *A preface to economic democracy*. Berkeley: University of California Press.

Dahl, R. A. (1998). *On democracy*. New Haven, CT: Yale University Press.

Dahrendorf, R. (1990). *Reflections on the revolution in Europe*. London: Chatto and Windus.

Dalton, R. (1994). *The green rainbow: Environmental groups in Western Europe*. New Haven, CT: Yale University Press.

Danziger, S., Corcoran, M., Danziger, S., Heflin, C., Kalil, A., Levine, J., et al. (2002). In R. Cherry & W. M. Rodgers III (Eds.), *Prosperity for all? The economic boom and African-Americans*. New York: Russell Sage Foundation.

Danziger, S., Danziger, S., Corcoran, M., Tolman, R., & Kalil, A. (1999). Barriers to employment among welfare recipients. *Focus, 20*(2), 30–34.

Danziger, S., & Gottschalk, P. (Eds.). (1993). *Uneven tides: Rising inequality in America*. New York: Russell Sage Foundation.

Davis, A. (1975). *An autobiography*. New York: Bantam.

Davis, A. (1983). Women, race and class. New York: Vintage.

Davis, A. (1998, Fall). What is the prison industrial complex? Why does it matter? *Colorlines*, pp. 12–17.

Davis, K., & Shoen, C. (1978). *Health and the War on Poverty*. Washington, DC: Brookings Institution.

Davis, R. (1999). *The web of politics: The internet's impact on the American political system*. New York: Oxford University Press.

Dear, R. B., & Patti, R. J. (1981). Legislative advocacy: Seven effective tactics. *Social Work, 26*, 289–297.

De Grazia, A. (1951). *Public & republic: Political representation in America*. New York: Knopf.

Demkovitch, L. (1984, November 24). Hospitals that provide for the poor are reeling from uncompensated costs. *National Journal, 16*, 2245–2249.

DeNavas-Walt, C., Proctor, B. D., & Mills, R. J. (2004). Income, poverty and health insurance coverage in the United States. *Current Population Report*. Washington, DC: U.S. Department of Commerce, Economics and Statistics Administration.

De Parle, J. (1994). *American dream: Three women, ten kids and a nation's drive to end welfare*. New York: Viking.

De Parle, J. (1999). *The welfare dilemma: A collection of articles*. New York: The New York Times.

De Parle, J. (2004, August 22). Raising Kevin. *New York Magazine*, pp. 27–31, 48, 52–53.

Devine, J. A., & Wright, J. D. (1993). *The greatest of evils: Urban poverty and the American underclass*. New York: Aldine de Gruyter.

Diamond, P., & Orszag, P. (2004). *Saving social security: A balanced approach*. Washington, DC: Brookings Institution.

Dizard, J. D., & Gadlin, H. (1990). *The minimal family*. Amherst: University of Massachusetts Press.

Dluhy, M. J., & Kravitz, S. (1990). *Building coalitions in human services*. Newbury Park, CA: Sage.

Dore, M. (1990). Functional theory: Its history and influence in contemporary social work. *Social Service Review, 64*(3), 358–374.

Dorr, R. C. (1910). *What eight million women want*. Boston: Small, Maynard.

Douglas, P. (1939). *Social Security in the United States: An analysis and appraisal of the federal Social Security Act*. New York: McGraw-Hill.

Downey, T. (2001, Summer). Republicans with hearts give Democrats hope. *Brookings Review*, 9–10.

Downs, S. W., & Sherraden, M. (1983, June). The orphan asylum in the nineteenth century. *Social Service Review, 57*, 272–290.

Drew, P. (1983). *A longer view: The Mary Richmond legacy*. Baltimore: University of Maryland, School of Social Work.

Dreyfuss, B. (2004, June). The seduction. *American Prospect*, pp. 18–23.

Dublin, T. (1979). *Women at work: The transformation of work and community at Lowell, Massachusetts, 1826–1860*. New York: Columbia University Press.

Duleep, H. O., & Regets, M. (1994). *The elusive concept of immigrant quality*. Discussion Paper PIRP–UI-28. Washington, DC: Urban Institute.

Duncan, G. (1985). *Years of poverty, years of plenty*. Ann Arbor: University of Michigan, Institute for Social Research.

Dunham, A. (1940). The literature of community organization. In *Proceedings of the National Conference of Social Work* (pp. 410–422). New York: Columbia University Press.

Dworkin, R. M. (1981). What is equality? *Philosophy and Public Affairs, 10*, 185–246, 283–345.

Dworkin, R. M. (1985). *A matter of principle*. Cambridge: Harvard University Press.

Edelman, M. (1988). *The construction of the political spectacle*. Chicago: University of Chicago.

Edelman, M. (2001). *The politics of misinformation*. New York: Cambridge University Press.

Edin, K., & Lein, L. (1997). *Making ends meet: How single mothers and welfare mothers survive welfare and low wage work*. New York: Russell Sage Foundation.

Edsall, T. B. (1984). *The new politics of inequality*. New York: W.W. Norton.

Edsall, T. B. (1989). The changing shape of power: A realignment in public policy. In S. Fraser & G. Gerstle (Eds.), *The rise and fall of the New Deal order, 1930–1980* (pp. 269–293). Princeton, NJ: Princeton University Press.

Edsforth, R. (2000). *The New Deal: America's response to the Great Depression*. Malden, MA: Blackwell.

Effrat, M. P. (1973). Approaches to community: Conflicts and complementarities. *Sociological Inquiry, 43*(3), 1–32.

Ehrenreich, B. (1986, July/August). Two, three many husbands. *Mother Jones*, pp. 8–9.

Ehrlich, R. (2002, May 1). Retirement in Chile is a private and heated matter. *Christian Science Monitor*.

Eisner, M. A. (2000). *From warfare state to welfare state: World War I, compensatory state building and the limits of the modern order*. University Park: Pennsylvania State University Press.

Ellwood, D. T. (1988). *Poor support: Poverty and the American family*. New York: Basic Books.

Elshtain, J. B. (2002). *Jane Addams and the dream of American democracy.* New York: Basic Books.

Elster, J. (1988). Is there or should there be a right to work? In A. Gutman (Ed.), *Democracy and the welfare state* (pp. 52–78). Princeton, NJ: Princeton University Press.

Ely, J. H. (1980). *Democracy and distrust: A theory of judicial review.* Cambridge, MA: Harvard University Press.

Entman, R. A., & Rojecki, A. (2000). *The black image in the white mind: Media and Race in America.* Chicago: University of Chicago Press.

Erikson, R. B., & Goldthorpe, J. H. (1992). *The constant flux: A study of class mobility in industrial societies.* Oxford, UK: Oxford University Press.

Esping-Andersen, G. (1987). Citizenship and socialism: De-commodification and solidarity in the welfare states. In M. Rein, G. Esping-Andersen, & L. Rainwater (Eds.), *Stagnation and renewal in social policy: Rise and fall of policy regimes* (pp. 78–101). Armonk, NY: M.E. Sharpe.

Esping-Andersen, G. (1990). *The three worlds of capitalism.* Oxford, UK: Polity.

Esping-Andersen, G. (1996). After the golden age? Welfare state dilemmas in a global economy. In G. Esping-Anderson (Ed.), *Welfare states in transition: National adaptations in global economies* (pp. 1–31). London: Sage.

Esping-Andersen, G. (2002a). Child centered social investment. In G. Esping-Andersen, D. Gallie, A. Hemeijck, & J. Miles (Eds.), *Why we need a new welfare state* (pp. 26–67). Oxford, UK: Oxford University Press.

Esping-Andersen, G. (2002b). A new gender contract. In G. Esping-Andersen, D. Gallie, A. Hemeijck, & J. Miles (Eds.), *Why we need a new welfare state* (pp. 68–95). Oxford, UK: Oxford University Press.

Esping-Andersen, G. (2002c). Toward the good society, once again? In G. Esping-Andersen, D. Gallie, A. Hemeijck, & J. Miles (Eds.), *Why we need a new welfare state* (pp. 1–28). Oxford, UK: Oxford University Press.

Esping-Andersen, G. (with Gallie, D., Hemrijck, A., & Miles, J.). (2002d). *Why we need a new welfare state.* Oxford, UK: Oxford University Press.

Estrada, L. F., Garcia, C., Macias, R., & Maldonado, L. (1988). Chicanos in the United States: A history of exploitation and resistance. In F. C. Garcia (Ed.), *Latinos and the political system* (pp. 50–78). Notre Dame, IN: University of Notre Dame Press.

Etzioni, A. (1995). *The new communitarian thinking: Persons, virtues, institutions, and communities.* Charlottesville: University Press of Virginia.

Etzioni, A. (1996a). Positive aspects of community and the dangers of fragmentation. In C. A. De Alcántara (Ed.), *Social futures, global visions* (pp. 89–102). Oxford, UK: Blackwell.

Etzioni, A. (1996b). The responsive community: The communitarian. *American Sociological Review, 61,* 1–11.

Ewen, D., & Hart, K. (2003). *State budget cuts create growing child-care crisis for low income working families.* Washington, DC: Children's Defense Fund.

Ezell, M. (2001). *Advocacy in the human services.* Belmont, CA: Brooks/Cole.

Fabricant, M., & Burghardt, S. (1992).*The welfare state crisis and the transformation of social service work.* Armonk, NY: M.E. Sharpe.

Falk, H. S. (1984). Editorial. *Journal of Education for Social Work, 20,* 2.

Families USA, Advocate Agency for Health Care Consumers. (2002). *Report on Medicare Reform.* Washington, DC: Author.

Feagin, J. (1985). *Racial and ethnic relations.* Englewood Cliffs, NJ: Prentice Hall.

Feeley, M., & Rubin, E. (1998). *Judicial policy making and the modern state.* New York: Cambridge University Press.

Ferrara, P. J., Goodman, J. C., & Matthews, M., Jr. (1995, October). Private alternatives to social security in other countries. *National Center for Policy Analysis* (NCPA Policy Report 200). Available: http://www.mcpa.org/studies

Figueira-McDonough, J. (1993). Policy practice: The neglected side of social work intervention. *Social Work, 38,* 179–188.

Figueira-McDonough, J. (1994a, Fall/Winter). Family policies: The failure of solidarity and the costs of motherhood. *Journal of Applied Social Sciences, 18*(1), 41–54.

Figueira-McDonough, J. (1994b). Gender and the social work curricula: Research and proposals. *Report to the Dean of the School of Social Work.* Tempe: Arizona State University.

Figueira-McDonough, J. (1995, December). Community organization and the underclass: Exploring new practice directions. *Social Service Review, 69,* 57–85.

Figueira-McDonough, J. (1996, November). *Teenage sexuality in underclass neighborhoods: Realism versus craziness. Partial report on the Study of Young People in Deprived Neighborhoods.* Paper delivered to the Department of Justice Studies, Arizona State University, Tempe.

Figueira-McDonough, J. (1997). Teenage sexuality, pregnancy and motherhood. In A. Schneider (Ed.), *Profile and status of black children in Arizona* (pp. 103–124). Tempe: Arizona State University.

Figueira-McDonough, J. (1998a). Environment and interpretation: Voices of young people in poor inner-city neighborhoods. *Youth and Society, 30*(2), 123–163.

Figueira-McDonough, J. (1998b). Toward a gender-integrated knowledge in social work. In J. Figueira-McDonough, F. E. Netting, & A. Nichols-Casebolt (Eds.), *The role of gender in practice knowledge: Claiming half of the human experience* (pp. 3–40). New York: Garland.

Figueira-McDonough, J. (2001). *Community analysis and praxis: Toward a grounded civil society.* New York: Brunner-Routledge.

Figueira-McDonough, J. (in press). Child care and the potential of breaking intergenerational poverty. In B. Arrighi (Ed.), *Children and poverty today.* Westport, CT: Praeger.

Figueira-McDonough, J., & Sarri, R. C. (2002). Increasing inequality: The ascendancy of neoconservatism and institutional exclusion of women. In J. Figueira-McDonough & R. C. Sarri (Eds.), *Women at the margins: Neglect, punishment, and resistance* (pp. 5–30). New York: Haworth Press.

Fischler, R. S. (1980). Protecting American Indian children. *Social Work, 25,* 341–349.

Fisher, D., Colton, T., Kleiman, N. S., & Schimble, K. (2004). *Between home and hard times: New York's families in economic distress.* New York: Center for an Urban Future. Available: http://www.nyfuture.org/content/report

Fisher, J. M. (Ed.). (1986). *Moral responsibility.* Ithaca, NY: Cornell University Press.

Fisher, J. (1990). The rank and file movement in social work, 1930–1936. *Journal of Progressive Human Services, 1* (1), 95–99.

Fisher, R. (1984). *Let the people decide: Neighborhood organizing in America.* Boston: Twayne Publishers.

Fix, M., & Passel, J. S. (1994). *Immigration and immigrants: Setting the record straight.* Washington, DC: Urban Institute.

Fix, M., & Passel, J. S. (2002). Assessing welfare reform's immigrant provisions. In A. Weil & K. Finegold (Eds.), *Welfare reform: The next act* (pp. 178–202). Washington, DC: Urban Institute.

Flacks, R. (1995). Think globally, act politically: Some notes towards new movement strategy. In M. Darnovsky, B. Epstein, & R. Flacks (Eds.), *Cultural politics and social movements* (pp. 251–363). Philadelphia: Temple University Press.

Flynn, E. E. (2002). Life at the margins: Older women living in poverty. In J. Figueira-McDonough & R. C. Sarri (Eds.), *Women at the margins: Neglect, punishment, and resistance* (pp. 203–228). New York: Haworth Press.

Flynn, J. P. (1982). *Social agency policy: Analysis and presentation for community practice.* Chicago: Nelson-Hall.

Follett, M. P. (1909). *The new state.* New York: Longman, Green.

The Foundation Directory. (1999). New York: Foundation Center.

Franklin, D. L. (1986). Mary Richmond and Jane Addams: From moral certainty to rational enquiry in social work practice. *Social Service Review, 60,* 504–526.

Franklin, J. (1970, December). Public welfare in the South during the Reconstruction era 1865–80. *Social Service Review, 44,* 329–392.

Fraser, S., & Gerstle, G. (1989). *The rise and fall of the New Deal order, 1930–1980.* Princeton, NJ: Princeton University Press.

Freire, P. (1970). *Pedagogy of the oppressed.* New York: Continuum.

Freire, P. (1973). *Education for critical consciousness.* New York: Continuum.

Freire, P. (1990). A critical understanding of social work. *Journal of Progressive Human Services, 1,* 3–10.

Fremstad, S., & Parrott, S. (2004, March 12). *The senate finance committee's TANF reauthorization bill.* Washington, DC: Center on Budget and Policy Priorities.

Freudenheim, M. (2004a, February 3). Companies limit health coverage to many retirees. *New York Times,* pp. A1, A12.

Freudenheim, M. (2004b, August 27). Record number of Americans not insured on health. *New York Times,* pp. C1–C2.

Freudenheim, M. (2004c, September 10). Cost of insuring worker's health increases 11.2%. *New York Times,* pp. A1, A4.

Friedman, L. L. (1982). *Gregarious saints: Self and community in America, 1830–1870.* Cambridge, MA: Cambridge University Press.

Frymer, P. (2003). Acting when elected officials won't: Federal courts and civil rights enforcement in U.S. labor unions, 1935–1985. *American Political Science Review, 97*(3), 483–499.

Fukuyama, F. (1992). *The end of history and the last man.* New York: Free Press.

Fullers, B., & Strah, A. (2001). The childcare and preschool workforce: Demographics, earnings and unequal distribution. *Educational Evaluation and Policy Analysis, 23*(1), 37–55.

Gale, W., & Orszag, P. R. (2004, May). The great tax shift. *American Prospect,* pp. 52–53.

Gale, W. G., Shoven, J. B., & Warshowsky, M. J. (Eds.). (2004). *Private pensions and public policies.* Washington, DC: Brookings Institution.

Galper, J. (1980). *Social work practice: A radical perspective.* Englewood Cliffs, NJ: Prentice Hall.

Gambrill, E. (1990). *Critical thinking in clinical practice*. San Francisco: Jossey Bass.

Gamson, W. (1990). *The strategy of social protest*. Belmont, CA: Wadsworth.

Gamson, W. (1995). Constructing social protest. In H. Johnston & B. Kladermans (Ed.), *Social movements and culture* (pp. 85–106). Minneapolis: University of Minnesota Press.

Gamson, W. A., & Schmeidler, E. (1984). Organizing the poor. An argument with Frances Fox Piven and Richard A. Cloward's *Poor People's Movements*. *Theory and Society, 13*(4), 567–587.

Ganow, M. (2000). Childcare subsidies: Strategies to provide outreach to eligible families. *Welfare Information Network, 4,* 10.

Gans, H. J. (2003). *Democracy and the news*. New York: Oxford University Press.

Garvin, C. D., Smith, A. D., & Reid, W. (1978). The work incentive experience. Montclair, NJ: Allanheld, Osmun/Universe Books.

Gershuny, J. (2000). *Changing times*. Oxford, UK: Oxford University Press.

Gewirth, A. (1978). *Reason and morality*. Chicago: University of Chicago Press.

Gewirth, A. (1982). *Human rights: Essays on justification and applications*. Chicago: University of Chicago Press.

Gibelman, M. (1995). *What social workers* do. Washington, DC: NASW Press.

Giddens, A. (1998). *Conversations with Anthony Giddens: Making sense of modernity*. Stanford, CA: Stanford University Press.

Gil, D. (1998). *Confronting injustice and oppression: Concepts and strategies for social workers*. New York: Columbia University Press.

Gilbert, N. (1979). The design of community planning structures. *Social Service Review, 53,* 654–664.

Gilbert, N. (1995). *Welfare justice: Restoring social equity*. New Haven, CT: Yale University Press.

Gilder, G. (1981). *Wealth and poverty*. New York: Basic Books.

Gillens, M. (1999). *Why Americans hate welfare: Race, media and the politics of antipoverty policy*. Chicago: University of Chicago Press.

Gillespie, E., & Shellhas, B. (Eds.). (1994). *Contract with America*. New York: Random House.

Glass, D. V. (1953). *Introduction to Malthus*. London: Watts.

Glazer, N. (1971, September). The limits of social policy. *Commentary, 52,* 51–58.

Glei, D. (1994). Age of mother by age of father, 1988. Unpublished data from *Sex and America's Teenagers, 1994*. Washington, DC: Alan Guttmacher Institute.

Gollander, D. (1993, Fall). Dorothea Dix and the English origins of the American asylum movement. *Canadian Review of American Studies, 23,* 149–176.

Gonnerman, J. (2003). *Life on the outside: The prison odyssey of Elaine Bartlett*. New York: Farrar, Straus and Giroux.

Goodin, R. E. (1985). *Protecting the vulnerable: A reanalysis of our social responsibility*. Chicago: University of Chicago Press.

Goodin, R. E. (1990). Stabilizing expectations: The role of earning related benefits in social welfare policy. *Ethics, 100,* 530–553.

Goodin, R. E. (1998). Social welfare as a collective social responsibility. In D. Schmidtz & R. E. Goodin (Eds.), *Social welfare and individual responsibility*. New York: Cambridge University Press.

Goodin, R. E., Heady, B., Ruud Muffels, R., & Dirven, H.-J. (1999). *The real world of welfare capitalism*. Cambridge, UK: Cambridge University Press.

Goodwin, S. (1997). *Comparative mental health policy: From institutional to community care*. Thousand Oaks, CA: Sage.

Gordon, L. (1990a). The new feminist scholarship on the welfare state. In L. Gordon (Ed.), *Women, the state, and welfare* (pp. 9–35). Madison: University of Wisconsin Press.

Gordon, L. (1990b). *Women, the state, and welfare.* Madison: University of Wisconsin Press.

Gordon, L. (1994). *Pitied but not entitled: Single mothers and the history of welfare, 1880–1935.* New York: Free Press.

Gorin, S., & Moniz, C. (1997). Social work and health care in the 21st century. In M. Reisch and E. Gambrill (Eds.), *Social work in the 21st century* (pp. 152–162). Thousand Oaks, CA: Pine Forge Press.

Gornick, J., & Meyers, M. K. (2003). *Policies that work for reconciling parenthood and employment.* New York: Russell Sage Foundation.

Gottschalk, M. (2000). *The shadow welfare state: Labor, business and the politics of health care in the United States.* Ithaca, NY: Cornell University Press.

Gourevitch, A. (2002, Summer).When low wages don't add up. *American Prospect,* pp. 32–33.

Gramsci, A. (1985). *Selections from cultural writings* (D. Forgacs & G. Nowell-Smith, Eds.; W. Boellower, Trans.). Cambridge, MA: Harvard University Press.

Grant Foundation. (1988). *The declining economic fortune of young Americans.* New York: Author.

Green, R. (1980). Native American women. *Signs: A Journal of Women in Culture and Society, 6,* 248–258.

Greenberg, E. (1985). *Capitalism and the American political ideal.* Armonk, NY: M.E. Sharp.

Greenberg, M. (2001, Summer). Welfare reform and devolution: Looking backward and forward. *Brookings Review, 19*(3), 20–24.

Greenstein, R. (2002, Summer). EITC, welfare reform's hidden ally. *American Prospect,* pp. 35–36.

Greenstein, R. (2004, March 21). What the trustees' report indicates about the financial status of social security. *Center for Budget and Policy Priorities.* Available: http://www.cbpp.org/3-23-04socsec.htm

Greenstein, R., & Orszag, P. (2004, April 2). Misleading comments about new Social Security and Medicaid projections. *Center on Budget and Policy Priorities.* Available: http://www.cbpp.org/3-22-04socsee-fact.htm

Greenstein, R., Orszag, P., & Kogan, R. (2004, June 14). The implications of the Social Security projections issued by the Congressional Budget Office. *Center on Budget and Policy Priorities.* Available: http://www.cbpp.org/6-14-04bud.htm

Griffin, C. S. (1965). *Their brother's keepers: Moral stewardship in the U.S., 1800–1865.* New Brunswick: Rutgers University Press.

Grimes, C. (1991, February). Wither the civil journalism bandwagon. *Jean Shorestein Center: Politics and Public Policy* (Paper D-36).

Gring-Pemble, L. (2003). *Grim tales: The rhetorical construction of American welfare policy.* Westport, CT: Praeger.

Gronbjerg, K. A. (1977). *Mass society and the extension of welfare.* Chicago: University of Chicago Press.

Gurin, A. (1971). Social planning and community organization. In *Encyclopedia of Social Work* (19th ed., vol. 2). Washington, DC: NASW Press.

Gutierrez, L., et al. (2005). Multicultural community practice strategies and inter-group empowerment. In M. Weil (Ed.), *Handbook of community practice.* Thousand Oaks, CA: Sage.

Gutman, H. G. (1983). Persistent myths about the Afro-American family. In M. Gordon (Ed.), *The American family in social-historical perspective.* New York: St. Martin's Press.

Haberkern, R. (2003, March 20). Helping parents with a criminal record find employment and achieve self-sufficiency. *Finance Project.* Available: http://www.financeprojectinfo.org

Habermas, J. (1975). *Legitimation crisis.* Boston: Beacon Press.

Hacker, J. S. (2002). *The divided welfare state: The battle over public and private social benefits in the United States.* New York: Cambridge University Press.

Hakim, C. (1996). *Key issues in women's work.* London: Athlone Press.

Halpern, D. (1995). *Mental health and the built environment: More than bricks and mortar?* London: Taylor and Francis.

Halpern, R. (1995). *Rebuilding the inner city: A history of neighborhood initiatives to address poverty in the United States.* New York: Columbia University Press.

Hansen, C. J., & Morris, R. (Eds.). (1999). *Welfare reform, 1996–2000: Is there a safety net?* Westport, CT: Auburn House.

Harrington, M. (1962). *The other America: Poverty in the United States.* New York: Macmillan.

Hasenfeld, Y. (1987). Power and social work practice. *Social Service Review, 61,* 490–497.

Haskins, R. (2001, Summer). Giving is not enough: Work and work supports are reducing poverty. *Brookings Review, 19,* 12–15.

Hawes, J. (1971). *Children in urban society: Juvenile delinquency in the nineteenth century America.* New York: Oxford University Press.

Hayek, F. A. (1976*). Law, liberty and legislation, volume 2: The mirage of social justice.* London: Routledge & Kegan Paul.

Hayes-Bautista, D. (1996). Poverty and the underclass: Some Latino cross currents. In M. R. Darby (Ed.), *Reducing poverty in America: Views and approaches* (pp. 69–81). Thousand Oaks, CA: Sage.

Hearings on Taxation: Hearings before the Committee on the Budget, House of Representatives, 97th Cong., 1, vol. 2, 97–202 (1981).

Heclo, H. (1974). *Modern social politics in Britain and Sweden.* New Haven, CT: Yale University Press.

Heclo, H. (1986). General welfare and the American political tradition. *Political Science Quarterly, 102,* 179–196.

Hefferman, W. J. (1992). *Social welfare policy: A research and action strategy.* New York: Longman.

Hefgot, J. (1972). Professional reform organizations and the symbolic representation of the poor. *American Sociological Review, 39*(4), 475–491.

Heidler, D., & Heidler, J. T. (2003). *Manifest destiny.* Westport, CT: Greenwood Press.

Hemerijck, A. (2002). The self-transformation of the European social model. In Esping-Andersen et al. (Eds.), *Why we need a new welfare state* (pp. 173–213). Oxford, UK: Oxford University Press.

Henry, C., Veschkul, M., & Rao, M. C. (2003). Childcare subsidies promote mothers' employment and children's development. *Institute for Women's Policy Research* (Publication # G14). New York: Homes for the Homeless and the Institute for Children and Poverty. Available: http://www2.homesforthehomeless.com

Herald, M. (2006). *Welfare Watchers,* April 17. Sacramento, CA: Western Center on Law and Poverty.

Herbert, B. (2003, November 29). Shh . . . , don't say poverty. *New York Times,* p. A17.

Hernandez, D. (1970). *Mexican-American challenge to a sacred cow.* Los Angeles: University of California, Mexican American Cultural Center.

Heskins, A. D. (1991). *The struggle for community.* Boulder, CO: Westview Press.

Hochman, S. (1997). School–community collaboratives: The missing links. In M. Reisch & E. Gambrill (Eds.), *Social work in the 21st century* (pp. 239–248). Thousand Oaks, CA: Pine Forge Press.

Hoefer, R. (2005). Altering state policy: Interest group effectiveness among state-level advocacy groups. *Social Work, 50*(3), 219–227.

Hofstadter, R. (1956). *The age of reform.* New York: Knopf.

Hofstadter, R. (1963). *The progressive movement, 1900–1915.* Englewood Cliffs, NJ: Prentice Hall.

Hofstadter, R. (1992). *Social Darwinism in American thought.* Boston: Beacon Press.

Homes for the Homeless and the Institute for Children and Poverty. (1998). *Report.* Available: www.homesforthehomeless.com

Hopps, J. G., & Morris, R. (Eds.). (2000). *Social work at the millennium.* New York: Free Press.

Horn, W. F. (2001, Summer). Wedding bell blues: Marriage and welfare reform. *Brookings Review,* pp. 39–42.

Horowitz, R. (1995). *Teen mothers—Citizens or dependents?* Chicago: University of Chicago Press.

Horseman, R. (1981). *Race and manifest destiny.* Cambridge, MA: Harvard University Press.

Howard, C. (1993). The hidden side of the American welfare state. *Political Science Quarterly, 108*(3), 403–436.

Howard, D. S. (1943). *The WPA and federal relief policy.* New York: Russell Sage Foundation.

Howe, R.-A. (1993). Legal rights and obligations: An uneven evolution. In R. Lerman & T. Ooms (Eds.), *Young unwed fathers: Changing roles and emerging policies* (pp. 141–169). Philadelphia: Temple University Press.

Hughes, J. (1977). *The government habit.* New York: Basic Books.

Iatridies, D. S. (2000). State social welfare: Global perspective. In J. G. Hopps & R. Morris (Eds.), *Social work in the millennium* (pp. 207–224). New York: Free Press.

Iglehart, A. P., & Becerra, R. M. (1995). *Social services and the ethnic community.* Needham Heights, MA: Allyn & Bacon.

Institute of Medicine. (1995). *Best intentions: Unintended pregnancy and the well being of children and families.* Washington, DC: Academic Press.

International Social Security Association. (1989). Development and trends in Social Security, 1978–1989. *International Social Security Review, 42*(3), 247–349.

Isserman, M., & Kazin, M. (1989). The failure and success of the new radicalism. In S. Fraser & G. Gerstle (Eds.), *The rise and fall of the New Deal, 1930–1980* (pp. 185–210). Princeton, NJ: Princeton University Press.

Jacobs, L. R., & Morone, J. R. (2005). *Healthy, wealthy and fair.* New York: Oxford University Press.

Jacobs, L. R., & Shapiro, R. (2000). *Politicians don't pander: Political manipulation and the loss of democratic responsiveness.* Chicago: University of Chicago Press.

Jansson, B. S. (1994). *Social policy: From theory to policy practice.* Pacific Grove, CA: Brooks/Cole.

Jansson, B. S. (2001). *The reluctant welfare state: American social welfare policies— past, present, and future.* Belmont, CA: Wadsworth/Thompson Learning.

Jansson, B. S. (2003). *Becoming an effective policy advocate: From policy practice to social justice* (4th ed.). Pacific Grove, CA: Brooks/Cole.

Jansson, B. S., Dempsey, D., McCroskey, J., & Schneider, R. (2005). Four models of policy practice: Local, state and national arenas. In M. Weil (Ed.), *Handbook of community practice.* Thousand Oaks, CA: Sage.

Jargowski, P. A. (1997). *Poverty and place: Ghettoes, barrios and the American city.* New York: Russell Sage Foundation.

Jarrett, M. (1919). The psychiatric thread running through all social case work. *Proceedings of the National Conference of Social Work.* New York: Russell Sage Foundation.

Jarrett, R. L. (1994). Living poor: Family life among single parent, African-American women. *Social Problems, 41*(1), 30–49.

Jencks, C. (1991). Is the American underclass growing? In C. Jencks & P. Peterson (Eds.), *The urban underclass* (pp. 28–100). Washington, DC: Brookings Institution.

Jencks, C. (1995). Can we replace welfare with work? In M. R. Darby (Ed.), *Reducing poverty in America: Views and approaches* (pp. 69–81). Thousand Oaks, CA: Sage.

Jencks, C. (2001, December 12). Who should get in? *New York Review of Books, 48,* 12.

Jencks, C. (2002, Summer). Liberal lessons from the welfare reform. *American Prospect,* pp. 14–18.

Jencks, C., & Peterson, P. (Eds.). (1991). *The urban underclass.* Washington, DC: Brookings Institution.

Jernegan, M. W. (1931a, June). The development of poor relief in colonial America. *Social Service Review, 5,* 175–198.

Jernegan, M. W. (1931b). *Laboring and dependent classes in colonial America, 1607–1783.* Chicago: University of Chicago Press.

Johnston, D. C. (2003). *Perfectly legal: The covert campaign to benefit the super rich—and cheat everyone else.* New York: Penguin Books.

Johnson, D. C. (2004, September 30). IBM makes a deal in move to close big pension case. *New York Times,* pp. A1, C4.

Jones, C. (1985). Types of welfare capitalism. *Government and Opposition, 20*(4), 328–343.

Jones, J. (1985). *Labor of love, labor of sorrow: Black women, work, and family from slavery to the present.* New York: Basic Books.

Jordan, B. (1990). *Social work in an unjust society.* London: Harvester Wheatsheaf.

Jordan, B. (1998). *The new politics of welfare.* London: Sage.

Jordan, B. (with Jordan, C.). (2000). *Social work and the third way: Tough love as social policy.* London: Sage.

Jost, T. S. (2003). *Disentitlement? The threats facing our public health-care programs and right–based response.* New York: Oxford University Press.

Joyce Foundation. (2002, April). *Welfare to work: What have we learned?* Report. Available: http://www.joycefdn.org/welrept/

Kahn, S. (1991). *Organizing: A guide for grassroots leaders.* Silver Springs, MD: NASW Press.

Kahn, S. (1994). *How people get power.* Washington, DC: NASW Press.

Kaplan, J. (2004, March). Addressing needs of adults sanctioned under TANF. *WIN Issues Brief, 8*(2). Available: http://www.financeprojectinfo.org/Publications/sanctionedclientsIN.htm

Karger, H. J. (1987). *The sentinels of order: A study of social control and the Minneapolis settlement house movement. 1915–1950.* New York: University Press of America.

Katz, B., & Allen, K. (2001, Summer). Cities matter: Shifting the focus of welfare reform. *Brookings Review,* pp. 30–33.

Katz, M. (1968). *The irony of early school reform.* Cambridge, MA: Harvard University Press.

Katz, M. (1986). *In the shadow of the poorhouse: A social history of welfare in America.* New York: Basic Books.

Katz, M. (1989). *The undeserving poor: From the war on poverty to the war on welfare.* New York: Pantheon.

Katz, M. (2001). *The price of citizenship: Redefining the American welfare state.* New York: Henry Holt.

Katz, M., Ducet, M., & Stern, M. (1982). *The social organization of early capitalism.* Cambridge, MA: Harvard University Press.

Katznelson, I. (2005). *When affirmative action was white: An untold history of racial inequality in the twentieth century.* Boston: W.W. Norton.

Kelso, R. (1969). *The history of public poor relief in Massachusetts, 1620–1920.* Montclair, NJ: Patterson Smith.

Kennedy, S. E. (1979). *If all we did was to weep at home: A history of white working class women in America.* Bloomington: Indiana University Press.

Kessler-Harris, A. (1982). *Out to work: A history of wage-earning women in the United States.* Oxford: Oxford University Press.

Ketterlinus, R. D., Henderson, M. A., & Lamb, M. E. (1990). Maternal age, sociodemographics, prenatal health and behavior: Influences on neonatal risk status. *Journal of Adolescent Health Care, 11*(5), 423–431.

Keynes, J. M. (1935). *The general theory of employment, interest and money.* New York: Harcourt Brace.

Kickingbird, K., Kickingbird, L., Chinitty, C., & Berkey, C. (1996). Indian sovereignty. In J. R. Wunder (Ed.), *Native American sovereignty,* vol. 6 (pp. 1–13). New York: Garland.

Kirby, D. (2001). *Emerging answers: Research findings on programs to reduce teen pregnancy.* Washington, DC: National Campaign to Reduce Teenage Pregnancy.

Kirby, J. (1980). *Black Americans in the Roosevelt era: Liberalism and race.* Knoxville: University of Tennessee Press.

Klass, G. M. (1985). Explaining America and the welfare state: An alternative theory. *British Journal of Political Science, 19*(4), 427–450.

Klehr, H. (1984). *The heyday of American communism.* New Haven: Yale University Press.

Kleinkauf, C. (1989). Analyzing social welfare legislation. *Social Work, 34,* 179–181.

Kleinman, L. (1993). The relationship between adolescent parenthood and inadequate parenting. *Children and Youth Services Review, 14*(4), 304–320.

Knickmeyer, R. (1972). Marxist approach to social work. *Social Work, 18*(1), 58–65.

Knox, V. (2002, Summer). Money also matters. *American Prospect*, pp. 26–28.

Korr, W. S., & Brieland, D. (2000). Social justice, human rights, and welfare reform. In J. G. Hopps & R. Morris (Eds.), *Social work at the millennium* (pp. 73–85). New York: Free Press.

Korsching, P. F., & Borich, T. O. (1997). Facilitating cluster communities: Lessons from the Iowa experience. *Community Development Journal, 32*(4), 342–352.

Koss, M. P. (1988). Hidden rape, sexual aggression and victimization in a national sample of students in higher education. In A. W. Burgess (Ed.), *Rape and sexual assault II* (pp. 3–26). New York: Garland.

Krugman, P. (2002, January 4). America polarized. *New York Times*.

Krugman, P. (2004, March 5). Social Security scares. *New York Times*, p. A23.

Ku, L., & Nimalendran, S. (2003, December 22). Losing out: States are cutting 1.2 to 1.6 million low-income people from Medicaid, SCHIP and other state health insurance programs. *Center on Budget and Policy Priorities*.

Lakoff, G. (2002). *Moral politics: How liberals and conservatives think*. Chicago: University of Chicago Press.

Lane, R. P. (1939). Community organization: A preliminary inquiry in its nature and characteristics. *Proceedings from the National Conference of Social Welfare*. New York: Columbia University Press.

Lause, T. (1979). Professional social work associations and legislative action: 1974–1977. *Journal of Sociology and Social Welfare, 6*, 255–273.

Lazarus, D. (2005, January 21). Social Security lessons. *San Francisco Chronicle*.

LeCroy, C. L. (2002). *The call to social work: Life stories*. Thousand Oaks, CA: Sage.

Leff, M. H. (1973, September). Consensus for reform: The mothers' pension movement in the Progressive era. *Social Service Review, 47*, 397–417.

Le Grand, J. (1982). *The strategy of equality: Redistribution and the social services*. London: Allen & Unwin.

Lehmbruch, G. (1984). Concentration and the structure of corporatist networks. In J. H. Goldthorpe (Ed.), *Order and conflict in contemporary capitalism*. Oxford: Clarendon Press.

Lelland, J. (2004, May 12). 73 options for Medicaid plan fuel chaos, not prescriptions. *New York Times*, pp. A1, A17.

Lens, V. (2005). Advocacy and argumentation in the public arena: A guide for social workers. *Social Work, 50*(3), 231–238.

Leonard, P. (1975). Towards a paradigm for radical practice. In R. Bailey & M. Brake (Eds.), *Radical social work* (pp. 36–61). New York: Vintage Press.

Lerman, P. (2004, August). I can't give you anything but love: Would poor couples with children be better off economically if they married? *Center for Law and Social Policy, Couples and Marriage Series* (Policy Brief Number 5).

Lerman, R. (2002a). Family structure and child bearing before and after the reform. In A. Weil & K. Finegold (Eds.), *Welfare reform: The next act* (pp. 33–52). Washington, DC: Urban Institute.

Lerman, R. (2002b). *Impacts of marital status and parental presence on the material hardship of families with children*. Washington, DC: Urban Institute.

LeSueur, M. (1982). Women are hungry. In E. Hedges (Ed.), *Ripening: Selected work, 1927–1980*. Old Westbury, NY: The Feminist Press.

Levitt, J., & Saegert, S. (1990). *From abandonment to hope: Community households in Harlem*. New York: Columbia University Press.

Lindeman, E. (1921). *The community: An introduction to the study of community leadership and organization.* New York: Association Press.

Little, D. (1991). *Varieties of social explanation: An introduction to the philosophy of social science.* Boulder, CO: Westview Press.

Litwak, E. (1985). Complementary roles for formal and informal support groups: A study of nursing homes and mortality rates. *Journal of Applied Behavioral Science, 21*(4), 407–425.

Longres, J. (1986). Marxian theory and social work practice. *Catalyst: A Socialist Journal of Social Services, 5*(4), 14–34.

Longres, J. (1995). Hispanic overview. *Nineteenth encyclopedia of social work* (19th ed., pp. 1214–1222). Washington, DC: NASW Press.

Longres, J. (1997). The impact and implications of multiculturalism. In M. Reisch & E. Gambrill (Eds.), *Social work in the 21st century* (pp. 39–47). Thousand Oaks, CA: Pine Forge Press.

Longres, J., & Mcleod, E. (1987). Consciousness raising and social work practice. *Social Case Work, 61*(5), 267–276.

Loprest, P. (2002). Making the transition from welfare to work: Successes but continuing concerns. In A. Weil & K. Finegold (Eds.), *Welfare reform: The next act* (pp. 17–32). Washington, DC: Urban Institute.

Lowenberg, S. (2004, March). The offshore thing. *American Prospect,* pp. 30–33.

Lubove, R. (1965). *The professional altruist: The emergence of social work as a career, 1880–1930.* Cambridge, MA: Harvard University Press.

Luna, Y. (2005). *Social constructions, social control and resistance: An analysis of welfare reform as a hegemonic process.* Unpublished doctoral dissertation, Arizona State University, Tempe.

Luna, Y., & Figueira-McDonough, J. (2002). Charity, ideology, and exclusion: Continuities and resistance in U.S. welfare reform. In J. Figueira-McDonough & R. C. Sarri (Eds.), *Women at the margins: Neglect, punishment, and resistance* (pp. 321–345). New York: Haworth Press.

MacIntyre, A. (1981). *After virtue.* London: Duckworth.

Mahaffey, M. (1981, March). *Orchestrating mass support for social change.* Symposium for Community Organization in the Eighties, Louisville, Kentucky.

Mahaffey, M., & Hanks, J. W. (1982). *Practical politics: Social work and political responsibility.* Silver Springs, MD: NASW.

Majone, G. (1996). *Regulating Europe.* London: Routledge.

Mannes, M. (1995). Factors and events leading to the passage of the Indian Child Welfare Act. *Child Welfare, 74,* 265–282.

Marshall, T. H. (1950). *Class, citizenship and social development.* New York: Doubleday.

Marwell, N. P. (2004). Privatizing the welfare state: Non-profit community based organizations as political actors. *American Sociological Review, 69,* 265–291.

Massey, D. S., & Denton, N. A. (1993). *American apartheid: Segregation and the making of the underclass.* Cambridge, MA: Harvard University Press.

Mather, M., & Rivers, K. L. (2003). *State profiles of child well being: Results from the 2000 Census.* Washington, DC: Ann E. Casey Foundation and Population Reference Bureau.

Matthaei, J. A. (1982). *An economic history of women in America.* New York: Schocken Books.

May, E. T. (1989). Cold war—warm hearth: politics and the family in the postwar era. In S. Fraser & G. Gerstle (Eds.), *The rise and fall of the New Deal, 1930–1980* (pp. 153–180). Princeton, NJ: Princeton University Press.

Mayo, M. (1980). Community development: A radical alternative. In R. Bailey & M. Brake (Eds.), *Radical social work* (pp. 129–142). New York: Pantheon.

McAdoo, H. P. (2002). The storm is passing over: Marginalized African-American women. In J. Figueira-McDonough & R. C. Sarri (Eds.), *Women at the margins: Neglect, punishment, and resistance* (pp. 91–100). New York: Haworth Press.

McCann, M. (1999). *Rights at work: Pay equity and the politics of legal mobilization.* Chicago: University of Chicago Press.

McDougall, W. (2004). *Freedom just around the corner: A new American history, 1585–1828.* New York: HarperCollins.

McGlen, N. E., & O'Connor, K. (1983). *Women's rights: The struggle for equality in the nineteenth and twentieth centuries.* New York: Praeger.

McKnight, G. (1998). *The last crusade: Martin Luther King, Jr., the FBI, and the poor people's campaign.* Boulder, CO: Westview Press.

McLanahan, S., & Teitler, J. (1999). The consequences of father absence. In M. E. Lamb (Ed.), *Parenting and child development in non-traditional families* (pp. 83–102). Mahwah, NJ: Erlbaum.

McKnealy offers rebuttal in controversy. (1959, April 8). *Newburgh News*, p. 13.

McPherson, J. (1982). *Ordeal by fire: The Civil War and Reconstruction.* New York: Knopf.

Mead, L. (1986). *Beyond entitlement: Social obligations of citizenship.* New York: Free Press.

Meier, A., & Rudwick, E. (1976). *From plantation to ghetto.* New York: Hill and Wang.

Meier, M. S. (1990). Politics, education and culture. In C. McWilliams (Ed.), *North from Mexico* (pp. 285–308). Westport, CT: Greenwood Press.

Meier, M. S., & Rivera, F. (1972). *The Chicanos: A history of Mexican-Americans.* New York: Hill and Wang.

Meriam, L., Brown, R. A., Cloud, H. R., & Everett, E. (1928). *The problem of Indian administration.* Baltimore: Johns Hopkins Press.

Merritt, D. B. (1995). *Public journalism and public life.* Hillside, NJ: Erlbaum.

Meyer, D. R., & Cancian, M. (2003). *W-2 child support demonstration evaluation final report.* Madison: University of Wisconsin, Institute of Poverty Research.

Meyers, M. K., Peck, L. R., Davis, E. E., Collins, A., Kreader, J. L., Georges, A., et al. (2002). *The dynamics of child care subsidy use: A collaborative study of five states.* New York: Columbia University, National Center for Children in Poverty.

Mezey, J., Greenberg, M., & Schumacher, R. (2002). *Unfinished agenda: Childcare for low income families since 1996.* Washington, DC: Center for Law and Social Policy.

Mill, J. S. (1912). *Utilitarianism, liberty, representative government.* London: Dent.

Mill, J. S. (1984). *Essays on equality, law and education* (J. M. Robson, Ed.). Toronto, Ontario, Canada: University of Toronto Press.

Miller, D. C. (1990). *Women and social welfare: A feminist analysis.* New York: Praeger.

Mills, R. J. (2000, September). *Health insurance: Consumer income.* Washington, DC: U.S. Census Bureau.

Mincy, R. B. (Ed.). (1994). *Nurturing young black males: Challenges to agencies, programs and social policy.* Washington, DC: Urban Institute.

Mink, G. (1990). The lady and the tramp: Gender, race, and the origins of the American welfare state. In L. Gordon (Ed.), *Women, the state, and welfare* (pp. 92–122). Madison: University of Wisconsin Press.

Minkoff, D. C. (1995). *Organizing for equality: The evolution of women's racial-ethnic organizations, 1955–1985.* New Brunswick, NJ: Rutgers University Press.

Mnookin, R. H. (1985). *In the interest of children: Advocacy, law reform and public policy.* New York: W. H. Freeman.

Mohl, R. (1971). *Poverty in New York, 1783–1825.* New York: Oxford University Press.

Mondros, J. (2005). Political, social, and legislative action. In M. Weil (Ed.), *Handbook of community practice.* Thousand Oaks, CA: Sage.

Moore, L. B. (1970). *Wage earners' budgets.* New York: Arno Press. (Original work published 1907)

Moreau, M. (1990). Empowerment through advocacy and consciousness raising: Implications of a structural approach to social work. *Journal of Sociology and Social Welfare, 17*(2), 53–67.

Moreau, M., & Leonard, L. (1989). *Empowerment through a structural approach to social work.* Ottawa, Ontario, Canada: Carlton University, School of Social Work.

Morgan, J., David, M., Cohen, W., & Brazer, H. (1962). *Income and welfare in the United States.* New York: McGraw-Hill.

Morone, J. A. (2003a). American ways of welfare. *Perspectives on Politics, 1*(1), 137–146.

Morone, J. A. (2003b). *Hellfire nation: The politics of sin in American history.* New Haven, CT: Yale University Press.

Morris, R. (2000). Social work's century of evolution as a profession: Choices made, opportunities lost. From the individual and society to the individual. In J. G. Hopps & R. Morris (Eds.), *Social work at the millennium* (pp. 43–70). New York: Free Press.

Moss, H. (1984). Institutional reform through litigation. *Social Service Review, 58,* 421–433.

Moynihan, D. P. (1965). *The Negro family: The case for national action.* Washington, DC: U.S. Government Printing Office.

Moynihan, D. P. (1969). *Maximum feasible misunderstanding: Community action and the War on Poverty.* New York: Free Press.

Mullaly, R. (1997). *Structural social work: Ideology, theory and practice.* Toronto, Ontario, Canada: McClelland & Stewart.

Mullenix, M. (1999, December). Transitional services for homeless families. *WIN Issues Brief, 3*(9).

Mulroy, E. A. (2002). Low income women and housing: Where will they live? In J. Figueira-McDonough & R. C. Sarri (Eds.), *Women at the margins: Neglect, punishment, and resistance* (pp. 151–171). New York: Haworth Press.

Mulroy, E. A., & Lane, T. (1992). Housing affordability, stress and single mothers: Pathway to homelessness. *Journal of Sociology and Social Welfare, 19*(3), 51–64.

Mulroy, E. A., & Shay, S. (1997). Non-profit organizations and innovation: A model of neighborhood based collaboration to prevent child mistreatment. *Social Work, 42,* 515–524.

Mumola, C. (2000, August). *Incarcerated parents and their children.* Washington, DC: Department of Justice, Bureau of Justice Statistics.

Murray, C. (1984). *Losing ground: American social policy 1950–1980.* New York: Basic Books.

Musgrave, R. (1986). *Public finance in a democratic society: Fiscal doctrine, growth and institutions*. New York: New York University Press.

Myles, J. (2002). A new social contract for the elderly. In G. Esping-Andersen et al. (Eds.), *Why we need a new welfare state* (pp. 130–132). Oxford: Oxford University Press.

Myles, J., & Pierson, P. (1997). Friedman's revenge: The reform of the liberal welfare state. *Politics and Society, 25,* 443–472.

Myles, J., & Quadagno, J. (2002). Political theories of the welfare state. *Social Service Review, 76,* 34–57.

Naples, N. A. (1991). Just what is needed to be done: Political practice of women community workers in low income neighborhoods. *Gender and Society, 5*(9), 478–496.

Naples, N. A. (1996). Activist mothering: Cross-generational continuity in community work of women from low income urban neighborhoods. In E. Chow, D. Wilkinson, & M. Zinn (Eds.), *Race, Class and Gender* (pp. 223–243). Thousand Oaks, CA: Sage.

Naples, N. A. (1997). The new "consensus" on the gendered social contract: The 1987–1988 U.S. congressional hearings on welfare reform. *Signs: Journal of Women in Culture and Society, 22*(4), 907–945.

Naples, N. A. (1998). *Grassroots warriors: Activist mothers, community work and war on poverty*. New York: Routledge.

Nash, G. B. (1979). *The urban crucible: Social change, political consciousness and the origins of the American Revolution*. Cambridge, MA: Harvard University Press.

Nathan, R. P., & Gais, T. L. (2001, Summer). Is devolution working? Federal and state roles in welfare. *Brookings Review*, pp. 25–29.

National Association of Social Workers. (1996). *NASW Code of Ethics (Revised)*. Washington, DC: Author.

National Association of Social Workers. (2003). *Social work speaks: Policy statements (2003–2006)*. Washington, DC: NASW Press.

National Immigration Law Center. (2004, January 9). *NILC reflection on President Bush's immigration reform proposal: A compelling vision but a seriously flawed proposal*. Available: www.nilc.org

National Law Center on Homelessness and Poverty. (2004). *Increasing homelessness and poverty violates international law*. Available: http://www.nlchp.org

National Low Income Housing Coalition. (2002). *Out of reach: Rental housing at what cost?* Available: http://www.nlihc.org

Nava, J. (1973). *Mexican Americans: Past, present and future*. New York: American Book Co.

Needleman, M. L., & Needleman, C. E. (1974). *Guerrillas in the bureaucracy: The community planning experiment in the U.S.* New York: Wiley.

Neubeck, K. J., & Casenave, N. A. (2001). *Welfare racism: Playing the race card against America's poor*. New York: Routledge.

Nisbet, R. (1980). *History of the idea of progress*. New York: Basic Books.

Norman, G., & Mitchell, D. J. (2000). *Pension reform in Sweden: Lessons for policy-makers*. Washington, DC: Heritage Foundation.

Nox, V. (2002, Summer). Money also matters. *American Prospect*, pp. A26–A31.

Nozick, R. (1974). *Anarchy, state and utopia*. New York: Saint Martin's Press.

O'Brien, P., & Harm, N. J. (2002). Women's recidivism and reintegration: Two sides of the same coin. In J. Figueira-McDonough & R. C. Sarri (Eds.), *Women at the margins: Neglect, punishment, and resistance* (pp. 296–317). New York: Haworth Press.

O'Dell, K. (2004). Addressing the housing needs of low income families. *Welfare Information Network Issue Notes, 1*(3), 1–6.

Offe, C. (1984). *Contradictions of the welfare state.* Cambridge: MIT Press.

Offe, C. (1998, January 5–6). *The German welfare state: Principles, performance and prospects.* Paper presented at the Conference on the Welfare State at the Century's End: Current Dilemmas and Possible Futures, Tel Aviv.

Offner, P., & Holzer, H. (2002, Summer). Forgotten men. *American Prospect,* pp. 36–37.

Ogburn, W. F. (1953). The changing functions of the family. In R. F. Winch & R. McGinnis (Eds.), *Selected readings in marriage and the family* (pp. 74–80). New York: Holt, Reinhart and Winston.

O'Hare, W. (2003, July). Goodbye Murphy Brown. *Kids Count.* Baltimore: Casey Foundation.

Okin, S. M. (1989). *Justice, gender and the family.* New York: Basic Books.

Ooms, T. (2002a, Fall). The role of the federal government in strengthening marriage. *Virginia Journal of Policy and the Law, 9,* 1.

Ooms, T. (2002b, April). Marriage plus. *American Prospect,* pp. 24–26.

Ooms, T., Buchet, S., & Parke, M. (2004, April). Beyond marriage licenses: Efforts to strengthen marriage and two-parent families. A state by state snapshot. *Center of Law and Social Policy.*

Organization for Economic Co-operation and Development. (1996). Social expenditures statistics of the OECD member countries (Provisional version). OECD Labor Market and Social Policy (Occasional Paper no. 17, OECD/GD(96)49). Paris: OECD.

Organization for Economic Co-operation and Development. (2003). Statistics portal. *Education at a Glance* (tables). Available: http://www.oecd.org

Organization for Economic Co-operation and Development. (2004). Health spending in most OECD countries rises with U.S. far outstripping others. *Statistics Portal.* Health. Available: http://www.oecd.org

Orland, M. E., & Folley, E. (1997, April). Beyond categorization: Defining barriers and potential solutions to creating effective comprehensive, community-based support systems for children and families. *The Finance Project.*

Orshansky, M. (1965, January). Analysis of the poverty population based on the economy of food plan. *Social Security Bulletin.*

Orszag, P. R. (2000, July 21). *Raising the amount that can be contributed to Roth IRAs: The dangers in the short run and the long run.* Washington, DC: Center on Budget and Policy Priorities.

Ozawa, M. N. (1997). Demographic changes and their implications. In M. Reisch & E. Gambrill (Eds.), *Social work in the 21st century* (pp. 8–27). Thousand Oaks, CA: Pine Forge Press.

Ozawa, M., & Yoon, H.-S. (2005). Leavers from TANF versus AFDC: How do they fare economically? *Social Work, 50*(3), 239–249.

Padilla, Y., & Sherraden, M. (2005). Community and social policy issues: Persistent poverty, economic inclusion, and asset building. In M. Weil (Ed.), *Handbook of community practice.* Thousand Oaks, CA: Sage.

Paradis, A. (1967). *The hungry years: The story of the great American Depression.* Philadelphia: Chilton.

Parenti, M. (1988). *Democracy for the few.* New York: St. Martin's.

Park, E., Nathanson, M., Greenstein, R., & Springer, J. (2003, December 8). The troubling Medicare legislation. *Center on Budget and Policy Priorities.* Available: http://www.cbpp.org

Parsons, T. (1951). *The social system.* Glencoe, IL: Free Press.

Passel, J. S., & Clark, R. (1998). *Immigrants in New York: Their legal status, incomes and taxes.* Washington, DC: Urban Institute.

Pateman, C. (1988). *The sexual contract.* Cambridge, UK: Polity Press.

Pear, R. (2004a, April 23). Agency to allow insurance cuts for the retired. *New York Times,* pp. A1, A16.

Pear, R. (2004b, August 22). Insurers object to new provision in Medicare law. *New York Times,* pp. A1, A18.

Pear, R. (2004c, January 10). Insurers to get 10.6% increase from Medicare. *New York Times,* pp. A1, A17.

Pear, R. (2004d, September 26). Medicare rules set off a battle on drug choices. *New York Times,* pp. A1, A20.

Pear, R. (2004e, April 2). Senate, torn by minimum wage, shelves major welfare bill. *New York Times,* p. A12.

Pear, R. (2004f, August 10). Survey finds beneficiaries largely fault Medicare law. *New York Times,* p. A12.

Pear, R. (2004g, February 15). U.S. nears clash with governors on Medicaid cost. *New York Times,* pp. A1, A15.

Pearce, D. M. (1985). Toil and trouble: Women workers and unemployment compensation. *Signs: Journal of Women in Culture and Society, 10*(31), 448–460.

Pearce, D. M. (2002). Welfare reform now that we know it: Enforcing women's poverty and preventing self-sufficiency. In J. Figueira-McDonough & R. C. Sarri (Eds.), *Women at the margins: Neglect, punishment, and resistance* (pp. 125–148). New York: Howard Press.

Peek, J., & Plotkin, C. (1951). Social caseworkers in private practice. *Smith College Studies in Social Work, 21*(3), 165–195.

Pelletiere, D., Wardrip, K., & Crowley, S. (2005). *Out of reach 2005.* Washington, DC: National Low Income Housing Coalition. Available: http://www.nlihc.org

Peretti, T. J. (1999). *In defense of a political court.* Princeton, NJ: Princeton University Press.

Peterson, M. D. (Ed.). (1966). *Democracy, liberty and property: The state constitutional conventions of the 1820's.* Indianapolis: Bobbs-Merrill.

Phillips, D. L. (1986). *Toward a just social order.* Princeton, NJ: Princeton University Press.

Phillips, K. (1990). *The politics of rich and poor: Wealth and the American electorate in the Reagan aftermath.* New York: Harper Perennial.

Pierson, P. (1994). *Dismantling the welfare state? Reagan, Thatcher and the politics of retrenchment.* Cambridge, UK: Cambridge University Press.

Pierson, P. (2004). *Politics in time: History, institutions, and social analysis.* Princeton: Princeton University Press.

Pinderhues, E. B. (1983, June). Empowerment for our clients and ourselves. *Social Case Work,* pp. 331–338.

Piven, F. F. (1974). The Great Society as political strategy. In R. A. Cloward & F. F. Piven (Eds.), *The politics of turmoil: Essays on poverty, race and the urban crisis* (pp. 267–270). New York: Pantheon.

Piven, F. F., & Cloward, R. A. (1971). *Regulating the poor: The functions of welfare.* New York: Pantheon.

Piven, F. F., & Cloward, R. A. (1974). *Poor people's movements: Why they succeed and how they fail*. New York: Pantheon.

Piven, F. F., & Cloward, R. A. (1982). *The new class war: Reagan's attack on the welfare state and its consequences*. New York: Pantheon.

Piven, F. F., & Cloward, R. A. (1997a). *The breaking of the American social contract*. New York: New Press.

Piven, F. F., & Cloward, R. A. (1997b). The decline of the labor party. In F. F. Piven & R. A. Cloward (Eds.), *The breaking of the American social compact* (pp. 17–40). New York: Free Press.

Platt, A. (1969). *Childsavers: The invention of delinquency*. Chicago: University of Chicago Press.

Plotnick, R., & Skidmore, F. (1975). *Progress against poverty: A review of the 1964–1974 decade*. New York: Academic Press.

Pontiglia, G. (2002). *Born twice*. New York: Knopf.

Porta, D., & Diani, M. (1999). *Social movements*. London: Blackwell.

Porter, E. (2004a, June 11). Not many jobs sent abroad, U.S. report says. *New York Times*, pp. A1, A6.

Porter, E. (2004b, August 19). Rising cost of health benefits cited as a factor in slump of jobs. *New York Times*, pp. A1, C2.

Porter, E. (2005, April 5). Illegal immigrants are bolstering social security with billions. *New York Times*, pp. A1, A20.

Portes, A., & Rumbaut, R. (2001). *Ethnicities: Children of immigrants in America*. Berkeley: University of California Press.

Poterba, J. M. (1997). The growth of 401(k) plans: Evidence and implications. In S. J. Schieber & J. B. Shoven (Eds.), *Public policy towards pensions*. Cambridge, MA: MIT Press.

Potter, J. (1984). Demographic development and family structure. In J. P. Greene & J. R. Pole (Eds.), *Colonial British America: Essays in the new history of the early modern era* (pp. 131–140). Baltimore: Johns Hopkins University Press.

President's Commission on Pension Policy. (1981). *Coming of age: Toward a national retirement income policy*. Washington, DC: U.S. Government Printing Office.

Provine, D. M. (2005). Judicial activism and American democracy. In K. L. Hall & T. McQuire (Eds.), *The judicial branch*. New York: Oxford University Press.

Putnam, M. C. (1887). Friendly visiting. *Proceedings of the Fourteenth Annual Conference of Charities and Corrections*. Boston: A. Williams.

Putnam, R. D. (1993a). *Making democracy work: Civic traditions in modern Italy*. Princeton: Princeton University Press.

Putnam, R. D. (1993b, Spring). The prosperous community: Social capital and public life. *American Prospect, 13,* 35–42.

Putnam, R. D. (2001). *Bowling alone: The collapse and revival of American community*. New York: Simon & Schuster.

Quadagno, J. (1987). Theories of the welfare state. *Annual Review of Sociology, 13,* 109–128.

Quadagno, J. (1994). *The color of welfare: How racism undermined the War on Poverty*. New York: Oxford University Press.

Radosh, R. (1971). *Debs*. Englewood Cliffs, NJ: Prentice Hall.

Rao, R. P. (1998). *Distributive justice: A third world response to Rawls and Nozick*. San Francisco: International Scholars Publications.

Rawick, G. P. (1972). *From sundown to sunup: The making of the black community*. Westport, CT: Greenwood.

Rawls, J. (1971). *A theory of justice*. Cambridge, MA: Harvard University Press.

Reagan, R. (1983). *Ronald Reagan talks to America*. Old Greenwich, CT: Devin-Adair.

Reamer, F. (1994). The evolution of social work knowledge. In F. Reamer (Ed.), *The foundation of social work knowledge* (pp. 1–12). New York: Columbia University Press.

Red Horse, J. G. (1980, October). American Indian elders: Unifiers of Indian families. *Social Casework, 61*, 490–493.

Reeser, L. C., & Epstein, I. (1990). *Professionalization and activism in social work: The sixties, the eighties, and the future*. New York: Columbia University Press.

Rehr, H., & Rosenberg, G. (2002). Social work and health care yesterday, today, and tomorrow. In J. G. Hopps & R. Morris (Eds.), *Social work at the millennium* (pp. 86–122). New York: Free Press.

Reich, R. B. (2002a). *I will be short: Essentials for a decent working society*. Boston: Beacon Press.

Reich, R. B. (2002b, March). Trickle down pain. *American Prospect*, p. 48.

Reich, R. B. (2003, October). The real supply side. *American Prospect*, p. 40.

Reich, R. B. (2004, January 29). The dead center. *New York Times*, p. A27.

Reisch, M. (1997). The political context of social work. In M. Reisch & E. Gambrill (Eds.), *Social work in the 21st century* (pp. 80–91). Thousand Oaks, CA: Pine Forge Press.

Reisch, M., & Andrews, J. (2001). *The road not taken: A history of radical social work in the United States*. New York: Brunner-Routledge.

Reisch, M., & Gambrill, E. (Eds.). (1997). *Social work in the 21st century*. Thousand Oaks, CA: Pine Forge Press.

Reisch, M., & Wenocur, S. (1986). The future of community organization in social work: Social activism and the politics of the profession building. *Social Service Review, 60*, 70–93.

Reisman, D. (1950). *The lonely crowd: A study of changing American character*. New Haven, CT: Yale University Press.

Resources for Welfare Decisions. (2004, January). The effects of litigation on the design and administration of welfare policies. *Welfare Information Network, 8*, 3. Available: http://www.financeproject.org/Publications/litigationRN.htm

Richmond, M. (1917). *Social diagnosis*. New York: Russell Sage Foundation.

Rieder, J. (1989). The rise of the silent majority. In S. Fraser & G. Gerstle (Eds.), *The rise and fall of the New Deal order, 1930–1980* (pp. 243–265). Princeton, NJ: Princeton University Press.

Riley, T.C., Pernice, C., Perry, M., & Kannel, S. (2002). *Why eligible children lose or leave SCHIP*. Portland, ME: National Academy of State Health Policy.

Rimlinger, G. (1971). *Welfare policy and industrialization in Europe, America and Russia*. New York: Wiley.

Rivera, F. G., & Erlich, J. L. (1998). *Community organizing in a diverse society* (3rd ed.). Needham Heights, MA: Allyn & Bacon.

Rochefort, D. A. (1981). Progressive and social control perspectives of social welfare. *Social Service Review, 55*(4), 568–591.

Rodriguez, J. (1999, July 30). Chile's private pension at 18: Current state and future challenges. *Cato Institute Project on Social Security privatization*. Available: http://www.socialsecurity.org.pubs

Rohter, L. (2005, January 27). Chile's retirees find shortfall in private plan. *New York Times,* pp. A1, C2.

Rollins, W. B., & Lefkowitz, B. (1961, September 6). Welfare à la Newburgh. *The Nation,* p. 158.

Rose, N. (1997). The future economic landscape: Implications for social work practice and education. In M. Reisch & E. Gambrill (Eds.), *Social work in the 21st century* (pp. 28–38). Thousand Oaks, CA: Pine Forge Press.

Rosen, J. (1996). *Getting the connections right: Public journalism and the troubles of the press.* New York: Twentieth Century Fund.

Rosenbaum, H. D., & Ugrinsky, A. (Eds.). (1994). *The presidency and domestic policies of Jimmy Carter.* Westport, CT: Greenwood Press.

Ross, D. C., & Cox, L. (2003). *Preserving recent progress on health coverage for children and families: New tensions emerge.* Washington, DC: Kaiser Commission Report on Medicaid and the Uninsured.

Ross, M. (1955). *Community organization: Theory and principles.* New York: Harper Brothers.

Rossi, P. H. (1989). *Down and out in America: The origins of homelessness.* Chicago: University of Chicago Press.

Rothman, D. (1971). *The discovery of the asylum: Social disorder in the new republic.* Boston: Little, Brown.

Rothman, J. (1968). Three models of community organization. In *Social work practice 1968* (pp. 16–47). New York: Columbia University Press.

Russell, D. (1975). *The politics of rape.* New York: Stein and Day.

Ryan, M. (1975). *Womanhood in America from colonial times to the present.* New York: View Points.

Salmond, J. (1967). *The Civilian Conservation Corps, 1933–1942: A New Deal case study.* Durham, NC: Duke University Press.

Sanchez, R. (2004, September 11). Guest worker bill is offering indenture servitude, disaster. *Arizona Republic,* p. 1.

Sandler, R., & Shoenbrod, D. (2003). *Democracy by decree: What happens when courts run government.* New Haven, CT: Yale University Press.

Sard, B., & Waller, M. (2002, April). *Housing strategies to strengthen welfare policy and support working families.* Washington, DC: Brookings Institution, Center on Urban and Metropolitan Policy and the Center on Budget and Policy Priorities.

Sass, S. A. (1997). *The promise of private pensions: The first 100 years.* Cambridge, MA: Harvard University Press.

Sawhill, E. (2001, Summer). Making welfare a way station, not a way of life. *Brookings Review,* pp. 4–7.

Sawhill, E. (2002, April 8). Is lack of marriage a real problem? *American Prospect,* pp. 28–30.

Saxton, P. (1991). Comments on social work and therapies. *Social Service Review, 65*(2), 314–319.

Scannapieco, M., & Jackson, S. (1996). Kinship care: The African American response to family preservation. *Social Work, 41,* 190–196.

Schackel, S. (1992). *Social housekeepers: Women shaping public policy in New Mexico, 1920–1940.* Albuquerque: University of New Mexico Press.

Scheingold, S. (2004). *The politics of rights: Lawyers, public policy and political change.* Ann Arbor: University of Michigan Press.

Scheirer, M. A. (1981). *Program implementation: The organizational center.* Beverly Hills, CA: Sage.

Schneider, A., & Ingram, H. (1993). Social construction of target populations: Implications for politics and policy. *American Political Science Review, 87*(2), 334–346.

Schneider, R. (2002). Influencing "state" policy: Social arena for the 21st century. *Social Policy Journal, 1*(1), 113–116.

Schorr, L. B. (1997). *Common purpose: Strengthening families and neighborhoods to rebuild America.* New York: Doubleday.

Schrag, P., et al. (2004). Special report: Children left behind. *American Prospect, 15*(2), 33–52.

Schram, S. F. (1995). *Words of welfare: The poverty of social science and the social science of poverty.* Minneapolis: University of Minnesota Press.

Schram, S. F. (2000). *After welfare: The culture of postindustrial social policy.* New York: New York University Press.

Schrecker, E. (2002). *The era of McCarthyism: A brief history with documents.* New York: Palgrave.

Schulman, R., Blank, H., & Ewen, D. (2001). *A fragile foundation: Child care assistance policies.* Washington, DC: Children's Defense Fund.

Schumacher, R., Greenberg, M., & Duffy, J. (2001). *The impact of TANF funding on childcare subsidy programs.* Washington, DC: Center for Law and Social Policy.

Schwartz, J. E. (1983). *America's hidden success: A reassessment of twenty years.* New York: W. W. Norton.

Seefeldt, K., & Smock, P. (2004, February). *Marriage on the public policy agenda: What policy makers need to know from research.* Ann Arbor: University of Michigan, National Poverty Center (PSC Research Report 04-554). Available: http://www.psc.isr.umich.edu/pubs/pdf/rr04-554.pdf

Seitz, V. R. (1995). *Women, development, and communities for empowerment in Appalachia.* Albany: State University of New York Press.

Sen, A. K. (1992). *Inequality reexamined.* Cambridge, MA: Harvard University Press.

Shapiro, V. (1990).The gender basis of American social policy. In L. Gordon (Ed.), *Women, the state, and welfare* (pp. 37–54). Madison: University of Wisconsin Press.

Shavit, Y., & Blossfeld, H. P. (1993). *Persistent inequalities.* Boulder, CO: Westview Press.

Sherraden, M. (1990). The business of social work. In *Encyclopedia of social work* (18th ed., 1990 supplement). Silver Springs, MD: NASW Press.

Sherraden, M. (1991). *Assets and the poor: A new American welfare policy.* Armonk, NY: M.E. Sharpe.

Sills, D. (Ed.). (1991). *International encyclopedia of the social sciences,* 438–446. New York: Macmillan/Free Press.

Skocpol, T. (1980). Neo-Marxist theories of the state and the New Deal. *Politics and Society, 10,* 155–201.

Skocpol, T. (1982). *Protecting soldiers and mothers: The political origins of social policy in the United States.* Cambridge, MA: Belknap Press of Harvard University Press.

Skocpol, T. (1995). *Social policy in the United States: Future possibilities in historical perspective.* Princeton, NJ: Princeton University Press.

Skocpol, T. (2004, January). A bad senior moment. *American Prospect*, pp. 26–29.

Skonkoff, J., & Phillips, D. (Eds.). (2002). *From neurons to neighborhoods: The science of early development*. Washington, DC: Academic Press.

Smith, D. F. (1990). *The conceptual practice of power: Feminist sociology of knowledge*. Boston: Northeastern University Press.

Sobel, R. (1975). *Herbert Hoover at the onset of the Great Depression, 1929–1930*. Philadelphia: Lippincott.

Social Security Administration. (2002). *Annual statistical supplement* (Table 4.AI). Washington, DC: Author.

Social Security Administration. (2004). *Social security programs throughout the world: Europe*. Available: http://www.ssa.gov

Social Security and Medicare Board of Trustees. (2005). *Annual report on the status of the Social Security and Medicare programs*. Washington, DC: U.S. Government Printing Office.

Soss, J. (2000). *Unwanted claims: The politics of participation in the U.S. welfare system*. Ann Arbor: University of Michigan Press.

Southern Governors' Association. (1988). *Study of the AFDC-Medicaid eligibility process in the southern states*. Washington, DC: Author.

Specht, H. (1968, May 29). *Disruptive tactics*. Paper presented at the National Conference on Social Welfare, San Francisco.

Specht, H. (1990, September). Social work and popular psychotherapies. *Social Service Review, 64*, 345–357.

Specht, H., & Courtney, M. (1994). *Unfaithful angels: How social work abandoned its mission*. New York: Free Press.

Special Report on Educating America. (2004, February). *Children left behind* (Contributors: P. Schrag, R. Rothstein, R. Borosage, R. Smith, E. Rosenfeld, G. Franke-Ruta, M. Yglesias, & A. McGravey). *American Prospect*.

Starr, P. (2004, January). The new politics of Medicare. *American Prospect, 2*.

Steiner, G. (1981). *The futility of family policy*. Washington, DC: Brookings Institution.

Steiner, J. (1925). *Community organization: A study of its theory and current practice*. New York: Century.

Stephens, J. D. (1996). The Scandinavian welfare states: Achievements, crisis and prospects. In G. Esping-Andersen (Ed.), *Welfare states in transition: National adaptations in global economies*. London: Sage.

Stern, M. (1992). *Calculating Visions: Kennedy, Johnson and civil rights*. New Brunswick, NJ: Rutgers University.

Stern, M. D. (2005). *Formulating responses in an egalitarian age*. Lanham, MD: Rowman & Littlefield.

Stiles, W. B., Shapiro, D. A., & Elliott, R. (1986). Are all psychotherapies equivalent? *American Psychologist, 41*, 165.

Stockman, D. (1986). *The triumph of politics*. New York: Harper & Row.

Stout, L. (1996). *Bridging the class divide and other lessons for grassroots organizing*. Boston: Beacon.

Stoutland, S. E. (1997). *Neither urban jungle nor urban village: Women, families, and urban development*. New York: Garland.

Strauss, J. (2000). *Fighting poverty with virtue: Moral reform and America's urban poor, 1825–2000*. Bloomington: Indiana University Press.

Strope, L. (2004, August 17). Income gap over two decades, data shows. *Chicago Tribune*.

Sullivan, W. (1982). *Restructuring public philosophy*. Berkeley: University of California Press.

Swartz, R., & Miller, B. (2002). *Welfare reform and housing*. Washington, DC: Brookings Institution.

Swenson, C. R. (1998). Clinical social works contribution to a social justice perspective. *Social Work, 43*(6), 527–537.

Swidler, A. (1986). Love and adulthood in American culture. In R. Bellah, R. Madsen, W. Sullivan, A. Swidler, & S. Tipton (Eds.), *Individualism and commitment in American life* (pp. 103–125). New York: Harper & Row.

Taylor, T. (1984). *The bureau of Indian affairs*. Boulder, CO: Westview Press.

Teixeira, R. A. (1992). *The disappearing American voter*. Washington, DC: Brookings Institution.

Temporary Assistance for Needy Families. (2003). Characteristics and financial status of TANF recipients. *Fifth Annual Report to Congress*, Chapter 10.

Thelen, K. (2003). How institutions evolve: Insights from comparative historical analysis. In J. Mahoney & D. Rueschmeyer (Eds.), *Comparative analysis in the social sciences* (pp. 208–240). Cambridge, UK: Cambridge University Press.

Theoharis, A. G. (1971). *Seeds of repression: Harry Truman and the origins of McCarthyism*. Chicago: Quadrangle Books.

Therborn, G. (1986). *Why some people are more unemployed than others*. London: Verso.

Therborn, G. (1989). Pillarization and popular movements, two variants of welfare capitalism: The Netherlands and Sweden. In F. G. Castles (Ed.), *The comparative history of public history*. Oxford: Polity.

Thrupkaew, N. (2002, Summer). No huddled masses need to apply. *American Prospect*.

Titmuss, R. (1958). *Essays on the welfare state*. New Haven, CT: Yale University Press.

Titmuss, R. (1967). *Choice and the "welfare state."* London: Fabian Society.

Tobin, J. (1970). On limiting the domain of inequality. *Journal of Law and Economics, 13*, 363–378.

Tolchin, S., & Tolchin, M. (1983). *Dismantling America*. New York: Houghton Mifflin.

Toner, R. (2004, January 30). Political memo. *New York Times*, pp. A1, A13.

Toner, R., & Rosenbaum, D. (2004, September 18). Social Security poses hurdles to the president. *New York Times*, pp. A1, A10.

Tonry, M. (1995). *Malign neglect: Race, crime and punishment*. New York: Oxford University Press.

Toulmin, S. E. (1958). *The use of argument*. Cambridge, UK: Cambridge University Press.

Townsend, P. (1979). *Poverty in the United Kingdom*. Harmondsworth, UK: Penguin.

Trattner, W. I. (1999). *From poor law to welfare state: A history of social welfare in America* (6th ed.). New York: Free Press.

Tretheway, A. (1997). Resistance, identity, and empowerment: A postmodern feminist analysis of human service organization. *Communication Monographs, 64*, 281–301.

Turner, D. C., Giorno, A., DeSerres, A., Vourc'h, A., & Richardson, R. (1998). *The macroeconomic implication of aging in the global context* (Papers 1, 2). Paris: Organization for Economic Co-operation and Development.

Tyrrell, Y. (1979). *Sobering up: From temperance to prohibition in antebellum America*. Westport, CT: Greenwood Press.

United Nations. (1997). *Demographic yearbook*. New York: United Nations, Department of Economic and Policy Analysis and Social Information and Policy Analysis.

Urban Institute. (1999). *National survey of America's families*. Washington, DC: Author.

U.S. Census Bureau. (1987). *Money income and poverty in the United States*. Washington, DC: U.S. Government Printing Office.

U.S. Census Bureau. (1997). Voting and registration in the election of November 1996. *Current population reports* (pp. 20–504). Washington, DC: U.S. Government Printing Office.

U.S. Census Bureau. (1998). *Current population survey*. Washington, DC: U.S. Government Printing Office.

U.S. Census Bureau. (2000). *Statistical abstract of the United States 1999* (Table 891). Washington, DC: U.S. Government Printing Office.

U.S. Census Bureau. (2002). Money income and poverty in the United States by race and ethnicity (Table B-2). *Current Population Reports*. Washington, DC: U.S. Government Printing Office.

U.S. Census Bureau. (2003a, August). Income, poverty, and health insurance in the United States. *Current Population Reports*. Washington, DC: U.S. Government Printing Office.

U.S. Census Bureau. (2003b). *Money, income, and poverty in the United States by race and ethnicity*. Washington, DC: U.S. Government Printing Office.

U.S. Conference of Mayors. (2002). *A status report on hunger and homelessness in American cities*. Available: http://www.usmayors.org

U.S. Department of Agriculture. (2001). Consumption and family living. *Report* (Chapter xiii). Available: http://www.USDA.gov.nass.pubs

U.S. Department of Agriculture. (2004). *Household food security in the United States, 2003*. Available: http://www.ers.usda.gov

U.S. Department of Commerce, Bureau of Economic Analysis. (2001, July 31). *National income and product income* (Table 6.11C). Washington, DC: U.S. Government Printing Office.

U.S. Department of Justice. (1997). *Statistical yearbook of immigration statistics*. Washington, DC: U.S. Government Printing Office.

U.S. Department of Justice, Bureau of Justice Statistics. (1999, August). Prisons 1998. *Report* (NCJ # 175688). Washington, DC: U.S. Government Printing Office.

U.S. Department of Justice. (2002). *Statistical yearbook of immigration statistics*. Washington, DC: U.S. Government Printing Office

U.S. General Accounting Office. (1987).*Work and welfare: Current AFDC work programs and implications for federal policy*. Washington, DC: U.S. Government Printing Office.

U.S. General Accounting Office. (2001). *More research needed on TANF family caps and other policies for reducing out-of-wedlock births*. Washington, DC: U.S. Government Printing Office.

U.S. General Accounting Office. (2003). Economic independence and well-being of children. *Performance and accountability series*. Washington, DC: Government Printing Office.

Van Hook, J., Glick, J. E., & Bean, F. (1999). Public assistance receipt among immigrants and natives: How the unit of analysis affects research findings. *Demography, 36*(1), 111–120.

Van Soetz, D. (Ed.). (1992). *Incorporating peace and social justice into the social work curriculum*. Washington, DC: Peace and Social Justice Committee, National Association of Social Workers.

Ventura, N. (2005, September). Stand up "with" others. *NASW California News, 32,* 13.

Ventura, S. J., & Martin, J. A. (1998). Final natality statistics, 1996. *Monthly Vital Statistics Report, 46*(11S), 66. Hyattsville, MD: National Vital Statistics.

Vieth, W. (2004, April 15). A plethora of tax breaks eases the sting, but at what price? *Los Angeles Times,* p. A18.

Vrana, D. (2004, September 10). Families pay $1,000 more than in 2000. *Los Angeles Times*, pp. A1, A23.

Vrana, D., & Kemper, V. (2004, January 15). More workers are likely to retire without company health benefits. *Los Angeles Times*, pp. A1, A24.

Wagner, D. (1989). Fate of idealism in social work: Alternative experiences of professional careers. *Social Work, 35*(4), 385–389.

Wagner, D. (2000). *What's love got to do with it? A critical look at American charity*. New York: New Press.

Waite, L. J., & Gallagher, M. (2000). *The case for marriage: Why married people are happier, healthier, and better off financially*. New York: Doubleday.

Wakefield, J. C. (1988a). Psychotherapy, distributive justice, and social work: Distributive justice as a conceptual framework for social work (Part I). *Social Service Review, 62,* 187–210.

Wakefield, J. C. (1988b). Psychotherapy, distributive justice, and social work: Psychotherapy and the pursuit of justice (Part II). *Social Service Review, 62,* 353–382.

Waller, M. (2006, March 17). Refresher course on welfare. *Economic Studies, 2.* Washington, DC: Brookings Institution.

Walruff, J. (2002). Teenage pregnancy: Mediating rotten outcomes and improving opportunities. In J. Figueira-McDonough & R. C. Sarri (Eds.), *Women at the margins: Neglect, punishment, and resistance* (pp. 229–249). New York: Haworth Press.

Walsh, M. W. (2004a, June 13). Healthier and wiser? Sure but not wealthier. *New York Times*, Section 3, pp. 1, 9.

Walsh, M. W. (2004b, May 21). United Methodist Church bucks the trend on employee pensions. *New York Times*.

Wandersee, W. D. (1981). *Women's work and family values, 1920–1940*. Cambridge, MA: Harvard University Press.

Warner, A. G. (1894). *American charities*. New York: Thomas K. Crowell.

Warner A. G. (1989). *American charities: A study in philanthropy and economics* (Introduction by M. J. Deegan). New Brunswick, NJ: Transaction Publishers. (Original work published 1919)

Warren, D. (1975). *Black neighborhoods: An assessment of community power*. Ann Arbor: University of Michigan Press.

Warren, D. (1981). *Helping networks: How people cope with problems in urban neighborhoods*. South Bend, IN: University of Notre Dame Press.

Warren, R. (1978). *The community in America*. Chicago: Rand McNally.

Warren, R. B., & Warren, D. I. (1980). *The neighborhood organizer's handbook*. South Bend, IN: University of Notre Dame Press.

Watson, B. (2005). *Bread and roses: Mills, migrants, and the struggle for the American Dream*. New York: Viking.

Weaver, R. K. (2000). *Ending welfare as we know it*. Washington, DC: Brookings Institution.

Weil, A., & Finegold, K. (Eds.). (2002). *Welfare reform: The next act*. Washington, DC: Urban Institute.

Weil, M., Gamble, D., & Williams, E. S. (1998). Women, communities and development. In J. Figueira-McDonough, E. Netting, & A. Casebolt (Eds.), *The role of gender in practice knowledge: Claiming half of the human experience* (pp. 241–286). New York: Garland.

Weimer, D. L., & Vinning, A. R. (1992). *Policy analysis: Concepts and practice*. Englewood Cliffs, NJ: Prentice Hall.

Weinberg, A. K. (1935). *Manifest destiny: A study of nationalist expansion in American history*. Baltimore: Johns Hopkins University Press.

Weiss, I. (2005). Is there a global common core to social work? A cross-national comparative study of BSW graduate students. *Social Work, 50*(2), 101–109.

Welfare Information Network. (2001, October). Earnings supplements and income disregards can ease the transition from welfare to work. *Resources for Welfare Decision Making, 5*, 12.

Welfare Information Network. (2004). The effect of litigation on the design and administration of welfare policies and programs. *Resources for Welfare Decision Making, 8*, 3. Available: http://financeprojectinfo.org

Welfare queen becomes issue in Reagan campaign. (1976, February 15). *New York Times*, p. A51.

Wellstone, P. (1978). *How the rural people got power*. Amherst: University of Massachusetts Press.

Wenocur, S. (1975). The social welfare workers movement: A case of New Left thought. *Journal of Sociology and Social Welfare, 3*(1), 3–20.

Wenocur, S., & Reisch, M. (1983). The social work profession and the ideology of professionalization. *Journal of Sociology and Social Welfare, 10*, 684–732.

Wenocur, S., & Soifer, S. (1997). Prospects for community organization. In M. Reisch & E. Gambrill (Eds.), *Social work in the 21st century* (pp. 198–208). Thousand Oaks, CA: Pine Forge Press.

Wertheimer, B. M. (1977). *We were there: The story of working women in America*. New York: Pantheon.

Wilensky, H., & Lebeaux, C. (1958). *Industrial society and social welfare*. New York: Free Press.

Wilson, W. J. (1987). *The truly disadvantaged: The inner city, the underclass, and public policy*. Chicago: University of Chicago Press.

Wilson, W. J. (1991). Public policy research and the truly disadvantaged. In C. Jenks & P. E. Peterson (Eds.), *The urban underclass* (pp. 480–481). Washington, DC: Brookings Institution.

Wilson, W. J. (1996). *When work disappears: The world of the new working poor*. New York: Knopf.

Wilson, W. J., & Neckerman, K. M. (1986). Poverty and family structure: The widening gap between evidence and public policy issues. In S. Danziger & D. N. Weinberg (Eds.), *Fighting poverty: What works and what doesn't* (pp. 232–259). Cambridge, MA: Harvard University Press.

Wineman, S. (1984). *The politics of human services*. Montreal, Quebec, Canada: Black Rose Books.

Winfrey, J. C. (1998). *Social issues: The ethics and economics of taxes and public programs*. New York: Oxford University Press.

Wirth, L. (1933). The scope and problems of the community. *Publications of the Sociological Society of America, 27,* 61–73.

Wisner, E. (1945, September). The puritan background of the New England poor laws. *Social Service Review, 19,* 381–390.

Withorn, A. (1984). *Serving the people: Social services and social change.* New York: Columbia University Press.

Withorn, A. (1986). Why do they hate me so much? A history of welfare and its abandonment in the U.S. *American Journal of Orthopsychiatry, 66,* 495–509.

Wolfe, B., & Vandell, D. L. (2002, Summer). Welfare reform depends on good child care. *American Prospect,* pp. 19–21.

Wolff, E. (2000, April). *Recent trends in wealth ownership, 1983–1998* (Working paper #300). Annandale-on-Hudson, NY: Bard College, Jerome Levy Economic Institute.

Wolters, R. (1970). *Negroes and the Great Depression: The problem of economic recovery.* Westport, CT: Greenwood Press.

Woods, R. A., & Kennedy, A. J. (1922). *The settlement horizon: National estimates.* New York: Russell Sage Foundation.

Woodsum, J. A. (1998). Native American women: An update. In J. Carrillo (Ed.), *Readings in American Indian law: Recalling the rhythm of survival* (pp. 226–234). Philadelphia: Temple University Press.

Wunder, J. R. (Ed.). (1996a). *Constitutionalism and Native Americans, 1903–1968.* New York: Garland.

Wunder, J. R. (Ed.). (1996b). *The Indian bill of rights, 1968.* New York: Garland.

Wunder, J. R. (Ed.). (1996c). *Native American law and colonialism, 1776–1903.* New York: Garland.

Wunder, J. R. (1996d). *Recent legal issues for American Indians, 1968 to the present.* New York: Garland.

Yates, J. V. N. (1824, January). Report to the secretary of state in 1824 on relief and settlement of the poor. *Assembly Journal* (Appendix B), 386–399.

Yates, J. (1997). Child support enforcement and welfare reform. *Welfare Information Network, 1,* 5.

Yglesias, M. (2003, December). The research wars. *American Prospect,* pp. 39–41.

Zemans, F. K. (1998). The accountable judge: Guardian of judicial independence. *Southern California Law Review, 72,* 625–656.

Zigler, E., & Styfco, S. J. (2001). Extended childhood intervention prepares children for school and beyond. *Journal of Medical Association, 285*(18), 2378–2380.

Zimbalist, S. E. (1977). *Historic themes and landmarks of social welfare research.* New York: Harper & Row.

Zucker, R. (2001). *Democratic distributive justice.* New York: Cambridge University Press.

Index _____

About the Author _____

Josefina Figueira-McDonough, PhD, is professor emerita of Social Work and of Justice and Social Inquiry at Arizona State University. Trained in social work and sociology at the University of Michigan, she has taught in both fields at the University of Michigan, Michigan State University, and Vanderbilt University. She has lectured or conducted research in Puerto Rico, Brazil, South Korea, Taiwan, Mozambique, Portugal, Spain, Italy, and Ireland. Her work on social justice has focused on deviance and control, the ecology of poverty, policy outcomes, community analysis, and curricula. This research has been supported by federal, state, and private grants and disseminated in social science as well as in social work journals. She is presently on the board of two international and interdisciplinary journals, *Social Intervention* and *Social Compass,* and is a member of the book committee of the National Association of Social Workers. Her most recent books include *Community Analysis and Praxis: Toward a Grounded Civil Society* (2001), *Serviço Social: Profissão e Identidade,* with A. Negreiros, A. Martins, and B. Henriques (2000), and *Women at the Margins: Neglect, Punishment and Resistance,* edited with Rosemary Sarri (2002).